SACRED TRUTHS OF THE DOCTRINE & COVENANTS

VOLUME TWO

LEAUN G. OTTEN
C. MAX CALDWELL

Deseret Book Company
Salt Lake City, Utah

To Our Families
—Forever—

© 1983 Leaun G. Otten and C. Max Caldwell

All rights reserved. No part of this book may be reproduced in any form or by any means without permission in writing from the publisher, Deseret Book Company, P. O. Box 30178, Salt Lake City, Utah 84130. This work is not an official publication of The Church of Jesus Christ of Latter-day Saints. The views expressed herein are the responsibility of the authors and do not necessarily represent the position of the Church or of Deseret Book Company.

Deseret Book is a registered trademark of Deseret Book Company.

First printing by LEMB, Inc., 1983
First printing by Deseret Book Company, 1993

Library of Congress Catalog Card Number 82-71791

ISBN 6-87747-098-2 (LEMB, Inc.)
ISBN 0-87579-784-9 (Deseret Book Company)

Printed in the United States of America
10   9   8   7   6   5   4   3

Acknowledgments

We are deeply grateful to the administration and staff of Religious Education of the Brigham Young University for their encouragement and assistance in the preparation and publication of this book.

We shall always be grateful for the devoted encouragement, strength, and support the authors have received from their families. The acomplishment of this work is a tribute to their sacrifice and loyalty.

Key to Abbreviations

AGQ	Answers to Gospel Questions
APPP	Autobiography of Parley P. Pratt
BofM	Book of Mormon
CHC	A Comprehensive History of the Church
CHMR	Church History and Modern Day Revelation
CR	Conference Report
D&C	Doctrine and Covenants
DCC	Doctrine and Covenants Commentary
DS	Doctrines of Salvation
DWW	Discourses of Wilford Woodruff
GD	Gospel Doctrine
GS	Gospel Standards
HC	History of the Church
IE	Improvement Era
JD	Journal of Discourses
LDSBE	L.D.S. Biographical Encyclopedia
LHCK	Life of Heber C. Kimball
MofF	Miracle of Forgiveness
PofGP	Pearl of Great Price
TPJS	Teachings of the Prophet Joseph Smith

Suggested Titles

Section

71	A Special Missionary Call to Joseph Smith and Sidney Rigdon
72	Second Bishop—Stewardships
73	Effective Use of Time
74	I Corinthians 7:14—Marriage Within the Church—Salvation of Children
75	Duties of Missionaries
76	The Vision (Degrees of Glory, Etc.)
77	Insights to the Book of Revelation
78	Purposes of the Law of Consecration
79	Power in Our Church Callings
80	Teach and Testify
81	Keys of the Kingdom—First Presidency—A Counselor
82	A Principle of Forgiveness—Judged By What We Know—A Law of Blessings
83	Women and Children Under the Law of Consecration
84	Priesthood
85	One Mighty and Strong—The Book of the Law—Salvation Only Through the Church
86	The Wheat and the Tares—Lawful Heirs to the Priesthood
87	Prophecy on Wars
88	The Olive Leaf
89	The Word of Wisdom
90	Keys of the Kingdom—Oracles of God
91	The Apocrypha
92	A Lively Member
93	How and What to Worship
94	Church Buildings
95	Chastisement for Delaying the Building of the Kirtland Temple
96	Dividing the French Farm—For What Purpose?
97	Zion
98	Purpose of the Law—Law of Forgiveness, Retribution, War
99	Law of Representation
100	How and What to Teach—Promises
101	Jackson County—Why Cast Out

102	The First High Council—A Church Court
103	Redemption of Zion—Zion's Camp
104	Order of the Church for the Salvation of Men
105	Zion Not to be Redeemed for a Little Season
106	Compensation for Full-time Calling—Children of Light
107	Priesthood and Church Government
108	Strengthen Your Brethren
109	Dedicatory Prayer—Kirtland Temple
110	The Appearance of the Savior—Keys Restored
111	Mission to Salem, Massachusetts—Follies
112	Thomas B. Marsh—The Lord's Instructions to a Quorum President
113	Insights to the Book of Isaiah
114	David W. Patten—A Man of Faith
115	The Name of the Lord's Church—Far West, Missouri Temple
116	Adam-ondi-Ahman
117	The More Weighty Matters
118	Twelve Apostles—Faith and Obedience
119	The Lord's Law of Tithing
120	Disbursement of Tithing Funds
121	Constitution of the Priesthood
122	Why Suffering?
123	Anti-Christ Literature and Works
124	Nauvoo Temple—Being Accepted of the Lord
125	Saints in Iowa
126	Brigham Young—His Acceptable Offering to the Lord
127	Baptisms for the Dead—Witnesses and Recordings
128	Baptisms for the Dead—Records in Heaven—Review of the Restoration
129	Three Grand Keys by which Messengers May Be Known
130	The Godhead—Conditions in Heaven
131	Three Heavens in the Celestial Kingdom—The More Sure Word of Prophecy
132	Celestial Marriage
133	The Appendix—The Gathering and the Second Coming
134	Governments and Man's Laws—Religion and Divine Laws
135	Martyrdom—Joseph and Hyrum Smith
136	Covenants and Promises—Camp of Israel
137	Joseph Smith's Vision of the Celestial Kingdom
138	Joseph F. Smith's Vision of the Redemption of the Dead

Table of Contents

Acknowledgements iii
Key to Abbreviations iii
Suggested Titles .... iv, v
Preface .... viii-xii
Chapter   1   Section 71 1
Chapter   2   Section 72 7
Chapter   3   Section 73 11
Chapter   4   Section 74 15
Chapter   5   Section 75 19
Chapter   6   Section 76 25
Chapter   7   Section 77 37
Chapter   8   Section 78 43
Chapter   9   Sections 79 and 80 49
Chapter   10   Section 81 53
Chapter   11   Section 82 59
Chapter   12   Section 83 63
Chapter   13   Section 84 67
Chapter   14   Section 85 77
Chapter   15   Section 86 85
Chapter   16   Section 87 91
Chapter   17   Section 88 99
Chapter   18   Section 89 115
Chapter   19   Section 90 127
Chapter   20   Section 91 131
Chapter   21   Section 92 135
Chapter   22   Section 93 139
Chapter   23   Section 94 145
Chapter   24   Section 95 149
Chapter   25   Section 96 153
Chapter   26   Section 97 157
Chapter   27   Section 98 163
Chapter   28   Section 99 171

Chapter	29	Section 100	177
Chapter	30	Section 101	183
Chapter	31	Section 102	193
Chapter	32	Section 103	199
Chapter	33	Section 104	203
Chapter	34	Section 105	209
Chapter	35	Section 106	217
Chapter	36	Section 107	221
Chapter	37	Section 108	235
Chapter	38	Section 109	239
Chapter	39	Section 110	245
Chapter	40	Section 111	251
Chapter	41	Section 112	257
Chapter	42	Section 113	263
Chapter	43	Section 114	267
Chapter	44	Section 115	271
Chapter	45	Section 116	277
Chapter	46	Section 117	281
Chapter	47	Section 118	285
Chapter	48	Sections 119 and 120	291
Chapter	49	Sections 121, 122, and 123	297
Chapter	50	Section 124	309
Chapter	51	Section 125	319
Chapter	52	Section 126	321
Chapter	53	Sections 127 and 128	327
Chapter	54	Section 129	335
Chapter	55	Section 130	339
Chapter	56	Section 131	347
Chapter	57	Section 132	353
Chapter	58	Section 133	365
Chapter	59	Section 134	371
Chapter	60	Section 135	377
Chapter	61	Section 136	383
Chapter	62	Section 137	389
Chapter	63	Section 138	393
Appendix			401
Selected Bibliography			409

Preface

Volume Two of Sacred Truths of the Doctrine and Covenants is a continuation of the approach to the study of the Doctrine and Covenants that was presented in Volume One. The authors call attention to the premises that served as a basis for the organization and presentation of the materials in both volumes. Inserted herein is a reproduced extract from the Introductory Chapter of Volume One:

Gospel Scholarship

A study of the Doctrine and Covenants is a study of the Lord's doctrine. By this study one also learns of man's opportunity to enter into covenants with the Lord that makes possible man's eventual exaltation. Such a study is not limited to historical events and sayings. The gospel scholar who studies the Doctrine and Covenants will seek not only to learn and understand the truths revealed by the Lord, but he will also endeavor to discover and make application of these truths in his own life. Ultimately, the purpose of all gospel scholarship is to enhance the opportunity for the individual to attain unto personal salvation. This concept of gospel scholarship is the basis upon which this book has been written.

There is another dimension of gospel scholarship. The way the gospel is taught, whether verbally or in written form, should be consistent with principles of simplicity. Two great gospel scholars have emphasized this dimension of gospel presentation:

> The Lord has a great many principles in store for us; and the greatest principles which he has for us are the most simple and plain. The first principles of the Gospel which lead us unto eternal life are the

simplest, and yet none are more glorious or important unto us. Men may labour to make a great display of talent, learning, and knowledge, either in printing or preaching. They may try to preach the mysteries and to present something strange, great, and wonderful, and they may labour for this with all their might, in the spirit and strength of man without the aid of the Holy Spirit of God, and yet the people are not edified, and their preaching will not give much satisfaction. It is the plainest and the most simple things that edify us the most, if taught by the Spirit of God; and there is nothing more important or beneficial unto us. (Wilford Woodruff, JD, Vol. 5, p. 50)

Make quality performance a goal. Seek the Spirit of the Lord. Study the scriptures. Work in unity. Stay close to the fundamentals so that what you teach will be true. Strengthen your lessons by making them simple. (Spencer W. Kimball, "Men of Example," p. 11)

Based upon these two fundamental principles of gospel scholarship (application of salvation principles and simplicity), this book presents information pertinent to each section of the Doctrine and Covenants. Each presentation provides the following:

1. Suggested Title

Each section of the Doctrine and Covenants has been given a suggested title which will serve as a capsulized summary of the content of the section. It will also serve as a guide to the gospel scholar and assist him to find and remember the content of the various sections. Several of the sections have been given titles by the Lord or by His Prophet, Joseph Smith, Jun. The Savior called Section 1, His "Preface" and Section 42, His "Law." The Prophet Joseph Smith referred to Section 76 as "The Vision" and Section 88 as "The Olive Leaf."

By formulating a title for each section of the Doctrine and Covenants, the gospel scholar will be able to more effectively use this volume of scripture. To assist in the effective use of these titles, a complete list of all section titles is provided in the front of the book and a cross-reference index of all titles is provided as an Appendix at the end.

2. Overview of Section Content

For each section of the Doctrine and Covenants, an overview is provided of the content of the section. This overview gives emphasis to the various doctrinal teachings and concepts as contained within the section. It is not strictly a listing of sequential verses except in those cases where it lends itself to a separation of concepts. This overview should aid the gospel scholar to become familiar with the content of each revelation.

3. Historical Setting

Each section of the Doctrine Covenants must be studied in light of its historical setting. President Joseph Fielding Smith has stressed the importance of this approach:

> You may take it up if you want to by topics, or doctrines, that is good; but you are not going to understand the Doctrine and Covenants, you are not going to get out of it all there is in it unless you take it up section by section; and then when you do that, you will have to study it with its setting as you get it in the history of the Church. (DS, Vol. 3, p. 199)

In this book, a historical setting for each section of the Doctrine and Covenants has been provided. This historical information is not exhaustive, but has been selected to assist the gospel scholar to better understand the content of each revelation.

4. Sacred Truths

As previously mentioned, an important dimension of gospel scholarship is the transfer of gospel principles into the behavioral patterns of the individual.

In this book, various gospel principles will be discussed from each section of the Doctrine and Covenants. An attempt has been made to point out the importance of applying these principles in a meaningful way to one's life and circumstances today.

All truth is sacred to the Lord. Truth becomes sacred to the individual when it is understood and applied. The Doctrine and Covenants is a depository of sacred truths as revealed by the Lord.

The Doctrine and Covenants—The Lord's Book

The Doctrine and Covenants is the Lord's book and serves as a means to help us become a pure people before the Lord (see D&C 100:16). In the Lord's preface to His book, He gave directions as to how His revelations in this dispensation should be used to bring about His purposes for the salvation of mankind:

1. Publish the Commandments

> Behold, this is mine authority, and the authority of my servants, and my preface unto the book of my commandments, which I have given them to publish unto you, O inhabitants of the earth. (D&C 1:6, underlining added)

Preface

The Lord wanted His book published. This was an essential step in the raising up of a pure people. Of course, Lucifer has always opposed purity in people and consequently took steps to prevent the publishing of the book. A mob gathered in Jackson County and destroyed the printing office of W.W. Phelps and most of the papers and publication work. Bishop Partridge and Charles Allen were tarred and feathered, and members of the Phelps family were thrown outside with their furniture. (See HC, Vol. 1, pp. 390-393)

Notwithstanding this opposition, the revelations were preserved and subsequently published. How grateful the world should be to have access to the Lord's book containing His revelations.

2. Search the Commandments

> Search these commandments, for they are true and faithful, and the prophecies and promises which are in them shall all be fulfilled. (D&C 1:37)

The Lord wants us to know the contents of His book. Once the book was published, the directive was given to "search" the contents.

President Kimball has emphasized the need to evaluate our scripture "searching" habits. He has said:

> ...I ask us all to honestly evaluate our performance in scripture study. It is a common thing to have a few passages of scripture at our disposal, floating in our minds, as it were, and thus to have the illusion that we know a great deal about the gospel. In this sense, having a little knowledge can be a problem indeed. I am convinced that each of us, at some time in our lives, must discover the scriptures for ourselves—and not just discover them once, but rediscover them again and again. (Ensign, September 1976, p. 4)

3. Teach the Commandments

> And also gave commandments to others, that they should proclaim these things unto the world;...(D&C 1:18)

The Lord commanded that the revelations contained in His book should be taught, not only to the Latter-day Saints, but to all the world by the mouth of His servants. (See D&C 1:1-6) Clearly, this commission to teach the contents of the Lord's book can only be fulfilled by those who come to know the contents of His book by searching and obtaining personal understanding. (See D&C 11:21)

Intent and Purpose of This Work

The purpose of this book is that it should serve as a supplement to the individual's study of the Doctrine and Covenants. It is not to be construed as a substitute for either studying or teaching the scriptures. This book should strengthen the individual's conviction that the scriptures are the source of truth and the depository of the gospel of Jesus Christ. This book is intended to direct the reader's attention to the scriptures and encourage an increased study thereof.

The authors accept full responsibility for the contents of this book. Any errors or mistaken conclusions that may be found herein are the responsibility of the authors. Earnest effort has been made to present the truth as it has been revealed by the Lord and taught by the General Authorities of the church.

Testimony

The Doctrine and Covenants is a testimony that the Savior lives and reveals His mind and will through His living prophets in this dispensation. The Lord continues to direct His church through revelation and thus provides divine guidance for the membership of His kingdom upon the earth. A safe and a wise course through the vicissitudes of mortality will always be clearly defined by the Lord's living oracles.

Chapter 1

Doctrine and Covenants Section 71

Suggested Title

A Special Missionary Call to Joseph Smith and Sidney Rigdon

Overview of Section Content

1. Joseph Smith and Sidney Rigdon are called on a special mission for a season (vs. 1-6)
2. Specific instructions and promises to Joseph Smith and Sidney Rigdon while on this mission (vs. 7-11)

Historical Setting

Joseph Smith, Jun.

After Oliver Cowdery and John Whitmer had departed for Jackson County Missouri, I resumed the translation of the Scriptures [Bible], and continued to labor in this branch of my calling with Elder Sidney Rigdon as my scribe, until I received the following: (HC, Vol. 1, p. 238)

Joseph Fielding Smith

...Ezra Boothe who apostatized after his return from Missouri, did all in his power to injure the Church. He was responsible for the publication of the earliest attacks against the Church. He also caused articles to be published in the press among which were some scandalous letters published in the Ravenna *Ohio Star*, which created a bitter spirit on the part of many people. December 1, 1831, the Lord gave a revelation to Joseph Smith and Sidney Rigdon (Sec. 71.) in which the Lord said: "Behold, thus saith the Lord unto you my servants Joseph Smith, Jun., and Sidney Rigdon, that the time has verily come that it is necessary and expedient in me that you should open your mouths in proclaiming my gospel, the things of the kingdom, expounding the mysteries thereof out of the scriptures, according to that portion of Spirit and power which shall be given unto you, even as I will." They were, therefore, released for the time of this mission from translating the scriptures [Bible], that they might go forth to confound their enemies . . . . (CHMR, Vol. 2. p. 40)

Sacred Truths

Introduction

In this special missionary call, the Lord counselled and taught Joseph Smith and Sidney Rigdon. In this chapter we will discuss two of the concepts about which the Lord spoke:

1. Power in the Ministry
2. Enemies of the Lord's work

Power in the Ministry

As these two men were called by the Lord to perform a special service in the ministry, they were instructed that they would have power in their ministry provided that they did the following:

1. *Proclaim the gospel* (See D&C 71:1)

The Lord expects those who have received the gospel to share it with those who have not received it. (See D&C 50:13-14; 60:2, 13; 62:3; 88:81) It is one thing to be good—it is quite another to do good. (See D&C 78:7)

2. *Proclaim the gospel out of the scriptures* (See D&C 71:1)

In order to teach the gospel out of the scriptures, one must first know the gospel out of the scriptures. One cannot teach what he does not know. Note that the time had come that it was necessary and expedient to teach from the scriptures. When the time comes for scriptural presentation, the time for scriptural preparation has passed for that presentation. It is one thing to know the gospel is true—it is quite another to know the gospel.

3. Proclaim the gospel by the power of the Spirit (See D&C 71:1)

Whenever one receives a "portion of Spirit" as it pertains to the gospel, he has received a spiritual witness and a personal understanding. Such is the nature of an individual testimony. When the gospel of Jesus Christ is taught by one who has a personal spiritual witness, there is an accompaniment of power in such teaching. This power brings the honest-in-heart a spiritual conviction of the gospel truth being taught. President Joseph F. Smith taught the importance of teaching the gospel by the power of the spirit. He said:

> ...It is my opinion that the Lord bears record to the testimonies of his servants unto those who hear those testimonies, and it is left with them whether or not they will harden their hearts against the truth and not listen to it, and abide the consequences. I believe the Spirit of the Almighty God is upon most of the elders who go out into the world to proclaim the gospel. I believe their words are accompanied by the testimony of the Spirit of God. But all men are not open to receive the witness and the testimony of the Spirit. And the responsibility will rest with them. Yet it may be possible the Lord withholds his Spirit from some, for a wise purpose in him, that their eyes are not opened to see and their minds not quickened to comprehend the word of truth. As a rule, however, it is my opinion that all men who are seeking after the truth and are willing to receive it, will also receive the witness of the Spirit which accompanies the words and testimonies of the servants of the Lord; while those whose hearts are hardened against the truth and will not receive it when it is borne record of to them, will remain ignorant and without a comprehension of the gospel. (GD, p. 360)

This same power in the ministry that was promised Joseph Smith and Sidney Rigdon is available to and needed by all who serve in any capacity in the ministry of the Lord. To latter-day parents, priesthood and auxiliary leaders, home and visiting teachers, and others of the Church, the Lord said:

> Now, behold this is wisdom; whoso readeth, let him understand and receive also;
> For unto him that receiveth it shall be given more abundantly, even power. (D&C 71:5-6)

Enemies of the Lord's Work

Whenever any of the Lord's authorized servants proclaim the gospel according to the Lord's pattern previously described in this chapter, the enemies of the Lord will come to realize the following:

1. *Their shame shall be made manifest* (D&C 71:7)

To the honest seeker of truth, who receives the gospel by the spirit, the shame of those who fight against the Lord's work will be readily discerned. The destructive efforts of Satanic forces will be spiritually detected.

2. *Their efforts are against the Lord* (See D&C 71:8)

It is comforting to the Lord's servant to realize that when he performs his tasks according to the Lord's pattern, those who reject his message are, in reality, rejecting the Savior. Those who resist and reason against the servant are resisting and reasoning against the Lord. President Joseph F. Smith taught:

> ...up to date everything that has been done to thwart the purposes of God and to frustrate his designs has been overruled for the good of Zion and for the spread of truth. And that will continue to be the case until the end, for they are fighting God's work, and not mine nor that of any other man. (GD, p.339)

3. *Their cause will not prosper* (See D&C 71:9)

There is a peace that comes to those who labor in the Lord's ministry. They know that no weapon formed against the Lord's servants will ever prosper. The Lord's work cannot be destroyed and will not fail. President Heber J. Grant has said:

> Our enemies have never done anything that has injured this work of God, and they never will. I look around, I read, I reflect, and I ask the question, Where are the men of influence, of power and prestige, who have worked against the Latter-day Saints? Where is the reputation, for honor and courage, of the governors of Missouri and Illinois, the judges, and all others who have come here to Utah on special missions against the Latter-day Saints? Where are there people to do them honor?...Where are the men who have assailed this work? Where is their influence? They have faded away like dew before the sun. We need have no fears, we Latter-day Saints. God will continue to sustain this work; He will sustain the right. If we are loyal, if we are true, if we are worthy of this gospel, of which God has given us a testimony, there is no danger that the world can ever injure us. (GS, pp. 85-86)

4. *They will be confounded by the Lord* (See D&C 71:10)

Enemies to the Lord's work are enemies to the Lord. Every one of such will eventually be confronted with the Lord's truth and be confounded in the Lord's own due time. President Lee counselled the Saints to keep the commandments and promised that the Lord will take care of their enemies. President Lee said:

> I always remember the word of the Lord when I hear these things said by those who are trying to tear down his work. The Lord has said: [Quoted D&C 71:7-11]...
>
> What he is trying to have us understand is that he will take care of our enemies if we continue to keep the commandments. So, you Saints of the Most High God, when these things come, and they will come—this has been prophesied—you just say,
>
> "No weapon formed against the work of the Lord will ever prosper, but all glory and majesty of this work that the Lord gave will long be remembered after those who have tried to befoul the name of the Church and those of its leaders will be forgotten, and their works will follow after them."
>
> We feel sorry for them when we see these things happen. (CR, October 1973, p. 167)

Summary and Conclusion

This is the Lord's work. Therefore, it must be attended to and accomplished His way. There are enemies and opposition to those who participate and represent the Lord in His work. Nevertheless, if His authorized servants will keep the commandments, the Savior will take care of their enemies and triumph over all.

Chapter 2

Doctrine and Covenants Section 72

Suggested Title

Second Bishop—Stewardships

Overview of Section Content

1. Newel K. Whitney called to be a Bishop in Kirtland (vs. 1-2, 8)
2. Stewards to render an account of their stewardships both in time and in eternity (vs. 3-4)
3. Several duties of Bishop Whitney (vs. 5-7, 9-14)
4. Certification of stewards for an inheritance in Zion (vs. 15-26)

Historical Setting

Joseph Smith, Jun.

Knowing now the mind of the Lord, that the time had come that the Gospel should be proclaimed in power and demonstration to the world, from the Scriptures, reasoning with men as in days of old, I took a journey to Kirtland, in company with Elder Sidney Rigdon on the 3rd day of December, to fulfil the above revelation [Section 71] On the 4th, several of the Elders and members assembled together to learn their duty, and for edification, and after some time had been spent in conversing about our temporal and spiritual welfare, I received the following:....(IIC, Vol. 1, p. 239)

Joseph Fielding Smith

...At a very early day after the organization of the Church the Lord revealed the need of a bishop to look after the temporalities and stewardships in the Church. Bishop Edward Partridge was called and sent to Zion to engage in the duties of his calling. On the 4th day of December, 1831, while the Prophet and Sidney Rigdon were engaged in their ministry refuting their enemies, a meeting of the elders was called and the Lord gave them a very important revelation. (CHMR, Vol. 2, pp. 40-41)

Sacred Truths

Introduction

In obedience to the Lord, as directed in Doctrine and Covenants 71:1-2, Joseph Smith and Sidney Rigdon proceeded on their special mission. They were not only to proclaim the gospel to their enemies and non-church members but they were also to meet with church members while on this mission.

While in a meeting with some of the elders of the church, interest was expressed concerning the temporal and spiritual welfare of the members. In response to this concern, the Lord gave this revelation (Section 72) in which He called Newel K. Whitney to serve as a bishop to the saints in Ohio. (See D&C 72:2, 8) It is important to note that the Lord called a man to serve as a bishop but also outlined some of the duties he would be expected to perform. No one can be expected to perform correctly unless he first understands his responsibilities.

In this chapter, we will discuss some of the revealed responsibilities of a bishop and the relationship of church members to their bishop.

Some Revealed Responsibilities of a Bishop

It should be understood that in discussing matters pertaining to a bishop, the discussion is not directed toward any particular man who is called to serve as a bishop. Rather, the discussion pertains to the office and calling of a bishop as an ecclesiastical position within the organizational framework of the church.

We will discuss the following five revealed responsibilities of a bishop:

1. Receive an account of members' stewardships (See D&C 72:3, 5)

The bishop is responsible to be aware of and look after the spiritual and temporal welfare of every member of his ward. The bishop obtains such an awareness through personal interviews as well as private discussions with other priesthood leaders. As he interviews people for temple recommends, tithing settlements, annual interviews of the youth, etc. he is, in actuality, receiving an accounting of the members' stewardships in time.

2. Keep the Lord's storehouse (See D&C 72:10)

Bishop's storehouses provide many essential commodities for the use and benefit of welfare recipients. Bishops help determine the amount and kinds of goods that are to be produced by church welfare projects. These will then be stored and distributed by the bishops.

3. Receive funds of the church (See D&C 72:10)

All contributions and offerings made by church members and others on a local level are received and receipted by the bishop. He is responsible for the accountability and disbursement of these funds. Though worthy church members may be called to assist, the bishop is responsible before the Lord for the appropriate care and handling of these funds.

4. Temporal assistance (See D&C 72:11-13)

The bishop is to assist when help is needed, in providing temporary, temporal relief to the worthy needy in his ward. Contributions and offerings of other church members make it possible for the bishop to provide this assistance when needs arise.

5. Certificates of verification (See D&C 72:15-18, 25)

The bishop, as a common judge in Israel, is responsible to the Lord to verify the worthiness of the members of his ward. In this revelation the Lord directed that such verification be given in the form of a certificate that confirmed the member's acceptance before the Lord. This certificate assured the worthy member of certain privileges and blessings that are promised to the faithful.

Bishops of the church, as judges in Israel, continue to issue certificates of worthiness, or acceptability, as they provide temple recommends, recommends for ordinances, certificates of membership, etc.

Relationship of Church Members to their Bishop

Our salvation is in the hands of the Lord. His bishops are called to aid Him in caring for the temporal and spiritual salvation of the church membership. Latter-day Saints must realize the importance of the office of a bishop. It is only through this office that anyone can receive the full benefits and blessings of church membership. For example, one's salvation and exaltation is contingent upon having received and remained worthy of the ordinances of the priesthood given in the temple. Everyone who has this privilege extended to them to enter the Lord's house is granted such privilege by the bishop who verifies his worthiness and acceptability before the Lord.

Parents in Zion are responsible to teach their children to understand and respect the office of their bishop. Their salvation is administered by the Lord through that office. Thus, our eternal destiny is affected by our relationship with the Lord through His authorized servant, the bishop.

Summary and Conclusion

The Lord has provided for the spiritual and temporal needs of His children. Bishops are called by the Lord through His prophet to aid in caring for and providing both spiritual and temporal assistance. Thus, the people are blessed as they sustain and hearken to the Lord's authorized representatives.

Chapter 3

Doctrine and Covenants Section 73

Suggested Title

Effective Use of Time

Overview of Section Content

1. Elders to continue preaching the gospel until conference convenes (vs. 1-2)
2. Joseph Smith and Sidney Rigdon are to resume translation of the Bible and also continue preaching (vs. 3-6)

Historical Setting

Joseph Smith, Jun.

...On the 10th of January, I received the following revelation making known the will of the Lord concerning the Elders of the Church until the convening of the next conference. (HC, Vol. 1, p. 241)

Hyrum M. Smith and Janne M. Sjodahl

A Conference had been appointed to be held at Amherst, Ohio, January 25th, 1832. The Elders (for their names see Sec. 75) while waiting for Conference time, were anxious to know the will of the

Lord, whereupon the Prophet received this Revelation, . . .(DCC, p. 431)

Sacred Truths

Introduction

In this revelation, the Lord responded to the desires of the elders, as discussed in the Historical Setting of this chapter. He also gave Joseph Smith additional instructions pertaining to:

1. A future conference of the elders (See D&C 73:2)
2. The resuming of the translation of the Bible (See D&C 73:3-4)

This translation had been temporarily suspended in lieu of a special missionary call given to Joseph Smith and Sidney Rigdon. (See D&C 73:3-4)

3. The continued preaching of the gospel (See D&C 73:4)

In this chapter, we will only discuss the Lord's counsel to the elders concerning their effective use of time.

Effective Use of Time

While waiting for conference to convene the elders desired to know what the Lord wanted them to do with their time. Note what the Lord said to these elders:

> For verily, thus saith the Lord, it is expedient in me that they should continue preaching the gospel, and in exhortation to the churches in the regions round about, until conference. (D&C 73:1)

In other words, while waiting, do something productive. This principle can be applied to all of us. How much time is lost while waiting at airports, doctor's and dentist's offices, for meetings to start, and a host of other like situations? Do something constructive while waiting, is the counsel of the Lord.

President Joseph F. Smith stressed the importance of this concept when he said:

> I desire to say to this congregation at this time that I have felt very strongly of late a desire, a responsibility, I may say, resting upon me, to admonish the Latter-day Saints everywhere to cease loitering away their precious time, to cease from all idleness. It is said in the revelations that the idler in Zion shall not eat the bread of the laborer, and there is vastly too much, in some parts—not universally, but there is far too much precious time wasted by the youth of

Zion, and perhaps by some that are older and more experienced and who ought to know better, . . . Read good books. Learn to sing and to recite, and to converse upon subjects that will be of interest to your associates, and at your social gatherings, instead of wasting the time in senseless practices that lead only to mischief and sometimes to serious evil and wrongdoing; instead of doing this, seek out of the best books knowledge and understanding. Read history. Read philosophy, if you wish. Read anything that is good, that will elevate the mind and will add to your stock of knowledge, that those who associate with you may feel an interest in your pursuit of knowledge and of wisdom. (GD, p. 235)

Summary and Conclusion

The Lord expects us to use our time wisely. We are accountable before Him for the use we make of the time given us to perform our labors.

Chapter 4

Doctrine and Covenants Section 74

Suggested Title

I Corinthians 7:14—Marriage Within the Church—Salvation of Children

Overview of Section Content

1. The law of Moses, part-member families, and marriage within the Church (vs. 1-5)
2. Little children are holy and sanctified through the Savior's atonement (vs. 6-7)

Historical Setting

Joseph Smith, Jun.

Upon the reception of the foregoing word [Section 73] of the Lord, I recommenced the translation of the Scriptures, and labored diligently until just before the conference, which was to convene on the 25th of January. During this period, I also received the following, as an explanation of the First Epistle to the Corinthians, 7th chapter, 14th verse: . . .(HC, Vol. 1, p. 242)

Sacred Truths

Introduction

The verse in question (Bible, I Cor. 7:14) appears in this revelation as verse 1. The problem that the apostle Paul was addressing in his letter to the Corinthian saints and his counsel to them can be categorized into three topics:

1. Part-member families
2. Marriage within the Church
3. Salvation of children

Part-Member Families

Paul was trying to convince the Corinthian saints that the converted member ought not to forsake the non-member spouse. (See D&C 74:1) The reason he gave for this counsel is explained by the following commentary:

> In the Corinthian Church, some evidently held that when the husband, or wife, had been converted, he, or she, ought to abandon the unconverted partner as unclean and contaminating. Not at all! St. Paul says, in substance, that the conversion of one of the partners has brought a sanctifying influence into the family. As Meyer puts it, "The non-believing partner in a marriage __ becomes partner—as if by sacred contagion—of the higher, divinely consecrated character of his consort." "Else," the Apostle argues, "were your children unclean." If the wife—this is the argument—must abandon a husband because he is not a Church member, she would also be obliged to abandon her children. But this is not required. (DCC, p. 432)

Marriage Within the Church

Paul continued his counsel to the saints and specifically addressed the question of the importance of marrying within the church. The problems of religious conflicts that arise within the part-member families can be avoided when the decision is made to marry within the church. (See D&C 74:2-6; See also Bible, II Cor. 6:14)

A modern prophet has given this same counsel. President Spencer W. Kimball has taught:

> Clearly, right marriage begins with right dating. A person generally marries someone from among those with whom he associates, with whom he goes to school, with whom he goes to church, with whom he socializes. Therefore, this warning comes with great emphasis. Do not take the chance of dating non-members

or members who are untrained and faithless. A girl may say, "Oh, I do not intend to marry this person. It is just a 'fun' date." But one cannot afford to take a chance on falling in love with someone who may never accept the gospel. True, a small percentage have finally been baptized after marrying Church members. Some good women and some good men have joined the Church after the mixed marriage and have remained devout and active. We are proud of them and grateful for them. They are our blessed minority. Others who did not join the Church were still kind and considerate and cooperative and permitted the member spouse to worship and serve according to the Church patterns. But the majority did not join the Church and, as indicated earlier, friction, frustration and divorce marked a great many of their marriages. (M of F, pp. 241-242)

Salvation of Children

A child is innocent because of the sanctifying power of the Savior's atonement until he begins to become accountable for his own actions. (See D&C 74:7) The restoration of the gospel has provided abundant insight to the status of children as the following scriptural references attest:

1. D&C 29:46-47
2. D&C 68:27
3. D&C 93:38
4. B of M, Moroni 8
5. B of M, Mosiah 3:16

Summary and Conclusion

We learn from this revelation that the gospel of Jesus Christ is not a divisive influence in the lives of members of families. Rather, the gospel is a unifying element and solidifies families both in mortality and in eternity.

Chapter 5

Doctrine and Covenants Section 75

Suggested Title

Duties of Missionaries

Overview of Section Content

1. The Lord's counsel and promises to His faithful missionaries (vs. 1-5, 10-12, 18-29)
2. The Lord calls several elders on missions (vs. 6-9, 13-17, 30-36)

Historical Setting

Joseph Smith, Jun.

A few days before the conference was to commence in Amherst, Lorain county, I started with the Elders that lived in my own vicinity, and arrived in good time. At this conference much harmony prevailed, and considerable business was done to advance the kingdom, and promulgate the Gospel to the inhabitants of the surrounding country. The Elders seemed anxious for me to inquire of the Lord that they might know His will, or learn what would be most pleasing to Him for them to do, in order to bring men to a sense of their condition; for, as it was written, all men have gone out of the way, so that none doeth good, no, not one. I inquired and received the following: . . .(HC, Vol. 1, pp. 242-243)

Sacred Truths

Introduction

On January 10, 1832, the Lord gave a revelation to several elders in response to their concern as to how they should effectively use their time until the convening of the conference of Jan. 25, 1833. (See D&C Section 73) At that time, the Lord told the elders:

> For, verily, thus saith the Lord, it is expedient in me that they should continue preaching the gospel, and in exhortation to the churches in the regions round about, until conference;
> And then, behold, it shall be made known unto them, by the voice of the conference, their several missions. (D&C 73:1-2)

During the conference, the revelation contained in D&C section 75 was given in fulfillment of the Lord's promise.

As noted in the Historical Setting of this revelation, the elders were anxious to know what they should do while on their missions that would be most pleasing to the Lord. In this chapter, we will discuss the following specific duties of the missionaries that the Lord revealed would be pleasing unto Him:

Responsibility to be a Missionary

Every person who has established a covenant relationship with the Lord by the ordinance of baptism, has promised he would do all things whatsoever the Lord might ask of him. In other words, each Latter-day Saint has given his name for service in the Lord's kingdom. To a small group of elders specifically and to all church members generally, the Lord said:

> Hearken, O ye who have given your names to go forth to proclaim my gospel, and to prune my vineyard.
> Behold, I say unto you that it is my will that you should go forth and not tarry, neither be idle but labor with your might. (D&C 75:2-3, See also D&C 42:4-7)

The Lord would be pleased if every young man and all church members everywhere would not tarry but would abide by and respond to the counsel given by a latter-day prophet, Spencer W. Kimball:

> A mission is not just a casual thing—it is not an alternative program in the Church. Neither is a mission a matter of choice any more than tithing is a choice, any more than sacrament meeting is a choice, any more than the Word of Wisdom is a choice. Of course,

we have our free agency, but the Lord has given us choices. We can do as we please. We can go on a mission or we can remain home. But every normal young man is as much obligated to go on a mission as he is to pay his tithing, attend his meetings, keep the Sabbath day holy, and keep his life spotless and clean. (Address to Seminary and Institute Personnel, BYU, June 28, 1968)

Every boy in every country in all the world who has been baptized and received the Holy Ghost will have the responsibility of bearing the message of the gospel to the people of the world. And this is also your opportunity, and it will contribute greatly toward your greatness. (CR, October 1974, p. 117)

The Lord has made clear through our prophets that we must take the gospel to the nations of the world—that all must be taught in their own language, even to the ends of the earth. There is no one else in the world to teach the nations except ourselves. And since there are a limited number of young men, it is proper that every member be a missionary, and to that end the Church has launched a great new program to cover the earth in accordance with the injunction of the Lord:

"Behold, I sent you out to testify and warn the people, and it becometh every man who hath been warned to warn his neighbor." (D&C 88:81)

Hence it is incumbent upon each person to prepare himself for that solemn obligation and privilege. (The New Era, June 1973, p. 8)

Labor With Your Might

Before the church was even organized in this dispensation, the Lord made it clear that to labor with Him in the work of the ministry included a commitment to labor with all of one's heart, might, mind and strength. (See D&C 4:2)

To elders who are engaged in the work of the Savior, the Lord gave counsel: "...neither be idle but labor with your might...." (D&C 75:3) Saving of souls requires great labor. Missionaries who please the Lord use their time in diligent and productive efforts to assist others to come to an understanding of the gospel plan of salvation.

President Henry D. Moyle has said:

> I shall go to my grave saying that missionaries...never rise in their entire life above the stature they carve out for themselves in the mission field. I ask the missionaries all over the world to write that in their book, and then read the book ten years from now. If perchance, they have not risen in that first ten years after they come home from

the mission field, above that status of mediocrity that they [may have] maintained in the mission field, [they should] get down on their knees, pray, and work a little harder and seek to overcome that tremendous handicap they placed upon themselves by their lack of application, lack of appreciation, and lack of dedication in the mission field. (Address to California Mission June 2, 1962)

Many missionaries have borne testimony that they obtained fruits from their labors only when they labored diligently in their callings. It required early rising, long hours of continual effort, and taking advantage of every opportunity to perform a labor in behalf of others who are so dependent upon their untiring efforts.

What To Teach

It pleases the Lord when His missionaries lift up their voices "...as with the sound of a trump, proclaiming the truth according to the revelations and commandments..." (D&C 75:4) A trump symbolizes a clear, far-reaching, penetrating message of truth. The message of the missionary will be in harmony with the sound of a trump when he proclaims the truth "...according to the revelations and commandments..." (See D&C 75:4; see also D&C 42:12 and 52:9, 36)

In 1839, the Quorum of Twelve Apostles wrote a letter addressed to the elders and members of the church throughout the world. In the letter they counseled as follows:

> Be careful that you teach not for the word of God the commandments of men, nor the doctrines of men, nor the ordinances of men, inasmuch as you are God's messengers. Study the word of God, and preach it and not your opinions, for no man's opinion is worth a straw. Advance no principles but what you can prove, for one scriptural proof is worth ten thousand opinions.... (HC, Vol. 3, pp. 395-396)

In a message from the First Presidency, President Harold B. Lee directed:

> I say that we need to teach our people to find their answers in the scriptures. If only each of us would be wise enough to say that we aren't able to answer any question unless we can find a doctrinal answer in the scriptures! And if we hear someone teaching something that is contrary to what is in the scriptures, each of us may know whether the things spoken are false—it is as simple as that. But the unfortunate thing is that so many of us are not reading the

scriptures. We do not know what is in them, and therefore we speculate about the things that we ought to have found in the scriptures themselves. I think that therein is one of our biggest dangers of today.

When I meet with our missionaries and they ask questions about things pertaining to the temple, I say to them, as I close the discussion, "I don't dare answer any of your questions unless I can find an answer in the standard works or in the authentic declarations of the presidents of the Church." (Ensign, December 1972, p. 3)

Pray For the Spirit

It is also pleasing unto the Lord when the missionaries stay in close communication with Him and seek direction in their labors. By so doing they can be taught " . . .all things that are expedient for them . . ." (D&C 75:10) As missionaries are instructed by the Holy Ghost, they are also strengthened in their capacity to teach others as well as to withstand the discouragements and disappointments that are inevitably a part of a missionary experience. Missionaries who pray always have the assurance that the Lord will " . . .be with them even unto the end." (D&C 75:11)

Leave a Blessing and a Witness

The Lord is pleased when His missionaries heed His counsel to leave a blessing in every home where they are received. They are also expected to testify and leave a witness of the truthfulness of the work of the ministry in which they are engaged. (See D&C 75: 19-22) Commenting on this divine commission, Elder Joseph Fielding Smith has said:

> The message and commission to these brethren is also of the greatest interest, in many respects similar to the commission the Savior gave his disciples when he sent them forth in their ministry throughout the land of Palestine. Whenever they entered a house and were received, they were to leave their blessing. From such houses as would not receive them and their message, they were to depart speedily shaking off the dust of their feet as a testimony against them. They were to remember also that one important duty which they were to fulfill and that was to be sure and bear testimony in every instance. If they performed their labors sincerely, humbly and diligently bearing witness of the restoration then it would be more tolerable for the heathen in the day of judgment, than for that house which rejected the message. If no warning had been left, however, then the judgment would be pronounced against the servant who was expected to deliver it. (D. & C. 4.) This statement

that it would be more tolerable for the heathen should be considered. If the heathen are to be judged without law and assigned to the terrestrial kingdom (D. & C. 45:54; 76:72.), then the chances for those who rejected the message would imply that they may find themselves in a lower kingdom, when the judgment comes. The elders who delivered the message were also to be the judges in the day of judgment against those who rejected their testimony. Missionaries of the Church should realize this fact. They are sent to warn the world and when they faithfully do their duty they will stand as witnesses against those who reject them, but if they fail to perform their duty, then those unto whom the message should have been given, will stand up as accusers in their turn, and the unfaithful servants will be condemned. (CHMR, Vol. 2, pp. 46-47)

Summary and Conclusion

We should be reminded that "Every member is a missionary" and the instructions in this revelation are applicable to all who are engaged in service to the Master. Missionaries, parents, priesthood, and auxiliary leaders and teachers throughout the church should remember that their service needs to be of such nature that it is pleasing unto the Lord.

Chapter 6

Doctrine and Covenants Section 76

Suggested Title

The Vision (Degrees of Glory, etc.)

Overview of Section Content

1. The greatness and goodness of the Lord (vs. 1-4)
2. Blessings promised to the faithful (vs. 5-10)
3. Circumstances under which the vision was received (vs. 11-19)
4. A vision of Jesus Christ (vs. 20-24)
5. A vision of Lucifer (vs. 25-29)
6. A vision of sons of perdition (vs. 30-49)
7. A vision of the celestial kingdom (vs. 50-70)
8. A vision of the terrestrial kingdom (vs. 71-80)
9. A vision of the telestial kingdom (vs. 81-88)
10. A comparison of the three kingdoms of glory (vs. 89-112)
11. The things of God are seen and understood by the power of the Holy Ghost (vs. 113-119)

Historical Setting

Joseph Smith, Jun.

Upon my return from Amherst conference, I resumed the translation of the Scriptures. From sundry revelations which had been received, it was apparent that many important points touching the salvation of man, had been taken from the Bible, or lost before it was compiled. It appeared self-evident from what truths were left, that if God rewarded every one according to the deeds done in the body, the term "Heaven," as intended for the Saints' eternal home must include more kingdoms than one. Accordingly, on the 16th of February, 1832, while translating St. John's Gospel, myself and Elder Rigdon saw the following vision: ... (HC, Vol. 1, p. 245)

Sacred Truths

Introduction

As an introduction to this great revelation, we should hear the words of the Prophet Joseph Smith as he commented on the majesty and magnitude of this heavenly vision:

> Nothing could be more pleasing to the Saints upon the order of the kingdom of the Lord, than the light which burst upon the world through the foregoing vision. Every law, every commandment, every promise, every truth, and every point touching the destiny of man, from Genesis to Revelation, where the purity of the scriptures remains unsullied by the folly of men, go to show the perfection of the theory [of different degrees of glory in the future life] and witnesses the fact that that document is a transcript from the records of the eternal world. The sublimity of the ideas; the purity of the language; the scope for action; the continued duration for completion, in order that the heirs of salvation may confess the Lord and bow the knee; the rewards for faithfulness, and the punishments for sins, are so much beyond the narrow-mindedness of men, that every honest man is constrained to exclaim: *"It came from God."* (HC, Vol. 1, pp. 252-253)
>
> I could explain a hundredfold more than I ever have of the glories of the kingdoms manifested to me in the vision, were I permitted, and were the people prepared to receive them. (HC, Vol. 5, p. 402)

Contained in this revelation are descriptive accounts of six visions. Each account is a record of what two men saw as they became witnesses of these things before all the world. That the visions are given to two men is in keeping with the divine law of witnesses as explained by President Joseph Fielding Smith:

> There is a law definitely stated in the scriptures governing testimony and the appointment of witnesses. This law the Lord has *always* followed in granting new revelation to the people.
>
> All down through the ages this law has been a fixed and definite one. If we had perfect records of all ages, we would find that *whenever the Lord has established a dispensation, there has been more than one witness to testify for him*. Paul in writing to the Corinthians said: "In the mouth of two or three witnesses shall every word be established." (DS, Vol. 1, p. 203)

This chapter will contain a discussion of information from each of the six visions and a comparison of the three kingdoms of glory.

A Vision of Jesus Christ

Joseph Smith and Sidney Rigdon are witnesses of the reality and living existence of Jesus Christ. Regardless of what the inhabitants of the world may think or say to the contrary, these men declared unequivocally:

> And now, after the many testimonies which have been given of him, this is the testimony, last of all, which we give of him: That he lives! (D&C 76:22)

As substantive evidence of this bold declaration and testimony, Joseph recorded that they knew whereof they spoke because they "...saw him...and...heard the voice bearing record that he is the Only Begotten of the Father..." (D&C 76:23)

What is the value of such a testimony? A witness and a faith that Jesus Christ lives is the most fundamental and valuable truth given to mankind. All else that is taught becomes meaningless without the understanding that Jesus is not a dead Christ. All saving truths that effect man's eternal destiny are based upon the existence of this one fundamental truth—that He lives. These are the greatest words ever spoken to mankind. It is sweet for living souls to know that He, who died, now lives. There is life after death.

Jesus Christ is not an ordinary being. The magnitude of His creative and atoning powers extend beyond the scope of mortal understanding. We learn from this vision that His work of creation is not limited to this world. Neither is the extent of His atonement as it applies to the lives of Father's children. The powers of the Savior's atonement also extend to the inhabitants of other worlds. (See D&C 76:24)

Commenting on the Savior's atonement, Joseph Smith wrote in poetic verse:

And I heard a great voice, bearing record from heav'n,
He's the Savior, and only begotten of God—
By him, of him, and through him, the worlds were all made,
Even all that career in the heavens so broad,

Whose inhabitants, too, from the first to the last,
Are sav'd by the very same Savior of ours;
And, of course, are begotten God's daughters and sons,
By the very same truths, and the very same pow'rs.
(Times and Seasons, Vol. 4, No. 6, dated Feb. 1, 1843, pp. 82-85; see also Millennial Star, Vol. 4, pp. 51-55; see also *The Vision*, by N. B. Lundwall, pp. 156-164)

A Vision of Lucifer

We learn from the account of this vision that Lucifer does exist and is a living personage. Both Joseph Smith and Sidney Rigdon beheld him and recorded the reality of his existence. (See D&C 76:28)

We also learn that Lucifer " . . .was in authority . . ." in the premortal life. (See D&C 76:25) Authority in the presence of God is known to us as priesthood. In other words, Lucifer held the priesthood. We know that Lucifer rebelled against his Heavenly Father. One of the great insights given in this vision was the way this rebellion was manifested.

Our Heavenly Father chose His first-born son (Jesus Christ) to carry out the plan of salvation and be the redeemer of the world. Lucifer rejected that selection and would not accept nor sustain the placement of Jesus Christ in authority over him and all others of Father's children. Because of his refusal to render obedience to his Father's decision he " . . .rebelled against the Only Begotten Son . . .[he] . . .was thrust down from the presence of God and the Son." (D&C 76:25; See also D&C 29:36; P of GP, Moses 1:19; 4:1-3)

It is imperative that members of The Church of Jesus Christ learn a great truth from the above account. Whenever they are tempted to rebel against authorized priesthood authority chosen by the Lord to direct His church, they are, in reality, playing the Lucifer game. If they do not cease, but continue in their rebellion, they will find themselves ultimately subjected to the same fate as Lucifer—cast out of Father's presence for rebellion.

There is yet another great insight to be gained from this vision. The heavens wept over Lucifer when he fell. (See D&C 76:26) Who wept and why? We were all there when he was cast out. We wept. After all, he was a spirit child of God and our spirit brother. The loss of any soul is the greatest tragedy that can ever take place in the heavens or on the earth. A true Latter-day Saint can distinguish between the evil, unworthy influence of sin and the value of the soul of the sinner. He rejects and deplores evil in any form. But his heart weeps over the potential loss of the sinner.

A Vision of Sons of Perdition

In this vision, Joseph Smith was taught the fate of the saints of God who yield themselves to and are finally overcome by the power of Satan. (See D&C 76:29-30) The covenant saints are a prime target of Lucifer. They alone can be taken to the depths of misery where he dwells, and become sons of perdition. They can rise higher and fall further than any other group of Father's children.

In this revelation, the Lord reveals five steps that will lead a covenant member of the church into the awful status of a son of perdition: (See D&C 76:31)

1. Know the power of God
2. Partake of God's power
3. Allow himself to be overcome by the power of the devil
4. Deny the truth
5. Defy God's power

The Lord describes the above actions in the following terms:

> Having denied the Holy Spirit after having received it, and having denied the Only Begotten Son of the Father, having crucified him unto themselves and put him to an open shame. (D&C 76:35)

The Prophet Joseph Smith discussed this sin as follows:

> All sins shall be forgiven except the sin against the Holy Ghost; for Jesus will save all except the sons of perdition. What must a man do to commit the unpardonable sin? He must receive the Holy Ghost, have the heavens opened unto him, and know God, and then sin against him. After a man has sinned against the Holy Ghost, there is no repentance for him. He has got to say that the sun does not shine while he sees it; he has got to deny Jesus Christ when the heavens have been opened unto him, and to deny the plan of salvation with his eyes open to the truth of it; and from that time he begins to be an enemy. This is the case with many apostates of the Church of Jesus Christ of Latter-day Saints.
>
> When a man begins to be an enemy to this work, he hunts me; he seeks to kill me, and never ceases to thirst for my blood. He gets the spirit of the Devil—the same spirit that they had who crucified the Lord of Life,—the same spirit that sins against the Holy Ghost. You cannot save such persons; you cannot bring them to repen-

tance: they make open war like the Devil, and awful is the consequence.(HC, Vol. 6, pp. 314-315)

In another revelation, the Lord referred to this unpardonable sin in the following words:

> The blasphemy against the Holy Ghost, which shall not be forgiven in the world nor out of the world, is in that ye commit murder wherein ye shed innocent blood, and assent unto my death, after ye have received my new and everlasting covenant, saith the Lord God....(D&C 132:27)

President Joseph Fielding Smith explained this concept as follows:

> ...Shedding innocent blood is spoken of in the scriptures as consenting to the death of Jesus Christ and putting him to shame. For those who have had the witness of the Holy Ghost, fighting with wicked hate against his authorized servants is the same, for if this is done to them, it is also done against him. For men who have had the light of the Holy Ghost to turn away and fight the truth with murderous hate, and those who are authorized to proclaim it, there is no forgiveness in this world, neither in the world to come. (IE, July 1955, p. 494)

As to the ultimate fate of sons of perdition, the Lord informs us that only they who become such, will have a full knowledge of the nature of such punishment. (See D&C 76:44-48) However, it should be understood that the sons of perdition will be resurrected, though they will not be redeemed from their sins nor will they inherit a kingdom of glory. (See D&C 76:36-39)

President George Q. Cannon explained the meaning contained in the above verses as follows:

> In many minds there has been a great misapprehension on the question of the resurrection. Some have had the idea, and have taught it, that the sons of perdition will not be resurrected at all. They base this idea, and draw this conclusion, from the 38th and 39th paragraphs of Section 76 of the book of Doctrine and Covenants....
>
> A careful reading of these verses, however, and especially of the preceding paragraphs, will show that the Lord does not, in this language, exclude even the sons of perdition from the resurrection. It is plain that the intention is to refer to them explicitly as the only ones on whom the second death shall have any power, "for ALL

THE REST shall be brought forth by the resurrection of the dead, through the triumph and the glory of the Lamb." This excluded class are the only ones on whom the second death shall have any power, and "the only ones who shall not be redeemed in the due time of the Lord after the sufferings of his wrath."

This is by no means to say that they are to have no resurrection. Jesus our Lord and Savior died for all, and all will be resurrected—good and bad, white and black, people of every race, whether sinners or not; and no matter how great their sins may be the resurrection of their bodies is sure. Jesus has died for them and they all will be redeemed from the grave through the atonement which He had made. (The Latter-day Prophets and The Doctrine and Covenants, Vol. 2, pp. 470-471)

A Vision of the Celestial Kingdom

Every Latter-day Saint should be encouraged in his quest for the celestial kingdom by what he learns from this vision. This eternal goal is attainable by all who truly desire to reach it. This glorious destiny is not restricted to people of position, specific parentage, or those who have achieved prestigious honors. The Lord informs us that the following are required for all men and women who desire celestial exaltaion: (See D&C 76:50-53)

1. Receive a testimony that Jesus is the Christ
2. Enter into covenants with the Lord through the ordinance of baptism
3. Keep the commandments
4. Receive the Holy Ghost
5. Be sealed by the Holy Spirit of Promise

The Lord described some of the blessings in store for exalted beings:

1. *Membership in the Church of the Firstborn.* (See D&C 76:54)

This is the status of resurrected beings who qualify for exaltation in the celestial kingdom. (See D&C 76:94-95; 88:4-5) For those in mortality who qualify as heirs of exaltation in the celestial kingdom, they have the promise of membership in the Church of the Firstborn and will be taken up to the literal fulfillment of their promises. (See D&C 78:20-21)

2. *Receive all things from the Father.* (See D&C 76:55-61)

Exalted beings receive of the fulness and the glory of our Heavenly Father. They are Gods and have power over all things, including life, death, things present and things future.

3. *Dwell in the presence of God.* (See D&C 76:62-70)

Exalted persons will enjoy the presence of the Father and the Son and will never lose that blessed privilege. They will also be privileged to reign with Christ on the earth during the millennium, having come forth in the first resurrection. These people enjoy the full benefits and blessings provided by the perfect atonement, having been made perfect through the mediator, Jesus Christ.

Those who receive the blessings of celestial exaltation do so because of their faith in Jesus Christ. Living by faith in Him provides protection against Lucifer and prevents being overcome by the powers of evil. Faith in the Savior provides power to overcome all things. (See D&C 76:31, 53, 60)

A Vision of the Terrestrial Kingdom

There are many of Father's children who live good and honorable lives. They live high standards of decency and integrity and reflect the moral principles of the Lord's gospel in their lives. One thing they lack, however, is the desire to enter into and keep covenants with the Lord. In this vision, the Lord identified these people as follows:

1. Those who die without law. (See D&C 76:72; see also D&C 45:54)

As an explanation of this verse, Elder Melvin J. Ballard has said:

> Now those who died without law, meaning the pagan nations, for lack of faithfulness, for lack of devotion in the former life, are obtaining all that they are entitled to. I don't mean to say that all of them will be barred from entrance into the highest glory. Any one of them who repents and complies with the conditions might also obtain celestial glory, but the great bulk of them will only obtain terrestrial glory. (Melvin J. Ballard, Crusader for Righteousness, p. 221)

2. Those who had been in spirit prison because they rejected the gospel in mortality. (See D&C 76:73-74)

Commenting on these verses, Elder Melvin J. Ballard has said:

> Any man or woman who has heard the Gospel and rejected it—not only those in the days of Noah, but any man or woman in this day who has had a good chance to receive and embrace the Gospel and enjoy its blessings and privileges, but who has been indifferent of these things, ignoring and neglecting them—such a person need not hope or anticipate that when he is dead the work can be done for him and he can gain celestial glory. Don't you Latter-day Saints get the notion that a man can live in defiance or total indifference, having had a good chance—not just a casual chance or opportunity—to accept the Gospel and that when he dies

you can go and do the work for him and have him receive every blessing that the faithful ones are entitled to. (Melvin J. Ballard, Crusader for Righteousness, p. 221)

3. ***Those who were honorable men of the earth.*** (See D&C 76:75-77)

Discussing this group, Elder Alvin R. Dyer said:

> Many noble and great bodies will possess this kingdom, receiving to an extent the glory of God as administered by the Son, but not of a fulness. These, for the most part, will be men who, during earth-life existence, sought the excellence of men; and some who gave of their time, talents and endeavor to the ways of manmade ideals of culture, science, and education, but thought not to include God and his ways in their search for a complete life. They receive more of the spirit of the world and of the wisdom which men teacheth, and, yet, are just men, however, neglecting that spirit which is of God. (Who Am I, pp. 552-553)

4. ***Those who were not valiant in the testimony of Jesus.*** (See D&C 76:79)

Elder Spencer W. Kimball explained the message of this verse:

> The Lord is at the helm, brothers and sisters, and he will continue to be there, and his work will go forward. The important question is whether we, as individuals, will be going in that same direction. It's up to us. This is a gospel of individual work. I wish our Latter-day Saints could become more valiant. As I read the seventy-sixth section of the Doctrine and Covenants, the great vision given to the Prophet Joseph Smith, I remember that the Lord says to that terrestrial degree of glory may go those who are not valiant in the testimony, which means that many of us who have recieved baptism by proper authority, many who have received other ordinances, even temple blessings, will not reach the celestial kingdom of glory unless we live the comandments and are valiant.
>
> What is being valiant? I believe that John, in the book of Revelation, says something about valiancy. He is speaking to the people at Sardis, one of the cities which Paul had proselyted. He is speaking to the Saints, mind you, not to the people in the world. He says: "I know thy works, that thou hast a name that thou livest, and art dead." (Rev. 3:1.)
>
> There are many people in this Church today who think they live, but they are dead to the spiritual things. And I believe even many who are making pretenses of being active are also spiritually dead. Their service is much of the letter and less of the spirit. (CR, April 1951, pp. 104-105)

A Vision of the Telestial Kingdom

The inhabitants of the telestial kingdom were the wicked people of the earth. They rejected the Lord's prophets and participated in such evil doings as lying, immorality, etc. (See D&C 76:98-103) They are not the sons of perdition but will be cleansed as a result of their sufferings in hell while in the spirit world. They will come forth in the last resurrection and inherit the lowest kingdom of glory. They have no claim upon the environments of the Savior or the Father, but will enjoy the ministrations of the Holy Spirit. (See D&C 76:81-86, 106)

On one occasion, the Prophet Joseph Smith wrote the account of the vision (D&C Section 76) in poetic verse. A portion of the poem pertains to the vision of the telestial kingdom and its inhabitants. The Prophet described them as follows:

> These are they that receive'd not the gospel of Christ,
> Or evidence, either, that he ever was;
> As the stars are all diff'rent in glory and light,
> So differs the glory of these by the laws,
>
> These are they that deny not the spirit of God,
> But are thrust down to hell, with the devil, for sins,
> As hypocrites, liars, whoremongers and thieves,
> And stay 'till the last resurrection begins.
>
> (Times and Seasons, Vol. 4, No. 6, Feb. 1, 1843, pp. 82-85; See also Millennial Star, Vol. 4, pp. 51-55; See also *The Vision*, by N. B. Lundwall, pp. 156-164)

A Comparison of the Three Kingdoms of Glory

At the conclusion of this revelation, the Lord gave some additional information concerning the three degrees of glory, most of which specifically pertained to the telestial kingdom. The Lord said that a great number of people will be heirs of this lesser degree of glory. He said they will be "...as innumerable as the stars in the firmament of heaven, or as the sand upon the seashore." (D&C 76:109)

We also learn from this comparison that once people are assigned to a kingdom of glory, there will not be an opportunity to advance to a higher degree of glory "...worlds without end." (D&C 76:112) President Spencer W. Kimball has said:

> After a person has been assigned his place in the kingdom, either in the telestial, the terrestrial or the celestial, or to his exaltation, he will never advance from his assigned glory to another glory. That is eternal! (M of F, pp. 243-244)

Section 76

Summary and Conclusion

As we contemplate the light and knowledge contained in this revelation, we are impressed with the magnitude and majesty of this vision. To emphasize the value and importance of these revealed truths, we refer to a statement made by Joseph Fielding Smith as follows:

> ...Section 76 of the Doctrine and Covenants in its sublimity and clearness in relation to the eternal destiny of the human family, has not been surpassed. It should be treasured by all members of the Church as a priceless heritage. It should strengthen their faith and be to them an incentive to seek the exaltation promised to all who are just and true. So plain and simple are its teachings that none should stumble or misunderstand. (CHMR, Vol. 2, p. 50)

In conclusion, the fundamental question with which we are all confronted is as follows: How do we stand in our relationship to a testimony of Jesus Christ? Sons of Perdition deny Him. (See D&C 76:3-5) Telestial people receive not the testimony of Jesus. (See D&C 76:82) Terrestrial people reject the testimony of Jesus in mortality, but afterwards receive it and/or fail to be valiant in the testimony of Jesus. (See D&C 76:74, 79) Celestial saints receive the testimony of Jesus and are true and faithful to it. (See D&C 76:51-53) Our eternal destiny is dependent upon our faithfulness to a testimony of Jesus Christ.

Chapter 7

Doctrine and Covenants Section 77

Suggested Title

Insights to the Book of Revelation

Overview of Section Content

1. The earth in its future state (vs. 1)
2. Insights to the creation, condition, and destiny of beasts (vs. 2-4)
3. John's vision of faithful elders in the spirit world (vs. 5)
4. The seven thousand-year periods of the earth's temporal existence (vs. 6-7, 12-13)
5. The missions of certain angels sent from God (vs. 8-10)
6. The one hundred and forty-four thousand high priests (vs. 11)
7. The mission of John the Revelator (vs. 14)
8. Two prophets to the Jewish nation (vs. 15)

Historical Setting

Joseph Smith, Jun.

     About the first of March, in connection with translation of the Scriptures, I received the following explanation of the Revelation of St. John: . . .(HC, Vol. 1, p. 253)

Joseph Fielding Smith

...After the return of the Prophet from Amhurst [sic], he resumed his translation of the Scriptures. About the first of March, while engaged in this work, questions arose in regard to the meaning of some of the figurative and symbolical writings of John in the book of Revelation. There are many things therein which the brethren did not understand, therefore the Prophet inquired of the Lord and received answer to his question.... (CHMR, Vol. 2, pp. 62-63)

Sacred Truths

Introduction

The Book of Revelation contains symbolic and figurative writings. This revelation (Section 77) contains many insights that assist the reader in understanding the content and teachings of the revelation given to John. Section 77 is arranged in a question and answer format, much of which is self-explanatory, or has been clearly explained by the leaders of the Church. However, some of the content of the section has not been sufficiently interpreted by appropriate church authority. In light of the foregoing comments, we will only discuss four topics in this chapter.

Creation, Condition, and Destiny of Beasts

The Lord has revealed the following pertaining to beasts and animals of the earth: (See D&C 77:2-4)

1. They will be resurrected and placed in their appropriate places in Heaven. As the fall of Adam affected animals, (see B of M, 2 Nephi 2:22) so also through the atonement will the animals be heirs of salvation in their respective spheres.

2. The spirits of animals are in the likeness of their bodies. The spirit is eternal and does not change. The spirit of an elephant looks like an elephant; the spirit of man looks like a man. This is true of all creatures under Heaven. Therefore, the body of the creature cannot change and evolve into something different and still look like its spirit. This principle is simply stated by the Lord that there might not be misunderstandings.

3. They will be given knowledge, including power to move and act and as such, have the capacity to enjoy their eternal happiness and destiny.

The Prophet Joseph Smith, Elder Joseph Fielding Smith, and the First Presidency have further explained and commented on these principles:

Joseph Smith, Jun.

John saw curious looking beasts in heaven; he saw every creature that was in heaven,—all the beasts, fowls and fish in heaven,—actually there, giving glory to God. How do you prove it? (See Rev. 5:13.) "And every creature which is in heaven, and on the earth, and under the earth, and such as are in the sea, and all that are in them, heard I saying, Blessing, and honor, and glory, and power, be unto Him that sitteth upon the throne, and unto the Lamb for ever and ever."

I suppose John saw beings there of a thousand forms, that had been saved from ten thousand times ten thousand earths like this,—strange beasts of which we have no conception: all might be seen in heaven. The grand secret was to show John what there was in heaven. John learned that God glorified Himself by saving all that His hands had made, whether beasts, fowls, fishes or men; and He will glorify Himself with them.

Says one, "I cannot believe in the salvation of beasts." Any man who would tell you that this could not be, would tell you that the revelations are not true. John heard the words of the beasts giving glory to God, and understood them. God who made the beasts could understand every language spoken by them. The four beasts were four of the most noble animals that had filled the measure of their creation, and had been saved from other worlds, because they were perfect: they were like angels in their sphere. We are not told where they came from, and I do not know; but they were seen and heard by John praising and glorifying God. (HC, Vol. 5, pp. 343-344)

Joseph Fielding Smith

We also learn from this revelation and the word of the Lord in other revelations that in the eternities the animals and all living creatures shall be given knowledge, and enjoy happiness, each in its own sphere, in "their eternal felicity." These creatures will not then be the dumb creatures that we suppose them to be while in this mortal life. (CHMR, Vol. 2, p. 69)

First Presidency

The Church of Jesus Christ of Latter-day Saints, basing its belief on divine revelation, ancient and modern, proclaims man to be the direct and lineal offspring of Deity. God Himself is an exalted man, perfected, enthroned, and supreme. By His almighty power He organized the earth, and all that it contains, from spirit and element, which exist co-eternally with Himself. He formed every plant that grows, and every animal that breathes, each after its own kind, spiritually and temporally—"that which is spiritual being in the likeness of that which is temporal, and that which is temporal in the likeness of that which is spiritual." He made the tadpole and the ape, the lion and the elephant; but He did not make them in His own image, nor endow them with Godlike reason and intelligence. Nevertheless, the whole animal creation will be perfected and perpetuated in the Hereafter, each class in its "distinct order or sphere," and will enjoy "eternal felicity." That fact has been made plain in this dispensation (Doctrine and Covenants, 77:3). (IE, Vol. 13, No. 1, Nov. 1909, p. 81)

Temporal Existence

The Lord makes it plain in this revelation, that the earth's temporal existence is to be seven thousand years. (See D&C 77:6-7, 12-13; See also D&C 29:22-23) As an explanation of the time period being considered, Elder Joseph Fielding Smith has said:

> By the seven thousand years of temporal existence is meant the time of the earth's duration from the fall of Adam to the end of time, which will come after the millenium and "a little season" which will follow. (CHMR, Vol. 2, p. 64)

Whatever conditions existed on this earth prior to the fall of Adam has not been made known to mankind. Likewise, the length of time the earth existed prior to the fall has not been made known. However, we do know there was no temporal activity or existence (such as sorrow, death, etc.) prior to the fall of Adam. The fall marked the beginning of such temporal experiences and the beginning of the earth's seven-thousand year period of temporal existence. Therefore, it is folly for a person with an understanding of the truths provided in this revelation to project the image of a temporal existence for this earth for millions of years into the past.

We have recorded chronology that accounts for nearly six thousand years of the earth's temporal history. We, in this dispensation, are living in the ending of the sixth thousand-year period, the time just prior to the earth's millennium, that is, the earth's seventh thousand-year period of temporal existence. Elder Orson F. Whitney explained this concept as follows:

> According to received chronology—admittedly imperfect, yet approximately correct—four thousand yers, or four of the seven great days given to this planet as the period of its "temporal existence," had passed before Christ was crucified; while nearly two thousand years have gone by since. Consequently, Earth's long week is now drawing to a close, and we stand at the present moment in the Saturday Evening of Time, at or near the end of the sixth day

of human history. Is it not a time for thought, a season for solemn meditation? Morning will break upon the millennium, the thousand years of peace, the Sabbath of the World! (The Latter-day Prophets and the Doctrine and Covenants, Vol. 3, p. 13)

An additional insight provided in this revelation, is that there is a key given to the chronological time-frame of the events described in John's Book of Revelation. We learn that each seal seen by John in his vision represents a separate sequential thousand-year period of the earth's temporal existence. By knowing which time period is involved, we can better understand and determine the meaning of the many symbolic references given by John. We can better follow the sequence of the earth's events from the fall of Adam to the end of the earth's temporal existence. And, of course, we are better able to discern the intended workings of God in our day as pertains to the restoration of His Kingdom and the events associated therewith for the salvation of man.

One Hundred Forty-Four Thousand

It is refreshing to receive correct understanding from the Lord as to the identity and mission of the 144,000. (See Bible, Revelation, chapter 7) The Lord said these are 144,000 high priests who are called to teach the gospel of Jesus Christ and gather as many as will come unto Him. (See D&C 77:11)

Elder Joseph Fielding Smith taught this principle as follows:

> This certainly is a great honor to be one of the 144 thousand who are specially called by the power of "the angels to whom is given power over the nations of the earth," to bring souls unto Christ. John the Apostle, had the great desire to bring souls to Christ. The three Nephite Disciples likewise sought this great honor and it was granted to them. It is one of the noblest desires that a man can have. It will be a wonderful blessing to those who are called in this great group. This 144 thousand will not be the only ones who worship the Father and the Son, for after speaking of the twelve thousand out of each of the tribes, John records: "After this I beheld, and, lo, a great multitude which no man could number, of all nations, and kindreds, and people, and tongues, stood before the throne, and before the Lamb, clothed with white robes, and palms in their hands; And cried with a loud voice, saying: Salvation to our God which sitteth upon the throne, and unto the Lamb. And all the angels stood round about the throne, and about the elders and the four beasts, and fell before the throne on their faces, and worshipped God." [Bible, Revelation 7:9-11] (CHMR, Vol. 2, pp. 71-72)

Two Prophets

Concerning the "...two prophets that are to be raised up to the Jewish nation in the last days,..." (D&C 77:15), Elder Parley P. Pratt has commented:

> John, in his 11th chapter of Revelations, gives us many more particulars concerning this event. He informs us that, after the city and temple are rebuilt by the Jews, the Gentiles will tread it under foot forty and two months, during which time there will be two prophets continually prophesying and working mighty miracles.
>
> And it seems that the Gentile army shall be hindered from utterly destroying and overthrowing the city, while these two prophets continue. But, after a struggle of three years and a half, they at length succeed in destroying these two prophets, and then overrunning much of the city; they send gifts to each other because of the death of the two prophets; and in the meantime will not allow their dead bodies to be put in graves; but suffer them to lie in the streets of Jerusalem three days and a half, during which the armies of the Gentiles, consisting of many kindreds, tongues and nations, passing through the city, plundering the Jews see their dead bodies lying in the street.
>
> But, after three days and a half on a sudden, the spirit of life from God enters them, and they will arise and stand upon their feet, and great fear will fall upon them that see them. And then they shall hear a voice from heaven saying, "Come up hither," and they will ascend up to heaven in a cloud, and their enemies beholding them.
>
> And having described all these things, then comes the shaking, spoken of by Ezekiel, and the rending of the Mount of Olives, spoken of by Zechariah. John says, "The same hour was there a great earthquake, and the tenth part of the city fell, and in the earthquake were slain of men seven thousand." And then one of the next scenes that follow is the sound of voices, saying, "The kingdoms of this world are become the kingdom of our Lord, and of his Christ; and he shall reign forever and ever." (Voice of Warning, pp. 49-50)

Summary and Conclusion

Section 77 of the Doctrine and Covenants provides the gospel scholar with an opportunity to better understand some of the messages and teaching of the Book of Revelation. The Lord has provided us valuable explanations of passages and statements that are not otherwise understood by those who study the vision given to John.

Chapter 8

Doctrine and Covenants Section 78

Suggested Title

Purposes of the Law of Consecration

Overview of Section Content

1. The Lord instructs His Saints to organize themselves to take care of the poor in Ohio and in Missouri (vs. 1-3, 9-13)
2. The Lord's purpose for having His Saints organized in Ohio and in Missouri (vs. 4-8, 14-15)
3. Adam holds the keys of salvation under the direction of the Savior (vs. 16)
4. Blessings promised to the faithful (vs. 17-22)

Historical Setting

Joseph Smith, Jun.

> Besides the work of translating, previous to the 20th of March, I received the four following revelations: . . . [Sections 78, 79, 80, 81] (HC, Vol 1, p. 255)

Joseph Fielding Smith

> ...During the early part of the year 1832, the Prophet and Sidney Rigdon continued the work of the revision of the Scriptures.

At the time the Prophet was still residing in the house of Father John Johnson, at Hiram [Ohio]. It was during this time that this important revelation was given to the members of the Priesthood who were assembled imparting instructions in relation to the plan of the "united order" or "order of Enoch," on which the promised Zion should be built. The Lord had revealed that it was only through obedience to his divine will, the celestial law, that Zion could be built. The members of the Church rejoiced when the Lord revealed to them the site on which the New Jerusalem, or City of Zion, should be built. Their enthusiasm, however, was not sufficient to carry them through to a conclusion in strict obedience to the divine will. In this revelation (Sec. 78) the Lord reveals his will in words of wisdom to all those holding the High Priesthood. The brethren had made inquiry for further light in relation to the plan of the Lord in relation to the "united order," or "order of Enoch." The Lord said if they would hearken he would speak in their ears "the words of wisdom, that salvation may be unto you in that thing which you have presented before me, saith the Lord God." The time had fully come, and "is now at hand; and behold, and lo, it must needs be that there be an organization of my people, in regulating and establishing the affairs of the storehouse for the poor of my people, both in this place (Ohio) and in the land of Zion."

. . . the Lord had revealed the law of consecration, and had indicated to the members the absolute necessity of living this law, if they would establish Zion. In January, 1831, the commandment was given that the little band of believers should "go to the Ohio," and there the Lord would give them his law (D&C 38:32.) In February 1841, [1831] just after the Saints had assembled in Ohio, the Lord said to them: "He that receiveth my law and doeth it, the same is my disciple; and he that saith he receiveth it and doeth it not, the same is not my disciple, and shall be cast out from among you." February 9, 1841, [1831] the promised law was given and it covered numerous subjects of vital importance to the Church. In this commandment the Lord said: "If thou lovest me thou shalt serve me and keep all my commandments. And behold, thou wilt remember the poor, and consecrate of thy properties for their support that which thou hast to impart unto them, with a covenant and a deed which cannot be broken." Then follows instructions how these properties are to be laid before the bishop of the Church and his counselors. "And it shall come to pass, that after they are laid before the bishop of my church, and after that he has received these testimonies concerning the consecration of the properties of my Church, that they cannot be taken from the Church, agreeable to my commandments, every man shall be made accountable unto me, a steward over his own property, or that which he has received by consecration, as much as is sufficient for himself and family." (D&C 42:29-32) Then follows the charge that "if there shall be properties in the hands of the church, or any individuals of it, more than is necessary for their support after this first consecration, which is a residue to be consecrated unto the bishop, it shall be kept to administer to those who have not, from time to time, that every man who has need may be amply supplied and receive according to his wants. Therefore the residue shall be kept in my storehouse, to administer to the poor and the needy, as shall be appointed by the high council of the church, and the bishop and his council." [D&C 42:33-34] All of this was to be by covenant, for "the salvation of my people." [D&C 42:36]

Now (in March 1832), the Lord says: "The time has come, and is now at hand," [D&C 78:3] for this great undertaking to be accomplished. (CHMR, Vol. 2, pp. 73-75)

Sacred Truths

Introduction

As noted in the Historical Setting of this chapter, the Lord had revealed the law of consecration at an earlier date. Then, in this revelation, the Lord informed the Latter-day Saints that the time had arrived for His people in Ohio and Missouri to live and practice the principles of the law of consecration. (See D&C 78:3) In order to organize the saints and instruct them further in the implementation of this law, the Lord directed Joseph Smith and others to journey to Missouri. (See D&C 78:9-12) In this revelation, the Lord emphasized two important purposes of this law as it pertained to the church as well as the individual lives of the Latter-day Saints. We will discuss these purposes in this chapter.

Equality

The Lord desires that His people attain heaven and equally share in heavenly things. But before this can be a reality, we must learn to be equal in earthly things. (See D&C 78:5-7) The term "equal", as used in this context, should not be understood to mean "dead-level equality." Or in other words, the Lord does not expect that all people will have the same quantity of the same things of the earth. Rather, in a subsequent revelation, the Lord explained equality as meaning that each person under the law should have equal claims or opportunities to obtain the necessary and desirable things of the earth. (See D&C 82:17)

This desired equality is obtained under this law through the processes of consecrating of resources and the development of individual stewardships. Each individual has opportunity to provide for his own needs and share his surplus with others who may be in need. Thus, the equality of the saints is assured and achieved when equal opportunity is afforded each individual. As a further explanation of this concept of equality, the following comments have been made:

Joseph Fielding Smith

> The saints are instructed that it is essential that they be equal in all things, else there can be no righteousness. What would the celestial kingdom be like, if there were not unity and equality prevailing there? So it should be in the Church on earth . . . .
>
> There should be equality in all temporal things. By being equal the Lord does not mean that every man should receive the same compensation for labor performed, but that each should receive according to his needs and thus equality may be maintained. Where there is no selfishness in the hearts of the people this desirable end can be accomplished, but it is bound to fail where jealousy and selfishness are not eliminated from the soul. It is essential that we be able to keep the celestial law of equality. (CHMR, Vol. 2, pp. 75-76)

George Q. Cannon

> The Lord has said that "if ye are not equal in earthly things, ye cannot be in obtaining heavenly things." He has revealed a plan by which this equality can be brought about. Yet, He does not design to make us of equal height; He does not design that we should all have the same colored hair or eyes, or that we should dress exactly alike. This is not the meaning of the word "equality," as it is used in the revelation; but it means to have an equal claim on the blessings of our Heavenly Father—on the properties of the Lord's treasury, and the influences and gifts of His Holy Spirit. This is the equality meant in the revelations, and until we attain to this equality we cannot be equal in spiritual things, and the blessings of God cannot be bestowed upon us until we attain to this as they otherwise would. (JD, Vol. 13, p. 99)

Independence

Another purpose of the law of consecration as stated by the Lord, is to provide a condition of independence for His church and the members thereof. (See D&C 78:14-15, 17-22) The Savior declared that His church is to ultimately be independent of all men and all organizations of men. The church's place is above all things that are not celestial. Latter-day Saints can see the hand of the Lord as He directs His church to purchase and operate production projects, printing presses, broadcasting facilities, etc. The church is developing independence.

The concept of independence extends beyond the church as an organization and becomes a desirable and sought-for objective in the lives of the church members. The church is a vehicle whereby the members may be prepared to become rulers. It is in the church that members are taught to render obedience, preside over and conduct the business of quorums and auxiliary organizations, listen to and apply eternal truths as given by inspired and authorized representatives of the Lord, and generally develop the attributes and qualities of character that provide freedom, confidence, and independence for the individual. It is no wonder that people in the church who more fully understand this principle are not only willing, but anxious to serve in the church and labor for the salvation of others.

Commenting on the intended destiny of the church and its people, Elder Joseph Fielding Smith has said:

> By the keeping of the covenant of consecration the Lord promised that the Church would stand independent above all other creatures beneath the celestial world. It is the will of the Lord, that eventually, the Church may take its rightful place above all other creatures upon the earth, or other spheres that are not celestial. This is the destiny of the Church, but the destiny of each of us individually depends on whether or not we will accept in faithfulness the covenants and obligations which are given us. The promise is that if we will be obedient we shall come up and be made rulers over many kingdoms. Those who receive the celestial exaltation will, without doubt, be made rulers over many kingdoms, and they will have power and authority to direct and to counsel those of lesser glories. Moreover, they will have the privilege of exaltation and of becoming creators in their own right as the sons of God. (CHMR, Vol. 2, p. 77)

Summary and Conclusion

Whatever else it may be, the law of consecration is a part of the Lord's program to develop celestial people. It provides a way by which the Lord's church and His people can have equal opportunity to achieve exaltation and stand independent above all non-celestial things.

Chapter 9

Doctrine and Covenants Sections 79 and 80

Suggested Titles

Section 79—Power in our Church Callings
Section 80—Teach and Testify

Overview of Section Content

Section 79

1. Jared Carter is called to preach the gospel (vs. 1)
2. Blessings and promises for faithfulness (vs. 2-4)

Section 80

1. Stephen Burnett and Eden Smith are called to preach the gospel (vs. 1-3)
2. A command to bear witness of the truth of the gospel (vs. 4-5)

Historical Setting

The contents of these two sections are such that they can be studied together. Historically, they were given to the Prophet Joseph Smith during the same period of time. (See Historical Setting for Chapter Eight, Section 78) In both of these sections, men are called to missionary service by the Lord.

Sacred Truths

Introduction
Inasmuch as these two sections both pertain to missionary calls we will discuss the contents of both in this chapter. We will discuss two major messages from these revelations.

Power In Our Church Callings
In every church calling there is an expectation that the servant will render service in accordance with the Lord's commandment to serve with all of one's "...heart, might, mind and strength..." (D&C 4:2) Though this is basic to every calling, labor alone is insufficient without the spiritual power that should accompany each calling.

From the calling given to Jared Carter (Section 79) we learn that this spiritual power accompanies one's labor when the servant is in harmony with the following:

1. Every servant of the Lord is given certain duties and responsibilities. There are also certain limits or restrictions within which he is authorized to labor. In other words, he is to labor within the boundaries of his calling and not encroach upon the jurisdiction of others in their individual assignments. The Lord instructed Jared Carter that he should labor within "...the power of the ordination wherewith *he* has been ordained,..." (D&C 79:1, italics added) When a servant labors diligently to perform the specific duties assigned to him, he is entitled to receive the power of the spirit which assists him in the successful performance of his labors. To illustrate:

A diligent bishop is entitled to inspiration in connection with matters pertaining to his ward but not in matters pertaining to the stake. A faithful missionary will have spiritual guidance in his assigned tasks, but will not be inspired in the direction of the entire mission.

President Joseph Fielding Smith stressed this concept when he said:

> The priesthood is the *power* to bless mankind, and all of those who hold the priesthood are expected to use it *within the sphere of their assignment* to bless their fellowmen. When any of us use this authority in righteousness, and as directed by the Holy Spirit, our acts are binding and will be recognized by the Lord both in time and in eternity. (CR, October 1970, p. 153, italics added)

2. Every person who is called to serve in the Lord's church is given proper authority to function in his assignment. However, there is need for each person, properly called, to seek for spiritual direction and understanding beyond his own knowledge and capabilities. The Lord directed Jared Carter to go forth "...in the *power* of the ordination..." (D&C 79:1, italics added) He was promised this spiritual assistance through the Holy Ghost which would "... teach him the truth and the way whither he shall go." (D&C 79:2)

The servant may not always see or understand the way to fulfill the needs of the Lord's people. But by laboring in harmony with the spirit of the Lord in his calling, he is able to be taught and shown how to accomplish his duties. Thus, he has power in his calling.

To illustrate the above principle, we refer to Elder Harold B. Lee. After having organized the Manchester Stake in Great Britain, he spoke of his experience there, where missionaries had previously labored in the early days of the Church:

> We were permitted, as we traveled in that same vicinity, to follow the course that Wilford Woodruff was directed under inspiration to go, from the potteries near Hanley down to Froomes Hill, probably some fifty or sixty miles to the south, where, directed by the Spirit, he found a people ready to receive the coming of the servants of the Lord. Within two days after his arrival there, after having met John Benbow and his wife and those who believed in the sect called the United Brethren, he had baptized six members, and in thirty days he had baptized forty-five preachers of the United Brethren, and one hundred sixty members, and obtained thereby the possession of one chapel and forty-five houses for use as meeting places. In eight months he had baptized over 1800—all 600 of the United Brethren with one exception—and 200 ministers of various denominations in the area.
>
> As a true missionary would, without boasting, he wrote this simple summary: "The power of God rested upon us and upon the mission in our field of labor . . . .The sick were healed, devils were cast out, and the lame made to walk." (CR, April 1960, p. 107)

Teach and Testify

When the Lord called Stephen Burnett and Eden Smith into the missionary service, He emphasized fundamental responsibilities of missionaries. Three times the Lord stressed the need for them to preach or declare His gospel. (See D&C 80:1, 3-4) Whatever else may be entailed with the preparation and sending of missionaries to the field, we should remember it is all for one purpose—to teach the gospel to the people of the world. It is true of all members of the church who are also considered to be responsible for sharing the gospel with others. Parents, priesthood leaders, home teachers, etc. are all expected to perform many duties. But one duty that is fundamental and universal to all callings is the teaching of the gospel. No one can be converted to the Lord and His gospel until he is first taught the gospel and given an opportunity to receive it.

All who teach the Savior's gospel must also testify and bear witness of its truthfulness. This is what is meant by the Lord's injunction to teach by the spirit. (See D&C 42:14) The Lord directed:

> ...declare the things which ye have heard, and verily believe, and know to be true. (D&C 80:4)

Of what were the missionaries to bear testimony? They were to testify of that which they had heard and been taught by the Lord's servants. Members of the church can also testify because they have heard the gospel taught in the organizations and meetings of the church. They may not yet know all the scriptural documentation for the various doctrines of the church. But they have heard those doctrines taught in the church and thus they, too, believe and know of its truth.

Summary and Conclusion

The work of the ministry is to assist the Lord in His work of saving the souls of mankind. Faithful servants have the power of the spirit enabling them to teach and testify to saving truths. Thus, this spiritual power influences and changes the lives of people and provides them the opportunity to obtain salvation in the Lord's kingdom.

Chapter 10

Doctrine and Covenants Section 81

Suggested Title
Keys of the Kingdom—First Presidency—A Counselor

Overview of Section Content
1. The Lord calls Frederick G. Williams to be a counselor to Joseph Smith (vs. 1)
2. The keys of the kingdom always belong to the Presidency of the High Priesthood (vs. 2)
3. Some of the duties of Frederick G. Williams as a counselor (vs. 3-5)
4. Promises given to Frederick G. Williams conditioned on his faithfulness (vs. 6-7)

Historical Setting

As noted previously (Chapter Eight, Section 78) this revelation was one of four received by Joseph Smith during the same period of time.

Joseph Fielding Smith

> ...now the time was at hand for the organization of the First Presidency....In March, 1832, the Lord revealed that the First Presidency of the Church should be organized....It was not until

March 18, 1833, that the First Presidency was organized, although Sidney Rigdon and Frederick G. Williams had been acting in the capacity of counselors to the Prophet Joseph Smith for several months, . . . (CHMR, Vol. 2, pp. 79-80)

Sacred Truths

Introduction

In anticipation of the organization of the First Presidency of the church, Frederick G. Williams was called as a counselor to the Prophet Joseph Smith. (See D&C 81:1) In this revelation, the Lord revealed that the keys of the kingdom are held by the First Presidency. He also defined some of the duties of a counselor in that presidency. In this chapter, we will discuss these two subjects.

Keys of the Kingdom

The Lord referred to " . . . the keys of the kingdom . . ." (D&C 81:2) What is meant by this term? President Joseph F. Smith explained as follows:

> The Priesthood in general is the authority given to man to act for God . . . . It is necessary that every act performed under this authority shall be done at the proper time and place, in the proper way, and after the proper order. The power of directing these labors constitutes the keys of the Priesthood. (GD, p. 136)

The restoration in the latter days consisted of the restoring of the authority to act in the name of the Lord and the keys for directing the use of this authority. Various heavenly messengers restored these keys to the Prophet Joseph Smith enabling him to direct the work of the kingdom throughout the earth.

One of the most important lessons we can learn is taught in this revelation. The keys of the kingdom of God ". . . belong always unto the Presidency of the High Priesthood." (D&C 81:2)

The Presidency of the High Priesthood hold the keys of the kingdom of God. The kingdom of God is the church. Therefore, the Presidency of the High Priesthood is also the Presidency of the church. Elder Harold B. Lee taught this principle:

> In the 81st Section of the Doctrine and Covenants, given March, 1832, the Lord through the Prophet Joseph Smith gave this revelation to Frederick G. Williams, in which he was called to be a counselor to the Prophet Joseph Smith, and he said this:

Section 81   55

> "...Frederick G. Williams...to be a high priest in my church, and a counselor unto my servant Joseph Smith, Jun.;" (Note now) "Unto whom I have given the keys of the kingdom, which belong always unto the Presidency of the High Priesthood."
>
> Our conclusion, therefore, must be that anyone holding the keys of the kingdom is also by that same token the president of the High Priesthood of the Church. That settles the matter which sometimes is discussed as to whether Peter might properly be referred to as the President of the Church in the Meridian of Time. To my thinking it would be a very proper reference because he held the keys of the kingdom. (Address to Seminary and Institute Faculty, BYU, July 17, 1958)

Referring to the two offices held by the First Presidency, Elder Joseph Fielding Smith explained:

> There is a difference between the office of President of the Church and President of the High Priesthood; however these two offices cannot be separated and must be held by the same person duly appointed and sustained by proper vote. As President of the Church the presiding officer presides over all the membership of the Church. As President of the High Priesthood he presides over all the Priesthood of the Church and has authority to regulate it, for he holds the keys of that Priesthood....
> ...The President of the Church holds the supreme authority....he, it is, who holds the right of decision and the right of revelation for the Priesthood and for the Church. (CHMR, Vol. 2, pp. 79-80)

It is important to know that the Lord directs His church through the First Presidency who hold the keys of His kingdom. Such knowledge gives us a place to look for direction from the Lord. Elder Harold B. Lee emphasized the importance of this principle as follows:

> Truman O. Angell, the architect of the Temple, was asked to write an article for the Millennial Star describing what the great temple would look like when it was built, so he went into some detail and in this description he said this: "on the two west corner towers, and on the west end, a few feet below the top of the battlements may be seen in bold or relievo, the great dipper or Ursa Major, with the pointers ranging nearly towards the North Star."

This was to impress the moral: The lost may find themselves by the Priesthood; . . . If you can impress nothing else upon a youth tell him if he wants to be safe in this day to keep his eyes upon the president of the High Priesthood of this Church and then you set him the example by doing likewise. (Address to Seminary & Institute Faculty, BYU, July 17, 1958)

Some Duties of a Counselor

The Lord called Frederick G. Williams to serve as a counselor in the First Presidency. In this revelation, the Lord taught him some of his duties. All those who are called to serve as counselors can benefit from that which is given in this section. The Lord stressed the following duties:

1. Be faithful in counsel (See D&C 81:3)

The Lord, in His wisdom, provided counselors to presiding authorities. This organizational concept makes it possible for counselors to share their insights, knowledge, opinions, and wisdom based upon their understanding and experience. The Lord expects counselors to give counsel when invited to do so. The very act of counseling together is for the purpose of arriving at an appropriate decision acceptable to the Lord. That decision is to be determined by the presiding authority under inspiration and when it is declared, counseling ceases. The calling to counsel has been fulfilled at that time. It is the solemn duty of the counselor to be loyal to carry out the decision in all faithfulness before God.

2. Pray always (See D&C 81:3)

The greatest counselors are those who seek counsel themselves from the Master Counselor. It should be remembered that one of the titles given to the Lord is "Counsellor." (See Bible, Isa. 9:6)

3. Proclaim the gospel (See D&C 81:3)

Every calling in the Lord's church includes the responsibility to teach the gospel. The calling of a counselor is not administrative only. He should use the opportunities afforded in his calling to share the principles and teachings of the gospel in order to assist in the ministry of saving the souls of men.

4. Succor, lift, and strengthen (See D&C 81:5)

Counselors are to assist in carrying the weight of responsibility that rests upon the presiding authority. President Harold B. Lee illustrated this role when he served as a counselor to President Joseph Fielding Smith. President Lee explained:

Section 81 57

As I thought of the role of President Tanner and myself as his counselors, I thought of a circumstance in the life of Moses, when the enemies of the church in that day were just as they are in this day. They were threatening to overcome and tear down and to stop the work of the church. As Moses sat upon a hill and raised the rod of his authority, or the keys of his priesthood, Israel prevailed over their enemies; but as the day wore on, his hands became heavy and began to droop at his side. And so they held up his hands so they would not be weakened and the rod would not be lowered. He would be sustained so that the enemies of the church would not prevail over the saints of the Most High God. (See Exod. 17:8-12)

I think that is the role that President Tanner and I have to fulfill. The hands of President Smith may grow weary. They may tend to droop at times because of his heavy responsibilities; but as we uphold his hands, and as we lead under his direction, by his side, the gates of hell will not prevail against you and against Israel....Let's keep our eye on the President of the Church and uphold his hands as President Tanner and I will continue to do. (CR, October 1970, p. 153)

Summary and Conclusion

The value of counselors who discharge their duties in accordance with the provisons of this revelation, is described by the Lord when He said:

And in doing these things thou wilt do the greatest good unto thy fellow beings, and wilt promote the glory of him who is your Lord. (D&C 81:4)

Chapter 11

Doctrine and Covenants Section 82

Suggested Title
A Principle of Forgiveness—Judged by What We Know—A Law of Blessings

Overview of Section Content
1. Requirements necessary to be free from sin (vs. 1-7)
2. Compliance with the Lord's will insures salvation (vs. 8-10)
3. Several brethren are called to manage the affairs of the church under the law of consecration for the benefit of all (vs. 11-21)
4. The Lord counsels His saints to be friendly and judge not and extends promises of peace and blessings (vs. 22-24)

Historical Setting
Joseph Smith, Jun.

On the 26th, I called a general council of the Church, [in Missouri] and was acknowledged as the President of the High Priesthood, according to a previous ordination at a conference of High Priests, Elders and members, held at Amherst, Ohio, on the 25th of January, 1832. The right hand of fellowship was given to me by the Bishop, Edward Partridge, in behalf of the Church. [in Missouri] The scene was solemn, impressive and delightful. During the intermission, a difficulty or hardness which had existed between Bishop Partridge and Elder Rigdon, was amicably settled, and when we came together in the afternoon, all hearts seemed to rejoice and I received the following . . . . (HC, Vol. 1, p. 267)

Joseph Fielding Smith

. . .The first of April 1832 the Prophet Joseph Smith with Newel K. Whitney and Jesse Gause, left for Missouri to fulfill the provisions of the revelation given in March (Sec. 78) in relation to the regulation and establishment of the storehouse for the benefit of the poor, and the consecration of properties in that land . . . .

. . .This revelation is one showing the "order of Enoch" as exercised in the Church in Enoch's day . . . . (CHMR, Vol. 2, pp. 85-86)

Sacred Truths

Introduction

This revelation was received by the Prophet Joseph Smith, while in Missouri organizing the saints within the provisions of the law of consecration. A portion of this revelation (See D&C 82:11-21) reviews some of the principles and purposes of the law of consecration that had previously been revealed by the Lord. (See D&C Sections 42, 51, and 78)

While in conference among the saints in Missouri, the Prophet referred to a problem that existed between two of the brethren in attendance at the conference. (See Historical Setting for this chapter) Shortly after their problem was resolved the Lord spoke about some of the conditional aspects of forgiveness and some of the consequences of unresolved sin. In this chapter we will discuss these two subjects.

Forgiveness is Conditional

The Lord said that if we expect to obtain His forgiveness for our sins, we must first forgive others. (See D&C 82:1; See also D&C 64:7-10) Many people have come to know that they cannot find a peace of conscience resulting from the Lord's forgiveness until they have purged their hearts of unrighteous feelings towards others. We must forgive all others, whether we may have been wronged in family, friendship, professional or other associations. We must be more Christ-like in our attitude if we expect the Lord to be merciful towards us. We all have much for which we need forgiveness. We are hardly justified in seeking the Lord's mercy until we are willing to extend the same to others.

If Latter-day Saints fail to comply with these principles, they sin against this greater light and knowledge and thus receive greater condemnation. (See D&C 82:3) The Prophet Joseph Smith taught:

> God judges men according to the use they make of the light which He gives them. (The Historical Record, Vol. 7, p. 515.)

This principle has a positive dimension, also. Those who live in harmony with this greater light are promised that such compliance will bring them freedom from sin. The Lord is bound to provide them salvation. (See D&C 82:8-10)

Some Consequences of Sin

Those who fail to refrain from sin will receive sore judgments from the Lord. (See D&C 82:2) Whatever the world's attitude may be towards a sinful act is not important. The world may excuse it, condone it, justify it, or even promote it, but the act is still sin and the Lord said that such behavior will reap justice and judgment as the penalty. (See D&C 82:4)

To those who have sought for and received forgiveness for their sins and then failed to continue to comply with the conditions of forgiveness, the Lord said their "...former sins return,..." (D&C 82:7) Discussing this concept, President Brigham Young said:

> If a person with an honest heart, a broken, contrite, and pure spirit, in all fervency and honesty of soul, presents himself and says that he wishes to be baptized for the remission of his sins, and the ordinance is administered by one having authority, is that man saved? Yes, to that period of time. Should the Lord see proper to take him then from the earth, the man has believed and been baptized, and is a fit subject for heaven—a candidate for the kingdom of God in the celestial world, because he has repented and done all that was required of him to that hour. But, after he is baptized and hands have been laid upon him for the reception of the Holy Ghost, suppose that on the next day he is commanded to go forth and preach the Gospel, or to teach his family, or to assist in building up the kingdom of God, or to take all his substance and give it for the sustenance of the poor, and he says, "I will not do it," his baptism and confirmation would depart from him, ...But if he says, with a willing heart and mind, "Here is my substance; I will not only pay the tenth of it, but the whole of it is at your feet; do with it as you please," does he not continue to be saved? Yes.

It is present salvation and the present influence of the Holy Ghost that we need every day to keep us on saving ground. When an individual refuses to comply with the further requirements of Heaven, then the sins he had formerly committed return upon his head; his former righteousness departs from him, and is not accounted to him for righteousness: but if he had continued in righteousness and obedience to the requirements of heaven, he is saved all the time, through baptism, the laying on of hands, and obeying the commandments of the Lord and all that is required of him by the heavens—the living oracles. He is saved now, next week, next year, and continually, and is prepared for the celestial kingdom of God whenever the time comes for him to inherit it. (JD, Vol. 8, p. 124)

Summary and Conclusion

The unrepentant sinner has no promise of salvation. His rewards are, instead, justice and judgment as determined by the Lord.

Those who live by the greater light of the Lord are promised forgiveness and salvation.

Chapter 12

Doctrine and Covenants Section 83

Suggested Title
Women and Children under the Law of Consecration

Overview of Section Content
1. Faithful widows have claim upon the church for their support (vs. 1-2, 6)
2. Women have claim upon their husbands for their support (vs. 2)
3. Widows who are not faithful (vs. 3)
4. Children have claim upon their parents or the church for their support (vs. 1, 4-6)

Historical Setting

Joseph Smith, Jun.

On the 28th and 29th, I visited the brethren above Big Blue river, in Kaw Township, a few miles west of Independence, and received a welcome only known by brethren and sisters united as one in the same faith, and by the same baptism, and supported by the same Lord. The Colesville branch in particular, rejoiced as the ancient Saints did with Paul. It is good to rejoice with the people of God. On the 30th, I returned to Independence, and again sat in council with the brethren, and received the following . . . .(HC, Vol. 1, p. 269)

Joseph Fielding Smith

> ...Following the solemn council the Prophet transacted considerable business "For the salvation of the Saints who were settling among a ferocious set of mobbers, like lambs among wolves." This is a good description of the conditions at that time. The Prophet tried to organize the members of the Church so that they might be independent of every evil and obstacle, by adherence to the covenants offered to them. He taught them to labor together in "mutual friendship and mutual love." On the 28th day of April he visited the brethren above the Big Blue river in Kaw Township, a few miles west of Independence. These were in large numbers, the saints of the Colesville branch. They welcomed him with rejoicing. On the 30th he returned to Independence and again sat in council with the brethren, and on that occasion the Lord gave him further light in relation to the claim of children on their parents, and also the claim of widows upon the Church....(CHMR, Vol. 2, pp. 89-90)

Sacred Truths

Introduction

While still in Missouri, the Prophet Joseph Smith received this revelation, which provided further light and knowledge concerning the law of consecration. Specifically, this section pertains to women and children under the law of consecration. In this chapter, we will discuss the provisions of this law as revealed for them.

Women in the Church

The Lord informs us that in marriage covenants, "Women have claim on their husbands for their maintenance, ..." (D&C 83:2) The word *claim* means rights, privileges, and/or entitlements. A wife has a right before the Lord to expect her husband to provide for her temporal necessities of life. She should not have to feel that she is a recipient of charity. He is not giving charity, but rather he is honoring his marriage covenant responsibility before God. A righteous woman will be grateful for the labors of her husband in her behalf, but is not obligated to feel indebted to him for her maintenance.

In discussing this principle, President Spencer W. Kimball has taught us a further application:

> Peter urged us to give honor unto our wives. (See 1 Pet. 3:7.) It seems to me we should be even more courteous to our wives and mothers, our sisters and our daughters, than we are to others. When

Paul said that a man who did not provide for his own and those of his own household was "worse than an infidel" (1 Tim. 5:8), I like to think of providing for our own as including providing them with affectional security as well as economic security. When the Lord told us in this dispensation that "women have claim on their husbands for their maintenance" (D&C 83:2), I like to think of maintenance as including our obligation to maintain loving affection and to provide consideration and thoughtfulness as well as food. (CR, October 1978, pp. 62-63)

When a sister is widowed, she no longer has a husband to provide for her maintenance. If her family is not able to provide for her temporal needs, and if she is a worthy member of the church, she then looks to the church for support. Under the law of consecration, she has claim on the church for her maintenance. (See D&C 83:1-2, 6) However, her claim is conditioned upon her worthiness as determined by the Lord's authorized representatives and the records of the church. President Joseph F. Smith has taught:

> When one comes to a bishop and asks for assistance because of his or her straitened circumstances, the first thing the bishop should do is to inquire if he or she is a tithe-payer. He should know whether the name is on the book of the law of the Lord, and if not on the book, if he or she has been derelict and negligent in relation to this principle of tithing, he or she has no claim upon the bishop, neither have their children; and if, under those circumstances, the bishop assists him, it will simply be out of pure charity and not because such have any claim upon the Church. (GD, p. 231)

Children in the Church

The Lord has also informed us that "All children have claim upon their parents for their maintenance until they are of age." (D&C 83:4) As with wives, so also with children. They are not recipients of charity, but have claim, before the Lord, upon their parents. Both mothers and fathers should be aware of their responsibility to their children. No child should be unattended by either parent as to his needs for food, clothing, shelter, etc. We should remember what President Kimball said, as quoted earlier in this chapter. Maintenance for children is more than providing them with temporal necessities. It includes the loving care and tender kindness that a child has a right to expect from both of his parents.

If children lose their parents and there is not sufficient family to provide for them, under the law of consecration, they have claim upon the church. President Joseph F. Smith said:

It is intended that the widows shall be looked after when they are in need, and that the fatherless and the orphans shall be provided for from the funds of the Church; that they shall be clothed and fed, and shall have opportunity for education, the same as other children who have parents to look after them. When a child is fatherless and motherless the Church becomes the parent of that child, and it is obligatory upon the Church to take care of it, and to see that it has opportunities equal with the other children in the Church. This is a great responsibility. Have we ever seen the day since the Church was organized when we could carry out this purpose of the Lord fully, and to our heart's content? We have not, because we never have had the means to do it with. But if men will obey the laws of God so that there shall be abundance in the storehouse of the Lord, we will have wherewith to feed and clothe the poor and the orphan and to look after those who are in need in the Church. (CR, October 1899, pp. 39-40)

Summary and Conclusion

Under the law of consecration, the Lord's church fills the role of a vicarious husband and a vicarious father for the widow and orphan in fulfillment of their claim for their maintenance.

Chapter 13

Doctrine and Covenants Section 84

Suggested Title
Priesthood

Overview of Section Content

1. The purpose of the Lord's church being estalished in the last days (vs. 1-5)
2. The lineage of the priesthood from Moses to Adam (vs. 6-18)
3. The greater priesthood and the power of godliness (vs. 19-22, 29)
4. The greater priesthood was taken from Israel in Moses' day. (vs. 23-25)
5. Keys and offices of the lesser priesthood (vs. 26-28, 30)
6. The offering and sacrifice of the sons of Moses (vs. 31-32)
7. The oath and covenant of the priesthood (vs. 33-48)
8. The whole world lieth in sin (vs. 49-53)
9. Chastisement and counsel to the church (vs. 54-61)
10. A commission to preach the gospel (vs. 62-102)
11. Counsel concerning contributions (vs. 103-105)
12. Utilizing and developing the strengths of the priesthood holder (vs. 106-110)
13. Counsel and assurances to the priesthood holders (vs. 111-120)

Historical Setting

Joseph Smith, Jun.

The Elders during the month of September began to return from their missions to the Eastern States, and present the histories of their several stewardships in the Lord's vineyard; and while together in these seasons of joy, I inquired of the Lord, and received on the 22nd and 23rd of September, the following revelation on Priesthood:....(HC, Vol. 1, pp. 286-287)

Joseph Fielding Smith

...In September 1832, the Elders who had been out through the eastern states returned to Kirtland and were anxious to be instructed further regarding Zion and in matters pertaining to their callings. In the presence of Six Elders, who united with the Prophet in earnest prayer, this revelation (Sec. 84) was given....(CHMR, Vol. 2, pp. 101-102)

Sacred Truths

Introduction

This revelation was given in response to elders' desires to learn more about Zion and their callings in the priesthood. It was natural for these elders coming home from missionary service to be anxious to learn all that they could about the establishment of Zion. This subject was uppermost in the minds of the saints at that time. Furthermore, these elders desired to know more about how they should continue to serve in their callings of the priesthood.

In this chapter, we will discuss this revelation under two topics:

1. Zion
2. Priesthood

Zion

Before the Lord restored His church in this dispensation, He revealed that the establishment of Zion was an integral part of the work of His kingdom in the last days. (See D&C 6:6; 11:6; 12:6; 14:6) In 1831, Joseph Smith was directed by the Lord to journey to Missouri that the Lord might reveal to him the location of the city of Zion, the New Jerusalem. (See D&C 52:2-5) After arriving in Missouri, Joseph learned by revelation that Independence, Missouri is to be the location for the city of Zion. He also was told that a temple would be built as part of the establishment of Zion. (See D&C 57:1-3)

The building of the New Jerusalem in the last dispensation was known by prophets in ages and dispensations long since past. Our scriptural records inform us that Enoch knew that the city of Zion, called the New Jerusalem would be built in the last days. (See P of GP, Moses 7:62-64) The prophet Ether recorded that he knew of the building of the New Jerusalem on the American continent. (See B of M, Ether 13:2-6) When the Savior appeared to the Nephite people He taught them that His church would build the city of New Jerusalem on the American continent in the latter days. (See B of M, 3 Ne. 21:12-23) Then, in our dispensation, after the Lord revealed to Joseph Smith the actual location for the city of Zion, Joseph wrote the following statement:

> We believe...that Zion (the New Jerusalem) will be built upon the American continent;...(P of GP, Articles of Faith, No. 10)

As the Savior told the Nephites, so he declared again in our day, that His church is responsible for the assembling of the saints and the building of the city of New Jerusalem, including the construction of the temple of the Lord. (See D&C 84:2-4)

As to the meaning of the term "generation" as used in this revelation, the following explanations have been given:

> "This statement has been a stumbling block to some and there have been various interpretations of the meaning of a generation. It is held by some that a generation is one hundred years; by others that it is one hundred and twenty-years; by others that a generation as expressed in this and other scriptures has reference to a period of time which is indefinite. The Savior said: "An evil and adulterous generation seeketh after a sign." This did not have reference to a period of years, but to a period of wickedness. A generation may mean the time of the present dispensation. Moreover, the statement is qualified in this revelation in the above quotation...."

> This is quite generally understood to be the meaning of this prophecy; but it is quite possible that a complete explanation of it cannot be obtained until it is fulfilled. That is the case with many divine predictions. When they are fulfilled they are clear. (DCC, p.497)

> ...we understand that certain things predicted through the Prophet Joseph Smith are to take place before this generation shall pass away, and the Lord will see to it that the generation in which those things were predicted will not all pass away until all shall be fulfilled, but there is no fixed period for a generation, no set time in the revelations of God, no year or date given when these things shall

take place, and it is folly for anybody to put a date to it. Leave that in the hands of the Lord and he will take care that his word is fulfilled; "not one jot or one tittle shall pass away," as Jesus declared, "but all shall be fulfilled." (Charles W. Penrose, CR, April, 1918, p. 21)

Priesthood

The information pertaining to priesthood that is revealed in this section is so extensive that it is not feasible to attempt a discussion on all aspects of this subject. We will only discuss selected portions of the revelation.

1. Priesthood lineage–Moses to Adam

Any authorized servant of the Lord can trace his priesthood lineage back to the Master. The Lord revealed in this section that Moses did not assume his authority. The authority of the priesthood was given him by one having that authority. This process is revealed by the Lord as having extended back to Adam. (See D&C 84:6-16)

As it was in ancient times, so it is today. Priesthood holders in the Lord's church can identify the source of their authority. The Lord sent messengers from heaven in this dispensation to confer priesthood authority upon the Lord's designated representatives. These men, in turn, bestowed that authority upon other righteous men according to the Lord's pattern, and this process continues in the church today. Every official and authorized act or ordinance performed by a priesthood holder has the same efficacy as if the Lord performed it. Therefore, those who perform as well as those who receive ordinances and blessings under the authority of the priesthood, realize that such experiences are appropriately done by the authority of the Master.

The Lord informs us that there was no man to bestow priesthood upon Adam, since he was first. He received his priesthood from the Lord. Adam was not a descendant of some other form of lower life. He did not evolve. He was born as a son of God, the first man of all men upon this earth. (See D&C 84:16; P of GP, Moses 1:34; Bible, Luke 3:38)

Elder Marion G. Romney, when speaking of Adam, said:

> It would please me immensely if...we could get away from using the language of those who do not believe in the mission of Adam. I have reference to words and phrases such as "primitive man," "prehistoric man," "before men learned to write," and the like. We sometimes use these terms in a way that offends my feelings; in a way which indicates to me that we get mixed up in our understanding of the mission of Adam. The connotation of these terms, as used by unbelievers, is out of harmony with our understanding of the mission of Adam.

"Adam fell that man might be." (2 Nephi 2:25.) There were no pre-Adamic men in the line of Adam. The Lord said that Adam was the first man. (Moses 1:34, 3:7; D. & C. 84:16.) It is hard for me to get the idea of a man ahead of Adam, before the first man. The Lord also said that Adam was the first flesh (Moses 3:7) which, as I understand it, means the first mortal on the earth. I understand from a statement in the book of Moses, which was made by Enoch, that there was no death in the world before Adam. (Moses 6:48; see also 2 Nephi 2:22.) Enoch said:

...death hath come upon our fathers; nevertheless we know them, and cannot deny, and even the first of all we know, even Adam.

For a book of remembrance we have written among us, according to the pattern given by the finger of God; and it is given in our own language. (Moses 6:45-46.)

I understand from this that Enoch could read about Adam in a book which had been written under the tutelage of Almighty God. Thus there were no prehistoric men who could not write because men living in the days of Adam, who was the first man, wrote.

I am not a scientist. I do not profess to know anything but Jesus Christ, and him crucified, and the principles of his gospel. If, however, there are some things in the strata of the earth indicating there were men before Adam, they were not the ancestors of Adam.

Adam was the son of God. He was our elder brother, not older than Jesus, but he was our brother in the same sense that Jesus was our brother, and he "fell" to earth life. He did not come up through an unbroken line of organic evolution. There had to be a fall. "Adam fell that men might be." (2 Nephi 2:25.)

I will go on now and read this scripture before I forget it:

For a book of remembrance we have written among us, according to the pattern given by the finger of God; and it is given in our own language.

And as Enoch spake forth the words of God, the people trembled, and could not stand in his presence. (Moses 6:46-47.)

Some men speak of the ancients as being savages, as if they had no intelligence. I tell you this man Enoch had intelligence, and Adam had intelligence, as much as any man that ever lived since or that lives now. They were mighty sons of God. (CR, April 1953, pp. 123-124)

On the subject of the origin of man, the First Presidency of the church has written an article which is worthy of careful study. (See IE, Vol. 13, No. 1, November 1909, pp. 75-81)

The first principle of the gospel is faith in the Lord Jesus Christ. His humble followers accept without reservation what He has revealed to mankind. The Lord said that Adam was the first man of all men upon the earth. Time will vindicate all truth.

2. The Greater Priesthood

We remember that this revelation was given in response to questions on Zion and Priesthood. In the first portion of this revelation the Lord mentioned the temple as a focal point and an integral part of Zion. (See D&C 84:4) There is also a relationship between the temple and the priesthood. The Lord revealed four of the functions of the greater priesthood: (See D&C 84:19-22)

a. It administers the gospel
b. It holds the key of the mysteries of the kingdom, the knowledge of God
c. Its ordinances manifest the power of godliness
d. Its power allows man to be in the presence of God

Some of the ordinances of the greater priesthood, in which these keys and powers are manifested, are administered only in the temples of the Lord. Thus, in answer to the inquiry of the elders, the Lord informed them that their obtaining of all the powers of the priesthood was contingent upon their righteous participation in all priesthood ordinances.

If any of us desire and expect to obtain eventual access to the powers of godliness and the fulness of the gospel, we must not neglect the opportunity that is available and afforded to us in the temples of the Most High.

Consistent with the Lord's timetable, He has extended all privileges and blessings of the priesthood to all of His worthy covenant children. (See D&C, Official Declaration—2)

3. The Lesser Priesthood

After the children of Israel rejected their opportunity to receive the ordinances of the greater priesthood, they were left with the lesser priesthood. (See D&C 84:23-26; see also Bible, Joseph Smith Translation, Exo. 34:1)

Some of the functions of the lesser priesthood are: (See D&C 84:26)

a. It holds the key of administering of angels
b. It holds the key of the preparatory gospel

The lesser priesthood provides us with the teachings and ordinances necessary to prepare us for the receiving of that which is administered by the greater priesthood, including the ordinances and teachings of the temple.

Section 84 73

4. The Oath and Covenant of the Priesthood

An oath, as it pertains to Diety, is a sworn statement or promise of the Lord describing that which will be or will come to pass. When the Melchizedek Priesthood is conferred upon a man, he receives the oath and covenant of the Father. (See D&C 84:40)

The oath that the Father makes is that the faithful Melchizedek Priesthood holder will be given all that the Father hath. (See D&C 84:38)

The covenant into which the priesthood holder enters is two fold: (See D&C 84:33)

  a. He promises to be faithful
  b. He promises to magnify his calling

Elder Delbert L. Stapley gave insight to the ramifications of the above-mentioned dimensions of the oath and covenant. He taught:

> According to a revelation on priesthood recorded in the 84th section of the Doctrine and Covenants, there are two main requirements of this oath and covenant. First is faithfulness, which denotes obedience to the laws of God and connotes true observance of all gospel standards. For better understanding of the oath and covenant of the priesthood, may I propound these questions:
>
> 1. Can a man be faithful who does not abide by the first two great commandments, to love the Lord God with all his heart, soul, strength, and mind, and his neighbor as himself?
>
> 2. Can a man be faithful who is not honest and truthful in all dealings and relationships with his fellow men?
>
> 3. Can a man be faithful who does not honor the Sabbath day and keep it holy, attend the Sacrament and priesthood metings; also worthily fulfil all other duties in keeping with his callings and obligations that day?
>
> 4. Can a man be faithful who does not plan and arrange for daily family prayer in the home?
>
> 5. Can a man be faithful who does not teach his children the true principles of the gospel of Christ and then set them a worthy example by living according to those truths?
>
> 6. Can a man be faithful who does not observe and keep the Word of Wisdom?
>
> 7. Can a man be faithful who does not pay an honest tithing and fast offering?
>
> 8. Can a man be faithful who does not obey the law of chastity and is not morally clean in his life and habits?

9. Can a man be faithful who does not, through obedience and sacrifice, prepare himself worthily for the holy temples of God where he can receive his endowments and sealings in the higher ordinances of the gospel and thus bind his family happily and eternally together in love and understanding?

10. Can a man be faithful who does not honor and obey the laws of the land?

Perhaps we could summarize by asking, "Can a man be faithful if he does not keep all the commandments of God?" The Savior counseled the man who came to him and inquired, "Good Master, what good thing shall I do, that I may have eternal life?"—by saying, "...if thou wilt enter into life, keep the commandments." (Matt. 19:16-17.) This counsel from the Lord is all inclusive and clearly points the way to joy and happiness.

These enumerated thoughts are just a few requirements associated with faithfulness, but each is important. As you meditate the full meaning of the word, other attributes that are important qualities of faithfulness will also impress and inspire your mind and heart for better understanding and personal resolves.

The second requirement of the oath and covenant of the Holy Priesthood is to magnify one's calling. To magnify is to honor, to exalt and glorify, and cause to be held in great esteem or respect. It also means to increase the importance of, to enlarge and make greater. Keeping this definition in mind, may I again resort to a few questions for more lucid understanding:

1. Can a man magnify his office and calling without honoring and abiding in the priesthood faithfully and worthily as a devoted and true servant of God?

2. Can a man magnify his calling without giving spiritual and humble dignity to his office?

3. Can a man magnify his calling who refuses to accept positions and responsibilities of trust when called upon to serve by his stake president, bishop, or other constituted authority?

4. Can a man magnify his calling if he is not obedient to gospel standards and requirements, and if he also fails to be amenable to the counsel and direction of righteous men who are properly called and approved by the people as their authorized leaders?

5. Can a man magnify his calling who refuses to sustain by his faith, prayers, and works those whom God has called and ordained to preside over him?

6. Can a man magnify his calling who does not use his priesthood in righteousness for the blessing and benefit of his fellow men?

7. Can a man magnify his calling who does not banish all iniquity from his soul, that he may gain favor with God and thus enjoy power in the use of the priesthood to bless people?

Again, may I summarize by asking, "Can a man magnify his calling who is not willing to sacrifice and consecrate all for the building of God's kingdom in righteousness, truth, and power in the earth?"

Here also by prayerful meditation you can add other important considerations applying to holders of the Holy Priesthood magnifying their callings, but these will suffice for the purpose of this talk.

To be faithful and devoted to priesthood obligations is the only way man can gain favor and power with God and have rightful claim upon him for blessings to himself, his family, and others to whom he may minister. The priesthood will not abide in force and power with him who does not honor it in his life by complying with the requirements of heaven. The Prophet Joseph Smith declared, "A man can do nothing for himself unless God direct him in the right way; and the priesthood is for that purpose." To magnify his calling in the priesthood a man must use it in righteousness and service to his fellow men. If he does so, he will gain power in its use and thus become enlarged in his gifts and abilities to perform greater service. Every man who receives the Holy Priesthood and is ordained according to the gifts and callings of God unto him, and faithfully magnifies his sacred calling, which fulfils the conditions of the oath and covenant, is sanctified by the Spirit unto the renewing of his body. He is then worthy to be numbered among the elect of God, having also received the Father's kingdom. By the power of the Spirit, which is light and truth, and through honoring the Holy Priesthood in faithfulness and obedience, a man develops holiness of life and character; therefore, he is set apart by this regeneration of soul for special and sacred trusts with the glorious promise for having continued in the oath and covenant of the priesthood, that "all that my Father hath shall be given unto him." (See D&C 84:38.)

The Lord is bound to fulfill this promise to those who abide by the conditions of the oath and covenant. (CR, April 1957, pp. 76-77)

Those who enter into the oath and covenant of the priesthood and "...breaketh this covenant after he hath received it, and altogether turneth therefrom, shall not have forgiveness of sins in this world nor in the world to come." (D&C 84:41) This penalty means they will lose the privilege of bearing the priesthood in eternity. Elder Joseph Fielding Smith discussed this penalty as follows:

Now when a man makes a covenant that he will receive the priesthood and magnify it, and then he violates that covenant, "and altogether turneth therefrom"—there is a chance to repent if he does not altogether turn therefrom—then there is no "forgiveness of sins in this world nor in the world to come." That does *not* mean that man is going to become a son of perdition, but the meaning is that *he will never again have the opportunity of exercising the priesthood and reaching exaltation*. That is where his forgiveness ends. He will not again have the priesthood conferred upon him, because he has trampled it under his feet; but as far as other things are concerned, he may be forgiven. (DS, Vol. 3, pp. 141-142)

5. *Enlightened Minds*

The Lord further counseled the elders as to their responsibilities as priesthood holders. They were informed that their minds had become darkened in times past as a result of their failure to: (See D&C 84:54-57)

a. Study the principles of the gospel in the Book of Mormon
b. Teach the principles of the gospel to others
c. Live the principles of the gospel

The Lord informed these priesthood holders that they were to be obedient to the above counsel that they might bring forth fruit pleasing unto the Lord. They were promised forgiveness inasmuch as they were faithful. (See D&C 84:58-61)

This counsel is applicable to all who hold the priesthood. If their minds are to be enlightened they must also comply with these responsibilities as outlined by the Lord.

6. *A Commission to Teach the Gospel*

Every Melchizedek Priesthood holder is responsible to the Lord for the preaching of the gospel of Jesus Christ to all the world. (See D&C 50:13-14) In this revelation the Lord emphasized the need and responsibility to perform this phase of priesthood work. (See D&C 84:62-102) He identified many ways by which this work could be done more effectively and promised many blessings to the faithful priesthood laborer. Any priesthood holder who accepts the counsel given by the Lord in this section will be responsive and willing to perform any call when it comes from the authorized representatives of the Lord.

Section 84

Summary and Conclusion

Zion (the New Jerusalem) will be built upon the American continent. This great objective is attainable through the righteous efforts of obedient priesthood holders and all who live and labor under priesthood direction.

Chapter 14

Doctrine and Covenants Section 85

Suggested Title

One Mighty and Strong—The Book of the Law—Salvation Only Through the Church

Overview of Section Content

1. The duty of the Lord's clerk in Zion in recording the names of the faithful (vs. 1-5)
2. One mighty and strong (vs. 6-8)
3. The book of remembrance (vs. 9-10)
4. The book of the law (vs. 11-12)

Historical Setting

Joseph Smith, Jun.

In answer to letters received from the brethren in Missouri, I wrote as follows: ...(HC, Vol. 1, p. 297)

Joseph Fielding Smith

...On the 27th day of November, 1832, the Prophet wrote to Elder William W. Phelps who was in Independence, Missouri, in charge of the printing and with authority to assist the bishop in matters concerning the establishing of the saints in their inheritances and expressed to him in words of tender fellowship, his love and confidence. Matters pertaining to the establishing and building up of Zion weighed heavily on the mind of the Prophet Joseph Smith. His anxiety was very great because of the grave responsibilities which had been placed upon his shoulders and the shoulders of his brethren to see that the covenants pertaining to consecration were faithfully kept. Especially was he concerned over the duties and responsibilities of the bishop in Zion, for they were very great. It was the duty of the bishop, assisted by his brethren, to see that justice was done, as the Lord pointed out in the revelations, in the matter of deciding and allotting inheritances in Zion. The history reveals that there were some things that had not been attended to in the spirit and according to the instructions which had been declared essential in the revelations. These matters caused the Prophet some anxiety and therefore he wrote to Brother Phelps stating that there were some things that were "lying with great weight" on his mind. By the Spirit of prophecy he uttered this prayer, as though it was a prayer in the heart of William Phelps.

"My God, great and mighty art Thou, therefore show unto Thy servant what shall become of all those who are essaying to come up unto Zion, in order to keep the commandments of God, and yet receive not their inheritance by consecration, by order or deed from the Bishop, the man that God has appointed in a legal way, agreeably to the law given to organize and regulate the Church, and all the affairs of the same."

Then the Prophet adds: "Brother William, in the love of God, having the most implicit confidence in you as a man of God, having obtained this confidence by a vision of heaven, therefore I will proceed to unfold to you some of the feelings of my heart, and to answer the question." Then what follows by the inspiration of the Spirit of the Lord has been accepted by the Church as a revelation. (D&C Sec 85) (CHMR, Vol. 2, pp. 111-112)

Sacred Truths

Introduction

At the time of this revelation (1832) the headquarters of the church was in Kirtland, Ohio. Bishop Edward Partridge was in Missouri and was responsible for organizing the saints there and administering the law of consecration in their behalf. William W. Phelps had been assigned to assist the Bishop in his duties. In the exercise of his office, Bishop Partridge had exceeded his authority on occasion. He had not always functioned in accordance with the instructions given him by the Prophet Joseph Smith, and therefore, was not in harmony with the Lord at that time.

Sensing this problem, Brother Phelps had written to Joseph Smith and sought his counsel on the matter. This revelation is an extract of an inspired letter written by Joseph Smith in answer to the concerns of Brother Phelps.

We will discuss this revelation in the following categories:

1. One mighty and strong
2. The book of the law
3. Salvation through the Church

One Mighty and Strong

It is vital to understand that the problem being addressed in this revelation existed in Missouri in 1832 and did not pertain to the church at large. The man referred to in the revelation who was attempting "...to steady the ark of God,..." (D&C 85:8) was Bishop Edward Partridge. His attitude and actions were very displeasing to the Lord. The Lord warned him that if he were to persist in his course of action the Lord would remove him from this mortal sphere and send one mighty and strong to take his place as a Bishop in Zion. (See D&C 85:7-8) Obviously, any such person called to serve as a replacement for Bishop Partridge would be called in the same manner he was. (See D&C 41:9; 68:14-21)

It should be understood that Bishop Edward Partridge responded to the Lord's counsel and warning and repented of his wrongdoing. By so doing he received forgiveness for his sins and found favor in the sight of the Lord. In November 1835, the Prophet Joseph Smith recorded the following revelation:

> Behold I am well pleased with my servant Isaac Morley, and my servant Edward Partridge, because of the integrity of their hearts in laboring in my vineyard, for the salvation of the souls of men. Verily I say unto you, their sins are forgiven them. (HC, Vol. 2, p. 302)

After the death of Bishop Partridge the Lord revealed that He had received him unto Himself. (See D&C 124:19)

The statements in this revelation partaining to "one mighty and strong" are no longer applicable. The warning was heeded and the replacement was not needed. For additional information and more in-depth discussion of this matter, see the statement issued by the First Presidency of the church. (See IE, Vol. 10, October, 1907, pp. 929-943)

The Book of the Law

Not only was there concern about Bishop Partridge, but other members of the church in Missouri were also failing to keep their commitments and covenants with the Lord. The Lord reminded them that the records of the church were being kept and would reflect their loyalty and obedience to His laws. (See D&C 85:1-5)

The Book of the Law of the Lord was the record that would reveal their faithfulness according to the terms and requirements of the law of consecration. Anyone, whose name was not recorded in that book would "...not find an inheritance among the saints of the Most High." (D&C 85:11)

The names of faithful saints are still being recorded upon certain records of the church. President Joseph F. Smith stressed the significance of having one's name appear upon such important documents as follows:

> I will read now a few verses from Section 85 of the Book of Doctrine and Covenants, commencing at the 9th verse:
>
> "And all they who are not found written in the book of remembrance, shall find none inheritance in that day, but they shall be cut asunder, and their portion shall be appointed them among unbelievers, where are wailing and gnashing of teeth.
>
> "These things I say not of myself; therefore, as the Lord speaketh, He will also fulfill.
>
> "And they who are of the High Priesthood, whose names are not found written in the book of the law, or that are found to have apostatized, or to have been cut off from the Church; as well as the lesser Priesthood, or the members, in that day, shall not find an inheritance among the Saints of the Most High;
>
> "Therefore it shall be done unto them as unto the children of the priests, as will be found recorded in the second chapter and sixty-first and second verses of Ezra."
>
> I am going to turn now to Ezra and see what is said there. We read:
>
> "61. And the children of the Priests; the children of Habaiah, the children of Koz, the children of Barzillai; which took a wife of the daughters of Barzillai the Gileadite, and was called after their name;
>
> "62. These sought their register among those that were reckoned by genealogy, but they were not found, therefore were they, as polluted put from the Priesthood.
>
> "63. And the Tirshatha said unto them, that they should not eat of the most holy thing, till there stood up a Priest with Urim and Thummim."
>
> This is the position the people will be in when they come to claim an inheritance in Zion, if their names are not found recorded in the book of the law of God. And I want to tell you that this refers directly to the law of tithing. In the first place it referred to the law of consecration, but that law, as has been explained, was not properly

kept, and inasmuch as people are under greater condemnation when they keep not the laws that are given them, the Lord in His mercy withdrew from the Latter-day Saints the law of consecration, because the people were not prepared to live it, and as long as it was in force and they kept it not they were under condemnation. The law of tithing was given in its place.

Some people may not care very much whether their names are recorded or not, but this comes from ignorance of the consequences. If their names are not recorded they will not only be cut off from the assistance which they would be entitled to from the Church if they needed it, but they will be cut off from the ordinances of the house of God; they will be cut asunder from their dead and from their fathers who have been faithful, or from those who shall come after them who shall be faithful, and they will be appointed their portion with the unbelievers, where there is weeping and gnashing of teeth. It means that you will be cut off from your fathers and mothers, from your husbands, your wives, your children, and that you shall have no portion or lot or inheritance in the kingdom of God, both in time and in eternity. It has a very serious and far reaching effect. It is therefore the more obligatory upon me and upon my fellow-servants in the church of God to make these matters known to the people, that our skirts may be free from their blood. (CR, October 1899, p. 42)

Salvation Through the Church

The Savior has made it very clear in this and other revelations that salvation can only be obtained through His church. (See D&C 85:11) It is not to be understood that the church saves souls, but rather full access to the Savior's atonement for sin comes only through His church. And why is membership in the Lord's church an essential part of one's salvation? The church is the depository of the Lord's priesthood authority and the only place where ordinances for salvation are authorized to be performed in His name. The Lord warned all who are cut off from or who choose to remain outside of His church that they have no claim upon salvation in His eternal kingdom. (See D&C 85:11; 50:8)

Summary and Conclusion

Edward Partridge repented and thus one mighty and strong was never sent by the Lord to take his place. Anyone who desires a place in the Lord's kingdom must have his name recorded in the Book of the Law of the Lord and remain true and faithful to the covenants he receives in the Lord's church.

Chapter 15

Doctrine and Covenants Section 86

Suggested Title
The Wheat and The Tares—Lawful Heirs to the Priesthood

Overview of Section Content
1. The sowing of the seed in the Savior's ministry (vs. 1-3)
2. The sowing of the seed in the last days (vs. 4-5)
3. The growing and the gathering of the wheat and the tares (vs. 6-7)
4. Priesthood blessings promised to those who are lawful heirs according to the flesh (vs. 8-11)

Historical Setting

Joseph Smith, Jun.

On the 6th of December, 1832, I received the following revelation explaining the parable of the wheat and tares. (HC, Vol. 1, p. 300)

Joseph Fielding Smith

...In this revelation the Lord has given a more complete interpretation than he gave to his apostles as recorded by Matthew. The reason for this may be accounted for in the fact that it is to be in these last days that the harvest is gathered and the tares are to be burned. In Matthew's account the Lord declares that he is the sower of good seed, and in the Doctrine and Covenants it is stated that the apostles were the sowers of the seed. There is no contradiction here. Christ is the author of our salvation and he it was who instructed the apostles, and under him they were sent to preach the Gospel unto all the world, or to sow the seed, and as the seed is his and it is sown under his command, he states but the fact in this revelation and also in the parable. (CHMR, Vol. 2, pp. 117-118)

Sacred Truths

Introduction

The parable of the wheat and the tares was given by the Savior during His earthly ministry and is recorded in the New Testament. (See Bible, Matt. 13:24-30, 36-43) As noted in the Historical Setting, Joseph Smith received this revelation as an explanation of this parable. We will discuss this revelation in the following two categories:
1. Sowing
2. Reaping

Sowing

The parable of the wheat and the tares represents the teaching of the gospel of Jesus Christ to the people of the world. That teaching effort is symbolized by the sowing of the good seed (wheat). In the midst of this effort, Satan teaches his false doctrine in opposition to the truth. Satan's efforts are symbolized by the sowing of the tares.

As the Savior explained this parable, we learn there have been two sowings of the good seed. The first sowing was the teaching of the gospel in the Savior's mortal ministry, the meridian of time. (See D&C 86:2) Because of Satan's false teachings, an apostasy took place, symbolized by the tares choking the wheat and the church being driven into the wilderness. (See D&C 86:3)

The second sowing is the restoration of the gospel to the earth in the last days, the dispensation of the fulness of times. (See D&C 86:4) Once again, Lucifer has sowed his false doctrine (tares) in opposition to the Lord's work. Because this apostate influence is amongst the Lord's people, the angels of heaven are desirous of cleansing the earth of evil doctrines and practices. (See D&C 86:5)

President Joseph Fielding Smith discussed this parable and gave the following insights concerning it:

Now in the parable as we have it in the book of Matthew, we do not have the distinction drawn betwen the sowing of the seed in the dispensation of the Meridian of Time and again the sowing of the seed in this Dispensation of the Fulness of Times. But here the Lord makes this clear. If we had the parable just as He gave it, I am sure that this distinction would be in it.

The sowing of the seed occurred twice—once by our Lord and His apostles at the time of his ministry (The wicked one sowed the tares and drove the Church into the wilderness. That has reference to the apostasy.); then again in this, our day, when the gospel is again restored, this same thing is repeated: The good seed is sowed; the wicked one comes along and sows the tares; and the angels are now waiting, pleading with the Lord, to reap down the earth. (BYU Speeches of the Year, March 21, 1967, p.4)

After the sowing of the seed, and before the time of the harvest, there is a time for growing. The Savior warned against an attempt to harvest before the crop is mature. (See D&C 86:6-7) In other words, we are warned against judging or categorizing the individual as to his spiritual worth before there has been adequate time for the distinction to be completely evident. No man is capable of determining the ultimate destiny of a human soul. Many changes may take place during the growing process that will effect the quality of the harvest. It would be a mistake to pre-judge or give up hope for anyone before the Lord's judgment is complete.

Reaping

Who are the reapers? Who does the reaping? Of necessity, they must be authorized representatives of the Lord. In this revelation they are referred to as servants of the Lord who are lawful heirs of the priesthood. (See D&C 86:8-11) We are very fortunate to have General Authorities of the Lord's church give insight to this scripture:

George Q. Cannon

Our lineage is not known to all of us. We may not know our origin; but this we may be assured of, that we who have received the truth are choice spirits . . .

Where do you think this nobility of character has come from? It has come from ancestors who obtained promises from God, through their faithfulness, in regard to their posterity. Our ancestors may have come through poverty and obscure channels, and some of them may not have possessed any noted characteristics; but when our ancestry is known, it will be found that the noblest men and women of God have been the progenitors of this people. (April 8, 1894, DW 48:701)

It was arranged before we came here how we should come and through what lineage we should come....As the Lord has taught us, . . .our Priesthood has been hid with God. He says:

> Therefore, thus saith the Lord unto you, with whom the priesthood hath continued through the lineage of your fathers—
>
> For ye are lawful heirs, according to the flesh, and have been hid from the world with Christ in God—
>
> Therefore your life and the priesthood have remained, and must needs remain through you and your lineage until the restoration of all things spoken by the mouths of all holy prophets since the world began. [D&C 86:8-10]

I am as convinced that it was predestined before I was born that I should come through my father as I am that I stand here (*Gospel Truth* , Vol. 2, p. 89.)

Joseph Fielding Smth

...During the ages in which we dwelt in the pre-mortal state we not only developed our various characteristics and showed our worthiness and ability, or the lack of it, but we were also where such progress could be observed. It is reasonable to believe that there was a Church organization there. The heavenly beings were living in a perfectly arranged society. Every person knew his place. Priesthood, without any question, had been conferred and the leaders were chosen to officiate. Ordinances pertaining to that pre-existence were required and the love of God prevailed. Under such conditions it was natural for our Father to discern and choose those who were most worthy and evaluate the talents of each individual. He knew not only what each of us *could* do, but what each of us *would* do when put to the test and when responsibility was given us. Then, when the time came for our habitation on mortal earth, all things were prepared and the servants of the Lord chosen and ordained to their respective missions. (*The Way to Perfection*, pp. 50-51)

Theodore M. Burton

One thing we often fail to realize is that our priesthood comes to us through the lineage of our fathers and mothers. The Lord explained it in these words: "Therefore, thus saith the Lord unto you, with whom the priesthood hath continued through the lineage of your fathers..." (D&C 86:8.)

"Oh," I can hear some of you say, "there must be something wrong with that statement, for I am the only member of my family who has joined the Church. How could I have received the priesthood from my parents?"

In this scripture the Lord was not talking about your priesthood line of authority. He was talking about your inherited right to receive and use priesthood power. This readiness to listen and believe is an inherited gift which enabled you to recognize and accept the truth. Jesus explained this thought as he said: "My sheep hear my voice, and I know them, and they follow me." (John 10:27.)

That spirit of acceptance is a manifestation of your inherited right to priesthood blessings. Such willingness to believe does not represent predestination, but it does represent foreordination. The Lord continues the revelation: "For ye are lawful heirs, according to the flesh, and have been hid from the world with Christ in God." (D&C 86:9.)

This means we receive a right to priesthood blessings from our blood ancestry. I hope you can understand that priesthood with its accompanying blessings is dependent to a great degree on family relationship.

What does the Lord mean by the expression "hid from the world with Christ in God"? He means that according to the plan of salvation you were reserved or held back in the heavens as special spirit children to be born in a time and at a place where you could perform a special mission in life. (CR, April 1975, p. 103)

Summary and Conclusion

The gospel of Jesus Christ has been restored to this earth. It is the second sowing of the seed according to the Lord's pre-determined plan. We are free to grow and develop in our spiritual standing before the Lord. If we are to be gathered unto the Lord, as wheat, it is essential that we hearken unto His authorized servants of the priesthood. By so doing, we retain our heirship as sons and daughters of God.

Chapter 16

Doctrine and Covenants Section 87

Suggested Title

Prophecy on Wars

Overview of Section Content

1. War will be poured out upon all nations (vs. 1-3)
2. Slaves to rise against masters; remnants of the land to vex Gentiles (vs. 4-5)
3. Calamities shall fall upon the earth's inhabitants (vs. 6-7)
4. Saints counseled to stand in holy places (vs. 8)

Historical Setting

Joseph Smith, Jun.

Appearances of troubles among the nations became more visible this season than they had previously been since the Church began her journey out of the wilderness. The ravages of the cholera were frightful in almost all the large cities on the globe. The plague broke out in India, while the United States, amid all her pomp and greatness, was threatened with immediate dissolution. The people of South Carolina, in convention assembled (in November), passed ordinances, declaring their state a free independent nation; and appointed Thursday, the 31st day of January, 1833, as a day of humiliation and prayer, to implore Almighty God to vouchsafe His blessings, and restore liberty and happiness within their borders. President Jackson issued his proclamation against this rebellion, called out a force sufficient to quell it, and implored the blessings of God to assist the nation to eradicate itself from the horrors of the approaching and solemn crisis.

On Christmas day [1832], I received the following revelation and prophecy on war: (HC, Vol. 1, p. 301)

Joseph Fielding Smith

...Scoffers have said it was nothing remarkable for Joseph Smith in 1832, to predict the outbreak of the Civil War and that others who did not claim to be inspired with prophetic vision had done the same. It has been said that Daniel Webster and William Lloyd Garrison in 1831 had predicted the dissolution of the Union. It is well known that senators and congressmen from the South had maintained that their section of the country had a right to withdraw from the Union for it was a confederacy, and in 1832, war clouds were to be seen on the horizon. It was because of this fact that the Lord made known to Joseph Smith this revelation stating that wars would shortly come to pass, beginning with rebellion of South Carolina, which would eventually terminate in war being poured out upon all nations and in the death and misery of many souls. It may have been an easy thing in 1832, or even in 1831, for someone to predict that there would come a division of the Northern States and the Southern States, for even then there were rumblings, and South Carolina had shown the spirit of rebellion. It was not, however, within the power of man to predict in the detail which the Lord revealed to Joseph Smith, what was shortly to come to pass as an outgrowth of the Civil War and the pouring out of war upon all nations. (CHMR, Vol. 2, pp. 122-123)

Sacred Truths

Introduction

This is a prophetic revelation. In it the Lord revealed that the United States of America would become a divided country for a time. He also revealed that war would be poured out upon all nations. One of the significant portions of this prophecy is the effect upon all nations that was to come as an outgrowth of the Civil War.

We will discuss this revelation under the following topics:

Section 87 93

1. Prophecy of Civil War
2. Prophecy of wars upon all nations
3. Slaves and remnants
4. Counsel to the saints

Prophecy of Civil War

This revelation was received in December, 1832. The prophecies pertaining to the Civil War and other predictions were well publicized from 1832 until the outbreak of the war in 1861. For instance, Elder Franklin D. Richards included this prophecy in the first published edition of the Pearl of Great Price in England in 1851. Elder Orson Pratt publicized this prophecy throughout his many missionary travels. Speaking of this endeavor he said:

> Well, it seems as if the Lord our God is giving the nation a pretty thorough warning. He told this nation by revelation, twenty-eight years before it commenced, of the great American war. He told all about how the Southern States should be divided against the Northern States, and that in the course of the war many souls should be cut off. This has been fulfilled.
>
> I went forth before my beard was gray, before my hair began to turn white, when I was a youth of nineteen, now I am fifty-eight, and from that time on I published these tidings among the inhabitants of the earth. I carried forth the written revelation, foretelling this great contest, some twenty-eight years before the war commenced. This prophecy has been printed and circulated extensively in this and other nations and languages. It pointed out the place where it should commence in South Carolina. That which I declared over the New England States, New York, Pennsylvania, Ohio, and many other parts in the East, when but a boy, came to pass twenty-eight years after the revelation was given.
>
> When they were talking about a war commencing down here in Kansas, I told them that was not the place; I also told them that the revelation had designated South Carolina, "and," said I, "you have no need to think that the Kansas war is going to be the war that is to be so terribly destructive in its character and nature. No, it must commence at the place the Lord has designated by revelation."
>
> What did they have to say to me? They thought it was a Mormon humbug, and laughed me to scorn, and they looked upon that revelation as they do upon all others that God has given in these latter days—as without divine authority. But behold and lo! in process of time it came to pass, again establishing the divinity of this work, and giving another proof that God is in this work, and is performing that which He spoke by the mouths of the ancient

prophets, as recorded in the Book of Mormon before any Church of Latter-day Saints was in existence. (JD, Vol. 13, p. 135)

President Wilford Woodruff recalled having recorded this revelation that was given to the prophet Joseph Smith:

> I traveled thousands of miles with Joseph Smith. I knew his spirit. Many of the revelations given through him has been fulfilled. I myself wrote the revelation that was given through him concerning the war that would take place in this country between the north and south. That revelation was published to the world for twenty years before the war. It broke out just as predicted, and I refer to it because it is one of the revelations that is fulfilled. (DWW, p. 31)

Prophecy of Wars Upon All Nations

The Lord prefaced this revelation by saying:

> Verily, thus saith the Lord concerning the wars that will shortly come to pass, . . . (D&C 87:1)

This revelation deals with multiple wars in addition to the Civil War. The Lord indicated that "...war shall be poured out upon all nations." (D&C 87:3) As to the time of the beginning of these wars, the Lord said it would be when Great Britain would seek help from other nations "...to defend themselves against other nations;..." (D&C 87:3)

Commenting upon this prophetic event, Elder B. H. Roberts has said:

> "And 'Then' War Shall Be Poured Out Upon All Nations:" This passage is from paragraph three of the revelation as published in the Doctrine and Covenants (Sec. 1xxxvii), the authorized book of collected revelations accepted by the church as one of its books of scripture. In early editions containing this revelation the "and *then* war," etc., was written "and *thus* war" etc. But a later reading of the manuscript copy of the revelation in the Church Historian's Office, discovered that in the manuscript copy it was written "then" not "thus;" which made a tremendous difference in the significance of the revelation, and greatly increased the prophetic value of it. The change was authorized and made in the copy of the revelation and was published in the *History of the Church*, Period I, 1902, Vol. I, pp. 301-2. Afterwards the same change was made in the Doctrine and Covenants. The change first appeared in the edition of 1921, Salt Lake City, and has been made in all subsequent editions.

It will be observed that in the revelation the statement is made that the southern states will call upon "other nations" to aid her in the war between the states; and specifies Great Britain as among these "other nations:" "And the southern states shall call upon other nations," it continues, "even the nation of Great Britain, as it is called, and they shall also call upon other nations in order to defend themselves against other nations; and *then* [when Great Britain does that] *war shall be poured out upon all nations."*

Take note that this mis-print in the revelation, "thus" instead of "then," was discovered and corrected in the first volume of the *History of the Church*, Period I, in 1902, twelve years before the outbreak of the World War of 1914.

England through many years trusted to the strength of her navy to guarantee the integrity of her far-flung empire; and her statesmen prided themselves on what they called England's policy of "Splendid Isolation." That is to say, her freedom from entangling alliances with continental European powers, and for matter of that, with other world powers. But when Germany began its rivalry in naval construction against England, some years before the outbreak of the World War of 1914-1918, then England lost her sense of security based upon the strength of her navy, and turned to other nations—"called upon other nations, in order to defend herself against other nations," then was the signal given for the "war upon all nations." (CHC, Vol. 1, pp. 300-301)

Slaves and Remnants

Additional statements of prophetic importance were to find fulfillment after or as an outgrowth of the Civil War. The Lord spoke of the following: (see D&C 87:4-6)

1. Slaves rising up against their masters
2. Remnants of the land vexing the Gentiles
3. Famine, plague, earthquake and other destructive phenomena

Speaking of the future fulfillment of these events, we note the following commentary:

> There are other parts which yet remain unfulfilled, but they, too, will come to pass, in time. "Slaves are to rise up against their masters" (v. 4), and the "Remnant" is to "vex the Gentiles with a sore vexation" (v. 5). There will, finally, be "famine, and plague, and earthquakes, and the thunder of heaven, and the fierce and

vivid lightning also," and thus the inhabitants of the Earth will feel the wrath of God (v. 6). (DCC, p. 537)

Commenting on the potential breadth of some of these prophecies, Elder Joseph Fielding Smith has taught:

> The rising up of slaves, it is thought by many, was fulfilled in the Civil War when many of the negroes found their way into the armies of the north and fought against their former masters. Others think this is yet to come. The history of this American continent also gives evidence that the Lamanites have risen up in their anger and vexed the Gentiles. This warfare may not be over. It has been the fault of people in the United States to think that this prophetic saying has reference to the Indians in the United States, but we must remember that there are millions of the "remnant" in Mexico, Central and South America. It was during our Civil War that the Indians in Mexico rose up and gained their freedom from the tyranny which Napoleon endeavored to inflict upon them contrary to the prediction of Jacob in the Book of Mormon, that there should be no kings among the Gentiles on this land. The independence of Mexico and other nations to the south has been accomplished by the uprising of the "remnant" upon the land. However, let us not think that this prophecy has completely been fulfilled. (CHMR, Vol. 2, p. 127)

Counsel to the Saints

Although this revelation contains prophecy of death, destruction, bloodshed, famine, etc., the Lord advises the saints that there is safety in the midst of all the turmoil. He counseled them to " . . .stand ye in holy places, and be not moved, until the day of the Lord come; . . ." (D&C 87:8)

What are holy places and where are they to be found? President Harold B. Lee has informed us as follows:

> The Lord has told us where these "holy places" are:
> And it shall come to pass among the wicked, that every man that will not take his sword against his neighbor must needs flee unto Zion for safety. (D&C 45:68.)
> Where is Zion?
> During the various periods of time or dispensations, and for specific reasons, the Lord's prophets, His "mouthpieces," as it were, have designated gathering places where the Saints were to gather. After designating certain such places in our dispensaton, the Lord then declared:

Until the day cometh when there is found no more room for them; and then I have other places which I will appoint unto them, and they shall be called stakes, for the curtains or the strength of Zion. (D&C 101:21.)

Thus, the Lord has clearly placed the responsibility of directing the work of gathering in the hands of His divinely appointed leaders. I fervently pray that all Saints and truth seekers everywhere will attune their listening ears to these prophet-leaders instead of to some demagogue who seeks to make capital of social discontent and gain political influence. (Stand Ye In Holy Places, p. 22)

Summary and Conclusion

The Lord revealed through His living prophet that war would be poured out upon all nations and that other destructive powers would be unleashed upon the earth. Some of these prophecies have been fulfilled. Other events are yet to take place. The Lord has afforded His saints safety if they heed His counsel to stand in "holy places."

Chapter 17

Doctrine and Covenants Section 88

Suggested Title
The Olive Leaf

Overview of Section Content
1. The Lord is pleased with those who are sanctified (vs. 1-2)
2. The Comforter promises eternal life to faithful saints (vs. 3-5)
3. The light of Christ (vs. 6-13)
4. The resurrection of all mankind and the kingdoms to which they will be assigned (vs. 14-35)
5. All kingdoms are governed by God's law (vs. 36-45)
6. All of God's kingdoms bear witness of him (vs. 46-47)
7. Only the righteous will comprehend God (vs. 48-50)
8. A parable of the Lord's visits to the inhabitants of his kingdoms (vs. 51-61)
9. Counsel and promises of the Lord to those who draw near unto him and are sanctified (vs. 62-76)
10. A commandment to teach all mankind the doctrine of the kingdom (vs. 77-83)
11. Judgments of God (vs. 84-91)
12. Sequence of events surrounding the resurrections (vs. 92-107)
13. The secret acts of men during the earth's temporal existence and the Savior's victory over Satan (vs. 108-116)

14. A commandment to build a temple and instructions to prepare to be in the house of the Lord (vs. 117-126)
15. The school of the prophets (vs. 127-141)

Historical Setting

Joseph Smith, Jun.

Two days after the preceding prophecy, [Section 87] on the 27th of December, I received the following:... (HC, Vol. 1, p. 302)

Hyrum M. Smith and Janne M. Sjodahl

...Joseph Smith sent a copy of the Revelation to Elder Phelps, who was the editor of the *Evening and Morning Star*, and accompanied it by a letter in which the Saints were admonished to repent. (DCC, p. 540)

Joseph Smith, Jun.

Brother William W. Phelps:
I send you the "olive leaf" which we have plucked from the Tree of Paradise, the Lord's message of peace to us; for though our brethren in Zion indulge in feelings towards us, which are not according to the requirements of the new covenant, yet, we have the satisfaction of knowing that the Lord approves of us, and has accepted us, and established His name in Kirtland for the salvation of the nations; for the Lord will have a place whence His word will go forth, in these last days, in purity; for if Zion will not purify herself, so as to be approved of in all things, in His sight, He will seek another people; for His work will go on until Israel is gathered, and they who will not hear His voice, must expect to feel His wrath. Let me say unto you, seek to purify yourselves, and also all the inhabitants of Zion, lest the Lord's anger be kindled to fierceness....(HC, Vol. 1, p. 316)

Sacred Truths

Introduction

This revelation is the Lord's message of peace to all those who stand approved before the Lord and are acceptable unto Him. In this revelation, the Lord invites all to repent and become partakers of His peace.

We will discuss the Lord's message of peace as contained in this revelation under the following topics:

Section 88

1. The Holy Spirit of Promise
2. The Light of Christ
3. The resurrection
4. Kingdoms and law
5. Sanctification
6. Doctrine of the kingdom
7. Secret acts of men—Satan overcome
8. School of the prophets

The Holy Spirit of Promise

What is the Holy Spirit of Promise? The Holy Spirit is the Holy Ghost that is promised to every faithful, covenant member of the Lord's church. The Holy Spirit provides a promise of eternal life to those who are worthy of its presence. (See D&C 88:3-5) Every ordinance that is performed for the salvation of souls in the Church of Jesus Christ must receive a stamp of approval by the Holy Ghost. (See D&C 132:7) This approval is given based upon the following:

1. Proper authority by which the ordinance is performed
2. Worthiness of the individual receiving the ordinance

Speaking on this subject, Elder Joseph Fielding Smith has said:

The Holy Spirit of Promise is the Holy Ghost who places the stamp of approval upon every ordinance: baptism, confirmation, ordination, marriage. *The promise is that the blessings will be received through faithfulness.*

If a person violates a covenant, whether it be of baptism, ordination, marriage or anything else, the Spirit withdraws the stamp of approval, and the blessings will not be received.

Every ordinance is sealed with a promise of a reward based upon faithfulness. The Holy Spirit withdraws the stamp of approval where covenants are broken. (DS, Vol. 1, p. 45)

It is possible that mistakes will occur and sins will be committed after such sealing action takes place. However, the stamp of approval can be regained upon sincere and genuine repentance when the individual receives forgiveness through the atonement of the Savior.

The Light of Christ

There is a relationship, as to their meaning, of several scriptural terms. The Lord has said:

For the word of the Lord is truth, and whatsoever is truth is light, and whatsoever is light is Spirit, even the Spirit of Jesus Christ. (D&C 84:45)

The glory of God is intelligence, or, in other words, light and truth. (D&C 93:36)

The terms light, truth, Spirit, and intelligence are frequently used interchangeably throughout the scriptures. An awareness of the synonimity of these terms aids one as he seeks knowledge and understanding from the scriptures.

We will discuss four functions of the light of Christ as contained in this revelation:

1. Creative Power

The Lord revealed that it was the light of Christ by which the sun, the moon, the earth and all things were created, or made. (See D&C 88:7-10) It is comforting and peaceful to the soul to know that God is at the helm and all things were created by Him through the righteous use of His power. By divine revelation, we know that this universe and all living things therein exist because of the acts of creation of our God. We do not exist as a by-product of chance. Such a philosophy is contrary to the revealed word of the Lord. The process of creation and the fact of such an event has been discussed by two apostles as follows:

Parley P. Pratt

> ...when the worlds were framed, God spake, and this divine fluid [light or spirit] went forth and executed the mandate, by controlling the elements in accordance with the will, pattern or design formed in the mind of Him that spake ...
>
> By this divine Spirit all things were designed and formed. (*Key to Theology*, p. 104)

Joseph Fielding Smith

> It is true that all life does come from the same source, but that is not the scum of the sea, a jellyfish or a pollywog. *God, our Father, is the creator of life, and he placed life on this earth in varied forms, and also on other worlds.* (DS, Vol. 1, p. 140)

The prophet Jacob emphasized these same truths when he declared:

> For behold, by the power of his word man came upon the face of the earth, which earth was created by the power of his word. Wherefore, if God being able to speak and the world was, and to

speak and man was created, O then, why not able to command the earth, or the workmanship of his hands upon the face of it, according to his will and pleasure? (B of M, Jacob 4:9)

2. Enlightening Power

The Lord said that His light is the means by which man's mind is enlightened. (See D&C 88:11)

One of the manifestations of this function of light is the conscience which is given to every soul that is born into the world. (See D&C 84:46;93:2) (For additional information, see DS, Vol. 1, p. 51)

The Lord counsels His children to seek additional enlightenment as follows:

> ...seek learning, even by study and also by faith. (D&C 88:118)
> ...the Spirit enlighteneth every man through the world, that hearkeneth to the voice of the Spirit. (D&C 84:46)

If we are desirous of being enlightened by our Father in Heaven, we must follow His admonition to "seek" such knowledge. Elder Melvin J. Ballard emphasized the importance of seeking light from the Lord as follows:

> There is a spirit in man, and the spirit of the Almighty giveth them understanding, but all this wealth that comes from our Father, comes to us through the spirit and not through the flesh. All his aid and his assistance reach us through the spiritual senses and the spiritual power. This light and this power that come from the presence of our Father are just as real as the light of the sun. As the light of the sun is to our physical body, so is the light or the power that cometh from God sensitive and sensible to our spiritual being, but the man who is spiritually asleep is in a lamentable condition, because he is without refuge, without help, without power and strength to combat the powers of evil that are seeking our undoing by and through the flesh. Just as for ages there has been in existence in the elements of the earth in which we live, that mysterious power called electricity, in abundance everywhere, and not yet harnessed, trapped, controlled and brought to the service of man until the devices men have discovered have been brought into place and now we are aquainted with it, we draw upon it, utilize it to tremendous advantage, just so there is a great storehouse of spiritual power and always has been...He is everywhere by the presence and power of his Spirit, and that power and presence and Spirit cannot be brought

to the children of men unless they seek after it. "Ask and ye shall receive, knock and it shall be opened unto you, seek and ye shall find." Men may walk in the midst of it, they may be anxious for it, and yet wholly oblivious to it unless they open the windows of their soul through prayer; for that is the way the soul touches and reaches this vast power and brings it available to man's use, to man's aid and to man's advantage. And if, therefore, these are our conditions, who can walk safely through the dangers and vicissitudes of life with all these enemies arrayed against us and be successful without the help of the Lord? No wonder he calls upon us to seek him. He cannot force that spirit upon us nor make us conscious of it, nor give it to us, unless we are willing to seek for it, unless we open our hearts. (IE, Vol. 26, pp. 989-991)

3. Life-Giving Power

It is because of the power and light of Jesus Christ that all things live. (See D&C 88:13) Such life-giving power was extended to all living things before the fall of Adam. There was no death before the fall. (See B of M, 2 Nephi 2:22) Life is sustained in our mortal existence because of the light that emanates from the Savior. One way the light of Christ sustains us in mortality is through the sun, the light of which is essential to life on the earth. (See D&C 88:7; P of GP, Abraham, Facsimile No. 2, Explanation Fig. 5)

In addition, the light of the Savior will provide life beyond the grave and make possible the resurrection of the body to a state of never-ending life.

Jesus Christ is truly "...the life of men and the light of men." (D&C 93:9) Thus, in time, every knee shall bow and every tongue shall confess that Jesus is the Christ. In other words, all will acknowledge that they are indebted to Him for their very lives. (See D&C 88:104; 76:110; B of M, Mosiah 27:31)

4. Governing Power

The light of Christ is the power by which all things are governed. (See D&C 88:13) It has been and can be appropriately described as priesthood, or power of God.

Righteous priesthood holders have access to this power by which they govern. This light and power is described by the Lord as follows:

> He that is ordained of God and sent forth, the same is appointed to be the greatest, notwithstanding he is the least and the servant of all.
>
> Wherefore, he is possessor of all things; for all things are subject unto him, both in heaven and on the earth, the life and the light, the

Spirit and the power, sent forth by the will of the Father through Jesus Christ, his Son. (D&C 50:26-27)

It is by this power the Lord governs the universe and all things therein.

Elders Joseph Fielding Smith and Charles W. Penrose discussed the magnitude of this governing power as follows:

Joseph Fielding Smith

> This Light of Christ is not a personage. It has no body. I do not know what it is as far as substance is concerned; but it fills the immensity of space and emanates from God. It is the light by which the worlds are controlled, by which they are made. It is the light of the sun and all other bodies. (DS, Vol. 1, p. 52)

Charles W. Penrose

> This spirit that pervades all things, which is the light and life of all things, by which our Heavenly Father operates, by which He is omnipotent, never had a beginning and never will have an end. It is the light of truth; it is the spirit of intelligence. (JD, Vol. 26, p. 23)

The Resurrection

The contents of this revelation as pertaining to the resurrection can be conveniently arranged and discussed under the following headings:

1. The literal resurrection of the body

One of the greatest messages of peace that has ever been proclaimed to mankind is that there will be a literal resurrection of the body. In a day when men are denying truth, it is comforting and refreshing to hear the Lord's words concerning the reality of the resurrection of the physical body. The Lord has revealed that the eternal spirit of man will be reunited with his physical body and thus the soul of man (spirit and body) becomes an eternal spiritual body. (See D&C 88:14-16, 27)

Elder James E. Talmage emphasized the literalness of man's resurrection. He said:

> It is peculiar to the theology of the Latter-day Saints that we regard the body as an essential part of the soul. Read your dictionaries, the lexicons, and encyclopedias, and you will find that nowhere, outside of the Church of Jesus Christ, is the solemn and eternal truth taught that the soul of man is the body and the spirit

combined. It is quite the rule to regard the soul as that incorporeal part of men, that immortal part which existed before the body was framed and which shall continue to exist after that body has gone to decay; nevertheless, that is not the soul; that is only a part of the soul; that is the spirit-man, the form in which every individual of us, and every individual human being, existed before called to take tabernacle in the flesh. It has been declared in the solemn word of revelation, that the spirit and the body constitute the soul of man; and, therefore, we should look upon this body as something that shall endure in the resurrected state, beyond the grave, something to be kept pure and holy. (CR, October 1913, p. 117)

We also learn from the Prophet Joseph Smith that there is an eternal nature to parts of the physical body. He said:

There is no fundamental principle belonging to a human system that ever goes into another in this world or in the world to come; I care not what the theories of men are. We have the testimony that God will raise us up, and he has the power to do it. If any one supposes that any part of our bodies, that is, the fundamental parts thereof, ever goes into another body, he is mistaken. (HC, Vol. 5, p. 339)

Commenting upon the fundamental parts of the body, Elder Harold B. Lee has said:

A chemist of renown gives what could be a definition of what Joseph Smith termed "fundamental parts." Here are his words: "Some biologists hold the view that there is an ultimate molecule of life hidden in the protoplasm, which holds the secret of the endless building up and breaking down." (Outlines of Science, Vol. 3, p. 718, Arthur Thompson) This same scientist then makes this significant statement in agreement with the Prophet: "The question may be asked, Do not the particles that compose man's body, when they return to mother earth, go to make or compose other bodies? No, they do not. Some philosophers have asserted that the human body changes every seven years. This is not correct, for it never changes. That is, the substances of which it is composed do not pass off and other particles of matter come and take their places. Neither can the particles which have comprised the bodies of men become parts of the bodies of other men, beasts, fowl, fish, insects or vegetables. They are governed by a divine law, and though they may pass from the knowledge of the scientific world that divine law still holds and governs and controls them."

In a discussion of this same subject, President John Taylor made this interesting comment: "It is true the body or the organization may be destroyed in various ways, but it is not true that the particles out of which it is created can be destroyed. They are eternal; they never were created. This is not only a principle associated with our religion...but also it is in accordance with acknowledged science. You may take, for instance, a handful of fine gold and scatter it in the street among the dust; again gather together the materials among which you have thrown the gold, and you can separate one from the other so thoroughly that your handful of gold can be returned to you; yes, every grain of it...every particle cleaving to its own elements." (The Gospel Kingdom, p. 24)

Now again we have a physician residing at Santa Monica, California, who makes this explanation: "We have bodies that are composed of bone, muscle, fat, blood, lymph, nerves and tissues. In all these tissues there is a building up and breaking down of complex chemical compounds. These substances are made into tissues. They give form and beauty to the body, and also supply energy. They are derived from the elements in food, drink and air. These are not the fundamental parts of the body, however, for they are used and then discarded, and new substances come to take their place. This is not true of the fundamental parts. They never change. A person may fast for a certain period of time, and become very emaciated, 'lose flesh' we say. People may live on their own tissues until they become almost 'skin and bone,' yet they live and can, when fed again, regain their former form and weight. During the fast, the fundamental parts of the body are not lost, but only the tissues that are taken into the body temporarily." (Dr. Joseph A. Ammussen, *Improvement Era*, Vol. 30, page 701) (Youth and the Church, pp. 187-189)

2. *The sequence of the resurrection*

We learn from this revelation that there are four phases of the resurrection process: (See D&C 88:92-107)

a. Celestial
b. Terrestrial
c. Telestial
d. Sons of Perdition

These four phases are known scripturally as the First and Second Resurrections, or the Resurrection of the Just and the Unjust. (See D&C 45:45, 54; 76:15-17, 50, 64-65, 85) The first resurrection (the just) includes the Celestial and the Terrestrial people. The second resurrection (the unjust) includes the Telestial people and the sons of perdition. Occasionally, reference is made to the "morning of the first resurrection." This term would apply to the first phase (Celestial) of the first resurrection. This phase is depicted by the sounding of the first trump at the time of the Savior's second coming. (See D&C 88:92-98) This sounding of the trump pertains to the saints of God who have died since the Savior's resurrection.

The second phase of the first resurrection, is depicted by the second trump. (See D&C 88:99) This phase is the resurrection of the Terrestrial people and is sometimes referred to as the afternoon of the first resurrection. This concludes the first resurrection.

The second resurrection consists of two groups. The Telestial will be first and is depicted by the sounding of the third trump. This event will occur at the conclusion of the thousand-year period of millennial peace. (See D&C 88:100-101) The second phase of the second resurrection is the resurrection of the sons of perdition and is depicted by the sounding of the fourth trump. (See D&C 88:102)

This message of peace from the Lord is the same message declared by His servant, the Apostle Paul:

> If in this life only we have hope in Christ, we are of all men most miserable.
> But now is Christ risen from the dead, and become the firstfruits of them that slept.
> For since by man came death, by man came also the resurrection of the dead.
> For as in Adam all die, even so in Christ shall all be made alive. (Bible, I Cor. 15:19-22)

3. The resurrection of the earth

Another unique doctrine contained in this revelation pertains to the earth. The earth is a living entity which eventually will die and be resurrected. (See D&C 88:25-26) From it comes life for all things that grow thereon. President Heber C. Kimball taught:

> Some say the earth exists without spirit; I do not believe any such thing; it has a spirit as much as any body has a spirit. How can anything live, except it has a living spirit? How can the earth produce vegetation, fruits, trees, and every kind of production, if there is no life in it? It could not, any more than a woman could produce children when she is dead: she must be alive to produce life, to manifest it, and show it to the world. (JD, Vol. 5, p. 172)

In its resurrected state, the earth will be a celestial dwelling place for celestial beings. (See D&C 88:17-26) Elder Joseph Fielding Smith provides additional insight as follows:

> The earth will be cleansed again. It was once baptized in water. When Christ comes, it will be baptized with fire and the power of the Holy Ghost. At the end of the world *the earth will die; it will be dissolved, pass away, and then it will be renewed, or raised with a resurrection*. It will receive its resurrection to become a celestial body, so that they of the celestial order may possess it forever and ever. Then *it will shine forth as the sun and take its place among the worlds that are redeemed*. When this time comes the terrestrial inhabitants will also be consigned to another sphere suited to their condition. Then the words of the Savior will be fulfilled, for the meek shall inherit the earth. (DS, Vol. 1, pp. 87-88)

Our earth is one of many such creations of the Lord. From the Lord's parable in this revelation, we learn that the Lord will visit the various earths and the inhabitants thereof. (See D&C 88:51-61) As pertaining to the Lord's visit to this earth prior to its resurrection, Elder Joseph Fielding Smith said:

> During the millennium, the Savior will spend one thousand years here which is one day according to the Lord. In Doctrine and Covenants, Section 88 it is written that the Savior will do the same thing in other worlds, visiting each in its turn. (AGQ, Vol. 3, p. 212)

Kingdoms and Law

Once again we are reminded that this revelation is the Lord's message of peace to us. It is solace to the soul to know that all things are governed by God's law. (See D&C 88:37-38, 42) He comprehends all things and all things are subject unto Him. Nothing in His universe is left to chance and nothing exists without His knowledge. He organized all things and all things are governed by Him. (See D&C 88:13, 41-43)

Of all of God's creations, only man has agency to be disobedient to the laws of God. (See B of M, Helaman 12:4-23) However, because of his agency, man can also choose to come unto God. If man chooses to come unto God in His kingdom, then man must choose to be obedient to the laws of God pertaining to that kingdom. (See D&C 88:38-39) Man receives his reward by obedience to which ever law he chooses to obey.

Sanctification

To be sanctified means to be cleansed and free from the effects of sin. Before anyone can be resurrected and inherit any degree of glory they must be sanctified before the Lord. The only ones who will be resurrected unclean will be the sons of perdition who will go to outer darkness and not inherit a kingdom of glory.

How is one sanctified? To inherit the celestial glory, one must render obedience to the law of Christ and repent of any transgressions thereof. Thus, an individual is sanctified by the law and through the mercy of Christ. To inherit the lesser kingdoms of glory one must abide by the laws pertaining to those kingdoms and suffer themselves for any unrepented transgressions of the law of Christ. (See D&C 88:21-24, 35)

The Lord has invited and commanded all His children to sanctify themselves through the law of Christ. Those who have an eye single to His glory by obeying His law have the immutable promise of the Lord that they will be filled with the Lord's light, comprehend all things, and see the face of the Lord. (See D&C 88:67-68)

Doctrine of the Kingdom

Because all things have been created and are governed by the Lord He expects His children to learn and gain knowledge of all these things. In this revelation, the Lord directed His children to seek learning of things pertaining to: (See D&C 88:77-79, 118)

1. The kingdom of God
2. The things of the heavens
3. The things of the earth
4. History
5. Prophecy
6. Nations, cultures, economies, etc.

What is the reason and purpose for this learning? The answer given by the Lord is:

> That ye may be prepared in all things when I shall send you again to magnify the calling whereunto I have called you, and the mission with which I have commissioned you.
>
> Behold, I sent you out to testify and warn the people, and it becometh every man who hath been warned to warn his neighbor. (D&C 88:80-81)

Elder Gordon B. Hinckley has illustrated the need for such knowledge. He taught:

> ...I want to plead with you to keep balance in your lives. Do not become obsessed with what may be called "a gospel hobby." A good meal always includes more than one course. You ought to have great strength in your chosen and assigned field of expertise. But I

warn you against making that your only interest. I glory in the breadth of this commandment to the people of the Church: [Quoted D&C 88:77-80]

In my life I have had opportunity to serve in many different capacities in the Church. Every time I was released in connection with a new calling, I felt reluctant to leave the old. But every call brought with it an opportunity to learn of another segment of the great program of the Church. I carry in my heart something of pity for those who permit themselves to get locked into one situation and never have an opportunity to experience any other. Missionaries not infrequently plead with their presidents that they be able to extend their missions. This is commendable and is usually indicative of the fact that they have been effective in their work. But a missionary's release usually is as providential as his call, as thereby there is opened to him other opportunities. And out of it all will come a balance in his life.

And beyond the Church there are other experiences to be had in other fields. There is so much work to be done in the communities in which we live. We are urged as citizens to make our contributions through participation in the processes of government. If we are to preserve in our communities those qualities which we so greatly cherish, we must become involved and expend time and effort in that labor. We can develop strength and gain much of experience in so doing while assisting with the pressing social problems that confront our society. We also need to know something about the world of business and science and mechanics in which we live.

It is imperative that we...read constantly the scriptures and other books related directly to the history, the doctrine, and the practices of the Church. But we ought also to be reading secular history, the great literature that has survived the ages, and the writings of contemporary thinkers and doers. In so doing we will find inspiration to pass on to our students, who will need all the balanced strength they can get as they face the world into which they move.

Brethren and sisters, grow in the knowledge of the eternal truths which you are called to teach, and grow in understanding of the great and good men and women who have walked the earth and of the marvelous phenomena with which we are surrounded in the world in which we live. Now and then as I have watched a man become obsessed with a narrow segment of knowledge, I have worried about him. I have seen a few such. They have pursued relentlessly only a sliver of knowledge until they have lost a sense of balance. At the moment I think of two who went so far and became so misguided in their narrow pursuits, that they who once had been effective teachers of youth have been found to be in apostasy and have been excommunicated from the Church. Keep balance in your lives. Beware of narrowness. Let your interests range over many good fields while working with growing strength in the field of your own profession. (Address to Church Educational System Religious Educators, Sept. 15, 1978)

Secret Acts of Men—Satan Overcome

As was noted in the discussion of Section 77 of the Doctrine and Covenants (See Chapter 7 of this volume), the earth's temporal existence began with the fall of Adam. We are told again by the Lord in Section 88 that the earth's temporal existence consists of seven thousand years. At the beginning of the seventh thousand-year period (the millennium), the unrepented secret acts of men will be revealed for each of the preceding six thousand-year periods. Likewise, shall the great and good works of the earth's history be reviewed for each of the same time periods. (See D&C 88:108-109) All things shall be made known. Nothing shall be hidden from view. Satan will then be bound for a thousand years. (See D&C 88:110)

At the end of the seventh thousand-year period, Satan shall be loosed. At that time he will gather his armies to do battle against Michael (Adam) and his armies. The conclusion of the battle will be the overcoming of Satan and the removal of him and his followers to their own place. They shall not have power or influence any more over the Lord's people. (See D&C 88:110-116)

School of the Prophets

The school of the prophets consisted of a group of the early church leaders coming together to be taught and instructed by and under the direction of the Prophet Joseph Smith. Elder Bruce R. McConkie commented on this school as follows:

> In the early days of this dispensation the Lord commanded the brethren to "teach one another the doctrine of the kingdom." [D&C 88:77] They were to learn all things pertaining to the gospel and the kingdom of God that it was expedient for them to know, as also things pertaining to the arts and sciences, and to kingdoms and nations. They were to "seek learning, even by study and also by faith," [D&C 88:118] and were to build a holy sanctuary or temple in Kirtland, which among other things was to be "a house of learning." [D&C 88:119] (D&C 88:74-81, 118-122)
>
> As part of the then existing arrangement to fulfill these com-

Section 88

mands, the Lord directed the setting up of the *school of the prophets* (D&C 88:112, 127-141), ...(Mormon Doctrine, pp. 611-612)

Summary and Conclusion

As children of God, we have been taught how to find peace. The Lord has not left us to wander without direction or to wonder without doctrine. Compliance with the word of God as contained in this revelation brings everlasting peace to the souls of all mankind.

Chapter 18

Doctrine and Covenants Section 89

Suggested Title
The Word of Wisdom

Overview of Section Content
1. Several reasons for the Word of Wisdom for the Latter-day Saints (vs. 1-4)
2. Instructions concerning the use of wine, strong, drinks, tobacco, and hot drinks (vs. 5-9)
3. Insructions concerning the use of herbs, fruit, beasts, fowls and grains (vs. 10-17)
4. Temporal and spiritual blessings promised to the obedient (vs. 18-21)

Historical Setting

Joseph Fielding Smith

...The only comment made by the Prophet Joseph Smith, February 27, 1833, when the revelation on the Word of Wisdom was received is: "I received the following revelation." In those early days of the Church men had not been trained when they came into the Church that their bodies were tabernacles which should be kept sanctified and cleansed physically and morally, as well as spiritually. The use of liquor, tobacco, and stimulants of various kinds, was very common. Tea and coffee were looked upon as foods, and the same to some extent was the attitude towards alcoholic beverages.... (CHMR, Vol. 2, pp. 145-146)

Brigham Young

...I think I am as well acquainted with the circumstances which led to the giving of the Word of Wisdom as any man in the Church, although I was not present at the time to witness them. The first school of the prophets was held in a small room situated over the Prophet Joseph's kitchen, in a house which belonged to Bishop Whitney, and which was attached to his store, which store probably might be about fifteen feet square. In the rear of this building was a kitchen, probably ten by fourteen feet, containing rooms and pantries. Over this kitchen was situated the room in which the Prophet received revelations and in which he instructed his brethren. The brethren came to that place for hundreds of miles to attend school in a little room probably no larger than eleven by fourteen. When they assembled together in this room after breakfast, the first they did was to light their pipes, and, while smoking, talk about the great things of the kingdom, and spit all over the room, and as soon as the pipe was out of their mouths a large chew of tobacco would then be taken. Often when the Prophet entered the room to give the school instructions he would find himself in a cloud of tobacco smoke. This, and the complaints of his wife at having to clean so filthy a floor, made the Prophet think upon the matter, and he inquired of the Lord relating to the conduct of the Elders in using tobacco, and the revelation known as the Word of Wisdom was the result of his inquiry. (JD, Vol. 12, p. 158)

Sacred Truths

Introduction

As noted in the Historical Setting, this revelation was given as a result of a question about the use of tobacco by some members of the church. The Lord gave instructions on the use of tobacco as well as other things pertaining to the health of man. In this chapter, we will limit our discussion to the following four areas:

1. The Word of Wisdom—A commandment
2. The Word of Wisdom—A bulwark against evil

3. The Word of Wisdom—A principle
4. The Word of Wisdom—A promise

The Word of Wisdom—A Commandment

The Lord addressed this revelation to all members of the church. (See D&C 89:1)

This revelation was given February 27, 1833 and at that time it was not given as a commandment, though it did reflect the will of the Lord to His church. (See D&C 89:2)

As to the reason why it was not given as a commandment in 1833 and for information pertaining to the acceptance of the revelation as a commandment in 1851, we refer to the words of two former prophets in the church:

Joseph F. Smith

> The reason undoubtedly why the Word of Wisdom was given—as not by "commandment or restraint" was that at that time, at least, if it had been given as a commandment it would have brought every man, addicted to the use of these noxious things, under condemnation; so the Lord was merciful and gave them a chance to overcome, before He brought them under the law. Later on, it was announced from this stand, by President Brigham Young, that the Word of Wisdom was a revelation and a command of the Lord. I desired to mention that fact, because I do not want you to feel that we are under no restraint. We do not want to come under condemnation. (CR, October 1913, p. 14)

Joseph Fielding Smith

> Question: "Will you please tell me if the Word of Wisdom has ever been presented to the Church as a commandment making its observation obligatory upon the members of the Church?"
>
> Answer: This question is one of a score that have been received in relation to the Word of Wisdom. Some of the questions are due to misunderstanding and others, apparently, seeking answers that will justify a violation or modification of the provisions enumerated in the revelation. The simple answer to this question is yes, such commandment has been given and repeated on several occasions. September 9, 1851, President Brigham Young stated that the members of the Church had had sufficient time to be taught the import of this revelation and that henceforth it was to be considered a divine commandment. This was first put to vote before the male members

of the congregation and then before the women and by unanimous vote accepted. President Joseph F. Smith at a conference meeting in October 1908, made the same statement, and this has been repeated from time to time.

It is true that when it was first revealed it was not given as a commandment made mandatory upon the members as the commandments of the Decalogue are. Nevertheless the meaning is clear, so that no member with sincere desire to do the will of the Lord will think of wilfully violating the counsel it contains. During the first few years after the organization of the Church, converts came out of the world who saw nothing wrong in the use of tobacco and the drinking of wine, and in some instances even stronger alcoholic beverages. To correct this evil, which reason teaches us is harmful to the body, and to cleanse the Church of such habits, the Lord gave this Word of Wisdom. No matter how we may look at it, the intent is clear that it should be faithfully observed. (AGQ, Vol. 1, pp. 197-198)

The Word of Wisdom—A Bulwark Against Evil

The Lord warned against some of the evils and designs of conspiring men as they existed in 1833 and forewarned against evils that would surface in future years. (See D&C 89:4)

This revelation is not a complete law of health since there are many positive as well as negative influences and practices that have an effect upon the health of our bodies that are not mentioned. However, it is a point of orientation. Those who catch the spirit of this revelation and build upon it as a foundation or a standard will reap the benefits of obedience to its principles. And what is the orientation or spirit of this revelation? It serves as a bulwark or protection against the enslavement of our bodies to harmful and addictive substances. Emphasizing the importance of the Word of Wisdom as a bulwark against evil, Elder Boyd K. Packer has said:

> The revelation received by the Prophet Joseph Smith on February 27, 1833, known as the Word of Wisdom, has been a bulwark and a protection to Latter-day Saints from that time to this. In our day it suddenly looms higher in importance. The introduction to the revelation includes the following: "Behold, verily, thus saith the Lord unto you: in consequence of evils and designs which do and will exist in the hearts of conspiring men in the last days, I have warned you, and forewarned you, by giving unto you this Word of Wisdom by revelation...." (D&C 89:4)

However much the Word of Wisdom has protected us over the years from the degrading influences of drunkenness, alcoholism and from the use of tobacco, it now stands as a protection against evil and designs which are a greater threat. Although there was no extensive scientific information to support the Word of Wisdom when it was given, that has come as the years have unfolded. And, now we find that adherence to the counsel contained in the Word of Wisdom is a shield before our youth, protecting them from the frightening invasion of narcotics.

Young people who keep the Word of Wisdom are not ordinarily likely to indulge—even experiment—with drugs. If there are strong family ties and a warm family homelife, the likelihood of their addiction is more remote than ever. Parents and ward priesthood and auxiliary leaders, particularly those who deal directly with youth, would do well to emphasize the Word of Wisdom. It is a shield and a protection to our young people against narcotics also.

Young Latter-day Saints are taught that our body is a sacred possession. It is the instrument of our mind and the foundation of our character. We should take nothing into our bodies that would harm the organs thereof; or that would tamper with the delicate processes of thinking and feeling. There needs to be a vigorous re-emphasis of this among the youth of the Church. The physical body is a priceless treasure. It should not be degraded by subjecting it to the influence of tobacco, nor alcohol in any form, nor, more dangerous than either of these, the slavery which comes through drug addiction.

Latter-day Saints may well count their blessings when they consider the instruction which the Lord has given through his servants regarding our well-being in difficult and dangerous times. The warning has come. Evils and designs will exist in the hearts of conspiring men in these days. Latter-day Saints can provide a certain immunity for themselves by following the counsel of the leadership of the Church. (Church News, March 6, 1971, p. 4)

The Word of Wisdom—A Principle

There is another reference point or principle in this revelation that serves as a standard for all members of the church. This commandment was "Given for a principle with promise...." (D&C 89:3) There is more to the Word of Wisdom than just physical or temporal laws of health. The Word of Wisdom involves a principle of spiritual dimension, even the principle of obedience. (See D&C 89:3, 18)

The spirit of this law is self-mastery. Aside from the physical harm that occurs to the body from indulgence in harmful substances, there is also spiritual damage done to the soul through disobedience to the commandment. It is only through obedience (the first law of heaven) that an individual can gain the spiritual stature necessary for an inheritance in the kingdom of heaven. Stressing the spiritual implications of the Word of Wisdom, two former prophets have taught:

Brigham Young

> ...I said to the Saints at our last annual Conference, the Spirit whispers to me to call upon the Latter-day Saints to observe the Word of Wisdom, to let tea, coffee, and tobacco alone, and to abstain from drinking spirituous drinks. This is what the Spirit signifies through me. If the Spirit of God whispers this to His people through their leader, and they will not listen nor obey, what will be the consequence of their disobedience? Darkness and blindness of mind with regard to the things of God will be their lot; they will cease to have the spirit of prayer, and the spirit of the world will increase in them in proportion to their disobedience until they apostatize entirely from God and His ways. (JD, Vol. 12, p. 117)

Heber J. Grant

> ...I am converted beyond the shadow of a doubt that no man or woman in this Church who does not observe the Word of Wisdom can grow and increase in a knowledge and testimony of the gospel as he or she could otherwise do. (Gospel Standards, p. 249)

The Word of Wisdom—A Promise

The Lord referred to the Word of Wisdom as "...a principle with promise...." (D&C 89:3) As to the obtaining the promises associated with this revelation, we note that they are conditioned upon the following: (See D&C 89:18)
 1. Keeping and following the counsel given in Section 89
 2. Living the commandments of the Lord

Commenting upon the necessity of fulfilling both of these requirements, President Harold B. Lee has taught:

> If you would escape from the devastation when God's judgments descend upon the wicked, as in the days of the children of Israel, you must remember and do what the Lord commands: "...all saints who remember to keep and do these saying"—meaning keep His great law of health, known as the Word of Wisdom—and in addition thereto walk "in obedience to the commandments," which would include honesty, moral purity, together

with all the laws of the celestial kingdom, then "the destroying angel shall pass by them, as the children of Israel, and not slay them." (Stand Ye In Holy Places, p. 24)

The promises mentioned by the Lord that will come to the faithful can be grouped into three categories as follows: (See D&C 89:18-21)

1. Health in the navel, marrow to the bones

This phrase appears but once in all of the revealed latter-day scripture in the standard works of the Church. The scriptures do not provide an explanation as to its meaning. To those who are worthy of this promise, the meaning will be manifest by the Lord in His own time and place.

2. Wisdom and Hidden Treasures of Knowledge

One of the finest explanations that provides insight to the meaning of this promise has been given by President Spencer W. Kimball:

> ...I sat one day with my attorney friend, Guy Anderson, across the directors' room table of my office in Arizona.
>
> In his slow, pleasant drawl, he said, "I came to congratulate you on your call to the apostleship and to visit with you before your move to Salt Lake City." We talked about what my call entailed, and then he told me of one of his experiences as a law student at George Washington University.
>
> A number of young members of the Church were students there. Since there were no stakes in the East at that time, they held a Sunday School class in a rented residence, and Congressman Don B. Colton from Utah was their teacher.
>
> This particular Sunday morning, they were considering the 89th section of the Doctrine and Covenants, the Lord's law of health.
>
> Brother Colton had made an impressive presentation on the Word of Wisdom, which is "the order and will of God in the temporal salvation of all saints in the last days."
>
> He emphasized also the further statement of the Lord: [Quoted D&C 89:4].
>
> The Lord is displeased when his earthly children imbibe in "wine or strong drink." He said, "...tobacco is not for the body-...and is not good for man.... And again, hot drinks, [tea and coffee] are not for the body."
>
> Brother Colton emphasized the promise made by the Lord to those who did observe this law of health and other commandments. Hear these rich promises: [Quoted D&C 89:18-21].

Then came a question from one of the students: "Brother Colton, the promise is that if one observes these laws, he shall find wisdom and great treasures of knowledge, even hidden treasures. Many of the men in this university use tobacco and liquor and break all commandments, including the law of chastity. Yet in some cases they excel academically. So far as I can tell my obedience to the Word of Wisdom has not made me superior intellectually to them. How do you account for that?"

Since closing time had come, Brother Colton held this difficult question for the next week.

On Friday, as usual, several of the congressman were eating luncheon at the House of Representatives' restaurant when Brother Colton joined them. The others began to joke in a friendly fashion, "Here comes the 'Mormon' congressman; this man from Utah won't drink nor smoke a cigarette nor even drink a cup of coffee." A congressman from a western state came to the defense, saying "Gentlemen, you may joke at Mr. Colton and have your fun at the expense of the 'Mormon' Church, but let me tell you an experience."

He told a story something like this:

"I was back in my home state, building political fences, shaking hands with voters, getting acquainted with my people. Sunday overtook me in a country town.

"I sat in the lobby of the hotel, reading the paper, and through the plate glass window I saw many people going in the same direction. My curiousity was stirred. I followed them to a little church and slid unobtrusively into a back seat and listened and observed.

"This church service was different. I had never seen one like it. A man called 'bishop' conducted the meeting. The singing was by the congregation, the prayer by a man from the audience, apparently called without previous notice. Soft music was played. All was silent as one young man knelt and said a prayer over bread, which he and his companion had broken into small pieces, and then several boys, probably 12 or 13 years of age, took plates of broken bread and passed it to the congregation. The same was done with little cups of water. After the choir sang an anthem, to my amazement (for I expected to hear a sermon), the bishop announced something like this: 'Brothers and sisters, today is your monthly fast and testimony service, and you may proceed to speak as you feel led by the Spirit. This time is not for sermons but to speak of your own soul and your inner feelings and assurances. The time is yours.'"

The western congressman paused and then continued.

"Never before had I experienced anything like this. From the congregation people arose. One man in a dignified voice said how he loved the Church and the gospel and what it meant in the life of his family.

"From another part of the chapel, a woman stood and spoke with deep conviction of a spectacular healing in her family as an answer to prayer and fasting, and closed with what the people called a testimony—that the gospel of Jesus Christ as taught by the Church was true; that it brought great happiness and a deep peace to her.

"Still another woman arose and bore witness of her sureness that Joseph Smith was truly a prophet of God and had been the instrument of the Lord in restoring the true gospel of Christ to the earth.

"A man from the choir, evidently a recent immigrant, seemed sensitive about his language. He was struggling with v's and his w's and verbs and construction. Two years ago, two young missionaries in far-away Holland had taught him the restored gospel. He told how happy his family had been since embracing it, and what a transformation had come in their lives!

"The old and the middle-aged and the youth responded; some were farmers, laborers; there were teachers and business and professional men. There was no ostentation, no arrogance, but a quiet dignity, a warm friendliness, a sweet spirituality.'

"Then came in succession several children. They spoke less of their knowledge of spiritual things but more of their love for their parents and for the Savior, of whom they had learned much in Primary, Sunday School, and family home evenings.

"Finally the bishop stood and in a few appropriate words of commendation expressed his own sureness; then he closed the meeting."

The western congressman noted that all around the table were intently listening. He continued:

"Never had time passed so rapidly. I had been entranced. And as each additional speaker had concluded in the name of Jesus Christ, I was moved—deeply stirred—and I pondered: How sincere! How sweet and spiritual! How sure these people seem to be of their Redeemer! How much at peace! What security they have in their spiritual knowledge, what strength and fortitude, and what purposeful lives!"

The congressman said, "I thought of my own children and grandchildren and their helter-skelter existence, their self-centered activities, their seeming spiritual vacuums, their routine lives in search of wealth and fun and adventure. And I said to myself with an enthusiasm new to me, 'How I wish my own posterity could have this sureness, this faith, this deep conviction. Why, these humble people seem to have a secret that most people do not enjoy—yes, that is it—something worth more than all else, real treasures, hidden treasures.'"

The luncheon ended. The congressmen went back to their offices.

Elder Colton was now again before his Sunday School class of young college men. He retold the Friday afternoon story and said that what the congressman had observed were "hidden treasures of knowledge" promised by the revelation. These mysteries of the kingdom relate to all truths, not merely to scientific accomplishments and legal cases and other secular things. He said that "treasures of knowledge" extended far beyond material things, out into the infinite areas not explored by many otherwise brilliant people. He repeated the Prophet's statements, which are proverbial among members of the Church: Knowledge is power. The glory of God is intelligence.

Knowledge is not merely the equations of algebra, the theorems of geometry, or the miracles of space. It is hidden treasures of knowledge as recorded in Hebrews, by which "the worlds were framed by the word of God" (Heb. 11:3); by which Enoch was translated that he should not see death; by which Noah, with a knowledge no other human had, built an ark on dry land and saved a race by taking seed through the flood.

Knowledge is that power which raises one into new and higher worlds and elevates him into new spiritual realms.

The treasures of both secular and spiritual knowledge are hidden ones—but hidden from those who do not properly search and strive to find them. The knowledge of the spiritual will not come to an individual without effort any more than will the secular knowledge or college degrees. Spiritual knowledge gives the power to live eternally and to rise and overcome and develop and finally to create.

Hidden knowledge is not unfindable. It is available to all who really search. Christ said, ". . .seek and ye shall find." (Matt. 7:7) Spiritual knowledge is not available merely for the asking; even prayers are not enough. It takes persistence and dedication of one's life. The knowledge of things in secular life are of time and are limited; the knowledge of the infinite truths are of time and eternity.

Of all treasures of knowledge, the most vital is the knowledge of God: his existence, powers, love and promises.

The Christ said: "He that hath my commandments, and keepeth them, he it is that loveth me: and he that loveth me shall be loved of my Father, and I will love him, and will manifest myself unto him." (John 14:21)

He further said: "If a man love me, he will keep my words: ...and we will come unto him, and make our abode with him." (John 14:23)

And the Prophet Joseph Smith explained: "And this means that the coming of the Father and the Son to a person is a reality—a personal appearance—and not merely dwelling in his heart." (D&C 130:3)

This personal witness, then, is the ultimate treasure.

One may acquire knowledge of space and in a limited degree conquer it. He may explore the moon and other planets, but no man can ever really find God in a university campus laboratory, in the physical test tubes of workshops, nor on the testing fields at Cape Kennedy. God and his program will be found only in deep pondering, appropriate reading, much kneeling in devout, humble prayer, and in a sincerity born of need and dependence.

These requirements having been fully met, there is no soul between the poles nor from ocean to ocean who may not positively obtain this knowledge, this hidden treasure of knowledge, this saving and exalting knowledge. (CR, October 1968, pp. 127-130)

3. *Physical Strength and Protection*

Every mortal being is susceptible to disease, accident, and other vicissitudes of mortality and no one is immune to these body-destroying experiences. However, collectively speaking, the Latter-day Saints have been promised blessings of health and strength. As to some of the dimensions of the meaning of this promise, President George Albert Smith has said:

...While Joseph Smith might write those words, [D&C 89] he couldn't fulfil that promise. I stand here today as one of the humblest among you, as the result of the observance of the requirements of that revelation and other commandments that God has given. Observance of that commandment has placed the membership of the Church of Jesus Christ of Latter-day Saints in the tops of these everlasting mountains in a class by themselves. Not only do we have the lowest death rate of any people in all the world, but we also have a high birth rate as well. That was the promise that was given by the Lord in the days of the Prophet Joseph Smith. The Lord said that the destroying angels should pass by us and not slay us if we kept his counsel. What has been another result? The age of men and women in the Church of Jesus Christ of Latter-day Saints has increased until the average term of life among us is longer than among any other people in the world. (CR, October 1945, p. 21)

Time has always vindicated the truth of the word of the Lord given through His living prophets. One illustration of the validity of these promises is provided by one scientific report as follows:

Mormons, Adventists Have Low Cancer Rate

Mormons neither drink nor smoke, and they stress clean living. They also die of cancer at about half the rate of other Californians, according to a study made by James E. Enstrom, a researcher at U.C.L.A. School of Public Health.

That is not surprising, since many cancers have been linked to tobacco and alcohol. But Enstrom has found that Mormons in Utah and California have strikingly lower cancer-death rates in sites that have never been clearly associated with tobacco, alcohol and diet. These include colo-rectal cancer, stomach cancer, breast cancer, uterine cancer, cancer of the kidneys, and cancer of the pancreas.

His findings are supported by a separate study of cancer deaths among Seventh-Day Adventists (whose religion has even stricter dietary regulations and bans on smoking and drinking) done by Dr. Roland L. Phillips of Loma Linda University at Loma Linda, Calif. Dr. Phillips found that the cancer-death rate for Seventh-Day Adventists in California is 50 to 70 percent lower—depending upon the site—than the rate for the entire state.

Enstrom feels that these findings indicate that total life-style—including drinking, smoking, exercise and dietary habits—plays an important but still unknown role in determining whether a person will die of cancer. Mormons also emphasize tight-knit family life. "Maybe man's emotional status is of greater importance than we have thought," says Dr. James O. Mason, commissioner of health services for the Mormon church headquarters in Salt Lake City. "Maybe the extra bit of harmony in some of our homes is good for physical as well as emotional health." (Reader's Digest, March 1975, pp. 49-50)

Summary and Conclusion

The Lord has given counsel and commandments in many areas of life. This revelation is one in which He addresses matters pertaining to our physical bodies and the blessings associated with the proper care thereof. Great promises and blessings await those who follow His counsel, keep His commandments and implement His concepts in their own standards of behavior.

Chapter 19

Doctrine and Covenants Section 90

Suggested Title
Keys of the Kingdom—Oracles of God

Overview of Section Content
1. Joseph Smith holds the keys of the kingdom and the right to receive revelation for the church (vs. 1-5)
2. Counselors in the First Presidency hold the keys of the kingdom with the prophet (vs. 6)
3. Some of the duties and responsibilities of the First Presidency (vs. 7-18)
4. Counsel given to various church members (vs. 19-31)
5. Joseph Smith presides over Zion (church in Missouri) (vs. 32-33)
6. A warning of the Lord to the saints in Zion (Missouri) (vs. 34-37)

Historical Setting

Joseph Smith. Jun.

　　March 8.—I received the following revelation: ... (HC, Vol. 1, p. 329)

Joseph Fielding Smith

> ...No explanation is given why this revelation was received, but it is one containing information of the greatest importance and may have come through the prayers of the brethren as indicated in this divine message. (CHMR, Vol. 2, p. 149)

We would call attention to the fact that approximately one year earlier (March 1832 - See Chapter 10, Section 81 Historical Setting) the Lord indicated there should be a First Presidency organized. At that time the Lord revealed that "...the keys of the kingdom...belong always unto the Presidency of the High Priesthood:" (D&C 81:2) In March 1833, the Lord reaffirmed this principle and taught the membership further pertaining to the keys held by the First Presidency.

Sacred Truths

Introduction

In this chapter we will discuss two of the major teachings contained in the revelation:
1. Keys of the kingdom
2. Oracles of God

Keys of the Kingdom

When the term "keys" is used in connection with the priesthood, it is understood to refer to the power to direct the use of priesthood authority. The Lord informed the Prophet Joseph Smith that the keys of the kingdom would be his to hold throughout this life and in the world to come. (See D&C 90:2-3) Joseph's presiding authority was to direct the work of salvation both in this world and in the spirit world. As to Joseph's administering the Lord's work for this dispensation in the spirit world, Elder Wilford Woodruff has taught:

> I used to have peculiar feelings about his [Joseph Smith's] death and the way in which his life was taken. I felt that if, with the consent and good feelings of the brethren that waited on him after he crossed the river to leave Nauvoo, Joseph could have had his desire, he would have pioneered the way to the Rocky Mountains. But since then I have been fully reconciled to the fact that it was according to the program, that it was required of him, as the head of this dispensation, that he should seal his testimony with his blood, and go hence to the spirit world, holding the keys of this dispensation, to

open up the mission that is now being performed by way of preaching the gospel to the "spirits in prison." (DWW, p. 35)

All who hold the priesthood in any capacity, are subject to someone else of higher authority. This was true of Joseph Smith. To illustrate: Michael (Adam) holds the keys for the salvation of all mankind under the direction of the Savior and Joseph Smith functions under the presiding authority of Michael. (See D&C 78:15-16) Each successor of the Prophet Joseph Smith holds the keys of the kingdom subordinate to him. President George Q. Cannon explained this principle as follows:

> You never heard President Young teach any other doctrine; he always said that Joseph stood at the head of this dispensation, that Joseph holds the keys, that although Joseph had gone behind the veil, he stood at the head of this dispensation and that he himself held the keys subordinate to him. President Taylor teaches the same doctrine, and you will never hear any other doctrine from any of the faithful Apostles or servants of God, who understand the order of the Holy Priesthood. (*Gospel Truth*, Vol. 1, p. 255)

We also learn from this revelation that the keys of the kingdom held by the President of the church are held jointly with him by the counselors in the First Presidency. (See D&C 90:6) The counselors use these keys under the direction of the President.

Oracles of God

An oracle of God is a person through whom the Lord speaks His mind and will to the people. The term oracle is also used to identify that which a prophet speaks, or the revelations that come, from the Lord to the people. The Lord informs the world in this revelation that it is through His prophet that His revelations will be given unto His church. (See D&C 90:4) Inasmuch as the prophet and his counselors constitute the First Presidency, it is through this presidency that the Lord will counsel, direct and give His oracles to the membership of His Church and to the world if they would receive it. (See D&C 90:6; 124:125-126) The Prophet Joseph Smith understood perfectly this order in the kingdom and declared as follows:

> ...the Presidents or Presidency are over the Church; and revelations of the mind and will of God to the Church, are to come through the Presidency. This is the order of heaven,... (TPJS, p. 111)

...Look to the Presidency and receive instruction. (TPJS, p. 161)

The Lord is constantly giving counsel to His church through those whom He has appointed, even the First Presidency of the church. In a later revelation, the Lord identified the relationship that exists between the Lord, the First Presidency, and the membership of the church. He said:

Whosoever receiveth my word receiveth me, and whosoever receiveth me, receive those, the First Presidency, whom I have sent, whom I have made counselors for my name's sake unto you. (D&C 112:20)

The Lord has warned the members of His church to beware how they look upon the First Presidency and the counsel and revelations that come through them. Those who treat lightly such counsel will stumble and fall and bring upon themselves condemnation from the Lord. (See D&C 90:4-5) Anyone who rejects and teaches contrary to the oracles of God that come through the First Presidency of the church is setting himself up as a source of wisdom and counsel to the people. Such a person, who fails to repent, will lose his place in the kingdom of God and will be found guilty of setting up a golden calf for the worship of the people. (See D&C 124:45-46, 84)

Summary and Conclusion

The principles taught in this revelation are crystal clear and cannot be misunderstood. The Lord has emphasized that there is but one place on the earth where the power to govern the affairs of His kingdom can be found and that place is the First Presidency of His church. Every legitimate and authoritative action done in this church is done by virtue of the keys of the authority vested in His Presidency.

It is also through that Presidency that the Lord's counsel, direction, and revelations will be given to His church. A true disciple of Jesus Christ is one who receives the laws of the Lord and is obedient to them. (See D&C 41:5) The true disciple looks to the First Presidency for those laws and follows their counsel and instruction. The true disciple is aware that the Lord's words are pure and binding upon him as a member of the church and are to be answered before the Lord on the day of judgment. (See D&C 41:12)

Chapter 20

Doctrine and Covenants Section 91

Suggested Title

The Apocrypha

Overview of Section Content

1. The Apocrypha contains both truth and error (vs. 1-2)
2. Joseph Smith is told that it is not needful for him to translate the Apocrypha (vs. 3)
3. The Apocrypha is beneficial to those who read by the Spirit (vs. 4-6)

Historical Setting

Joseph Smith, Jun.

March 9.—Having come to that portion of the ancient writings called the Apocrypha, I received the following:...(HC, Vol. 1, p. 331)

Joseph Fielding Smith

...On the 9th of March 1833, while the Prophet was busy considering the translation of the Scriptures, he inquired of the Lord regarding the Apocrypha of the Old Testament. He received the answer that it was not necessary for him to translate this record, for it contained many things that were not true having been interpreted by the hands of men. However, in the main it was correctly translated but its value was not of sufficient import for time to be taken to revise it.... (CHMR, Vol. 2, p. 153)

Sacred Truths

Introduction

To more fully appreciate the teachings contained in this revelation, some understanding of the Apocrypha, its meanings, origin, etc., will be helpful. To aid in this understanding, statements from two General Authorities are provided as follows:

James E. Talmage

> The Apocrypha embrace a number of books of doubtful authenticity, though such have been at times highly esteemed. Thus, they were added to the Septuagint, and for a time were accorded recognition among the Alexandrine Jews. However, they have never been generally admitted, being of uncertain origin. They are not quoted in the New Testament. The designation *apocryphal*, meaning hidden, or secret, was first applied to the books by Jerome. The Roman church professes to acknowledge them as scripture, action to this end having been taken by the Council of Trent (1546); though doubt as to the authenticity of the works seems still to exist even among Roman Catholic authorities. The sixth article in the Liturgy of the Church of England defines the orthodox view of the church as to the meaning and intent of Holy Scripture; and, after specifying the books of the Old Testament which are regarded as canonical, proceeds in this wise: "And the other books (as Hierome [Jerome] saith) the church doth read for example of life and instruction of manners; but yet doth it not apply them to establish any doctrine; such are these following:—The Third Book of Esdras; The Fourth Book of Esdras; the Book of Tobias; The Book of Judith; The rest of the Book of Esther; The Book of Wisdom; Jesus, the Son of Sirach; Baruch the Prophet; The Song of the Three Children; The Story of Susanna; Of Bel and the Dragon; The Prayer of Manasses; The First Book of Maccabees; The Second Book of Maccabees." (*Articles of Faith*, pp. 244-245)

Section 91   133

Bruce R. McConkie

These apocryphal writings were never included in the Hebrew Bible, but they were in the Greek Septuagint (the Old Testament used by the early apostles) and in the Latin Vulgate. Jerome, who translated the Vulgate, was required to include them in his translation, though he is quoted as having decided they should be read "for example of life and instruction of manners" and should not be used "to establish any doctrine." Luther's German Bible grouped the apocryphal books together (omitting 1st and 2nd Esdras) at the end of the Old Testament under this heading: "Apocrypha: these are books which are not held equal to the sacred scriptures, and yet are useful and good for reading."

The Apocrypha was included in the King James Version of 1611, but by 1629 some English Bibles began to appear without it, and since the early part of the 19th century it has been excluded from almost all protestant Bibles. The American Bible Society, founded in 1816, has never printed the Apocrypha in its Bibles, and the British and Foreign Bible Society has excluded it from all but some pulpit Bibles since 1827. (*Mormon Doctrine*, p. 39)

The Apocrypha

From this revelation, we learn four things pertaining to the apocrypha of the Old Testament:

1. Truth

The Lord revealed that there are many truths contained in the apocrypha. (See D&C 91:1) The Church of Jesus Christ of Latter-day Saints is the depository of truth. All truth comes from God, therefore, it is part of the gospel of Jesus Christ.

2. Error

The Lord revealed that there are many untruths contained in the apocrypha. (See D&C 91:2) The Lord's church cannot accept untruth in any form. It is not a part of the gospel of Jesus Christ.

3. Translation

The Lord revealed to Joseph Smith it was "...not needful that the Apocrypha should be translated." (D&C 91:3) The Lord said it was not needful. In other words, the contents of the Apocrypha are not essential to the salvation of mankind.

4. Reading

The Lord revealed the way by which the reader of the apocrypha might recognize that portion which is true. The Spirit manifests truth and when one reads by the Spirit, he is enlightened and is able to obtain the benefit therefrom. (See D&C 91:4-6)

Summary and Conclusion

The principle revealed in this revelation can be applied to the study of any subject. If information is true, the Spirit will manifest it. If it is not true, there will be no spiritual witness given. Each of us should live in such a way that we can receive spiritual manifestations and be guided by the truth.

> ...the only perfect and absolute way to gain a sure knowledge of any truth in any field is to receive personal revelation from the "Holy Spirit of God." (Bruce R. McConkie, "Honest Truth Seekers," Letter dated July 1, 1980)

Chapter 21

Doctrine and Covenants Section 92

Suggested Title

A Lively Member

Overview of Section Content

1. The United Order is directed to receive Frederick G. Williams as a member (vs. 1)
2. Frederick G. Williams is to be a lively member in the United Order (vs. 2)

Historical Setting

Joseph Smith, Jun.

> For your satisfaction, I here insert [In a letter of April 21, 1833 to the brethren in Zion] a revelation given to Shederlaomach [Frederick G. Williams], the 15th of March, 1833, constituting him a member of the United Firm. (HC, Vol. 1, p. 340)

Hyrum M. Smith and Janne M. Sjodahl

> In the Revelation given on April 26th, 1832 (Sec. 82), the Lord instructed the Prophet Joseph, Oliver Cowdery, Martin Harris, Sid-

ney Rigdon, Newel K. Whitney, and a few others (v. 11) to unite their temporal interests under the rule of the Order of Enoch. In this Revelation the brethren in that organization are commanded to receive, as a member, Frederick G. Williams, whom the Lord had declared to be the equal of Joseph Smith and Sidney Rigdon in holding the keys of the kingdom (Sec. 90:6).....(DCC, pp. 586-587)

Sacred Truths

Introduction

In this concise revelation to Frederick G. Williams the Lord revealed two important concepts that are fundamental to all members of the church:
1. Membership
2. A lively member

Membership

The Lord instructed the United Order to "...receive him [Frederick G. Williams] into the order." (D&C 92:1) What does it mean to *receive* a member into church organizations? As members of the church we are commonly invited to receive and welcome new members into our wards and quorums and extend a hand of fellowship to them when they come. There have been some unfortunate circumstances when people have been overlooked, ignored or in some way made to feel unwelcome and left out. Various factors may contribute to this condition—unintentional oversight, financial status, mental or physical impairments, cultural or ethnic differences, etc. It is important to note that the Lord placed no conditions on the receiving of Brother Williams into the United Order. His membership was to be accepted on equal terms with the other members without regard to his background or other qualifications. Members of the church should receive an unconditional welcome into any ward or church organization in which they have legitimate membership status. They are to be *received* by the group.

A Lively Member

The Lord spoke plainly to Frederick G. Williams as to his responsibility as a member of the United Order. He was directed to "...be a lively member in this order;..." (D&C 92:2) To be lively means to be active, involved, doing, etc. There is no room for being passive in the Lord's kingdom. (See D&C 58:27-28) One cannot simply watch and observe the activity of the kingdom and maintain a spiritually growing status in the church. The importance of such activity has been stressed by President Harold B. Lee as follows:

Now, brethren, we are going out now with a determined activity to bring these our brethren into activity—activity of some kind. One of the mission presidents, with a group of his missionaries back in the Eastern States some years ago, was meeting in a hall with pillars that ran down the center of the hall, and he said to one of the missionaries, "Get up and push that pillar over."

"Well," said the missionary, "I can't."

"Why?"

"Because the weight of that ceiling is all on top of the pillar."

Then the president asked, "Suppose that weight were lifted off. Could you push the pillar over then?"

The missionary replied, "Why, sure, I think I could."

Then the president said, "Now, brethren, you and I are just like one of those pillars. As long as we have a weight of responsibility in this church, all hell can't push us over; but as soon as that weight is lifted off, most of us are easy marks by the powers that drag us down."

Now we want to put a weight of responsibility on every holder of the priesthood and on every father in every home. You must remember that if we are to multiply the number of those who are so-called inactives, who haven't been to the temple, by the average-size family, you are counting up to hundreds of thousands of members of this church who, unless we do something about it, will not be sealed together in the temple and will not, therefore, belong together in family relationships in the hereafter.

Remember that activity is the soul of spirituality. (*CR*, October 1971, p. 129)

Summary and Conclusion

This revelation stresses two of the responsibilities of church members:
1. Receive others into full fellowship in the organizations of the church.
2. Be personally active and involved in the work of the Lord.

Chapter 22

Doctrine and Covenants Section 93

Suggested Title

How and What to Worship

Overview of Section Content

1. The Savior's promises to the sanctified (vs. 1, 20-22, 27-28)
2. The eternal nature of Jesus Christ (vs. 2-5)
3. The record of John and his testimony of Jesus Christ (vs. 6-18)
4. Proper worship—Purpose of this revelation (vs. 19)
5. Nature of intelligence, light, and truth (vs. 23-26, 29-30, 36-37, 39)
6. Nature and agency of man (vs. 31-35, 38)
7. Church leaders commanded to teach their families light and truth (vs. 40-50)
8. Instructions to the First Presidency (vs. 51-53)

Historical Setting

Joseph Smith, Jun.

>   May 6. [1833]—I received the following: . . .(HC, Vol. 1, p. 343)

139

The Prophet Joseph Smith has not given any explanation as to the events surrounding the obtaining of this revelation. This is one of the most significant of all the revelations received in this dispensation.

Sacred Truths

Introduction

The purpose of this revelation was given by the Savior:

> I give unto you these sayings that you may understand and know how to worship, and know what you worship, that you may come unto the Father in my name, and in due time receive of his fulness. (D&C 93:19)

What is worship? It is often described as an act or process of showing reverence or honor and respect to a Supreme Being. However, worship also includes the establishment of a spiritual relationship with the Lord. This relationship makes possible a constant spiritual communication experience with God. It is the way by which man is able to "...pray always..." (D&C 93:49)

We note in the above quoted verse (D&C 93:19) that the Lord identified three aspects of this subject of worship which will be discussed in this chapter:

1. How to worship
2. What to worship
3. Purpose of worship

How to Worship

In order to attain the level of worship described above, it is essential that we properly prepare ourselves. The personal preparation necessary is described by the Lord in five steps: (see D&C 93:1)

1. Forsake sins
2. Come unto the Lord
3. Pray to the Lord
4. Obey the voice of the Lord
5. Keep the Lord's commandments

Not only did the Lord stress the need for each individual to sanctify and prepare himself for worship, He also taught us another way by which we are able to strengthen our worship experience. He called our attention to the content of scriptures which teach us more about Him and which help us to come closer to Him by searching for and receiving the scriptural witnesses. (See D&C 93:6-18)

Elder Spencer W. Kimball emphasized some of the dimensions of proper worship as follows:

> One may acquire knowledge of space and in a limited degree conquer it. He may explore the moon and other planets, but no man can ever really find God in a university campus laboratory, in the physical test tubes of workshops, nor on the testing fields at Cape Kennedy. God and his program will be found only in deep pondering, appropriate reading, much kneeling in devout, humble prayer, and in a sincerity born of need and dependence.
>
> These requirements having been fully met, there is no soul between the poles nor from ocean to ocean who may not positively obtain this knowledge, this hidden treasure of knowledge, this saving and exalting knowledge. (*CR*, October 1968, p. 130)

What to Worship

We worship God our Father and His son Jesus Christ for they are one in the Godhead. (See D&C 93:2-4) The Savior personified the Father in two ways:

1. The Father gave His fulness to Jesus Christ. This included all power in heaven and on earth including the glory of the Father. (See D&C 93:4, 17)

2. Jesus Christ was the Only Begotten of the Father in the flesh. The Father of the Savior's physical body was the Eternal Father in Heaven. (See D&C 93:4, 11)

Because of the powers inherited through His heavenly parentage, Jesus Christ was able to perform both portions of the atonement for mankind:

1. From His Father, the Savior inherited power over physical death and was thus able to provide the resurrection for all.

2. Because Jesus was totally obedient to the commandments of His Father, He conquered all sin and opened the doors of salvation to the penitent as He redeemed them from their sins.

The Savior is referred to as: "The Word" (D&C 93:8), "The light and the Redeemer of the world," the "Spirit of truth," "The life . . . and light of men" (D&C 93:9), "The Only Begotten" (D&C 93:11). It is important to understand that when the above scriptural terms are used, they have reference to Jesus Christ as He personifies the Father. These sayings help us to understand and know the beings whom we worship. (See D&C 93:19)

One of the purposes of knowing how Jesus personified his Father is that we can learn how we can do the same. Man can also progress and likewise manifest works of righteousness and achieve the rewards of the Gods. (See D&C 93:19-20, 28) From this revelation we learn some of the ways by which Jesus Christ obtained the fulness of the Father. (See D&C 93:2-17)

Purpose of Worship

This revelation contains at least two aspects of purposeful worship:

1. Obtaining the fulness of the Father (See D&C 93:19)

Though the Savior was not born with a fulness of all truth, He kept Father's commandments and grew from grace to grace until He received a fulness of the glory of the Father and all power in Heaven and on earth. (See D&C 93:12-17) All of Father's children are eligible to receive a fulness of truth if they will keep the Savior's commandments. By so doing, they will eventually obtain and know all things. (See D&C 93:27-28)

Thus we learn that true and purposeful worship consists in the day-to-day keeping of the Lord's commandments.

Once we understand the purpose of what we are to do as individuals, we are then better prepared and responsible to share that experience with our families. The Lord reminded some of the church leaders that they were responsible to teach their children light and truth and to keep the commandments and thereby bless their families with the opportunity to obtain a fulness of the Father's glory. (See D&C 93:40-50)

From this revelation, we learn many things about truth:

1. The Savior represents the fulness and spirit of truth (vs. 9, 11, 26)
2. Definition of truth (vs. 24)
3. How to obtain a fulness of truth (vs. 28)
4. Truth is equated with intelligence and light (vs. 29, 36)
5. Truth acts within the limits God places upon it (vs. 30)
6. Truth is the basis upon which man is judged (vs. 32-35)
7. Truth forsakes and provides power over evil (vs. 37)
8. Truth is lost through disobedience (vs. 39)
9. Children are to be taught truth (vs. 40)
10. Parents are condemned for failure to teach truth (vs. 42-47)

2. Overcoming evil (See D&C 93:36-37, 49)

The Lord revealed that God's glory (light and truth) is manifested through the Lord Jesus Christ. All light and truth emanates from Him and is the power by which evil is overcome. As noted earlier, the power to overcome evil is obtained by keeping the commandments of the Lord. By so doing we become spiritually closer to the Savior and qualify ourselves for the obtaining of the intelligence that flows from Him.

Elder Joseph Fielding Smith explained this concept as follows:

> We very frequently quote from one of the revelations the words of the Lord to this effect, that "The glory of God is intelligence," and I wonder if we ourselves really comprehend what it means. We stop in the middle of a sentence. That is not the end of the sentence, for the Lord says, "The glory of God is intelligence, or in other words light and truth." And then he adds that "light and truth forsaketh that evil one."
>
> When we have the Spirit of the Lord we have intelligence—light and truth...It is pure intelligence, if you please, and he who has it has the power to discern between right and wrong, truth and error, and he will follow righteousness. (*CR*, October 1933, p. 60)

Summary and Conclusion

This revelation teaches us that all men ought to submit themselves in obedience to and humble worship of God the Father and His Son Jesus Christ.

It is only through the proper worship of God that mankind can be sanctified and attain unto eternal life and receive the fulness of the Father.

Chapter 23

Doctrine and Covenants Section 94

Suggested Title
Church Buildings

Overview of Section Content
1. A commandment to build the Kirtland Stake, beginning at the temple (vs. 1-2)
2. Instructions for the erection of a house for the work of the First Presidency (vs. 3-9)
3. Instructions for the erection of a printing house (vs. 10-12)
4. Appointment of and inheritances for the Lord's building committee (vs. 13-15)
5. These two houses are to be built when the Lord directs (vs. 16-17)

Historical Setting

Joseph Smith, Jun.

The same date (May 6th) [1833] I received the following:... (HC, Vol. 1, p. 346)

Joseph Fielding Smith   ...A conference of high priests assembled April 30, 1833, in the school room in Kirtland and took steps to raise means to pay the rent for the house where their meetings had been held during the past season. John P. Green was appointed to take charge of a branch of the Church in Parkman County....The next day the conference again convened and took into consideration the necessity of building a schoolhouse, for the accommodation of the elders, who were to come together to receive instruction preparatory to taking missions and continuing in the ministry according to the revelation of March 8, 1833. [D&C Sec. 90] By unanimous voice of the conference, Hyrum Smith, Jared Carter and Reynolds Cahoon were appointed a committee to obtain subscriptions for the purpose of erecting such a building....later the Lord gave a revelation with directions for the building of this house....(CHMR, Vol. 2, pp. 164-165)

Sacred Truths

Introduction

As noted in the Historical Setting the church did not own any buildings at that time. The church had reached a point in its growth where it was necessary to have facilities to carry out its programs, meetings, and activities. In this revelation, the Lord gave instructions on the subject of church buildings. We will discuss four areas of instruction that He gave.

The Kirtland Temple

A city includes homes as residents for individuals and families. The Savior desired to dwell among His saints. To do so necessitated that a house be built for Him. It is appropriate that His home should be in the center of all others. Thus, in the city of Kirtland (a stake of Zion) the Lord instructed that the city should be constructed as an extension outward from His house. (See D&C 94:1-2) To those who understand the spiritual meaning of a temple, there is a peace and satisfaction in knowing that they may drive by, be neighbors to, and on occasion enter the Lord's home.

The Building for the First Presidency

The Lord instructed the church to erect a building for the work of the First Presidency. And what is the work of the Presidency? It is to preside over and direct the affairs of the Lord's kingdom under the direction of the Lord. To function in this role, requires revelation from the Lord. (See D&C 94:3)

To facilitate the flow of revelation and make it possible for the Lord to work closely with the Presidency, the Lord directed that the building be dedicated unto Him and be kept spiritually clean and free from the influence of the forces of evil. (See D&C 94:6-9) The Lord promised that if these conditions were met His glory and His presence would be there. (See D&C 94:8)

Dr. Norman Vincent Peale visited the First Presidency in their office facilities and had a very spiritual and uplifting experience. His account of that occasion is as follows:

> I met with these men of God in the room which Woodrow Wilson said was the most beautiful room in the United States—and it is indeed magnificent. There were these three dedicated Christian leaders—President Kimball, President N. Eldon Tanner, and President Marion G. Romney. We had a pleasant conversation and finally, at the close, I said to the president, because I felt that he was so deeply spiritual, "President Kimball, will you bless me?"
>
> He replied, "You mean you want me to give you a blessing such as I give our people?"
>
> I said, "Yes."
>
> So he came around behind me with the other two presidents and they put their hands on my head and President Kimball in his quiet, sincere, loving manner prayed for me by name. He asked the Lord to be near to me and love me and to take care of me and to guide me. As he prayed, I began to be very broken up and touched, and then of a sudden I had a wondrous feeling of the Presence and I said to him, "Sir, He is here; I feel His presence." (Church News, February 9, 1980, p. 11)

A non-member of the church bore testimony of the fulfillment of the Lord's promise. The Lord said His presence would be there—and it is so.

The Building for Printing

The Lord instructed the saints to erect a building that would accomodate the printing needs of the church. (See D&C 94:10-12) It is a blessing to the church today to have the capability of printing and publishing the scriptures and many other items for the use and benefit of mankind. It is vital that the church be independent and not reliant upon other sources to provide the vast quantities of printed materials so necessary for the dissemination to the world of the truths of the gospel of Jesus Christ.

The Building Committee

In this revelation the Lord called men to serve as a committee to build His houses. (See D&C 94:13-15) The need for such a committee has not diminished since the time of this revelation. As the church has grown, its need for buildings and various physical facilities has dramatically increased.

Now, even more than in 1833, there is a need for someone to be responsible for the planning, approving, constructing and maintaining of buildings erected and dedicated to the Lord for His purposes. Hence, the church still has need of a building committee which functions under the direction of the First Presidency

Summary and Conclusion

The Lord referred to the temple as "...my house." (D&C 94:1) In connection with the building for the First Presidency, the Lord said, "...my glory...and my presence shall be there." (D&C 94:8) The Lord spoke of the printing building as "...a house unto me,..." (D&C 94:10) The building committee is charged by the Lord with the responsibility "...to build mine houses,..." (D&C 94:15)

The above summation of this revelation reminds us that the Lord has a building program, and is concerned about the physical facilities of His church. Buildings of the church are the Lord's buildings. Members of the Lord's church ought to be anxious to assist in erecting, renovating and properly maintaining the Lord's buildings. The buildings serve as a means for, not an object of our worship.

Chapter 24

Doctrine and Covenants Section 95

Suggested Title
Chastisement for Delaying the Building of the Kirtland Temple

Overview of Section Content
1. The Lord's chastisement of His saints for their failure to build the Kirtland Temple and fulfill His righteous purposes (vs. 1-12)
2. The Lord's instructions as to how to build His temple (vs. 13-17)

Historical Setting

Joseph Smith, Jun.

The same day [June 1, 1833] I received the following:...(HC, Vol. 1, p. 350)

Joseph Fielding Smith

...the Lord gave another revelation (Sec. 95) in which He rebuked the elders of the Church for their delay in building another house which they had been commanded to build....
...It was Dec. 27, 1832, that the Lord gave the command to the Church that his house should be built, in which he said: "Organize yourselves; prepare every needful thing; and establish a house of

prayer, a house of order, a house of God." (Sec. 88:119) The elders of the Church it would appear, had not taken this command seriously, presumably it had been overlooked in the consideration of so many wonderful things in that particular revelation.... The Kirtland Temple was necessary before the apostles (who had not yet been called), and other elders of the Church could receive the endowment which the Lord had in store for them. The elders had been out preaching the Gospel and crying repentance ever since the Church was organized and many great men had heard and embraced the truth, nevertheless elders could not go forth in the power and authority which the Lord intended them to possess until this Temple was built where he could restore keys and powers essential to the more complete preaching of the Gospel and the administering in its ordinances....

...Four days after the Lord had rebuked the brethren for their neglect without waiting for subscriptions, the brethren went to work on the Temple. Elder George A. Smith, a recent convert, hauled the first load of stone for the Temple. Hyrum Smith and Reynolds Cahoon commenced digging the trench for the walls, and they finished the same with their own hands....(CHMR, Vol. 2, pp. 166-168)

Sacred Truths

Introduction

In this revelation, the Lord chastised the saints for their failure to begin to build a temple as they had been previously commanded.

All of us are imperfect. We all need to be corrected or reproved from time to time. On occasion, we may also find ourselves in the role of the chastiser. How wise we would be if we looked to the Lord's example and followed His pattern of chastising correctly. This revelation contains a pattern that we should follow. The pattern contains three responsibilities of the chastiser.

The Chastiser's Love

Three times in the first verse of this revelation, the Lord expressed His love. Before He delivered any chastisement, the Lord made certain the saints knew of His love for them. (See D&C 95:1) Love includes feelings or emotions. Very often chastisement is given under stress of emotions that overshadow love. Anger is commonly a motivation for reproof. Most people would be well-advised to wait until anger is calmed in order that love can be communicated according to the Lord's pattern. Love is an essential factor when one assumes the role of the chastiser.

Sometimes chastisement includes some form of punishment. Such punishment must still be bestowed as an act and expression of love. The heavens wept over the loss of Lucifer. (See D&C 76:26) The Lord wept over the wicked inhabitants of the earth because He knew of their eventual suffering. (See P of GP, Moses 7:28-38)

People with responsibility to direct the actions of others and who truly love those people with whom they labor, will not avoid or shirk their responsibility to chastise when it is needed. When there was a need to chastise, the Lord took action and by so doing, the problem was solved. (See D&C 95:2-12)

When one is chastised by someone who loves him, that chastisement needs to be seen as an act of love. We are all in need of rebuke from time to time, and when such is given according to the Lord's pattern, we should be grateful that someone loved us enough to correct us. Benjamin F. Johnson, one of Joseph Smith's close friends, noted the following about the prophet Joseph Smith:

> Joseph, the Prophet, as a friend was faithful, long suffering, noble and true to that degree that the erring who did love him were reminded that the rod of a friend was better than the kiss of an enemy, while others who "sopped in his dish" but bore not reproof became his enemies and, like Law, Marks, Foster, Higbee and others who hated him, conspired to his death. (They Knew the Prophet, p. 89)

The Chastisement—Motive

From this revelation we learn that the Lord's motive for chastising or correcting, was to help the people overcome mistakes and assist them in obtaining forgiveness. (See D&C 95:1) There is no more righteous motive for chastisement than a desire to help others obtain freedom from mistakes of the past and extend forgiveness to them in an act of brotherly love.

Before acting in the role of a chastiser, a person should wisely inquire of himself: "What is my motive?"

The Chastiser Prepares A Way

Again, we learn from this revelation that when the chastisement ceases, the chastiser is responsible to show the one who has erred how to proceed to correct his mistake. (See D&C 95:1) It is one thing to tell a person that he is wrong. It is quite another to show him how to do things right.

When the saints failed to begin to build the Kirtland temple, the Lord not only chastised them for their failure, but He also revealed to them how to proceed in the accomplishment of their assigned task. (See D&C 95:13-17)

Summary and Conclusion

Most people will have the responsibility of chastising or correcting others from time to time. Whenever such occasion arises, we should be reminded of the need to perform our task correctly and follow the Lord's pattern:

1. Love is expressed and extended to one being chastised.
2. The motive of the chastiser is that of correcting and forgiving.
3. The chastiser teaches how to improve and overcome mistakes.

Chapter 25

Doctrine and Covenants Section 96

Suggested Title
Dividing the French Farm—For What Purpose?

Overview of Section Content
1. How to divide the French Farm and the purposes for which the farm was purchased (vs. 1-5)
2. Counsel and blessings promised to John Johnson (vs. 6-9)

Historical Setting

Joseph Smith, Jun.

March 23.—A council was called for the purpose of appointing a committee to purchase land in Kirtland, upon which the Saints might build a Stake of Zion. Brother Joseph Coe, and Moses Dailey were appointed to ascertain the terms of sale of certain farms; and Brother Ezra Thayre to ascertain the price of Peter French's farm. The brethren agreed to continue in prayer and fasting for the ultimate success of their mission. After an absence of about three hours Brothers Coe and Dailey returned and reported that Elijah Smith's farm could be obtained for four thousand dollars; and Mr. Morley's for twenty-one hundred; and Brother Thayre reported that Peter French would sell his farm for five thousand dollars. The council

153

decided to purchase the farms, and appointed Ezra Thayre and Joseph Coe to superintend the purchase; and they were ordained under the hands of Sidney Rigdon, and set apart as general agents of the Church for that purpose. (HC, Vol. 1, p. 335)

Joseph Smith, Jun.

June 4.—A...conference assembled...and took into consideration how the French farm should be disposed of. [divided] The conference could not agree who should take charge of it, but all agreed to inquire of the Lord, accordingly we received the following:...(HC, Vol. 1, p. 352)

Sacred Truths

Introduction

It would be well to remember that the Lord had commanded the Latter-day Saints to build a city for a stake of Zion in Kirtland, Ohio. (See Historical Setting of the chapter. Also see D&C 94:1) In order to fulfill this requirement the saints purchased several farms in the vicinity of Kirtland. Not understanding how to divide the Peter French farm into lots for inheritances, direction was sought and received from the Lord pertaining to this matter. The solution to the problem falls into two categories.

Priesthood Leadership

The Lord's house is a house of order. All things pertaining to His kingdom function under the direction of His authorized priesthood leaders. Therefore, the Lord specified that the Bishop in Kirtland was to be responsible for the dividing of the French farm. (See D&C 96:1-3)

For What Purpose?

The dividing of the farm into lots by the Bishop was not to be an end in and of itself. The Lord's counsel continued as He stressed the purpose of their work. Any work of value or worth must have a goal or purpose. As we review the purposes identified by the Lord for dividing the French farm we note there are several important principles being taught. To illustrate:

1. *For the benefit of those seeking inheritances* (See D&C 96:3)

All Latter-day Saints should be seeking celestial inheritances. Every activity, function, organization and program in the Savior's church exists for the beneift of those seeking inheritances in the kingdom of God. Once we have a purpose for our work, we also have a standard by which the work can be evaluated. Every Latter-day Saint who labors in the Lord's kingdom might evaluate the effectiveness of his labors by asking himself the following question: "Am I performing my work in such a way that it is a benefit and an assist to those who are earnestly seeking an inheritance in the Lord's celestial kingdom?"

2. *For the purpose of teaching the gospel* (See D&C 96:4)

The purpose of all church activity is to teach the gospel. The gospel is taught by both precept and example. The assignments and callings given to Latter-day Saints should serve as a means to teach the gospel to others by the way we perform in our individual responsibilities. The French farm was to be used as a means of spreading the gospel. It is also intended that our homes, church buildings, church farms, etc. should be a base for promulgating the blessings of the gospel into the lives of the Lord's children.

3. *For the purpose of subduing the hearts of the children of men* (See D&C 96:5)

The Lord also revealed that the dividing of the French farm should serve as a means of subduing the hearts of the children of men. In other words, every program of the Lord's Church is an invitation to all to accept the Lord. Such acceptance is in reality a commitment and a surrendering of the heart to the Lord and His work. Such is a purpose for all that we do in the church.

Summary and Conclusion

As we labor in the Lord's kingdom there may be occasions when we momentarily forget the purpose of our endeavors. Is the program we are administering the most important object in view? Do we get so involved in the building of chapels, decorating their interiors, harvesting the products of church farms, fulfilling temple assignments, and performing many other functional and important matters that we forget the purpose of it all?

Many people labor in the Lord's kingdom with a clear vision of the purposes of the Lord's work. Where labor is performed with this perspective, there will be found strength in the stakes of Zion. (See D&C 96:1)

Chapter 26

Doctrine and Covenants Section 97

Suggested Title

Zion

Overview of Section Content

1. Many saints in Zion (Missouri) blessed because of their faithfulness (vs. 1-2)
2. The Lord's counsel and instructions to the school in Zion (vs. 3-9)
3. The Lord's counsel and instructions concerning the building of a temple in Zion (vs. 10-17)
4. Blessings promised to the pure in heart in Zion (vs. 18-21)
5. Zion will escape the Lord's scourge if she is obedient (vs. 22-28)

Historical Setting

Joseph Smith, Jun.

August 2.—I received the following:...(HC, Vol. 1, p. 400)

Joseph Fielding Smith

...On the second day of August 1833, the Prophet received a revelation concerning Zion. While he was aware of the fact that trouble was brewing in Jackson County and the spirit of opposition was very great he did not know that the mob had risen and had destroyed property and violently handled some of the brethren. In this revelation the Lord said that he desired to make known his will concerning the brethren in Zion. Many of them had truly humbled themselves and were seeking wisdom. Because of their repentance they would be blessed, for the Lord was merciful to the meek, and all who will not humble themselves will be brought to judgement....(CHMR, Vol. 2, p. 189)

Hyrum M. Smith and Janne M. Sjodahl

A brief statement of the condition of the Church at this time may be of some help to the younger students of these Revelations.

In Kirtland, the work on the Temple had commenced. On the 5th of June, 1833, George A. Smith hauled the first load of stone for that sacred building, . . .

On the 25th of June 1833, the First Presidency sent letters of instruction to William W. Phelps, Edward Partridge, and the brethren in Zion, and enclosed plans for the future city of Zion and its temples . . .

In the month of July, however, a mob in Jackson County, led by a Rev. Pixley, began to move against the Saints.

On the 20th of July, the mass meeting convened. Inflamed by falsehood strewn broadcast by religious fanatics and political office-seekers, the meeting demanded the discontinuance of the printing office, the closing of the store, and the cessation of all mechanical labor. When the brethren refused to comply with this law-defying dictum, the mob broke down the printing establishment, seized Edward Partridge and Charles Allen, daubed them with tar from head to foot and covered them with feathers, on the public square. Others were frightened from their homes by threats and yells. On the 23rd, the very same day on which the corner stones of the Kirtland Temple were laid, the brethren in Missouri, in order to prevent bloodshed, signed an agreement with the mob leaders to leave the country before the 1st of April, 1834. The brethren immediately sent Oliver Cowdery to Kirtland to report to the First Presidency. He arrived there early in September, 1833.

The Revelation in Sec. 97 was received before the arrival in Kirtland of Oliver Cowdery, and, consequently, before the Prophet knew any particulars of the storm of persecution that raged in the land of Zion. (DCC, pp. 608-609)

We call attention to the printing office incident described in the above quotation. This was a mob effort designed to destroy the Book of Com-

Section 97   159

mandments (later known as the Doctrine and Covenants) which was in the process of being printed in that office.

Sacred Truths

Introduction

The mob actions mentioned in the Historical Setting of this chapter pertain to persecution of the saints in Jackson County, Missouri in 1833. Efforts on the part of the saints to establish Zion took place from 1831 to 1833. This revelation is the Lord's will concerning the saints in Jackson County at the time of this mob action (See D&C 97:1)

In this chapter, we will discuss three topics from this revelation. Though this counsel was directed to the saints in Missouri in 1833, there are principles that have application to the members of the church today.

School of Elders—in Zion

In order to help the priesthood holders better understand their callings and responsibilities, a school was organized for the elders in Missouri. Parley P. Pratt was called to preside over and teach the elders. In this revelation, the Lord indicated that He was pleased that the school was functioning under the able direction of Elder Pratt. (See D&C 97:3-5)

The Lord was desirous that the priesthood brethren should be assembled together and be schooled in the truths of the restored gospel of Jesus Christ. The need for such schooling has continued and is still of utmost importance in the church today.

To the faithful priesthood holder who is willing to keep his covenants by sacrifice and who regularly attends his priesthood quorum class to be schooled in the ways of the Lord, the promises of the Lord given in this revelation are applicable. Such a person is accepted of the Lord and is assured of the fruits of his labors as he serves in the Lord's Kingdom for the salvation of souls.

Parley P. Pratt described his labors and sacrifices in conducting the school of elders in Zion:

> In the latter part of summer and in the autumn, I devoted almost my entire time in ministering among the churches; holding meetings; visiting the sick; comforting the afflicted, and giving counsel. A school of Elders was also organized, over which I was called to preside. This class, to the number of about sixty, met for instruction once a week. The place of meeting was in the open air, under some tall trees, in a retired place in the wilderness, where we prayed, preached and prophesied, and exercised ourselves in the gifts of the Holy Spirit. Here great blessings were poured out, and

many great and marvelous things were manifested and taught. The Lord gave me great wisdom, and enabled me to teach and edify the Elders, and comfort and encourage them in their preparations for the great work which lay before us. I was also much edified and strengthened. To attend this school I had to travel on foot, and sometimes with bare feet at that, about six miles. This I did once a week, besides visiting and preaching in five or six branches a week. (APPP, pp. 93-94)

A Temple—In Zion

When the Lord first revealed the location for the city of Zion, He identified the place for the location of a temple. (See D&C 57:1-3) Later, in June 1833, the First Presidency instructed the brethren in Missouri (Zion) to begin immediately to build the first portion of the temple complex. (See HC, Vol. 1, pp. 362-364) Then, in August of 1833, the Lord reminded the saints that they were to build the temple and that it should be done speedily. (See D&C 97:10-11)

Why the urgency for erecting the temple edifice at that time? The Lord said that the salvation of Zion was contingent upon it. (See D&C 97:12) The need for the temple was emphasized by the Lord when He described it as a place of instruction for all laborers in His kingdom that they may be perfected in their understanding of all things pertaining to the Kingdom of God. (See D&C 97:13-14) The temple was to be a place where the Lord would be manifested to the pure in heart. (See D&C 97:15-17)

The saints in Missouri were facing heavy Satanic opposition. They needed the power of the Lord that would be obtainable in the House of the Lord. The importance of temples as a key to the development of spiritual strength has been emphasized in the following commentary:

> God was, if we may say so reverently, anxious that His people should rear a Temple in which they could be endowed with power from on high before the conflict with the adversary. The history of Temples teaches us that the people of God have been strong, or weak, in proportion to the faithfulness with which they have attended to their sanctuaries. The history of the Temple of Jerusalem is, as Dr. Joseph Angus, in his *Bible Handbook*, notes, "an index to the history of the Jews. When it fell, they were scattered; as it rose from its ruins, they gathered round it again; and history dates the captivity, with equal accuracy, from the destruction of the Temple, or from the first capture of Jerusalem." Speaking of the Temples in this dispensation, someone has declared that the completion of the Nauvoo Temple was the salvation of the Church from annihilation, although the Saints were forced to flee into the desert. Since the

completion of the Salt Lake Temple, the adversary has had less power to injure the Church than he had before. If we remember that the Temples are the palaces of God, where His Presence is manifested, we can understand why, when the adversary was marshalling his forces against the Church, our Lord urged the Saints to build the Temple speedily. We can also understand why the evil one planned to have them scattered before they could rear that sacred edifice. (DCC, p. 612)

Prosperity—In Zion

Obedience is the basis upon which all blessings are received. The saints in Missouri were promised that they would prosper, become great, and not be moved out of their place if they would be obedient unto that which the Lord required of them in this revelation. Such obedience produces a people who are pure in heart. This is the requirement for prosperity in Zion. (See D&C 97:18-21)

The saints were also warned that if they failed to be obedient the vengeance of a just God would be upon them and they would not prosper in the land of Zion. (See D&C 97:22-28)

Elder Parley P. Pratt referred to the failure of the saints collectively to be obedient to this revelation. He observed:

> This revelation was not complied with by the leaders and Church in Missouri, as a whole; notwithstanding many were humble and faithful. Therefore, the threatened judgment was poured out to the uttermost, as the history of the five following years will show. (APPP, p. 96)

Summary and Conclusion

The principle of obedience is stressed by the Lord in this revelation. The key to Zion's future, salvation, and prosperity was and is this first law of heaven. When saints are obedient in erecting and properly using temples of the Lord, they have the assurance of having the power of the Lord in their midst.

Chapter 27

Doctrine and Covenants Section 98

Suggested Title

Purpose of Law - Law of Forgiveness, Retribution, War

Overview of Section Content

1. The Lord's comfort and promises to the afflicted saints (vs. 1-3)
2. Constitutional law is source of freedom (vs. 4-8)
3. Honest and wise leaders are needed (vs. 9-10)
4. A commandment to forsake evil and keep covenants with the Lord (vs. 11-15)
5. The saints to seek to turn hearts of children and fathers to each other for heavenly inheritance (vs. 16-18)
6. Many Kirtland saints are reproved (vs. 19-22)
7. The law of retribution—patience, not vengeance (vs. 23-32)
8. The law of war (vs. 16, 33-38)
9. The law of forgiveness (vs. 39-48)

Historical Setting

Joseph Smith, Jun.

August 6.—I received the following:...(HC, Vol. 1, p. 403)

Joseph Fielding Smith

...Seventeen days after the mobbing of the saints in Missouri, the Prophet received a revelation in which the Lord said that the prayers of saints were heard in heaven, and counsel was given them to be patient in their afflictions and not seek vengeance against their enemies. Oliver Cowdery did not leave Independence on his special mission until after the 23rd day of July, and if he arrived in Kirtland before the 6th of August when this revelation was received, it certainly was a miraculous journey considering the distance and the means he had of transportation. Just when he arrived we do not know, but the Prophet had learned that difficulties of a serious nature had commenced in Jackson County. Naturally the members of the Church there were extremely aroused and it was only natural that in their hearts there should be some spirit of retaliation and revenge upon their enemies. Because of this the Lord gave this revelation....(CHMR, Vol. 2, p. 191)

Joseph Fielding Smith

...The law of forgiveness and retribution depicted in the latter half of this revelation is most worthy of careful study. This law applies to individuals and to families, as well as to the Church at large....(CHMR, Vol. 2, p. 193)

Sacred Truths

Introduction

It is natural for people's feelings to be aroused when they suffer unjust abuses. The saints in Missouri were no exception. When they were subjected to mobocracy, some felt a desire to retaliate.

In this revelation the Lord counselled the saints how to proceed in order that their lives and their behavior might stand approved before the Lord. The principles embodied in this revelation are applicable to all people.

In this chapter we will discuss the following:

1. Promise and counsel to the saints
2. Purpose of law
3. Law of forgiveness and retribution
4. Law of war

Promise and Counsel to the Saints

The Lord introduced His revelation to the afflicted saints by assuring them that He was aware of their suffering and persecutions. His love for them was manifested when He acknowledged their prayers and counselled them to trust Him and be patient through their trials and tribulations. (See D&C 98:1-2)

The promise extended to the saints in this revelation is one of the great evidences of His hand in the affairs of men. He said:

> ...all things wherewith you have been afflicted shall work together for your good, and to my name's glory, saith the Lord. (D&C 98:3)

It is not difficult to see the complete turnabout that has taken place in the posture and position of The Church of Jesus Christ of Latter-day Saints in the world. Its image is changing from one of being despised and hated to one of respect, dignity, and admiration. The name of the Lord is being vindicated and His work is one of glory as it becomes the means of salvation to Father's children throughout the nations of the earth.

The Lord is true and faithful. In His preface to His book of Doctrine and Covenants, He said that every promise contained within the book would be fulfilled. (See D&C 1:37) It is truly a witness and testimony to us that the Lord lives as we see His word being fulfilled.

Purpose of Law

All promises of the Lord are contingent upon compliance with the conditions upon which the promises were made. The Lord revealed certain principles which must be understood and practiced before His saints could expect the blessings and promises previously mentioned. In order to teach the purpose of law, the Lord said:

> I, the Lord God, made you free, therefore ye are free indeed; and the law also maketh you free. (D&C 98:8)

This statement specifically referred to the inspired constitutional law of the land. (See D&C 101:79-80) The principle, however, is universally applicable to all of God's laws.

The purpose of all of God's laws is to make men free. Obedience to law provides freedom from sorrow, regret, tyranny, and all unrighteousness in all of its many forms. Obedience to law is the way by which men obtain happiness and peace. A great treatise as to the benefits of laws was given by President N. Eldon Tanner as follows:

> All the laws of God and the laws of nature and the laws of the land are made for the benefit of man, for his comfort, enjoyment, safety, and well-being; and it is up to the individual to learn these laws and to determine whether or not he will enjoy these benefits by obeying the law and by keeping the commandments. My whole

purpose today is to show that laws exist for our benefit and that to be happy and successful we must obey the laws and regulations pertaining to our activities; and these laws will function either to our joy and well-being or to our detriment and sorrow, according to our actions. (CR, April 1970, p. 62)

As to the laws of the land, how does one know whether any given law is constitutional and justifiable before the Lord? The revelation of the Lord provides the answer. Any law that supports the principle of freedom in maintaining the rights and privileges of mankind is constitutional in the eyes of the Lord. (See D&C 98:5-6) Any law that restricts or diminishes the right of free agency of an individual is not constitutional. Counselling the priesthood brethren of the Lord's church, Elder Marion G. Romney said:

> We who hold the Priesthood must beware concerning ourselves, that we do not fall into the traps he [Satan] lays to rob us of our freedom. We must be careful that we are not led to accept or support in any way any organization, cause, or measure which, in its remotest effect, would jeopardize free agency, whether it be in politics, government, religion, employment, education, or any other field. It is not enough for us to be sincere in what we support. We must be right! (CR, October 1960, p. 75)

However, constitutional laws alone do not necessarily insure a righteous environment as a blessing for the people. The Lord said "...when the wicked rule, the people mourn." (D&C 98:9) We not only must support constitutional laws but we are enjoined by the Lord to seek for and uphold honest men to administer righteous laws. (See D&C 98:10) The Lord expects His people to be righteously involved in the political processes. The importance of such activity was stressed by Elder James E. Talmage as follows:

> Only the other day I was asked, in the course of conversation with an intelligent gentleman, not a member of our Church:
> "Is the 'Mormon' Church in politics?"
> I answered him: "Most assuredly it is in politics, and also in business, in statesmanship, in all the affairs of life, teaching the people to do what is right so far as it possibly can."
> "Well, has the Church any candidates in the pending election?"
> "Yes, indeed," said I, "the Church has a full ticket, and is counseling its members just how to vote."
> Now, let me tell you just how you should vote, just as I told him. The Church is telling its members to look upon the franchise as a sacred gift, to exercise it according to their very best judgement

Section 98 **167**

before the Lord, and the Church's ticket is the ticket of the best men, according to the best judgment of the people, to whichever party they belong. Vote the party ticket if you honestly feel that to be best, or vote for the men you think will most effectively subserve the needs of country, state, and people.

You have your agency and you know that you are free; therefore do not offend the Lord, by going contrary to what you believe, honestly and after thought and prayer, to be right. But above all, do not say that because your brother does not see things just as you do in the political field, he necessarily is wrong. I was very much touched by the president's words—that he was pained at the evidence that had come to view, that some brethren condemn their fellows because these do not look on things as those of the first class do in matters political. Our religion should purify our politics, and make us honest, tolerant, and bold, to do that which is required of citizens, and to exercise our rights at the polls. Our religion should make us honest in business, truthful in all our doings. To be so is to be in line with the keeping of the commandments of the Lord. I pray that this may continue to be a characteristic of the Latter-day Saints, in the name of Jesus Christ. (CR, October 1920, p. 66)

As one reflects upon the counsel of the Lord pertaining to the purpose of law, a fundamental principle is apparent. Our righteous attitude and obedience to laws inspired of the Lord are pre-requisite to our righteous relationship with Him.

Law of Forgiveness and Retribution

To teach the saints how to dispel their feelings of hate and revenge toward their persecutors, the Lord counselled the saints to seek redress, not revenge. (See D&C 98:23-24) If they did not obtain justice under the laws of the land, they were to bear their afflictions patiently before the Lord. Even if their enemies were to come upon them a second and third time, they still were not to revile. Instead, the saints were to warn their enemy. The Lord further stated, that after the third time, the Lord would give the saints power over their enemy. (See D&C 98:25-29)

To illustrate the above principle, we recall that the saints were driven from Jackson County, Missouri in 1833. In 1838, they were also driven from the state of Missouri. In 1845, they were driven from Illinois. On each of these three occasions, the saints collectively followed the counsel of the Lord in this revelation. They did not retaliate. Thus, the blessings promised in this revelation have literally been fulfilled for the benefit of the church. There are many third and fourth generation descendants who are now reaping the blessings because of the obedience of their forefathers. (See D&C 98:30)

The Lord also instructed the saints concerning forgiveness. Feelings of forgiveness towards a person who has wronged us ought to be in our hearts continually and unconditionally. In terms of action towards or against a wrongdoer, however, our dealings with an offender ought to be consistent with the Lord's counsel in this revelation. He admonished us not to limit the number of times we are willing to work with a wrongdoer if he is seeking forgiveness. (See D&C 98:39-40) As to those who do not seek forgiveness there are steps to be followed and action to be taken as outlined by the Lord. (See D&C 98:41-48)

Law of War

We live in a time of war and unrest. The earth will not have peace until the Savior comes. As citizens of nations and members of the true church of Jesus Christ, we need to know and follow the Lord's counsel concerning our involvement in war. In this revelation He said:

> Therefore, renounce war and proclaim peace, and seek diligently to turn the hearts of the children to their fathers, and the hearts of the fathers to the children. (D&C 98:16)

The Lord's people are peacemakers and their message is one of peace. However, our ability to live in peace depends upon our retention of our freedom under the law. Sometimes our freedoms are threatened and we are required to defend our country, homes, families and God-given rights of free agency. When it becomes necessary to defend ourselves in times of war, the Lord has given us His law pertaining to such action. (See D&C 98:32-38) Further counsel has been given by President Harold B. Lee as follows:

> What is the position of the Church with respect to war? A declaration of the First Presidency given during World War II is still applicable in our time. The statement said: "...the Church is and must be against war. The Church itself cannot wage war unless and until the Lord shall issue new commands. It cannot regard war as a righteous means of settling international disputes; these should and could be settled—the nations agreeing—by peaceful negotiations and adjustments."
>
> There is a scripture that has direct bearing there: "And now, verily I say unto you concerning the laws of the land, it is my will that my people should observe to do all things whatsoever I command them.
>
> "And the law of the land which is constitutional, supporting

that principle of freedom in maintaining rights and privileges, belongs to all mankind, and is justifiable before me.

"Therefore, I, the Lord, justify you, and your brethren of my church, in befriending that law which is the constitutional law of the land;

"And as pertaining to law of man, whatsoever is more or less than this, cometh of evil." (D&C 98:4-7.)

Note particularly that the revelation is directed to members of the Church. Therefore, it is applicable to persons of all nations, not just those in the land we call America.

There are many who are troubled and their souls harrowed by the haunting question of the position of the soldier who in combat duty kills the enemy. Again, the First Presidency has commented:

"When, therefore, constitutional law, obedient to those principles, calls the manhood of the Church into the armed sevice of any country to which they owe allegiance, their highest civic duty requires that they meet that call. If, hearkening to that call and obeying those in command over them, they shall take the lives of those who fight against them, that will not make of them murderers, nor subject them to the penalty that God has prescribed for those who kill, beyond the principles to be mentioned shortly: for it would be a cruel God that would punish his children as moral sinners for acts done by them as the innocent instrumentalities of a sovereign whom he had told them to obey and whose will they were powerless to resist." God is at the helm. (The New Era, August 1971, pp. 4-5)

Summary and Conclusion

The principles taught in this revelation are just as pertinent now as they were when they were addressed to the saints in Missouri. If people are to stand approved of the Lord, they must follow His counsel and choose to be obedient to laws inspired of Him.

Chapter 28

Doctrine and Covenants Section 99

Suggested Title

Law of Representation

Overview of Section Content

1. John Murdock is called as a missionary to represent the Lord (vs. 1-4)
2. The Lord will bring judgment upon the ungodly (vs. 5)
3. Additional counsel given to John Murdock (vs. 6-8)

Historical Setting

Hyrum M. Smith and Janne M. Sjodahl

    This is a Revelation calling Elder John Murdock to go on a mission to the Eastern States. He was one of the men who received the gospel in Kirtland when Oliver Cowdery and companions passed through that city on the first western journey to the Lamanites, and together with Sidney Rigdon, Edward Partridge, Isaac Morley, Lyman Wight, and others, he was called to the ministry at that time. He held many important positions in the Church and discharged his duties faithfully. One of his children, Joseph S., died at the age of eleven months, as a result of exposure during the night of mob assault upon the Prophet at Hiram. Emma Smith, the

Prophet's wife, had given birth to twins on the 30th of April, 1831. On the same date the home of the Murdocks had been blessed with twin children, Joseph S. and Julia. Sister Emma Smith's babies lived but three hours, and, when Sister Murdock passed away, Sister Emma took the motherless infants to rear. During the mob outrage, the infant boy contacted a cold that ended fatally, a few days later. (DCC, p. 629)

Sacred Truths

Introduction

Previous to this revelation, John Murdock's wife, Julia, had passed away April 30, 1831, leaving him a widower with five small children. (See LDSBE, Vol. 2, p. 363)

In this revelation, the Lord called John Murdock on a mission. However, his first responsibility was to his family. Therefore, the Lord directed him to delay his mission departure until after adequate arrangements were made with Bishop Partridge in Zion to care for the children during his absence. (See D&C 99:1, 6-8) As noted in the Historical Setting, the infant twins had been taken by Joseph and Emma Smith to raise. The other three children were sent to Missouri and placed under the care of Bishop Partridge, a friend of the family.

The Law of Representation

Embodied in this revelation is one of the great principles of the restored gospel of Jesus Christ. Here, the Lord reveals the way by which He directs the affairs of His kingdom. Whenever there is priesthood on the earth, the Lord works through those authorized priesthood holders. They represent the Lord and function as His agents in the work of the Lord's kingdom.

In the call given to John Murdock, the principle or law of representation was emphasized. The Lord said to him "...who receiveth you receiveth me;...whoso rejecteth you shall be rejected of my Father..." (D&C 99:2, 4) This is an eternal law that was manifested in ancient times. (See Bible, Numbers 14:27; 16:41; B of M, 1 Ne. 3:5-6)

In the present dispensation, this principle has been emphasized by many latter-day prophets. Following are excerpts from talks given by three general authorities of the church on this subject:

Orson F. Whitney

Inherent in the Priesthood is the principle of representation. So plenary and far-reaching are its powers, that when those holding this authority are in the line of their duty, and possess the spirit of their calling, their official acts and utterances are as valid and as binding as if the Lord himself were present, doing and saying what his servants do and say for him. (Section 1:38; 84:35-39)

This is what it means to bear the Priesthood. It constitutes men agents of the Almighty, transacting sacred business in the interest of the one who sent them. These agents should represent their Principal fairly and faithfully, reflecting, as far as possible, his intelligence and goodness, living so near to him that when their letter of instructions (the written word) falls short, the Spirit that indited it, resting upon them as a continual benediction, can give "line upon line" of revelation, flash upon flash of inspired thought, to illumine and make plain the path they are to tread...

When the Son of Man, sitting upon "the throne of his glory," (Matthew 25:31) shall require of all nations and of all men a final accounting, and shall put to them the crucial question: "How did you treat my servants whom I sent unto you?" Happy the nation or the man who can reply: "Lord, I showed them the respect to which they were entitled—I honored them as I would have honored Thee."

Grievous the sin and heavy the penalty incurred by those who mistreat the servants of the Master. (Saturday Night Thoughts, pp. 219-221. Taken from: Roy W. Doxey, The Latter-day Prophets and The Doctrine and Covenants, Vol. 3, pp. 367-368)

David O. McKay

The greatest safeguard we have for unity and strength in the Church is found in the priesthood, by honoring and respecting it. Oh, my brethren—presidents of stakes, bishops of wards, and all who hold the priesthood—God bless you in your leadership, in your responsibility to guide, to bless, to comfort the people whom you have been appointed to preside over and to visit. Guide them to go to the Lord and seek inspiration so to live that they may rise above the low and the mean, and live in the spiritual realm.

Recognize those who preside over you and, when necessary, seek their advice. The Savior himself recognized this authority on earth. You will remember the experience that Paul had just as he neared Damascus with papers in his pocket to arrest all who believed in Jesus Christ. A light suddenly shone about him, and he heard a voice saying, "Saul, Saul, why persecutest thou me?"

And Saul said: "Lord, what wilt thou have me to do? And the Lord said unto him, Arise, and go into the city, and it shall be told thee what thou must do." (Acts 9:4, 6.)

He could have told Saul in a few words what he should do, but there was a branch of the Church in Damascus, presided over by a humble man named Ananias, and Jesus recognized that authority. He knew Saul's nature. He knew that in the future it would be difficult for Saul to recognize the authority of the Church, as instances later proved. Saul had to receive from the very man whom he was going to arrest instructions regarding the gospel of Jesus Christ.

Here is a lesson for all of us in this Church. Let us, too, recognize the local authority. The bishop may be a humble man. Some of you may think you are superior to him, and you may be, but he is given authority direct from our Father in heaven. Recognize it. Seek his advice and the advice of your stake president. If they cannot answer your difficulties or your problems, they will write to the General Authorities and get the advice needed. Recognition of authority is an important principle. (CR, October 1967, pp. 6-7)

Harold B. Lee

Now, I want to refer particularly to this one verse, and then make a few comments about magnifying the priesthood. Notice what the Lord said: "And I will lay my hand upon you [Edward Partridge] by the hand of my servant Sidney Rigdon, and you shall receive my Spirit, the Holy Ghost, even the Comforter, which shall teach you the peaceable things of the kingdom." [D&C 36:2]

The other night I had a group of young Cub Scouts, who are about the age to become ordained deacons, and I said to these young men, "When you get to be deacons, what will be the duties of a deacon?"

And they all said, "The duty of the deacon is to pass the sacrament."

And I said, "Now I would like you to think of this a little differently. That isn't the way to explain the duty of a deacon. What does it mean to pass the sacrament? When a deacon carries the emblems of the bread and water which have been blessed to the good of those to whom it shall be passed, it is then a renewal of a covenant that if they will keep the commandments of God and remember the Lord Jesus Christ, for whom those emblems stand, they will have the Spirit of the Lord to be with them."

A deacon, then, has the responsibility of representing the Lord to carry these emblems and thus be the Lord's agent in submitting these to the body of the Church

When you ask a teacher what are his duties, he may answer,

"Well, it's to do home teaching." But you may wish to say to him, "When you do home teaching you are representing the Lord, to visit the home of each member, to see that they are doing their duty, and to see that they are all keeping the commandments of God." The duties of a priest—the priest "is to preach, teach, expound, exhort, and baptize, and administer the sacrament; and to visit the house of each member, and exhort them to pray vocally and in secret and attend to all family duties." They should have in mind when they are acting in those capacities, it is as though they were acting for and responsible to the Lord when they perform their duties.

When we officiate in the name of the Lord, as holders of the priesthood, we are doing it in the name and in behalf of our Heavenly Father. Priesthood is the power by which our Heavenly Father works through men, through deacons, through teachers, through priests, and I have a feeling that we are not impressing that upon our young men. They are not taking the understanding of their priesthood as seriously as they might. If they did, they would always want to appear as President Tanner has said of Bishop Featherstone. They would always want to appear at their best when they are exercising their priesthood. Their hair would be properly groomed; their clothing and appearance would reflect the sanctity they should feel in the performance of their priesthood duties. I have had that same feeling. I have never performed an ordinance, such as administering to the sick, without first excusing myself, if I were out in the garden or somewhere, until I was properly clothed, to make the best appearance I could, because I felt in so doing I was drawing close to the Lord himself, and I want to appear at my best in his presence.

Brethren, I am afraid that some of our elders do not understand this, that when they are officiating as elders of the Church, or as seventies or as high priests, it is as though when they perform the ordinance, the Lord through them is acting upon the heads of those for whom they minister. I have often thought one of the reasons why we are not magnifying our priesthood is because we don't understand that as holders of the priesthood, He is working through us by the power of the holy priesthood, and I would wish that we could all have that feeling, and so teach our young people what it means to hold the priesthood and to magnify it. (CR, April 1973, pp. 128-129)

Summary and Conclusion

An authorized servant of the Lord represents the Savior in His kingdom upon the earth. Members of the church would do well to recognize and remember the dignity of the offices of the priesthood. Likewise, it is important to follow direction and counsel of the Lord that is given through those who are His designated representatives. It would be well to remember what the Lord said near the conclusion of His mortal ministry: "...Inasmuch as ye have done it unto one of the least of these my brethren, ye have done it unto me." (Bible, Matthew 25:40)

Chapter 29

Doctrine and Covenants Section 100

Suggested Title

How and What to Teach—Promises

Overview of Section Content

1. The Lord gives assurance to Joseph Smith and Sidney Rigdon concerning their families (vs. 1)
2. The purpose of the mission of Joseph Smith and Sidney Rigdon at this time (vs. 2-4)
3. How and what to teach—promises (vs. 5-8)
4. Joseph the revelator—Sidney the spokesman (vs. 9-12)
5. The Lord will establish Zion (vs. 13-17)

Historical Setting

Joseph Smith, Jun.

October 5.—I started on a journey to the east, and to Canada, in company with Elders Rigdon and Freeman Nickerson, . . .

On the 11th of October, we left Westfield, and continuing our journey, staid that night with a man named Nash, an infidel, with whom we reasoned but to no purpose. On the 12th, arrived at Father Nickerson's, at Perrysburg, New York, where I received the following revelation: . . .(HC, Vol 1, pp. 416, 419-420)

Hyrum M. Smith and Janne M. Sjodahl

It is a very striking fact that The Church of Jesus Christ of Latter-day Saints, ever since its organization, has proceeded on its onward course, no matter what the outward circumstances have been. There has been no turning back, no hesitation, no vacillation. As a mighty ship with its precious cargo, the waves may have been breaking over it from stem to stern; it may have been assailed by hostile craft from above and from below, and from all sides. There may have been disaffection and even mutiny among the crew, but the command has always sounded clear and high above the storm and the din of conflict. "Forward, full speed!"

These reflections are suggested by the fact that while the enemies in Missouri were gathering their lawless forces for an assault upon the Church there, the Lord inspired the Prophet Joseph to go on a mission and proclaim the gospel message. He was not to mind the enemies. His calling was to testify to the world. And he went on this mission as far as Canada, as full of faith and hope as if there had been no storm-clouds in the sky. What a testimony to his divine commission! (DCC, p. 630)

Sacred Truths

Introduction

While on a mission to Canada and other places in the eastern United States, Joseph Smith became concerned about his family and their well-being. He made the followig entry in his journal, dated October 11, 1833: "I feel very well in mind. The Lord is with us, but have much anxiety about my family." (HC, Vol. 1, p. 419) In this revelation dated October 12, 1833, the Lord assured Joseph and Sidney Rigdon that their families were well and were in the care of the Lord. (See D&C 100:1)

The Lord also gave assurance to Joseph as to the eventual redemption and status of Zion. (See D&C 100:13-17) At that time, the saints in Missouri were suffering at the hands of mobocrats. But the Lord made it clear that His work would not be thwarted and He would still raise up a pure people and establish Zion upon the earth.

Having given these brethren peace of mind concerning their families and the future status of Zion, the Lord instructed them concerning the way He desired them to carry out their responsibilities as teachers and ministers of the gospel. He directed them as to how and what they were to teach and gave them certain promises if they would be obedient to His direction.

How and What to Teach

In the presentation of the gospel message, these brethren were told to "...speak the thoughts that I shall put into your hearts, ..." and teach "...in solemnity of heart, in the spirit of meekness, in all things." (D&C 100:5, 7)

Since the Lord said He would put the thoughts into their hearts, does this give license to assume there is no need for personal preparation on gospel subjects? No. Previously, the Lord had counselled: "...treasure up in your minds continually the words of life, and it shall be given you in the very hour that portion that shall be meted unto every man." (D&C 84:85) When teachers of the gospel prepare in this manner, they are then useful to the Lord and He will inspire them in their selection of what to teach.

In his presentation of the inspired selection of gospel truths, the teacher is to have solemnity of heart and the spirit of meekness. Solemnity does not eliminate humor in good taste, but it does not allow for making light of sacred things. Meekness, of course, means humble courage.

Those who are obedient to the above counsel of the Lord, will enjoy and benefit from the blessings and promises given by the Lord in this revelation.

Promises

The faithful gospel teacher is promised by the Lord that he "...should not be confounded before man; For it shall be given you in the very hour, yea, in the very moment, what ye shall say." (D&C 100:5-6) Many missionaries and teachers of the gospel can attest to the validity of this promise. One great teacher, Elder Jedediah M. Grant, had the following experience:

> In the early part of President Grant's ministry...he gained quite a reputation as a ready speaker, frequently responding to invitations to preach from such subjects or texts as might be selected at the time of commencing his sermon, by those inviting him. In time it became a matter of wonder with many as to how and when he prepared his wonderful sermons. In reply to their queries he informed them that he never prepared his sermons as other ministers did. "Of course, I read and store my mind with a knowledge of gospel truths," said he, "but I never study up a sermon." Well, they did not believe he told the truth, for, as they thought, it was impossible for a man to preach such sermons without careful preparation. So, in order to prove it, a number of persons decided to put him to test, and asked him if he would preach at a certain time and place, and from a text selected by them. They proposed to give him the text on his arrival at the place of meeting, thus giving him no time to prepare. To gratify them he consented. The place selected was

Jeffersonville, the seat of Tazewell county, at that time the home of the late John B. Floyd, who subsequently became secretary of war, and many other prominent men. The room chosen was in the court house. At the hour appointed the house was packed to its utmost capacity. Mr. Floyd and a number of lawyers and ministers were present and occupied front seats. Elder Grant came in, walked to the stand and opened the meeting as usual. At the close of the second hymn, a clerk, appointed for the occasion, stepped forward and handed the paper (the text) to Elder Grant, who unfolded it and found it to be blank. Without any mark of surprise, he held the paper up before the audience, and said: "My friends, I am here today according to agreement, to preach from such a text as these gentlemen might select for me. I have it here in my hand. I don't wish you to become offended at me, for I am under promise to preach from the text selected; and if any one is to blame, you must blame those who selected it. I knew nothing of what text they would choose, but of all texts this is my favorite one. You see the paper is blank (at the same time holding it up to view). You sectarians down there believe that out of nothing God created all things, and now you wish me to create a sermon from nothing, for this paper is blank. Now, you sectarians believe in a God that has neither body, parts nor passions. Such a God I conceive to be a perfect blank, just as you find my text is. You believe in a church without Prophets, Apostles, Evangelists, etc. Such a church would be a perfect blank, as compared with the Church of Christ, and this agrees with my text. You have located your heaven beyond the bounds of time and space. It exists nowhere, and consequently your heaven is blank, like unto my text." Thus he went on until he had torn to pieces all the tenets of faith professed by his hearers, and then proclaimed the principles of the gospel in great power. He wound up by asking, "Have I stuck to the text and does that satisfy you?" As soon as he sat down, Mr. Floyd jumped up and said: "Mr. Grant, if you are not a lawyer, you ought to be one." Then turning to the people, he added: "Gentlemen, you have listened to a wonderful discourse, and with amazement. Now, take a look at Mr. Grant's clothes. Look at his coat: his elbows are almost out; and his knees are almost through his pants. Let us take up a collection. As he sat down another eminent lawyer Joseph Stras, Esq., still living in Jeffersonville, arose and said: "I am good for one sleeve in a coat and one leg in a pair of pants, for Mr. Grant." The presiding elder of the M. E. church, South, was requested to pass the hat around, but he replied that he would not take up a collection for a "Mormon" preacher. "Yes you will," said Mr. Floyd; "Pass it around," said Mr. Stras, and the cry was taken up and repeated by the audience, until, for the sake of peace, the minister had to yield. He accordingly marched around with a hat in his hand, receiving contributions, which resulted in a collection sufficient to purchase a fine suit of clothes, a horse, saddle and bridle for Brother Grant, and not one contributor a member of the Church of Jesus Christ of Latter-day Saints, though some joined subsequently. And this from a sermon produced from a blank text. (LDSBE, Vol. 1, pp. 57-58)

The faithful gospel teacher is also promised that "...the Holy Ghost shall be shed forth in bearing record unto all things whatsoever ye shall say." (D&C 100:8)

It is not the burden of the gospel teacher to prove that the church and its message is true. He does not need to defend it; he does need to declare it and bear witness that it is true. The promise given by the Lord is that the Holy Ghost will also bear witness of the messages of truth declared by the humble teacher. The hearer of the message may or may not receive and accept the witness of the Spirit. But it is a certainty that the witness will be given. Commenting on this promise, two Presidents of the church have said:

Brigham Young

Nothing short of the Holy Ghost will do us any lasting good. I told you, in the beginning of my remarks, the truth as it is in heaven and on the earth, as it is with the angels, and with prophets, with all good people, and with every sinner that dwells upon the earth. There is not a man or woman who on hearing the report of the Book of Mormon but the spirit of the Almighty has testified to them of its truth; neither have they heard the name of Joseph Smith but the Spirit has whispered to them "he is the true Prophet." (Quoted by B. H. Roberts, CR, April 1905, pp. 44-45)

Joseph F. Smith

I was struck by a remark made by one of the brethren with respect to the many people who saw and heard the Prophet Joseph Smith and yet didn't believe that he was a prophet of God, or a man raised up by the Almighty to lay the foundations of this great latter-day work. It was said that the Lord had not revealed it unto them. Now, I do not dispute that statement, nor call it in question; but it occurred to me that there are thousands of men who have heard the voices of the inspired servants of God, unto whom the Almighty has borne record of the truth, and yet they have not believed it. It is my opinion that the Lord bears record to the testimonies of his servants unto those who hear those testimonies, and it is left with them whether or not they will harden their hearts against the truth and not listen to it, and abide the consequences. I believe the Spirit of the Almighty God is upon most of the elders who go out into the world to proclaim the gospel. I believe their words are accompanied by the testimony of the Spirit of God. But all men are not open to receive the witness and the testimony of the Spirit. And the responsibility will rest with them. Yet it may be possible the Lord withholds his Spirit from some, for a wise purpose in him, that their eyes are not opened to see and their minds not quickened to comprehend the word of truth. As a rule, however, it is my opinion that all men who are seeking after the truth and are willing to receive it, will also receive the witness of the Spirit which accompanies the words and testimonies of the servants of the Lord; while those whose hearts are hardened against the truth and will not receive it when it is borne record of to them will remain ignorant and without a comprehension of the gospel. I believe there are tens of thousands of people who have heard the truth and have been pricked in their hearts, but they are seeking every refuge they possibly can to hide themselves from their convictions of the truth. It is among this class that you will find the enemies of the cause of Zion. They are opposing the truth in order to hide themselves from their convictions of the truth. There are men, possibly within the sound of my voice—certainly within the limits of this city—who have read our books, who have listened to the discourses of the elders, and who are familiar with the doctrines of the Church; but they will not acknowledge—openly, at least—the truth of this gospel and the divinity of this work. Well, the responsibility rests with them. God will judge them and deal with them in his own way and time. (GD, pp. 360-361)

Summary and Conclusion

Gospel truths cannot be understood or known except by the power and the witness of the Holy Ghost. This witness is given to every hearer of the gospel as a means whereby he may distinguish between truth and error. Granted his free agency, the hearer may then choose to accept or reject the message and the witness; but if he has been taught it the Lord's way he is thereafter responsible for his decision.

Chapter 30

Doctrine and Covenants Section 101

Suggested Title

Jackson County - Why Cast Out

Overview of Section Content

1. Afflictions of saints in Missouri a result of their transgressions (vs. 1-8)
2. Saints to be protected at the time the Lord's indignation falls upon all nations (vs. 9-15)
3. The Lord will gather His people to Zion and her stakes according to the parable of the wheat and the tares (vs. 16-21, 63-68)
4. Saints counselled to stand in holy places and prepare for the Lord's second coming (vs. 22-23)
5. Some conditions and events at the Savior's second coming and His millennial reign (vs. 24-34)
6. Promises extended to the faithful saints (vs. 35-42)
7. A parable concerning the redemption of Zion (vs. 43-62)
8. Saints counselled to purchase land in Zion (vs. 69-75)
9. Saints to importune for redress according to constitutional law (vs. 76-95)
10. Saints counselled not to sell their properties to the enemies of the Lord (vs. 96-101)

Historical Setting

Joseph Smith, Jun.

Thursday night, the 31st of October, gave the Saints in Zion abundant proof that no pledge on the part of their enemies, written or verbal, was longer to be regarded; for on that night, between forty and fifty persons in number, many of whom were armed with guns, proceeded against a branch of the Church, west of the Big Blue, and unroofed and partly demolished ten dwelling houses; and amid the shrieks and screams of the women and children, whipped and beat in a savage and brutal manner, several of the men: while their horrid threats frightened women and children into the wilderness...

On Friday, the first of November, women and children sallied forth from their gloomy retreats, to contemplate with heartrending anguish the ravages of a ruthless mob, in the lacerated and bruised bodies of their husbands, and in the destruction of their houses, and their furniture. Houseless and unprotected by the arm of the civil law in Jackson county, the dreary month of November staring them in the face and loudly proclaiming an inclement season at hand; the continual threats of the mob that they would drive every "Mormon" from the county; and the inability of many to move, because of their poverty, caused an anguish of heart indescribable.

On Friday night, the 1st of November, a party of the mob proceeded to attack a branch of the Church settled on the prairie, about twelve or fourteen miles from the town of Independence...

The same night, (Friday), another party in Independence commenced stoning houses, breaking down doors and windows and destroying furniture....

Thursday, November 7th, the shores of the Missouri river began to be lined on both sides of the ferry, with men, women and children; goods, wagons, boxes, chests, and provisions; while the ferrymen were busily employed in crossing them over. When night again closed upon the Saints, the wilderness had much the appearance of a camp meeting. Hundreds of people were seen in every direction; some in tents, and some in the open air, around their fires, while the rain descended in torrents. Husbands were inquiring for their wives, and women for their husbands; parents for children, and children for parents. Some had the good fortune to escape with their families household goods, and some provisions; while others knew not the fate of their friends, and had lost all their effects. The scene was indescribable, and would have melted the hearts of any people upon earth, except the blind oppressor, and the prejudiced and ignorant bigot...

The Saints who fled from Jackson county, took refuge in the neighboring counties, chiefly in Clay county, the inhabitants of which received them with some degree of kindness. Those who fled to the county of Van Buren were again driven, and compelled to flee, and these who fled to Lafayette county, were soon expelled, or the most of them, and had to move wherever they could find protection.
(HC, Vol. 1, pp. 426-427, 437-438)
(See map end of chapter)

Joseph Smith, Jun.

December 16. (1833)—I received the following: (HC, Vol. 1, p. 458)

Hyrum M. Smith and Janne M. Sjodahl

In his letter to the scattered Saints in Missouri, dated December 10th, 1833, the Prophet stated that the spirit withheld from him definite knowledge of the reason why the calamity had fallen upon Zion. Here is another striking evidence of his sincerity. If he had been in the habit of writing revelations without divine inspiration, he could have done so at this time. but it is perfectly evident that he did not speak in the name of the Lord except when prompted to do so by the Spirit. On the 16th of December, however, this Revelation was received concerning the Saints in Zion . . . (DCC, p. 637)

Sacred Truths

Introduction

At the inception of mob action in Jackson County, Missouri, the Lord counselled the saints and instructed them in the course of action they should pursue. (See D&C Sections 97 and 98) Many did not heed His counsel. Had they been obedient and followed His instructions they would never have been driven out of Jackson County.

Approximately six weeks after the saints were driven from the county, the Lord gave to His prophet, a revelation (D&C Section 101) explaining why the expulsion of the saints. He also counselled them concerning the redemption of Zion and the promises that would be fulfilled concerning Zion at His second coming and during His millennial reign.

In this chapter, we will discuss the following topics:

1. Why the saints were cast out of Zion—why afflictions
2. Promises concerning the saints and Zion

3. A parable concerning the redemption of Zion
4. Zion, the Lord's second coming, and the millennial reign

Why the Saints Were Cast Out of Zion—Why Afflictions

The saints suffered extreme hardship and suffering at the hands of mobocrats in Jackson County, Missouri. In this revelation, the Lord revealed two reasons why afflictions come upon His people.

1. Transgression

Disobedience is the father of discomfort. The Lord had made it clear when the land of Zion was first revealed to the saints that obedience was a fundamental requirement for the establishment of Zion. (See D&C 58:6) Yet, they had not been obedient. They were covetous, contentious, and had set aside the counsel of the Lord. In summation, their disobedience brought about their afflictions. (See D&C 101:2, 6-8)

Afflictions resulting from disobedience to the Lord's law reflect a cause and effect condition, the same as when blessings result from obedience to the law. President Marion G. Romney explained this principle as follows:

> ...nearly a hundred and fifty years ago the Lord said that the conduct of the inhabitants of the earth, unless reformed, would bring disaster. He diagnosed its cause, predicted its coming, and prescribed the means by which it can be avoided.
>
> The inhabitants of the earth, He said—explaining the cause of the impending disaster—"have strayed from mine ordinances, and have broken mine everlasting covenant;
>
> "They seek not the Lord to establish his righteousness, but every man walketh in his own way, and after the image of his God....
>
> "Wherefore," He continued, "I the Lord, knowing the calamity which should come upon the inhabitants of the earth, called upon my servant Joseph Smith, Jun., and spake unto him from heaven, and gave him commandments;
>
> "And also gave commandments to others, that they should proclaim these things unto the world." (D&C 1:15-18)...
>
> He [the Lord] knew from widespread experience how we should have to conduct ourselves in order to avoid the calamities which have repeatedly vexed and devastated the inhabitants of the earth.
>
> So knowing, He instructed the first generation of men, beginning with Adam, and He has instructed every succeeding generation on how to live in order to persist and prosper. He has told them that if they would follow His directions, they would be blessed and

Section 101

flourish upon the earth. At the same time He has warned that if they persisted in disregarding His directions, they would bring upon themselves calamities and disaster....

Obedience invokes "peaceful and beneficient cooperation of the elements."

Disobedience "may" and repeatedly has produced "calamity in the form of destructive phenomena."

Total disobedience in the days of Noah "brought about the Deluge." (Dr. James E. Talmage, *Improvement Era*, June 1921, p. 738.)...

and let it not be supposed, now, that the Lord takes pleasure in these calamities. He does not. He graphically foretells the inevitable consequences of men's sins for the purpose of inducing them to repent and thereby avoid the calamities....

As the Lord has repeatedly warned that breaking His commandments would bring on calamity, so has He promised that observance of His commandments would avert calamity and bring blessings.

As disobedience brought on the flood, so obedience sanctified Enoch's Zion.

"And the Lord blessed the land, and they...did flourish.

"And the Lord called his people Zion, because they were of one heart and one mind, and dwelt in righteousness." (Moses 7:17-18.)

As in ancient America the rebellious were destroyed by earthquake, whirlwind, and fire at the time of Christ's crucifixion, so the righteous survivors developed a society which enjoyed perfect peace for several hundred years. (See 4 Ne. 2, 16.)

(CR, April 1977, pp. 74-76)

2. Trial of faith

From the beginning of time, the Lord has allowed His people to suffer affliction as a means of refining and perfecting them. In this revelation, He refers to this purpose of affliction of His people as follows:

Therefore, they must needs be chastened and tried, even as Abraham, who was commanded to offer up his only son.

For all those who will not endure chastening, but deny me, cannot be sanctified....

And all they who suffer persecution for my name, and endure in faith, though they are called to lay down their lives for my sake yet shall they partake of all this glory.

(D&C 101:4-5, 35)

Speaking of the trial of Abraham's faith when he was commanded to offer his son Isaac as a sacrifice, President George Q. Cannon explained why such trials are sometimes given:

> ...why did the Lord ask such things of Abraham? Because, knowing what his future would be and that he would be the father of an innumberable posterity, he was determined to test him. God did not do this for His own sake; for He knew by His foreknowledge what Abraham would do; but the purpose was to impress upon Abraham a lesson, and to enable him to attain unto knowledge that he could not obtain in any other way. That is why God tries all of us. It is not for His own knowledge; for He knows all things beforehand. He knows all your lives and everything you will do. But He tries us for our own good, that we may know ourselves; for it is most important that a man should know himself. He required Abraham to submit to this trial because He intended to give him glory, exaltation and honor; He intended to make him a king and a priest, to share with Himself the glory, power and dominion which He exercised.
> (CR, April 1899, p. 66)

Promises Concerning the Saints and Zion

Though many of the saints had been disobedient to the will of the Lord concerning Zion, He did not forsake them. (See D&C 101:9) They had been unjustly dealt with by the mobs and the Lord assured them of His continuing concern for them. While the saints were living under very trying and difficult circumstances, the Lord extended to them many promises, some of which are listed as follows:

1. The Lord will be merciful (vs. 9)
2. Justice will prevail upon the enemies of the saints (vs. 10-11)
3. Covenant Israel will be saved (vs. 12, 38-42)
4. Scattered Israel shall be gathered in Zion and her stakes according to the parable of the wheat and the tares (vs. 13, 17-21, 63-68)
5. They that mourn shall be comforted (vs. 14)
6. Martyrs for the Lord shall be crowned with glory (vs. 15, 35-37)
7. The city of Zion (New Jerusalem) shall be established in Jackson County, Missouri. (vs. 16-20)

From an historical perspective, we see the hand of the Lord in the fulfilling of many of these promises. Shall we not yet expect to see the remainder fulfilled according to His word? (See D&C 1:37)

Section 101   189

A Parable Concerning the Redemption of Zion

The Lord has stated unequivocally that a city of Zion will be established in Jackson County, Missouri. A vital requirement that is crucial to the establishment of Zion is the erection of a temple as a house of the Lord. The importance of erecting such an edifice for the salvation of Zion has been abundantly stressed throughout the Lord's revelations. (See D&C 57:1-3; 84:1-4; 97:10-17) When the saints failed to build a house unto the Lord, they were driven from the appointed land of Zion.

In this revelation, the Lord gave a parable stressing the cause of their being scattered and the need for a temple in the eventual redemption of Zion. (See D&C 101:43-62) To assist in understanding the symbolic meaning of the parable, we quote the following explanation of the imagery:

Nobleman - Savior
Vineyard - Earth
Choice piece of land - Jackson County, Mo.
Servants - Church members
Olive Trees - Settlements of the saints
Watchmen - Officers of the Church
Tower - Temple
Servant - Joseph Smith

> ...the Temple, the site of which was dedicated Aug 3, 1831, would have been the tower from which the movements of the enemy could have been observed by inspiration. But as nothing more was done to complete that tower, the enemy came by night and broke down the hedge, and the servants of the nobleman fled, leaving the enemy in possession...
>
> (DCC, p. 647

One of the important factors to remember from this parable is that the saints took lightly the counsel given by the Lord, concerning the need for a temple for the salvation of His people. Furthermore, it is likewise clear from the parable that all things the Lord has commanded concerning Zion will eventually be fulfilled. There will be a temple and a city will be established when the land of Zion is redeemed in the Lord's way and in the Lord's own due time.

At the present time, the Lord's people are being gathered unto stakes of Zion. Temples are being erected in order that ordinances of salvation might be performed for the living and the dead. May we not fail to learn a crucial lesson from this revelation. The need for a temple and its influence is just as critical for the saints today as it was in the earlier days of the church. Our salvation still depends upon it.

Zion, the Lord's Second Coming, and the Millennial Reign

One of the purposes for gathering the Lord's people unto the stakes of Zion, is to prepare them for the eventual redemption of Zion and for the second coming of the Lord. (See D&C 101:22-23)

The Savior's second coming will usher in the millennial period wherein many glorious conditions will abound and Zion shall flourish in all her beauty upon the earth. In various revelations, the Lord has described some of the millennial conditions that will prevail during that golden era of peace. Following are some of those conditions He has revealed:

1. Satan shall be bound (See D&C 43:30-31; 45:55; 101:28)
2. Change from mortality to immortality will take place in the twinkling of an eye (See D&C 43:32; 101:29-31)
3. Children shall grow up without sin unto salvation (See D&C 45:58)
4. The Savior shall be seen in the midst of the righteous as their king and lawgiver. (See D&C 45:58-59; 101:23)
5. All corruptible things will be removed from the earth and all things remaining shall be whole or new. (See D&C 101:24-25)
6. Enmity shall cease (See D&C 101:26)
7. All righteous petitions shall be granted (See D&C 101:27)
8. All things shall be revealed (See D&C 101:32-34)

Mortal man does not comprehend all that the Lord has planned for the future. It would be folly to attempt to explain beyond what the Lord has revealed. The important thing to remember is that the Lord will reign under conditions specified by Him.

Summary and Conclusion

Disobedience was the major cause for the afflictions and expulsion of the saints in Missouri in 1833. Even though the saints were driven out of Jackson County, the Lord still holds forth the promise of an eventual redemption of Zion in that place. Obedience to the Lord's law is a requirement for all who would participate in the cause of Zion in any age. Only the righteous will be privileged to enjoy a personal association with the Savior in the millennial Zion.

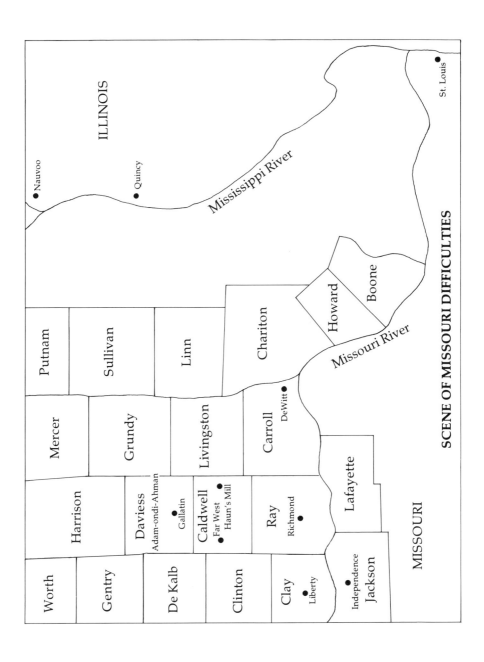

Chapter 31

Doctrine and Covenants Section 102

Suggested Title
The First High Council—A Church Court

Overview of Section Content
1. The first high council appointed to settle important difficulties in the church (vs. 1-5)
2. Procedures for the administrative functioning of the first high council (vs. 6-11)
3. Church court procedures for the first high council (vs. 12-23, 34)
4. A council of high priests abroad (vs. 24-26, 28)
5. Guidelines concerning appeals, jurisdiction, and decisions (vs. 27, 29-33)

Historical Setting

Joseph Smith, Jun.

At a council of the High Priests and Elders, (Orson Hyde, clerk,) at my house in Kirtland, on the evening of the 12th of February, I remarked that I should endeavor to set before the council the dignity of the office which had been conferred on me by the ministering of the angel of God, by His own voice, and by the voice of this Church; that I had never set before any council in all the order in which it ought to be conducted, which, perhaps, has deprived the councils of some or many blessings.

And I continued and said, no man is capable of judging a matter, in council, unless his own heart is pure; and that we are frequently so filled with prejudice, or have a beam in our own eye, that we are not capable of passing right decisions.

Our acts are recorded, and at a future day they will be laid before us, and if we should fail to judge right and injure our fellow-beings, they may there, perhaps, condemn us; there they are of great consequence, and to me the consequence appears to be of force, beyond anything which I am able to express. Ask yourselves, brethren, how much you have exercised yourselves in prayer since you heard of this council; and if you are now prepared to sit in council upon the soul of your brother. (HC, Vol. 2, pp. 25-26)

Joseph Smith, Jun.

On the 18th of January [February] I reviewed and corrected the minutes of the organization of the High Council, and on the 19th of February, the Council assembled according to adjournment, from the 17th, (Oliver Cowdery and Orson Hyde, clerks,) when the revised minutes were presented and read to the Council. I urged the necessity of prayer, that the Spirit might be given, that the things of the Spirit might be judged thereby, because the carnal mind cannot discern the things of God. The minutes were read three times, and unanimously adopted and received for a form and constitution of the High Council of the Church of Christ hereafter; with this provision, that if the President should hereafter discover anything lacking in the same, he should be privileged to supply it. (HC, Vol. 2, p. 31)

Sacred Truths

Introduction

By revelation from the Lord, the Prophet Joseph Smith was directed to organize a high council in Kirtland, Ohio. (See D&C 102:1) This first high council consisted of twelve high priests, presided over by a presidency. The council was appointed by revelation for the purpose of performing the functions of a duly-constituted church court. (See D&C 102:2) On Feb. 17, 1834, the first high council was organized and the minutes of that first organizational meeting were adopted as a constitution for high councils when functioning as church courts. Those minutes comprise the content of Section 102 of the Doctrine and Covenants.

In this chapter, we will discuss two aspects of a high council court:

Section 102

1. The unique nature of a high council court
2. Purpose of church courts

The Unique Nature of a High Council Court

When a high council functions as a church court, the members are equally divided into two groups. One group represents the interests of the church and the other group represents the interests of the accused. This court is unique in that neither of these two groups constitute a prosecution, defense, or jury element. Instead, their function is to prevent insult and injustice to either the church or the accused. Members of the council who are assigned to speak are to carry out this function for and in behalf of the respective parties. (See D&C 102:12-18)

After the high councilors have spoken, the reponsibility for giving a decision rests with the president assisted by his two counselors. The high councilors are then called upon to sustain the decision. (See D&C 102:19)

The decision of the president is final unless:

1. An error is discovered in the decision. In such case, a rehearing is scheduled and the error is corrected. (See D&C 102:20-23)
2. An appeal is made. If either of the parties are dissatisfied with the decision, an appeal may be made to the office of the First Presidency. Whatever decision is made by the First Presidency is final and is not subject to further appeal. (See D&C 102:27, 33)

(There are other church tribunals. For further information on their functions and jurisdictions, see *Priesthood and Church Government*, pp. 206-232.)

Purpose of Church Courts

We learn from this section that church courts are courts of love and that there is a need to be sensitive to the feelings and needs of the accused. Emphasis is given to the need to provide equity and fairness and protect the accused, as well as the church, from insult and injustice. (See D&C 102:16-17) When a church court functions within the framework of these guidelines, they are fulfilling their purpose as courts of love.

The need for and purpose of church courts has been well expressed by two General Authorities of the church as follows:

Robert L. Simpson

> Priesthood courts of the Church are not courts of retribution. They are courts of love. Oh, that members of the Church could understand this one fact.

The adversary places a fear in the heart of the transgressor that makes it so difficult for him to do what needs to be done; and in the words of James E. Talmage, "As the time of repentance is procrastinated, the ability to repent grows weaker; neglect of opportunity in holy things develops inability." (*Articles of Faith*, p. 114.) This simply means that doing what needs to be done will never be easier than right now. As in all other paths and guideposts that have been provided for us to achieve our eternal destiny of exaltation, there are no shortcuts....

Be not disillusioned by doctrine of the adversary that there will likely be a magic point in eternity when all of a sudden selfish and improper actions are automatically eliminated from our being. Holy writ has confirmed time and time again that such is not the case, and prophets through the ages have assured us that now is the time to repent, right here in this mortal sphere. It will never be easier than now; and returning to Brother Talmage's thought, he who procrastinates the day or hopes for an alternate method that might require less courage waits in vain, and in the meantime, the possibilities grow dimmer. He is playing the game as Satan would have him play it, and exaltation in the presence of God grows more remote with each passing day. (CR, April 1972, p. 32)

Stephen L. Richards

...I have taken the position, with which I think my brethren accord, that *every case of infraction* and I speak now of those infractions violative of the laws of God which involve moral turpitude, every infraction *against the laws of God should be dealt with*. I do not say how. I leave that to the inspired wisdom of the judges. Knowingly permitting a serious infraction of divine law to pass unnoticed is no kindness to the offender. He will never gain forgiveness except on the terms the Lord has prescribed, and which I have tried to outline.

And I ask you as a final question, How can we ever hope to maintain the dignity of the church and the majesty of the law of the Lord without exercising disciplinary action through the tribunals which the Lord has set up. So I think I am justified in calling upon the Bishoprics, the High Councils, the Stake Presidencies, the Mission Presidencies, and the officers of quorums to be watchmen on the towers of Zion, to guard and forewarn the people against the incursion of sin, to teach in plainness and without equivocation the law of the Lord, to uphold the law, and righteously and mercifully enforce it for the blessing of our membership in the Church and all mankind. (CR, April 1954, pp. 12-13)

Summary and Conclusion

God's house is a house of order. The Lord has structured His kingdom in such a way that His eternal laws can provide blessings to the citizens of His kingdom. Church courts are one of the ways by which the Lord can and does bless His children.

Chapter 32

Doctrine and Covenants Section 103

Suggested Title

Redemption of Zion - Zion's Camp

Overview of Section Content

1. The saints in the land of Zion were scattered because of their iniquities (vs. 1-4)
2. Redemption of Zion promised to the faithful who were scattered (vs. 5-7, 11-20)
3. Warning given to the unfaithful in Zion (vs. 8-10)
4. The call to organize Zion's Camp (vs. 21-28)
5. Assignments given to several brethren (vs. 29-40)

Historical Setting

Joseph Smith, Jun.

>February 24.—I received the following: (HC, Vol. 2, p. 36)

Joseph Fielding Smith

>...The high council of the Church met February 24, 1834, at the house of the Prophet for the purpose of receiving the message of Lyman Wight and Parley P. Pratt, delegates from the brethren in Missouri who came to Kirtland to report on conditions among the

exiles driven from Jackson County. Hyrum Smith and Joseph Coe were appointed to act in the stead of John Smith and John P. Greene who were absent. When the council was called to order and prayer had been offered by the Prophet, these two brethren delivered their message in relation to the condition of the brethren in Clay County, Missouri. They stated that the brethren there were anxious to know how and by what means Zion was to be redeemed. In Clay County they had been able to obtain food and raiment from the citizens in exchange for their labor, but the idea of being driven from their homes pained them, and they desired to know what the Lord would direct in the matter of reinstating them in their lands. (CHMR, Vol. 3, pp. 17-18)

Hyrum M. Smith and Janne M. Sjodahl

In a previous Revelation (Section 101:55-60), it was made known to the Prophet that he would be required, at some future time, to lead "the strength of mine house" to the land of Zion, in order to "redeem" it. The Revelation in this Section was received four months and twelve days afterwards, directing him to begin to gather up the strength of the Church for a relief expedition. Elders Lyman Wight and Parley P. Pratt had just arrived in Kirtland, from Missouri, with a message from the Saints. A meeting of the High Council was called. The messengers from Zion told the Council that the scattered Saints had obtained food and clothing in exchange for labor, and that they were quite comfortable for the time being; but they were grief-stricken because they had been driven from their homes in Zion, and they earnestly desired to know, if possible, how and by what means Zion was to be redeemed. This Revelation, given before the meeting of the Council was held, is an answer to that very question. When the messengers had stated the case, the Prophet had the answer ready. He had prepared to announce that he was going to Zion and that he would call for volunteers to accompany him. The Council endorsed this, and between thirty and forty men volunteered to go, whereupon the Prophet Joseph was elected Commander-in-Chief of the expedition. (DCC, pp. 659-660)

Sacred Truths

Introduction

As noted in the Historical Setting of this chapter, the saints who had been driven from Jackson County, Missouri, were anxious to know how they might regain possession of their lands and redeem the land for the establishment of Zion. Section 103 is the Lord's response to their concerns. He assured them that Zion could still be redeemed provided the saints in Zion and in Ohio would follow His instructions.

Conditional Promise of Redemption

In the beginning of this revelation, the Lord reviewed the reasons for the persecution of the saints in Jackson County and their subsequent expulsion. (See D&C 103:1-4) He then decreed that Zion could yet be redeemed on conditions of strict obedience of the saints both in Missouri and Ohio.

The saints in Missouri were promised a reinstatement to their lands provided they hearkened to the Lord from that very hour. But if they failed to hearken, their enemies would continue to prevail against them. (See D&C 103:5-11)

The saints in Ohio were to assist in the redemption of their brethren in Zion by sending a relief expedition. Ideally, this expedition was to consist of 500 men with sufficient funds to purchase land as previously commanded by the Lord. (See D&C 103:22-23, 30-34) (Note: Revelation had been previously given instructing the saints to save money in order to purchase land in Missouri. See D&C Sections 48, 57, 58, 101)

This relief expedition, which consisted of approximately 200 men, was subsequently known as Zion's Camp. It was led by the Prophet Joseph Smith who is referred to in this revelation as "...a man, who shall lead them like as Moses led the children of Israel." (D&C 103:16) When the Prophet Joseph Smith led Zion's Camp to Missouri, he did so in fulfillment of the parable of the redemption of Zion. (See D&C 101:55-56; 103:21)

Summary and Conclusion

Subsequent history reveals that Zion was not redeemed at that time because of the failure of the saints to render prompt and complete obedience to the Lord's instructions.

An appropriate question might be asked: How many blessings and opportunities have we forfeited for failure to render prompt and unconditional obedience? Or will we, instead, hearken to the Lord from this very hour?

Chapter 33

Doctrine and Covenants Section 104

Suggested Title

Order of the Church For The Salvation of Men

Overview of Section Content

1. Faithful and unfaithful covenant members of the united order (vs. 1-10)
2. Every man in the united order is accountable in his stewardship over earthly things (vs. 11-13, 54-57)
3. The Lord prepared all things in the earth to provide for His saints in His own way (vs. 14-18)
4. Stewardships, counsel, and blessings promised to several brethren (vs. 19-46)
5. The united orders in Kirtland and in Zion are to function independently (vs. 47-53)
6. A sacred treasury to be established for printing scriptures (vs. 58-66)
7. A general treasury to be established (vs. 67-77)
8. The saints are counseled to pay their debts and are promised deliverance out of financial bondage (vs. 78-86)

Historical Setting

Joseph Smith, Jun.

April 23.—Assembled in Council with Elders Sidney Rigdon, Frederick G. Williams, Newel K. Whitney, John Johnson, and Oliver Cowdery; and united in asking the Lord to give Elder Zebedee Coltrin influence over Brother Jacob Myres, to obtain the money which he has gone to borrow for us, or cause him to come to this place and bring it himself. I also received the following: . . . (HC, Vol. 2, p. 54)

Joseph Fielding Smith

The Church being in dire distress financially, brethren had been sent out to see if they could not collect funds for its relief, both in Kirtland and for Zion. A strong appeal to Orson Hyde was issued April 7, 1834. (See D.H.C. 2:48.) In the minutes of a conference held at Norton, Medina County, Ohio, the deliverance of Zion was earnestly discussed. The Prophet Joseph Smith who was present said in the course of his remarks that "if Zion is not delivered, the time is near when all of this Church, wherever they may be found, will be persecuted and destroyed in like manner;" that is in the manner in which the saints in Jackson County were destroyed. Destruction in this sense means to be persecuted, mobbed and scattered, their property being lost to them.

. . .On the 10th of April, a council of the United Order was held. It was there agreed that the Order, as it was then organized, be dissolved, and each member have his stewardship set off to him. Previously to this time, the United Order of Zion and of Kirtland stood as one unit. On April 23, 1834, the Prophet received an important revelation concerning the "Order of the Church for the benefit of the poor." (D&C 104) (CHMR, Vol. 3, p. 23)

Sacred Truths

Introduction

At the time of this revelation, the church was experiencing financial difficulties. As these temporal stresses mounted, it became increasingly more difficult to accomplish the spiritual objectives of the church. Hence, the Lord gave this revelation " . . .for the benefit of my church, and for the salvation of men until I come—." (D&C 104:1) Thus, the Lord gave the church counsel pertaining to their temporal affairs.

In this chapter we will discuss the following topics:

Section 104 205

1. The Lord provides—His way
2. Debt—The Lord's counsel

The Lord Provides—His Way

Perhaps the most fundamental principle pertaining to our temporal salvation was revealed by the Lord as follows:

> I, the Lord, stretched out the heavens, and built the earth, my very handiwork; and all things therein are mine. (D&C 104:14)

Inasmuch as all things are the Lord's, then it is His prerogative to determine the way in which the resources of the earth are used. To the Latter-day Saints, the Lord said it is His purpose to provide for His saints with the following stipulation: It must need be accomplished in His own way. (See D&C 104:15-16) And what is His way?

> . . .behold this is the way that I, the Lord have decreed to provide for my saints, that the poor shall be exalted, in that the rich are made low.
> For the earth is full, and there is enough and to spare; yea, I prepared all things, and have given unto the children of men to be agents unto themselves. (D&C 104:16-17)

To enhance our understanding of the meaning of these verses, we refer to the following statements by General Authorities:

Joseph Fielding Smith

> In speaking of the exaltation of the poor, the Lord did not intend to convey, as some may think, that he was to take from the rich and make them poor, but that through this divine law there would come an equality and in humility all would be made rich in the abundance that would be gathered into the storehouse of the Lord, and every man should be provided with an abundance.
> "For the earth is full, and there is enough and to spare; yea, I prepared all things, and have given unto the children of men to be agents unto themselves." (v. 17) The abundance of the earth is so plentiful, through the mercies of the Father, that all could have "enough and to spare" if the commandments of the Lord were strictly kept. (CHMR, Vol. 3, pp. 24-25)

Harold B. Lee

> We have come, yes, in a day when "The way of the Lord," as He described it, would be applied, when the poor would be exalted, or

in other words stimulated to success and pride, and uplifted because the rich have been made low, or in other words, because the rich have been made humble and willing to give of their substance, their time, and their talent, and their wisdom, and their example that the poor might be thus guided and directed. (CR, October 1941, p. 113)

Marion G. Romney

The poor can be exalted when and only when they are enabled to obtain independence and self-respect through their own industry and thrift. Our duty is to enable them to do this.

"The rich are made low" when they evidence their obedience to the second great commandment—"Thou shalt love thy neighbor as thyself" (Matt. 22:39)—by imparting of their substance "according to the law of [the] gospel, unto the poor and the needy." (D&C 104:18) (CR, October 1976, p. 168)

Spencer W. Kimball

The Lord's way builds individual self-esteem and develops and heals the dignity of the individual, whereas the world's way depresses the individual's view of himself and causes deep resentment.

The Lord's way causes the individual to hasten his efforts to become economically independent again, even though he may have temporary need, because of special conditions, for help and assistance. The world's way deepens the individual's dependency on welfare programs and tends to make him demand more rather than encouraging him to return to economic independence. (CR, April 1976, p. 172)

The organizational vehicle to accomplish the above purposes of the Lord is at the discretion of the Lord. When this revelation (Section 104) was given, the concepts were to be applied within the framework of the united order. The Lord specified that the order should be re-structured at that time, for the benefit of the saints both in Ohio and Missouri. (See D&C 104:47-53)

In later years, the vehicle designed by the Lord to provide for His saints, was the Church Welfare Program in all of its many ramifications.

Debt—The Lord's Counsel

Another fundamental principle of temporal salvation concerns financial indebtedness. The Lord's counsel to His church was given: "... .it is my will that you shall pay all your debts." (D&C 104:78) Meeting one's financial obligations is a matter of honesty and integrity with one's fellow men in order to stand approved of the Lord. Stressing the importance of this quality of character and performance of duty, President N. Eldon Tanner has said:

> Now among our fellowmen, neighbor to neighbor, it is important that we keep our covenants, our pledges, our agreements. A young man came to me not long ago and said, "I made an agreement with a man that requires me to make certain payments each year. I am in arrears, and I can't make those payments, for if I do, it is going to cause me to lose my home. What shall I do?"
> I looked at him and said, "Keep your agreement."
> "Even if it costs me my home?"
> I said, "I am not talking about your home. I am talking about your agreement; and I think your wife would rather have a husband who would keep his word, meet his obligations, keep his pledges or his covenants, and have to rent a home than to have a home with a husband who will not keep his covenants and his pledges."
> I don't know whether everyone here agrees with me or not; in fact, I am wondering. There are too many today, I feel, who are prepared to take the easy way out of paying their debts by not paying them and take whatever action is necessary to keep them free. It is important, brethren, that we keep our pledges and our covenants and keep our name good. A man's good name is worth more than any material thing he could have. (CR, October 1966, pp. 99-100)

Under certain economic circumstances, there are some justifiable debts. However, one should realize there are undesirable financial burdens connected with indebtedness. One such burden has been emphasized and discussed by President J. Reuben Clark:

> It is a rule of our financial and economic life in all the world that interest is to be paid on borrowed money. May I say something about interest?
> Interest never sleeps nor sickens nor dies; it never goes to the hospital; it works on Sundays and holidays; it never takes a vacation; it never visits nor travels; it takes no pleasure; it is never laid off work nor discharged from employment; it never works on reduced hours it never has short crops nor droughts; it never pays taxes; it buys no food; it wears no clothes; it is unhoused and without home and so has no repairs, no replacements, no shingling, plumbing, painting, or whitewashing; it has neither wife, children, father, mother, nor kinfolk to watch over and care for; it has no expense of living; it has neither weddings nor births nor deaths; it has no love,

no sympathy; it is as hard and soulless as a granite cliff. Once in debt, interest is your companion every minute of the day and night; you cannot shun it or slip away from it; you cannot dismiss it; it yields neither to entreaties, demands, or orders; and whenever you get in its way or cross its course or fail to meet its demands, it crushes you.

So much for the interest we pay. Whoever borrows should understand what interest is; it is with them every minute of the day and night. (CR, April 1938, pp. 102-103)

Summary and Conclusion

The Lord has organized this earth. It belongs to Him. He has provided adequate resources for all of His children provided those resources are utilized in accordance with His revealed directions to His prophets. His counsel is given according to the needs and circumstances of His people. Hence, wise Latter-day Saints give heed to and follow the programs of the Lord as directed by the Lord's authorized leadership. Such a practice preserves and strengthens the dignity of the individual.

Chapter 34

Doctrine and Covenants Section 105

Suggested Title

Zion Not To Be Redeemed For A Little Season

Overview of Section Content

1. Why Zion was not redeemed (vs. 1-4, 6-9, 16-17)
2. Some requirements of church members before Zion can be redeemed (vs. 5, 10-15, 29, 31)
3. Blessings promised to the faithful members of Zion's Camp (vs. 16, 18-19)
4. Counsel and promises extended to the saints living in Zion (vs. 20-28, 30, 32)
5. Counsel and promises to the first or presiding elders of the church (vs. 33-37)
6. Saints admonished to sue for peace and be faithful (vs. 38-41)

Historical Setting

Joseph Smith, Jun.

Cornelius Gillium, the sheriff of Clay county, came to our camp to hold consultation with us. I marched my company into a grove near by and formed in a circle, with Gillium in the center. Gillium commenced by saying that he had heard that Joseph Smith was in the camp, and if so he would like to see him. I arose and replied, "I am the man." This was the first time that I had been discovered or made known to my enemies since I left Kirtland. Gillium then gave us instruction concerning the manners, customs, and the dispositions of the people, and what course we ought to pursue to secure their favor and protection, making certain inquiries, to which we replied, which were afterwards published, and will appear under date of publication.

I received the following:—

(HC, Vol. 2, p. 108)

Hyrum M. Smith and Janne M. Sjodahl

Zion's Camp arrived at Fishing River on the 19th of June, 1834. On the 22nd, Sheriff Gillium, of Clay County, visited the Camp in order to find out the intentions of the brethren. The Prophet addressed him and his companions and then issued a signed statement in which the following occurs, "We are willing for twelve disinterested men, six to be chosen by each party, and these men shall say what the possessions of those men are worth who cannot live with us in the County: and they shall have their money in one year; and none of the 'Mormons' shall enter that County to reside, until the money is paid. The damages that we have sustained in consequence of being driven away, shall also be left to the twelve men; or, they may all live in the County if they choose, and we will never molest them if they let us alone and permit us to enjoy our rights. We want to live in peace with all men; and equal rights is all we ask." The opponents refused to listen to this fair proposition.

The very day on which Sheriff Gillium visited the Camp, the Prophet received this Revelation.

(DCC, pp. 679-680)

Sacred Truths

Introduction

Four months prior to the receipt of this revelation, the Lord had assured the saints that Zion could be redeemed provided that His intructions were heeded and His commandments were obeyed. (See D&C Section 103) At that time, the Lord instructed Joseph Smith to organize a company of men (Zion's Camp) to go to Missouri for the purpose of rendering assistance to the scattered saints. Members of the church in Ohio were also directed to contribute money to aid in the redemption of Zion.

The saints in Ohio only partially responded to the Lord's requests. They failed to contribute sufficient money and men for this expedition. In spite of these shortcomings, approximately two hundred men did go to Missouri. After their arrival at Fishing River in Clay County, Missouri, a revelation was given to Joseph Smith on June 22, 1834. (Section 105)

In this revelation, the Lord declared that Zion would not be redeemed at that time and revealed several requirements that must be met before the eventual redemption of Zion. In this chapter we will discuss two topics.

Zion Not To Be Redeemed In 1834

The Lord informed the members of Zion's Camp that because of the transgressions of the people, Zion was not to be redeemed at that time. (See D&C 105:2, 9)

As to the nature of those transgressions, the Lord declared:

> But behold, they have not learned to be obedient to the things which I required at their hands, but are full of all manner of evil, and do not impart of their substance, as becometh saints, to the poor and afflicted among them. (D&C 105:3)

Speaking of this disobedience, Elder Joseph Fielding Smith commented as follows:

> In that day when branches of the Church were called upon to assist their brethren they said, "Where is their God? Behold, he will deliver them in time of trouble, otherwise we will not go up unto Zion, and will keep our moneys." There were many who refused to go with the Prophet in Zion's Camp or send money to help their afflicted brethren. Because of this lack of faith and obedience, instead of redeeming Zion at that time, the Lord declared that Zion should have to "wait for a little season." This waiting was for the purpose of preparing the members of the Church, through faith, obedience, experience in suffering if they would not repent, so that they would eventually be willing to be obedient. To this day we have failed and Zion is not redeemed. We can hasten its redemption if we will be united in purpose and keep all of the commandments the Lord has required of us. This redemption could not come until there was an endowment from on high (CHMR, Vol. 3, pp. 37-38)

To illustrate the unrighteousness of some of the saints, an incident experienced by Zion's Camp was recorded by Elder Heber C. Kimball, a member of the camp:

> While we were here [Clay County, Missouri], the brethren being in want of some refreshment, Brother Luke Johnson went to Brother Burgett to get a fowl, asking him for one to make a broth for Elder Wilcox and others; but Brother Burgett denied him it, saying "In a few days we expect to return back into Jackson County, and I shall want them when I get there." When Brother Johnson returned he was so angry at Burgett for refusing him, he said, "I have a great mind to take my rifle and go back and shoot his horse." I told Luke to never mind; that such actions never fail to bring their reward.
>
> Judge how we felt, after having left the society of our beloved families, taking our lives in our hands and traveling about one thousand miles through scenes of suffering and sorrow, for the benefit of our brethren, and after all to be denied of a small fowl to make a little soup for brethren in the agonies of death. Such things never fail to bring their reward, and it would do well for the Saints never to turn away a brother who is penniless and in want, or a stranger, lest they may one day or other want a friend themselves. (LHCK, p. 62)

The saints failed in their efforts to redeem Zion. An opportunity was lost. One of the great events of the world's history had to be deferred to a future time. The revelations of the Savior had authorized the time, the place, and the people and one of the great prophets of all time stood at the head in leadership of the cause of Zion. But the saints did not have sufficient faith to render obedience and follow their living prophet. The Lord was not able to establish Zion at that time.

What a lesson for the saints living today. Zion is yet to be redeemed. What does the Lord expect of us?

Some Requirements For The Eventual Redemption of Zion

The Lord said that Zion would have to wait for a little season before it could be redeemed. (See D&C 105:9) He also said that His people must be prepared in order to accomplish this great mission. (See D&C 105:10) Following are some of the requirements that must be met by the Lord's church and His people before they are prepared to redeem Zion:

1. The saints must learn obedience. (See D&C 105:3, 6)

In order to learn obedience, people must be given opportunity to obey. Being obedient and learning obedience are not necessarily the same. One may be obedient because he has no choice. In order to learn obedience, an individual must confront opposition and have the freedom of choice. Then, when he chooses correctly, he has learned to be obedient. (See Bible, Heb. 5:8-9) Thus, as Latter-day Saints choose to obey the laws of tithing, Sabbath observance, etc. they are experiencing a great exercise in learning obedience.

2. The saints must be united. *(See D&C 105:4-5)*

Unity is a celestial law. Unity can only be achieved when we are obedient. We must be "one" with the leaders, teachings, and practices of the church. The Savior prayed that His followers might all be one (See Bible, John 17:20-22) Such unity is a necessity for Zion's redemption.

3. The saints must be taught more perfectly. (See D&C 105:10)

Within the church there are many programs that aid in the fulfillment of this requirement. The church places great emphasis upon the teaching of the gospel to the members. There are seminaries and institutes that provide religious education for youth and young adults. For adult members, there are various education-oriented lectures and workshops. The priesthood quorums and auxiliary classes are taught from church-approved curriculum that presents messages from the scriptures and lessons pertaining to the mission of the church. These are but a few examples. Suffice it to say, one of the major thrusts of the church is to perfect the saints. Knowledge must be obtained before perfection can be achieved.

4. The saints need experience and know more perfectly concerning their duty. (See D&C 105:10)

Part of the effectiveness of the church is the opportunity the members have to participate in so many of its varied activities and programs. Through this participation and personal involvement, the saints gain experience and better learn their duty. One illustration of this concept is the preparation opportunity that is afforded the rising generation in student wards and stakes on university and college campuses. The majority of church assignments there are filled by students and young people affiliated with the university environment. Thus, they are gaining needed experience and are learning more perfectly their duty.

5. The saints need to be endowed with power. (See D&C 105:11-12)

The Lord has endowed His church with power in many ways since this revelation (Section 105) was given. The restoration of the Quorum of Twelve Apostles, temple ordinances and privileges, welfare programs, priesthood correlation, worldwide missionary efforts, and restoration of certain keys of priesthood are but a few of the many ways the Lord has endowed His church with power from on high.

6. The saints must be sanctified. (See D&C 105:31)

Sanctification means to be clean before the Lord. This is accomplished by first knowing and then abiding by the law of the Lord. (See D&C 43:8-10) In essence, obedience and repentance are the means by which one qualifies for sanctification. Prophets and leaders of the church are continually teaching and encouraging the saints to place their lives in order according to the revealed laws of the Lord. The degree to which the saints respond to these urgings determines the level of sanctification within the church.

Summary and Conclusion

In retrospect, we note that the efforts and journeys of Zion's Camp did not result in the redemption of Zion. As to the accomplishments of the camp and the way by which Zion is to be eventually redeemed, Elder Orson F. Whitney has explained:

> Thus ended that remarkable expedition; remarkable for its object, for the issues involved, for its tragic episodes, examples of heroism and miraculous manifestations of divine power. What had it achieved? some may ask. Nay, might not many be tempted to query, was not the mission of Zion's Camp a failure?
>
> "What have you accomplished?" was the sneering taunt of the apostate and of those weak in faith, met by the remnant of the little band on their return to Kirtland. "Just what we went for"; the meek, though firm reply of such men as Heber C. Kimball and Brigham Young.
>
> And they were right. To them it was no failure. The trial of their faith was complete. Their offering, like Abraham's, had been accepted. They had been weighed in the eternal balance, and were not found wanting.
>
> But what of Zion and her redemption?
>
> Let the word of the Lord, the God of Enoch, the God of Joseph give answer:
>
> "...THE REDEMPTION OF ZION MUST NEEDS COME BY POWER." [D&C 103:15]
>
> Power dwells in unity, not in discord; in humility, not pride; in sacrifice, not selfishness; obedience, not rebellion.
>
> Zion's Camp, if it failed at all in fulfilling its mission, failed for precisely similar reasons to those which had caused the expulsion of the Saints from Jackson County; reasons which, in ancient times, kept Israel wandering for forty years in the wilderness, within sight of their coveted Caanan, which they were not permitted in that generation to possess. Like Moses, these modern pilgrims beheld, as from Pisgah's top, their promised land. Like Moses, on account of transgression, they were not permitted to "cross over." No doubt there were Calebs and Joshuas in the Camp, who were worthy. But

the great event, in the wisdom of the Highest, was not then destined to be.

It was left for a future generation and its Joshua to go up in the might of the Lord and redeem Zion. (LHCK, pp. 63-64)

As to the progress of the church in some of the ways the Lord has directed the saints, President Spencer W. Kimball has said:

The people are attending their meetings and looking after their personal responsibilities. The temples are increasing in numbers, and the work at the temples indicates great spirituality. The educational program is pleasing, with the university and colleges, the institutes and seminaries, and the ecclesiastical organizations of the Church all teaching. And knowledge is expanding and testimonies are deepening.

The construction program continues to expand throughout the land so that whereas many church buildings throughout the world are turned into bars or are boarded up and abandoned, we are building almost daily new chapels throughout the world, and they are filled with happy, faithful people.

We are not satisified or boastful, but keep in mind constantly what the Savior has said to us:

"If ye continue in my word, then are ye my disciples indeed;

"And ye shall know the truth, and the truth shall make you free." (John 8:31-32)

(CR, October 1974, p. 4)

Chapter 35

Doctrine and Covenants Section 106

Suggested Title

Compensation for Full-Time Calling—Children of Light

Overview of Section Content

1. Warren A. Cowdery called to be a presiding officer in the church (vs. 1-2)
2. Compensation for full-time calling in the church (vs. 3)
3. The second coming of the Lord will not overtake the children of light as a thief in the night (vs. 4-5)
4. Counsel and promises given to Warren A. Cowdery (vs. 6-8)

Historical Setting

Joseph Smith, Jun.

It now being the last of the month, and the Elders beginning to come in, it was necessary to make preparations for the school for the Elders, wherein they might be more perfectly instructed in the great things of God, during the coming winter. A building for a printing office was nearly finished, and the lower story of this building was set apart for that purpose, (the school) when it was completed. So the Lord opened the way according to our faith and works, and blessed be His name.

No month ever found me more busily engaged than November; (1834) but as my life consisted of activity and unyielding exertions, I made this my rule: *When the Lord commands, do it* . . .

I continued my labors daily, preparing for the school, and received the following: . . .

(HC, Vol. 2, pp. 169-70)

Sacred Truths

Introduction

Warren A. Cowdery was an older brother to Oliver Cowdery. In this revelation, he was called to a presiding assignment and was directed to devote his whole time in his calling. (See D&C 106:3) Among the things the Lord discussed with Brother Cowdery were the following topics that will be discussed in this chapter:

1. Compensation for full-time calling
2. Children of light

Compensation For Full-Time Calling

In Section 42 of the Doctrine and Covenants, the Lord revealed His law to His church. Among the laws revealed was that which pertained to remuneration for full-time service in the church. The Lord has provided that when He calls individuals to full-time service, it is His will that those individuals should receive compensation for their labors from the funds of the church. (See D&C 42:70-73)

In this revelation (Section 106) the Lord reaffirmed this law. He reminded Brother Cowdery, that when one devotes his whole time to his holy calling" . . . the laborer is worthy of his hire." (D&C 107:3)

Discussing the functional application of this law, Elder Bruce R. McConkie has taught:

> In the true church we neither preach for hire nor divine for money. We follow the pattern of Paul and make the gospel of Christ without charge, lest we abuse or misuse the power the Lord has given us. Freely we have received and freely we give, for salvation is free. All who thirst are invited to come and drink of the waters of life, to buy corn and wine without money and without price.
>
> All our service in God's kingdom is predicated on his eternal law which states: "The laborer in Zion shall labor for Zion; for if they labor for money they shall perish." (2 Ne. 26:31)
>
> We know full well that the laborer is worthy of his hire, and that those who devote all their time to the building up of the kingdom

must be provided with food, clothing, shelter, and the necessaries of life. We must employ teachers in our schools, architects to design our temples, contractors to build our synagogues, and managers to run our businesses. But those so employed, along with the whole membership of the Church, participate also on a freewill and voluntary basis in otherwise furthering the Lord's work. Bank presidents work on welfare projects. Architects leave their drafting boards to go on missions. Contractors lay down their tools to serve as home teachers or bishops. Lawyers put aside *Corpus Juris* and the Civil Code to act as guides on Temple Square. Teachers leave the classroom to visit the fatherless and widows in their afflictions. Musicians who make their livelihood from their artistry willingly direct church choirs and perform in church gatherings. Artists who paint for a living are pleased to volunteer their services freely. (CR, April 1975, p. 77)

Children of Light

Every calling in the church is designed to help those who serve as well as those who are served to prepare to meet and be in the presence of the Lord. When Warren A. Cowdery was given his calling, he was also reminded that it is of utmost importance to be prepared for the coming of the Lord. The Lord referred to those who are prepared as "children of light." (D&C 106:5)

There need not be any reason for a Latter-day Saint to be unprepared at the time of the Lord's coming. The light of the gospel has flowed into the church through inspired prophets since the first days of restoration. If any member of the church rejects the light of the Lord that is given through the Lord's prophets or the Lord's Spirit, it is as though he were "...walking in darkness at noon-day." (D&C 95:6)

Those who keep the commandments and follow the Lord's authorized representatives are entitled to the Holy Spirit which enlightens one's mind and enables one to comprehend spiritual things. These are they who not only see and understand the signs of the times, but are wise enough to live in accordance with the Lord's counsel—the gospel light. The coming of the Lord will not overtake them as does a thief who succeeds under cover of darkness when people are not prepared for him.

Summary and Conclusion

The Lord provides for all of His children. Those who devote full time in His service are compensated for their labors. And those who labor to keep the Lord's commandments and are obedient to His counsel are given the vision and assurance of eternal life in His kingdom.

Chapter 36

Doctrine and Covenants Section 107

Suggested Title

Priesthood and Church Government

Overview of Section Content

1. Two priesthoods—Melchizedek and Aaronic (vs. 1-7)
2. Power and authority of the Melchizedek Priesthood (vs. 8-12, 18-19)
3. Power and authority of the Aaronic Priesthood (vs. 13-17, 20)
4. Presiding priesthood quorums and some of their duties (vs. 21-35, 38-39, 58)
5. Standing high councils (vs. 36-37)
6. Priesthood patriarchal order from Adam to Noah (vs. 40-52)
7. Adam blessed his posterity at Adam-ondi-Ahman (vs. 53-57)
8. Presiding priesthood officers and some of their duties (vs. 59-67, 85-98)
9. The office of a bishop (vs. 68-76)
10. Some church tribunals (vs. 76-84)
11. Every man to learn his duty and act in his office (vs. 99-100)

Historical Setting

Joseph Smith, Jun.

Kirtland, March 12, 1835.—This evening the Twelve assembled, and the Council was opened by President Joseph Smith, Jun., and he proposed we take our first mission through the Eastern

States, to the Atlantic Ocean, and hold conferences in the vicinity of the several branches of the Church for the purpose of regulating all things necessary for their welfare.

It was proposed that the Twelve leave Kirtland on the 4th day of May, which was unanimously agreed to . . . .

This afternoon the twelve met in council, and had a time of general confession. On reviewing our past course we are satisfied, and feel to confess also, that we have not realized the importance of our calling to that degree that we ought; we have been light-minded and vain, and in many things have done wrong. For all these things we have asked the forgiveness of our Heavenly Father; and wherein we have grieved or wounded the feelings of the Presidency, we ask their forgiveness. The time when we are about to separate is near; and when we shall meet again, God only knows; we therefore feel to ask of him whom we have acknowledged to be our Prophet and Seer, that he inquire of God for us, and obtain a revelation, (if consistent) that we may look upon it when we are separated, that our hearts may be comforted. Our worthiness has not inspired us to make this request, but our unworthiness. We have unitedly asked God our Heavenly Father to grant unto us through His Seer, a revelation of His mind and will concerning our duty the coming season, even a great revelation, that will enlarge our hearts, comfort us in adversity, and brighten our hopes amidst the powers of darkness . . . .

In compliance with the above request, I inquired of the Lord, and received for answer the following: . . .

(HC, Vol. 2, pp. 209-210)

Sacred Truths

Introduction

The first Quorum of Twelve Apostles in this dispensation was organized Feb. 14, 1835. Six weeks later these new apostles were preparing to go on their first mission. They desired that they might be instructed further as pertaining to their callings and priesthood duties. This revelation (Section 107) was given in response to their righteous request. In addition to the information given to the Twelve concerning their office and calling, the Lord also revealed much information pertaining to other priesthood offices and functions of church government.

In this chapter, we will discuss the items listed in the Overview of Section Content, excluding item No. 7. This item will be discussed in chapter 45 of this book.

Two Priesthoods—Melchizedek and Aaronic

It was necessary that the Lord instruct His new apostles pertaining to the Priesthood which they held. They were told that the authority given to them was after the order of the Son of God, but that it was to be called after Melchizedek, who had served anciently as a great high priest. (See D&C 107:2-4; also see B of M, Alma 13:14-19)

All Priesthood comes from the Lord. It is the authority by which the Lord's agents represent Him and act in His name. The Lord revealed that there are two functions of His priesthood, namely Melchizedek and Aaronic. (See D&C 107:1) As an explanation of the relationship of these two priesthoods, Joseph Smith has taught:

> There are two Priesthoods spoken of in the Scriptures, viz., the Melchizedek and the Aaronic or Levitical. Although there are two Priesthoods, yet the Melchizedek Priesthood comprehends the Aaronic or Levitical Priesthood, and is the grand head, and holds the highest authority which pertains to the priesthood, and the keys of the Kingdom of God in all ages of the world to the latest posterity on the earth; and is the channel through which all knowledge, doctrine, the plan of salvation and every important matter is revealed from heaven. (TPJS, pp. 166-167)

Power and Authority of the Melchizedek Priesthood

There are at least two primary functions of the Melchizedek Priesthood:

1. *The right of presidency* (See D&C 107:8-12)

There is order in the Lord's church. The new apostles learned that the Melchizedek Priesthood includes the right of presidency and has power and authority over all offices in the church. They were also informed that all offices in the priesthood as well as the church members function under the presiding authority of the Presidency of the High Priesthood.

All organizations of the church, including priesthood quorums and auxiliaries, are subject to the presiding authority of the priesthood leaders in the ward and stake. These local priesthood leaders are likewise responsible to the power and authority of the Presidency of the High Priesthood. No one need ever be deceived. The Lord will not govern His church, nor any individual or organization of people on the earth, contrary to this designated priesthood organization. Such is the blessing of knowing how the Lord's people are to be governed.

2. *Keys to spiritual blessings* (See D&C 107:18-19)

The gift of the Holy Ghost and all subsequent spiritual ordinances and blessings are conferred upon the Lord's people by the power and authority of the Melchizedek Priesthood. Some of the spiritual blessings promised to the faithful through this priesthood were explained by President Spencer W. Kimball as follows:

> ...the priesthood is the power and authority of God delegated to man on earth to act in all things pertaining to the salvation of men. It is the means whereby the Lord acts through men to save souls. Without this priesthood power, men are lost. Only through this power does man "hold the keys of all the spiritual blessings of the church," enabling him to receive "the mysteries of the kingdom of heaven, to have the heavens opened" unto him (see D&C 107:18-19), enabling him to enter the new and everlasting covenant of marriage and to have his wife and children bound to him in an everlasting tie, enabling him to become a patriarch to his posterity forever, and enabling him to receive a fullness of the blessings of the Lord. (*The Ensign,* June 1975, p. 3)

Power and Authority of the Aaronic Priesthood

All things that come from God are sacred. (See D&C 63:64) The Aaronic Priesthood was restored to the earth under the direction of our Father in Heaven. This priesthood is the right or authority to represent Him in His service among the people of the earth. To represent Him is a sacred obligation and all official acts of the Aaronic Priesthood ought to be seen and treated as sacred moments in the lives of the participants. Those who serve as Aaronic priesthood holders and those who are served by the Aaronic Priesthood are blessed because they participate in sacred acts performed by and through the authority of the Lord's priesthood.

It was important that the new Quorum of Apostles should understand that the Aaronic Priesthood, which includes the office of Bishop, has the authority "...to administer in outward ordinances, the letter of the gospel..." (D&C 107:20) Explaining some of the specific duties of the Aaronic priesthood, President John Taylor taught as follows:

> ...There are two distinctive general Priesthoods, namely, the Melchizedek and Aaronic, including the Levitical Priesthood...they are both conferred by the Lord; that both are everlasting, and administer in time and eternity...the second Priesthood is called the Priesthood of Aaron; because it was conferred upon Aaron and his seed throughout all their generations...the lesser Priesthood is a part of, or an appendage to the greater, or the Melchizedek Priesthood, and has power in administering outward ordinances. The lesser or Aaronic Priesthood can make appointments for the greater, in preaching, can baptize, administer the

Section 107 225

sacrament, attend to the tithing, buy lands, settle people on possessions, divideinheritances,look after the poor, take care of the properties of the Church, attend generally to temporal affairs; act as common judges in Israel, and assist in ordinances of the Temple, under the direction of the greater or Melchizedek Priesthood. They hold the keys of the ministering of angels and administer in outward ordinances, *the letter of the Gospel,* and the baptism of repentance for the remission of sins. . . .It is further evident that as the Melchizedek Priesthood holds the keys of all the spiritual blessings of the church, and that the Presidency thereof has a right to officiate in all the offices of the Church, therefore that Presidency has a perfect right to direct or call, set apart and ordain Bishops, to fill any place or position in the Church that may be required for that ministry to perform in all the Stakes of Zion, or throughout the world. (IP, pp. 30-31, 33-34, 1899—Quoted in Latter-day Prophets and the Doctrine and Covenants, Vol. 4, pp. 4-5)

(*Note*: As pertains to the office of bishop and literal descendant of Aaron as mentioned in verses 15-17 of this revelation, see *Sacred Truths of the Doctrine and Covenants,* Vol. 1, p. 338.)

Presiding Priesthood Quorums and Some of Their Duties

There are three general presiding priesthood quorums in the Lord's Church:

1. *The First Presidency* (See D&C 107:22)

This is the highest priesthood quorum of the church. All others function under their authority and direction. Members of this quorum hold all the keys of the kingdom of God. They direct the use of the Lord's power and authority throughout the world.

2. *The Quorum of Twelve Apostles* (See D&C 107:23-24, 33-35, 38-39, 58)

Each member of the Quorum of Twelve Apostles holds the keys of the kingdom in concert with the other members of the Quorum and function under the direction of the First Presidency of the Church. The Quorum of Twelve Apostles is equal in authority and power to the First Presidency. (See D&C 107:24, 33)

As to how and when the Quorum of the Twelve Apostles are equal to the First Presidency, President Joseph F. Smith taught:

. . .I want here to correct an impression that has grown up to some extent among the people, and that is, that the Twelve Apostles possess equal authority with the First Presidency in the Church.

This is correct when there is no other Presidency but the Twelve Apostles; but so long as there are three presiding elders who possess the presiding authority in the Church, the authority of the Twelve Apostles is not equal to theirs. If it were so, there would be two equal authorities and two equal quorums in the Priesthood, running parallel, and that could not be, because there must be a head. Therefore, so long as there is a First Presidency in the church they hold supreme authority in the church, and the Twelve Apostles are subject unto them and do not possess the same authority as they do as a presiding quorum. When the Presidency are not here, or when the Lord takes away the man who is called to be the President of the Church, and the quorum of the three Presidents is thereby dissolved, then the authority of the Twelve rises to the dignity of Presidents of the Church and not till then. Some people have thought also that the quorum of Seventies possess equal authority with the First Presidency and with the Twelve. So they would if there was no Presidency and no Twelve, and only seventy Elders called Seventies in the Church, but their Authority is not equal to that of the First Presidency while the First Presidency lives, nor to that of the Twelve Apostles. (Elders Journal IV, No. 3, Nov. 1, 1906, p. 43)

These two highest priesthood quorums are equal as explained above. Therefore, the way by which a successor to the President of the Church is called is clearly outlined by the Lord and is not left to speculation. President Harold B. Lee discussed this subject of succession as follows:

> To those who ask the question: How is the President of the Church chosen or elected? the correct and simple answer should be a quotation of the fifth Article of Faith: "We believe that a man must be called of God, by prophecy, and by the laying on of hands, by those who are in authority to preach the Gospel and administer in the ordinances thereof."
>
> The beginning of the call of one to be President of the Church actually begins when he is called, ordained, and set apart to become a member of the Quorum of the Twelve Apostles. Such a call by prophecy, or in other words, by the inspiration of the Lord to the one holding the keys of presidency, and the subsequent ordination and setting apart by the laying on of hands by that same authority, places each apostle in a priesthood quorum of twelve men holding the apostleship.
>
> Each apostle so ordained under the hands of the President of the Church, who holds the keys of the kingdom of God in concert with all other ordained apostles, has given to him the priesthood

Section 107

authority necessary to hold every position in the Church, even to a position of presidency over the Church if he were called by the presiding authority and sustained by a vote of a constituent assembly of the membership of the Church.

The Prophet Joseph Smith declared that "where the president is not, there is no First Presidency." Immediately following the death of a President, the next ranking body, the Quorum of the Twelve Apostles, becomes the presiding authority, with the President of the Twelve automatically becoming the acting President of the Church until a President of the Church is officially ordained and sustained in his office.

Early in this dispensation, because of certain conditions, the Council of Twelve continued to preside as a body for as long as three years before the reorganization was effected. As conditions in the Church became more stabilized, the reorganization was effected promptly following the passing of the President of the Church.

All members of the First Presidency and the Twelve are regularly sustained as "prophets, seers, and revelators," as you have done today. This means that any one of the apostles, so chosen and ordained, could preside over the Church if he were "chosen by the body [which has been interpreted to mean, the entire Quorum of the Twelve], appointed and ordained to that office, and upheld by the confidence, faith, and prayer of the church," to quote from a revelation on this subject, on one condition, and that being that he was the senior member, or the president, of that body. (See D&C 107:22.)

Occasionally the question, is asked as to whether or not one other than the senior member of the Twelve could become President. Some thought on this matter would suggest that any other than the senior member could become President of the Church only if the Lord reveals to that President of the Twelve that someone other than himself could be selected.

The Lord revealed to the first prophet of this dispensation the orderly plan for the Church leadership by a predetermined organization of the earthly kingdom of God. He gave these specific guidelines, as we might speak of them:

"Of the Melchizedek Priesthood, three Presiding High Priests, chosen by the body, appointed and ordained to that office, and upheld by the confidence, faith, and prayer of the church, form a quorum of the [First] Presidency of the Church.

"The twelve traveling councilors are called to be the Twelve Apostles, or special witness of the name of Christ in all the world—thus differing from other officers in the Church in the duties of their calling.

"And they form a quorum, equal in authority and power to the three presidents previously mentioned." (D&C 107:22-24)

With reference to this subject, the fourth President of the Church, Wilford Woodruff, made a few observations in a letter to President Heber J. Grant, then a member of the Twelve, under date of March 28, 1887. I quote from that letter: "...when the President of the Church dies, who then is the Presiding Authority of the Church? It is the Quorum of the Twelve Apostles (ordained and organized by the revelations of God and none else). Then while these Twelve Apostles preside over the Church, who is the President of the Church[?] It is the President of the Twelve Apostles. And he is virtually as much the President of the Church while presiding over Twelve men as he is when organized as the Presidency of the Church, and presiding over two men." And this principle has been carried out now for 140 years—ever since the organization of the Church. Then President Woodruff continued:

"As far as I am concerned it would require...a revelation from the same God who had organized the church and guided it by inspiration in the channel in which it has travelled for 57 years, before I could give my vote or influence to depart from the paths followed by the Apostles since the organization of the Church and followed by the inspiration of Almighty God, for the past 57 years, by the apostles, as recorded in the history of the Church." (CR, April 1970, pp. 123-124)

(*Note*: For additional information on the principle of succession, see President Spencer W. Kimball, CR, April 1970, pp. 117-122.)

As to the process by which a successor is chosen to be President of the church, President N. Eldon Tanner has explained:

I would like to explain to you exactly what took place following the unexpected death of President Harold B. Lee on 26 December 1973. I was in Phoenix, Arizona, to spend Christmas with my daughter and her family, when a call came to me from Arthur Haycock, secretary to President Lee. He said that President Lee was seriously ill, and he thought that I should plan to return home as soon as possible. A half-hour later he called and said: "The Lord has spoken, President Lee has been called home."

President Romney, Second Counselor, in my absence was directing the affairs of the Church, and was at the hospital with Spencer W. Kimball, President of the Council of the Twelve. Immediately upon the death of President Lee, President Romney turned to President Kimball and said, "You are in charge." Remember, the Prophet Joseph Smith had said that without the President there was no First Presidency over the Twelve.

Not one minute passed between the time President Lee died and the Twelve took over as the presiding authority of the Church.

Following President Lee's funeral, President Kimball called a meeting of all of the Apostles for Sunday, December 30, at 3 p.m. in the Salt Lake Temple Council Room. President Romney and I had taken our respective places of seniority in the council, so there were fourteen of us present.

Following a song, and prayer by President Romney, President Kimball, in deep humility, expressed his feelings to us. He said that he had spent Friday in the temple talking to the Lord, and had shed many tears as he prayed for guidance in assuming his new responsibilities and in choosing his counselors.

Dressed in the robes of the holy priesthood, we held a prayer circle; President Kimball asked me to conduct it and Elder Thomas S. Monson to offer the prayer. Following this, President Kimball explained the purpose of the meeting and called on each member of the quorum in order of seniority, starting with Elder Ezra Taft Benson, to express his feelings as to whether the First Presidency should be organized that day or whether we should carry on as the Council of the Twelve. Each said, "We should organize now," and many complimentary things were spoken about President Kimball and his work with the Twelve.

Then Elder Ezra Taft Benson nominated Spencer W. Kimball to be the President of the Church. This was seconded by Elder Mark E. Petersen and unanimously approved. President Kimball then nominated N. Eldon Tanner as First Counselor and Marion G. Romney as Second Counselor, each of whom expressed a willingness to accept the position and devote his whole time and energy in serving in that capacity.

They were unanimously approved. Then Elder Mark E. Petersen, second in seniority in the Twelve, nominated Ezra Taft Benson, the senior member of the Twelve, as President of the Quorum of the Twelve. This was unanimously approved.

At this point all the members present laid their hands upon the head of Spencer W. Kimball, and President Ezra Taft Benson was voice in blessing, ordaining, and setting apart Spencer W. Kimball as the twelfth President of The Church of Jesus Christ of Latter-day Saints.

Then, with President Kimball as voice, N. Eldon Tanner was set apart as First Counselor and Marion G. Romney as Second Counselor in the First Presidency of the Church. Following the same procedure, he pronounced the blessing and setting apart of Ezra Taft Benson as President of the Quorum of the Twelve.(CR, October 1979, pp. 62-63)

From this revelation, the new apostles learned some of their duties pertaining to their calling:

1. They are special witnesses of the name of Jesus Christ in all the world. (See D&C 107:23)
2. They hold the keys and responsibility for carrying the gospel message to all the world. (See D&C 107:35)
3. They are to ordain and set in order all other officers of the church. (See D&C 107:38-39, 58)

When one remembers that a new Quorum of Twelve Apostles asked for revelation and guidance, one can readily understand the significance of the information contained in this revelation.

3. The Quorum of Seventy. (See D&C 107:25-26, 34)

The Quorum of Seventy are primarily responsible for the missionary efforts of the church. They are to perform their labors under the jurisdiction and presiding authority of the Quorum of Twelve Apostles.

The decisions of all three of these presiding priesthood quorums are to be unanimous in all holiness and righteousness. (See D&C 107:27-32) The way by which this unanimity is achieved was taught by Elder Stephen L Richards:

> There are some, perhaps who may feel that it is subversive of individual freedom of thought and expression to be controlled by the interpretations of our leaders. I wish to assure them that any feeling of con[s]traint will disappear when once they secure the genius and true spirit of this work. Our unanimity of thought and action does not arise, as some suppose, from duress or compulsion in any form. Our accord comes from universal agreement with righteous principles and common response to the operation of the Spirit of our Father. It is actuated by no fear except one. That is the fear of offending God, the Author of our work. (CR, October 1938, p. 116)

Standing High Councils

In this revelation, the Lord referred to "standing High Councils." (See D&C 107:36-37) As an explanation of the meaning of this phrase, we quote from an article written by Elder Roy W. Doxey:

In 1835 when Doctrine and Covenants section 107 was revealed there were two high councils, one in Ohio and the other in Missouri. The one in Ohio was the first organized, and the minutes of that organization are recorded in section 102. These minutes constitute in some respects guidelines for high councils today, especially in the functioning of courts. Since it was the only high council in the Church when it was organized (February 1834), the Kirtland high council was presided over by the First Presidency and had general jurisdiction throughout the Church. This placed the high council in a unique position. (See D&C 102:9-10) In reference to that high council, President John Taylor said:

"In Kirtland, Ohio, a great many things were revealed through the Prophet. There was then a First Presidency that presided over the High Council, in Kirtland: and that High Council and another which was in Missouri, were the only High Councils, in existence. As I have said, the High Council in Kirtland was presided over by Joseph Smith and his Counselors; and hence there were some things associated with this that were quite peculiar in themselves. It is stated that when they were at a loss to find out anything pertaining to any principles that might come before them in their councils, , that the presidency were to inquire of the Lord and get revelation on those subjects that were difficult for them to comprehend." (*Journal of Discourses*, 19:241)

Thus, the Kirtland high council, having general jurisdiction throughout the Church, differed from the high council in Missouri, and from stake high councils today. With the First Presidency presiding, the Kirtland high council formed "a quorum equal in authority in the affairs of the church, in all their decisions, to the quorum of the presidency [First Presidency], or to the traveling high council [Twelve Apostles]." (D&C 107:36)

In the next verse (37), the Lord refers to the high council in Missouri (Zion), which did not have the First Presidency as presiding officers, as being "equal in authority in the affairs of the church, in all their decisions, to the councils of the Twelve at the stakes of Zion." Thus, this high council, and any other stake high council of twelve members referred to as "councils of the Twelve at the stakes of Zion," was to be of equal standing to each other. (*Ensign*, July 1982, pp. 31-32)

Priesthood Patriarchal Order From Adam to Noah

The priesthood holders of this last dispensation need to know that the Lord's priesthood has been the directing authority upon this earth since the time of earth's creation. The Lord revealed to His newest apostles the way by which that priesthood was handed down from Adam to each succeeding generation until Noah.

The ancient patriarchs mentioned in this revelation were not just names in a family pedigree. They were also priesthood holders—righteous patriarchs presiding over families in the power of priesthood authority. (See D&C 107:40-52)

From these verses we are reminded of a fundamental principle. Whenever the Lord has dealt with His children, in all dispensations, His direction has been given through His authorized priesthood representatives.

Presiding Priesthood Officers

Every priesthood quorum president is given authority and responsibility as follows: (See D&C 107:85-89)

1. Preside over the priesthood quorum members
2. Sit in council with the priesthood quorum members
3. Teach the priesthood quorum members

The importance of these revealed duties of quorum presidents was stressed by Elder David O. McKay:

> Presidents of quorums: The Lord has said to you, as you will read in the 107th section of the Doctrine and Covenants, that it is your duty to meet with your quorum. If you are the president of a deacon's quorum, you are to meet with twelve deacons, and preside over them, to sit in counsel with them, and to teach them their duties. O, deacons, throughout the world! respond to that call. Do your duty, Bishops, you who hold the presidency of the Aaronic Priesthood; guide the young men in this activity. Are they slothful? Are they inactive? If they are, some of the results of inactivity mentioned before as befalling the idle individual will afflict the quorum in your ward. Mark it, it will not fulfill its place in the councils of the Church, unless it be active as a council, as a quorum. This is true of the Teachers, of the Priests, the Elders, the Seventies, the High Priests, and all. (CR, October 1909, p. 92)

The Office Of A Bishop

The calling of a Bishop in this last dispensation includes three primary responsibilities: (See D&C 107:13-15, 71-72)

1. Preside over the Aaronic Priesthood
2. Administer the temporal things of the church

3. Be a judge in Israel

Bishops do not preside over Melchizedek Priesthood quorums. When Presidents of Melchizedek Priesthood quorums perform their duties in accordance with the responsibilities revealed in this revelation, the Bishops are better able and more free to discharge their duties as the Lord has revealed they should.

Some Church Tribunals

Provision has been made by the Lord, through revelation, that every member of His church is subject to and entitled to the benefits of church court actions. Should the need arise, even the President of the church might be tried before a judge in Israel, the Presiding Bishop, together with a council of twelve high priests. Thus God is no respecter of persons. All members of the Lord's church can be disciplined or cleared of charges as circumstances warrant. (See D&C 107:76-84)

Priesthood Duty—Learn and Act

The Lord concluded this revelation on priesthood by directing each priesthood holder as follows: "Wherefore, now let every man learn his duty, and to act in the office in which he is appointed, in all diligence." (D&C 107:99)

Each man is expected to grow and develop, through study and service, towards the eternal goal of Godhood. The program of the church is designed to allow each man that individual opportunity. Elder James E. Faust commented as follows:

> President Lee placed the emphasis on *let*, in the sense of permitting or allowing those given responsibilities to function within their callings without unnecessary restrictions. (CR, April 1973, p. 114)

Summary and Conclusion

The new apostles of this dispensation were taught a number of important things contained in this revelation that would be helpful to them in the discharge of their duties in their ministry. Among other things they were informed of the following:

1. In all dispensations the Lord has directed His work through authorized priesthood holders. This pattern continues today.
2. Within the Church of Jesus Christ there is a head. All priesthood holders and members of the Lord's church are subject to and function under the Presidency of the High Priesthood (First Presidency).
3. There are quorums of priesthood, presiding priesthood officers, and

specific duties and callings pertaining to these officers and quorums within the priesthood organization.

    4. All priesthood holders are expected to exercise their priesthood for righteous purposes. Each man is to learn his duty and act accordingly.

Chapter 37

Doctrine and Covenants Section 108

Suggested Title

Strengthen Your Brethren

Overview of Section Content

1. Lyman Sherman assured of his forgiveness (vs. 1)
2. Counsel and promises concerning Lyman Sherman's spiritual standing (vs. 2-6, 8)
3. Lyman Sherman directed to strengthen his brethren (vs. 7)

Historical Setting

Joseph Smith, Jun.

>Saturday, 26.—Commenced again studying the Hebrew language, in company with Brothers Parrish and Williams. In the meantime, Brother Lyman Sherman came in, and requested to have the word of the Lord through me; "for," said he, "I have been wrought upon to make known to you my feelings and desires, and was promised that I should have a revelation which should make known my duty."
>
>(HC, Vol. 2, p. 345)

Sacred Truths

Introduction

Lyman Sherman was one of the seven presidents of the First Quorum of Seventy. He sought information through the Prophet Joseph Smith, concerning his spiritual standing before the Lord.

This revelation (Section 108) is an answer to his inquiry. The Lord's response to Lyman Sherman can be grouped into two subject areas:

Lyman Sherman's Spiritual Standing

The Lord assured Lyman Sherman that he was spiritually clean before the Lord at that time. (See D&C 108:1) Thus, he was worthy to be ordained and included among the first or presiding elders of the church. (See D&C 108:2-6) He was called to be a member of the Quorum of Twelve Apostles, thus fulfilling the promise extended to him by the Lord in this revelation. He died before he could be ordained and therefore his name does not appear in the list of men who have served in the Quorum of Twelve Apostles.

Priesthood callings extended to the faithful by the Lord are eternal. Death does not diminish nor take away a man's priesthood calling in the Lord's kingdom. We may be sure Lyman Sherman continues to serve among the presiding elders in the spirit world. (See D&C 124:130; 138:57)

Strengthen Your Brethren

The second area of counsel to Lyman Sherman dealt with his relationship with his brethren. The Lord instructed him to strengthen his brethren in the following four ways: (See D&C 108:7)

1. All conversation

Regardless of our position or station in life, we all may have an influence upon someone by the way we speak about the leaders of the church. We may be the means by which someone follows or fails to follow counsel of the leaders. Someone's decision on this matter may be a direct result of the influence we have on their confidence in the leadership of the church. Speaking of the effect our conversations may have upon the attitude of others, Elder George F. Richards taught:

> When we say anything bad about the leaders of the Church, whether true or false, we tend to impair their influence and their usefulness and are thus working against the Lord and his cause. When we speak well of our leaders, we tend to increase their influence and usefulness in the service of the Lord. In his absence our brother's character when assailed, should be defended, thus doing to others as we would be done by. The Lord needs the help of all of us. Are we helping or are we hindering? (CR, April 1947, p.24)

2. All Prayers

Many times the presiding authorities of the church have testified that they have been strengthened because of the prayers of the membership. One illustration of such testimony was given by President Spencer W. Kimball:

> I have all my life sustained my leaders, praying for their welfare, and I have in these past years felt a great power coming to me from similar prayers of the saints, raised to heaven on my behalf. (BYU Speeches of the Year, 1979, p. 164)

Prayer is a powerful tool. People can be strengthened through the prayers of others. There can be no doubt but that the leaders of the church are stronger because of the prayers of the membership in their behalf than they would be without the united faith and prayers of the saints.

3. All Exhortations

Exhortations means teachings. As members of the Lord's church we are responsible to teach what the presiding brethren teach. We have no right to interpret or teach anything contrary to what they have said. We can strengthen the brethren by teaching and stressing that which they have declared to be true. Through our teaching, their witness is extended by repetition to additional listeners. Thus, their strength and effectiveness is increased.

4. All Doings

When our actions, or doings, are in harmony with what the presiding brethren counsel, we are strengthening their position as well as our own. Where our lives reflect the counsel of church authorities, their influence is extended through our lives and thus they become a stronger influence for good in the earth. Strong leadership derives much of its strength from support.

It is not to be suggested that church leaders are infallible. They are mortal men. However, the Lord works through these men to bless the membership of His church. Such blessings are predicated upon the membership following their counsel, regardless of their human weaknesses. The prophet Joseph Smith taught the saints to look past the human weakness of the leadership and render obedience to their counsel. He said:

> I showed them that it was generally in consequence of the brethren disregarding or disobeying counsel that they became dissatisfied and murmured; and many when they arrive here, were dissatisfied with the conduct of some of the Saints, because every-

thing was not done perfectly right, and they get angry, and thus the devil gets advantage over them to destroy them. I told them I was but a man, and they must not expect me to be perfect; if they expected perfection from me, I should expect it from them; but if they would bear with my infirmities and the infirmities of the brethren, I would likewise bear with their infirmities. (TPJS, p. 268)

Summary and Conclusion

We must remember that it was the Lord who said to "strengthen your brethren." We cannot avoid the responsibility to act in this manner. It is a serious thing to fail in this assignment and we should be aware of the importance attached to this simple phrase that has so many ramifications to its meaning. The prophets have stressed this subject repeatedly. We refer to two of them:

Joseph Smith, Jun.

> O ye Twelve! and all Saints! profit by this important Key—that in all your trials, troubles, temptations, afflictions, bonds, imprisonments and death, see to it, that you do not betray heaven; that you do not betray Jesus Christ; that you do not betray the brethren; that you do not betray the revelations of God, whether in Bible, Book of Mormon, or Doctrine and Covenants, or any other that ever was or ever will be given and revealed unto man in this world or that which is to come. Yea, in all your kicking and flounderings, see to it that you do not this thing, lest innocent blood be found upon your skirts, and you go down to hell. All other sins are not to be compared to sinning against the Holy Ghost, and proving a traitor to the brethren. (TPJS, p. 156)

(*Note*: See also Bible, Proverbs 6:16-19)

Harold B. Lee

> Conversion must mean more than just being a "card carrying" member of the Church with a tithing receipt, a membership card, a temple recommend, etc. It means to overcome the tendencies to criticize and to strive continually to improve inward weaknesses and not merely the outward appearances. (CR, April 1971, p. 92)

Chapter 38

Doctrine and Covenants Section 109

Suggested Title
Dedicatory Prayer—Kirtland Temple

Overview of Section Content
1. The Kirtland Temple was built to fulfill the commandment of the Lord (vs. 1-5)
2. Various blessings promised to the faithful in the house of the Lord (vs. 6-21)
3. Blessings and power of the Lord requested for the righteous saints (vs. 22-49)
4. Blessings requested for all mankind (vs. 50-57)
5. Blessings requested for the House of Israel (vs. 58-67)
6. Blessings requested for the ultimate success of the church, its leaders, and their families (vs. 68-80)

Historical Setting

Joseph Smith, Jun.

>The dedicatory prayer was then offered:
>The following prayer was given by Revelation to Joseph, the Seer, and was Repeated in the Kirtland Temple at the time of its Dedication, March 27, 1836.
>
>(HC, Vol. 2, p. 420)

Joseph Fielding Smith

...Long before the doors of the temple were opened on the morning of the dedication, March 27, 1836, the people had assembled. When the doors were opened the people were admitted as far as the capacity of the building would permit. The First Presidency acted as ushers in the seating and each quorum of the Priesthood was seated in their order. When the building was filled to capacity the doors were closed and those who could not enter were forced to wait until another session...

...The Prophet then arose and presented the prayer of dedication. This prayer was given previously by revelation and is found in the Doctrine and Covenants, Section 109. Naturally this is a comprehensive commandment that the temple should be built and speaks of the purpose for which it was built...

(CHMR, Vol. 3, pp. 74-75)

Sacred Truths

Introduction

Section 109 of the Doctrine and Covenants is a revealed prayer that was given for the dedication of the Kirtland Temple. Speaking about the dedication of buildings unto the Lord, President Joseph Fielding Smith taught:

...When we dedicate a house to the Lord, what we really do is dedicate ourselves to the Lord's service, with a covenant that we shall use the house in the way He intends that it shall be used...Dedicatory prayers for temples, however, are formal and long and cover many matters of doctrine and petition. This pattern was set by the Prophet Joseph Smith in the dedication of the Kirtland Temple. The prayer given on that occasion was revealed to him by the Lord; all prayers used since then have been written by the spirit of inspiration and have been read by such of the Brethren as have been appointed to do so. The prayer I have prepared for dedication of this Provo Temple is no exception.

(Church News, Feb. 12, 1972)

We learn from President Smith's statement that the Lord's people are under covenant with the Lord to use His dedicated buildings properly. It matters how we act in the building, how we treat the physical facilities, how we dress when we enter, how and what we teach within the walls of the building. We should come to the building prepared to contribute, not detract, from the spirit which should be there.

There are many things we can learn from this revealed prayer. (D&C Section 109) We can become more sensitive to the blessings already received and those blessings which should be earnestly sought for. In this chapter, we will discuss the revelation as outlined in the Overview of Section Content.

The Kirtland Temple—Fulfillment of the Lord's Commandment

Whenever the Lord has given His people access to the fulness of the gospel, He has also commanded His people to build a house unto Him. This is one of the identifying characteristics of the Lord's church. Hence, in this dispensation, He commanded His saints, through His prophet, to build a temple unto the Most High in Kirtland, Ohio. (See D&C 88:119) No man or group of men can assume this privilege unto themselves. When a temple is built unto the Lord, it is built because the Lord commands it. Therefore, as temples continue to be built, so the observer can correctly conclude that revelation continues to flow from the Lord to His prophet. In this prayer (Section 109), it is acknowledged that the Lord gave the commandment to His servants to build His house. The servants, in turn, requested the Lord to accept of their workmanship. (See D&C 109:1-5)

Blessings Promised in the House of the Lord

When the Lord commanded the saints to build His house in Kirtland, He promised that certain blessings would flow unto the faithful from that house. (See D&C 88:119)

After the temple was completed, the prophet was inspired to pray for the realization of the previously promised blessings. (See D&C 109:6-21) And what were the blessings sought for in behalf of the saints of the latter-day dispensation?

1. The faithful who enter the temple will feel and acknowledge the power of the Lord. They can testify that they have been in the Savior's home on earth. (See D&C 109:10-13)
2. The true worshippers in the house of the Lord will be taught and learn wisdom. They will better understand and apply the teachings of the scriptures and the admonitions of the Lord's anointed. (See D&C 109:14)
3. The saints may grow up in the Lord, receive a fulness of the Holy Ghost, be correctly organized, and be prepared to obtain all needful things. (See D&C 109:15)
4. The temple will be a place for fasting and prayer, faith, glory, learning, and order as a house of God. (See D&C 109:8, 16)

Blessings and Power of the Lord Requested

This revealed prayer contains a plea that those who are endowed with power in the temple might withstand the onslaught of wickedness and evil in the world. Further, that those faithful servants might have power to seal their testimonies of truth against the wicked. The righteous servants should also have the power to bless the honest-in-heart throughout the earth.

Those who receive the ordinances and blessings of the temple have a power for righteousness that comes from the Lord. They can better withstand evil and can better propagate truth as an influence for good to all of Father's children. Those who are armed with this power of the Lord shall be established by the Lord with an honorable name in His house to be remembered throughout generations to come. (See D&C 109:22-49)

It is little wonder that the missionaries of the Lord's church are given an opportunity to participate in temple ordinances before embarking upon their missionary service as servants of the Lord. Nor is it difficult to see why the Lord's people are continually encouraged to attend regularly and be faithful participants in the sacred activities and ordinances of temple worship.

Blessings Requested for All Mankind

The Lord inspired the Prophet Joseph Smith to pray for various groups of people in the earth:

1. The enemies of the church (See D&C 109:50-53)
2. The nations of the earth (See D&C 109:54)
3. The leaders of America (See D&C 109:54)
4. The rulers and leaders of other nations (See D&C 109:55)
5. The peoples of the earth (See D&C 109:55)
6. The churches in the world (See D&C 109:55)
7. The poor, needy, and afflicted (See D&C 109:55)

Why might the Lord give counsel to pray for these people of the earth? Perhaps there are many reasons, but one is given by the Lord in this revelation. Hearts of the people of the world need to be softened. They can then more readily accept and respond favorably to the Lord's servants who leave His temple endowed with power to proclaim the message of the gospel for all mankind. (See D&C 109:56-57)

Members of the church have been encouraged and requested to pray for the leaders of nations for this very purpose.

Blessings Requested for the House of Israel

Joseph Smith was inspired to pray for an event that was impossible to bring about by the powers of mortal man. A plea was made in this prayer for

Section 109

the restoration of Israel, both temporally and spiritually. (See D&C 109:58-67)

Except for the intervening powers of the Lord, the scattered Jews could never have been restored to Jerusalem and the lands of their inheritance. What a testimony of the inspiration behind this revelation. Joseph Smith had no power to bring about the marvelous fulfillment of this prophetic prayer. In 1836, there was no indication of the return of Israel that was begun in the century following this declaration of desire. The Lord is at the helm.

Blessings Requested for the Ultimate Success of the Church

Regardless of the status of an individual either in or out of the church, every person needs to be adequately prepared to meet the Savior at His second coming. Every church teaching and program is designed to reach this sacred and spiritual goal. This is the mission of the church. Those who are adequately prepared will meet the Master at His coming and enjoy His glory in His millennial reign. For this we should pray. (See D&C 109:68-80)

Summary and Conclusion

Many blessings are petitioned for in this dedicatory prayer. These blessings are being and will yet be realized among the inhabitants of the earth.

When the servants of God are endowed with power in the Lord's home, then the temple and the servants become a means by which the Lord blesses mankind. The influence of that endowment becomes a worldwide power for good.

Chapter 39

Doctrine and Covenants Section 110

Suggested Title

The Appearance of the Savior—Keys Restored

Overview of Section Content

1. The Savior's appearance in and His acceptance of the Kirtland Temple (vs. 1-7)
2. Blessings to be poured out from the house of the Lord (vs. 8-10)
3. Restoration of certain priesthood keys by Moses, Elias, and Elijah (vs. 11-16)

Historical Setting

Joseph Smith, Jun.

Sunday, 3.—Attended meeting in the Lord's House, and assisted the other Presidents of the Church in seating the congregation, and then became an attentive listener to the preaching from the stand. Thomas B. Marsh and David W. Patten spoke in the forenoon to an attentive audience of about one thousand persons. In the afternoon, I assisted the other Presidents in distributing the Lord's Supper to the Church, receiving it from the Twelve, whose privilege it was to officiate at the sacred desk this day. After having performed this service to my brethren, I retired to the pulpit, the veils being dropped, and bowed myself, with Oliver Cowdery, in solemn and

245

silent prayer. After rising from prayer, the following vision was opened to both of us.— . . .

(HC, Vol. 2, pp. 434-435)

Joseph Fielding Smith

. . .After the dedication of the Kirtland Temple, council and spiritual meetings were held in the building almost daily. Sunday, April 3, 1836, was one of the most eventful days in the history of the Church. A general meeting was held in the Lord's House. In the forenoon Elders Thomas B. Marsh and David W. Patten spoke to an audience of about one thousand persons. In the afternoon the Sacrament was administered by the Presidency and the apostles. After this ordinance the Prophet and Oliver Cowdery retired to the pulpit, the veils were dropped, and these two men bowed before the pulpit in silent prayer, and the following vision was manifested before them . . .

It is interesting to know that on the third day of April, 1836, the Jews were celebrating the feast of the Passover, and were leaving the doors of their homes open for the coming of Elijah. On that day Elijah came, but not to the Jewish homes, but to the Temple in the village of Kirtland near the banks of Lake Erie, to two humble servants of the Lord who were appointed by divine decree to receive him.

(CHMR, Vol. 3, pp. 78, 84)

Sacred Truths

Introduction

In the dedicatory prayer of the Kirtland Temple, the Prophet Joseph Smith asked the Lord to " . . .accept the dedication of this house unto thee . . . ." (D&C 109:78) One week after the dedication, the Lord appeared to the Prophet Joseph Smith and Oliver Cowdery and accepted the temple as a house of the Lord. (See D&C 110:7) He also promised certain blessings would be forthcoming from His house.

In addition to the Savior's appearance, three other heavenly messengers appeared and restored certain keys of the priesthood to Joseph Smith and Oliver Cowdery.

In this chapter, we will discuss the following:

1. The resurrected Savior
2. Blessings to flow from the Lord's house

The Resurrected Savior

It would be difficult for a mortal being to describe a celestial personage and do so within the communicative limitations of mortal language. When Joseph described the Savior, he used descriptive language which conveyed illustrations that are familiar to mortal man.

Describing the Savior's eyes, Joseph said they "...were as a flame of fire;..." (D&C 110:3) A flame of fire has an intensity about it that demands one's attention. To look into the Savior's eyes, would be an experience demanding one's total attention and respect. Joseph also noted that the Lord's entire countenance had a brilliance that "...shone above the brightness of the sun;..." (D&C 110:3) There is a brilliance associated with the glory that accompanies the members of the Godhead.

The voice of the Lord was described "...as the sound of the rushing of great waters...." (D&C 110:3) Anyone who has heard the rushing of great quantities of water, knows there is a penetrating power associated with that experience. People in Book of Mormon lands also heard the voice of the resurrected Savior. That experience was described as follows:

> And it came to pass that while they were thus conversing one with another, they heard a voice as if it came out of heaven; and they cast their eyes round about, for they understood not the voice which they heard; and it was not a harsh voice, neither was it a loud voice; nevertheless, and notwithstanding it being a small voice it did pierce them that did hear to the center, insomuch that there was no part of their frame that it did not cause to quake; yea, it did pierce them to the very soul, and did cause their hearts to burn. (B of M, 3 Nephi 11:3)

As the Savior spoke to Joseph Smith and Oliver Cowdery, He identified Himself as Jehovah (the God of the Old Testament) who was slain, was resurrected, and lives today. (See D&C 110:4) We have another witness in this dispensation from the living Christ Himself as to the reality of His atonement and resurrection. We also have two mortal witnesses who saw Him and heard His divine declaration: "...I am he who liveth...." (D&C 110:4)

Blessings to Flow From the Lord's House

The Lord declared to Joseph Smith and Oliver Cowdery:

> Yea the hearts of thousands and tens of thousands shall greatly rejoice in consequence of the blessings which shall be poured out, and the endowment with which my servants have been endowed in this house.

And the fame of this house shall spread to foreign lands; and this is the beginning of the blessing which shall be poured out upon the heads of my people. Even so. Amen. (D&C 110:9-10)

We learn from the above verses that two great blessings were to flow from the Lord's house in Kirtland.

1. The hearts of vast multitudes of people will rejoice because of that with which the Lord's servants were to be endowed in that house.
2. The fame of the Kirtland Temple would spread to foreign lands.

Now, how was this to be fulfilled? What endowment was given in Kirtland that has served as a blessing to tens of thousands of people throughout the world? Why would the Kirtland Temple, a small building in a rural community in Ohio, find fame in foreign lands?

Three ancient prophets appeared to Joseph and Oliver and restored priesthood keys to them that have provided untold numbers of people throughout the earth with reasons to rejoice over their blessings.

Moses restored the keys of the gathering of Israel from the four parts of the earth. (See D&C 110:11) All those who have been gathered into the kingdom of God throughout the countries of the world are recipients of the blessings that have resulted from the restoration of keys in the Kirtland Temple.

Elias also appeared and restored keys. Who is Elias and what did he restore? Elias is Noah. (See Joseph Fielding Smith, CR, April 1960, p. 72) He restored the keys of the dispensation in which Abraham lived. (See D&C 110:12) Therefore, all of the blessings given to Abraham are now available to all mankind through the ordinances of The Church of Jesus Christ of Latter-day Saints. These blessings include eternal marriage vows with promises of eternal posterity and family relationships through the patriarchal order of the priesthood. Because of the restoration of these keys in the Kirtland Temple, multitudes of Father's children have been recipients of these blessings that have flowed from that house.

Elijah also restored keys of the priesthood. (See D&C 110:13-15) As to the nature of these keys, President Joseph Fielding Smith has taught:

> ...Elijah restored to this Church and, if they would receive it, to the world, the keys of the sealing power; and that sealing power puts the stamp of approval upon every ordinance that is done in this Church and more particularly those that are performed in the temples of the Lord. (CR, April 1948, p. 135)

Every family (both living and dead) who have received ordinances of the priesthood, can be assured that the power to keep those ordinances intact throughout all eternity was restored in the Kirtland Temple. The blessings that have flowed from that temple have given literally millions of people great cause to rejoice. The fame of that house is now known throughout foreign lands. The powers restored in that temple are presently being utilized and manifested in temples of the Lord in the various nations of the earth.

Summary and Conclusion

April 3, 1836 was a momentous day in the lives of the earth's inhabitants of this dispensation. On that day, the Savior and three other celestial beings appeared to two mortal servants of the Lord.

The priesthood keys restored that day in the Kirtland Temple have blessed multitudes of mankind, both in mortality and in the spirit world. These blessings have not come because of the powers of mortal men. They are the result of the concern of the Lord for His children. As these blessings are manifested in our lives today, there is an accompanying testimony that the Great Jehovah, the Redeemer of the world, lives to bless all mankind through His church upon the earth.

Chapter 40

Doctrine and Covenants Section 111

Suggested Title

Mission to Salem, Massachusetts—Follies

Overview of Section Content

1. Directions given to Joseph Smith and others pertaining to the missionary efforts in Salem, Massachusetts (vs. 1-4, 7-11)
2. Debt—The Lord's promise (vs.5)
3. Zion—The Lord's promise of mercy (vs. 6)

Historical Setting

Joseph Smith, Jun.

On Monday afternoon, July 25th, in company with SidneyRigdon, Brother Hyrum Smith, and Oliver Cowdery, I left Kirtland, . . .and the next evening, about ten o'clock we arrived at Buffalo, New York, . . .

. . .we took passages on a line boat for Utica, where we arrived about eight o'clock a.m. of the 29th, just in time to take the railroad car for Schenectady, the first passenger car on the new road . . . .

On the 30th, at seven o'clock a.m. we went on board the steamer *John Mason*, which took us to the Erie, lying over the bar . . .

From New York we continued our journey to Providence, on board a steamer; from thence to Boston, by steam cars, and arrived in Salem, Massachusetts, early in August, where we hired a house, and occupied the same during the month, teaching the people from house to house, and preaching publicly, as opportunity presented; visiting occasionally, sections of the surrounding country, which are rich in the history of the Pilgrim Fathers of New England, in Indian warfare, religious superstition, bigotry, persecution, and learned ignorance.

(HC, Vol. 2, pp. 463-464)

B. H. Roberts

...While the Prophet gives a somewhat circumstantial account of this journey to Salem and his return to Kirtland in September, he nowhere assigns an adequate cause for himself and company making it—the object of it is not stated. Ebenezer Robinson, for many years a faithful and prominent elder in the Church, and at Nauvoo associated with Don Carlos Smith—brother of the Prophet—in editing and publishing the *Times and Seasons*, states that the journey to Salem arose from these circumstances. There came to Kirtland a brother by the name of Burgess who stated that he had knowledge of a large amount of money secreted in the cellar of a certain house in Salem, Massachusetts, which had belonged to a widow (then deceased), and thought he was the only person who had knowledge of it, or of the location of the house. The brethren accepting the representations of Burgess as true made the journey to Salem to secure, if possible, the treasure. Burgess, according to Robinson, met the brethren in Salem, but claimed that time had wrought such changes in the town that he could not for a certainty point out the house "and soon left." They hired a house and occupied it and spent their time as per the narrative of the Prophet already quoted. While in Salem the Prophet received a revelation in which the folly of this journey is sharply reproved:...

(CHC, Vol. 1, p. 411)

Sacred Truths

Introduction

As one examines the purpose of the prophet's mission to Salem, Massachusetts, it would appear to be strange and unusual. However, it is not so strange or unusual when we note the economic conditions of the church and the nation at that time. The Kirtland Temple had just been completed and indebtedness surrounded that endeavor.

Speculation in lands and property was rife in the United States. Reeling under the pressure of indebtedness, the prophet sought relief for the church. Apparently, this endeavor considered all legal options. Unclaimed money was certainly a legal venture. Sincerity, however, may not always be indicative of wisdom. While in Salem, Massachusetts, the prophet received a revelation from the Lord in which He described Joseph's journey as a folly. (See D&C 111:1)

In this chapter we will discuss the nature of and the handling of follies.

The Nature of Follies

What is a folly? It could be described as an honest mistake, an unwise decision, or a sincere error in judgment.

So many misunderstandings that occur among families, friends, associates, etc. are the result of follies. Normally, there is no intention to hurt or offend. However, honest mistakes are made. The major problem isn't the folly, or unwise behavior, itself, but the lack of spiritual maturity to recognize a folly and deal with it properly.

When a folly is committed and not recognized as such, the general result is the ego or self-esteem of the individual, as well as his personal dignity, suffers abuse.

From the first verse of this revelation, we may begin to see the wisdom and perfection of the Savior:

> I, the Lord your God, am not displeased with your coming this journey, notwithstanding your follies. (D&C 111:1)

The recognition of follies by weak mortals is a giant step forward along the path of spirituality. The following is an illustration of such growth and advancement.

A father had a new windshield installed in his automobile. As he arrived home and drove into the driveway, he noticed his daughter playing on the lawn with the family dog. She was throwing rocks for the dog to retrieve. She threw a rock in the direction of the driveway and mistakenly hit the windshield of the car. The new windshield was shattered. What might be the usual reaction of the parent? Verbal or physical abuse would be the norm. However, this father was sensitive as to how the Lord would have him respond to this unintentional mistake and proceeded to assess the situation spiritually. "Folly," said he. "This behavior was not intended to do harm." The spiritual maturity here portrayed demonstrates that this father had the ability to recognize a folly. It seems such a simple thing, yet many people fail to separate the intent of the deed from the result of the act and the accompanying emotional climate. Hence, they launch forth on a course that is detrimental to the individual as well as to themselves.

The Handling of Follies

What is the mental or emotional condition of the child of God at the time he or she commits a folly? In most cases, their self-esteem plummets to a low level and their embarrassment is obvious. It is important to observe, in the case of Joseph Smith, how the Lord, after assessing the behavior to be a folly, moved to protect the ego of His youthful prophet; to salvage as much as possible from a difficult situation. We note His positive course of action:

> I have much treasure in this city for you, for the benefit of Zion, and many people in this city, whom I will gather out in due time for the benefit of Zion, through your instrumentality.
>
> Therefore, it is expedient that you should form acquaintance with men in this city, as you shall be led, and as it shall be given you....
>
> Concern not yourselves about your debts, for I will give you power to pay them....
>
> ...And inquire diligently concerning the more ancient inhabitants and founders of this city;
>
> For there are more treasures than one for you in this city. (D&C 111:2-3, 5, 9-10)

We would call attention to three important principles:

1. The most valuable treasure on this earth is the soul of a man. Apparently, Joseph Smith had allowed his concern for the church's financial needs to, momentarily, take precedence. Priorities were reestablished by the Savior.

2. The sincerity of the prophet's intent was recognized and help was assured.

3. The Lord helped Joseph to make the best of the situation. With reference to the Lord's direction for Joseph to "inquire...concerning the...ancient inhabitants....," (D&C 111:9) we quote the following:

> ..."ancient inhabitants" refers more particularly to the ancestors of the Prophet. The Revelation was given at Salem, the county seat of Essex County, Massachusetts. It was in that county that Robert Smith, the first of the Smith family in America, settled. It was the residence of many more of the pioneer immigrants to America, whose descendants joined the Church. At Salem, the county seat, the records for all the towns in the county were kept, and the Smiths' record, among others, were there. The matter of genealogy

evidently entered into the inquiry concerning the "ancient inhabitants".... (DCC, p. 729)

Summary and Conclusion

So many mistakes fall into the category of follies. The ability to recognize a folly is Christlike.

A positive approach to protect the ego of the individual might include a review of priorities, the acknowledgement of a sincere intent, and the implementation of the kind of action that becomes helpful and useful.

Chapter 41

Doctrine and Covenants Section 112

Suggested Title

Thomas B. Marsh—The Lord's Instructions to A Quorum President

Overview of Section Content

1. The Lord's instructions and counsel to Thomas B. Marsh, President of the Quorum of Twelve Apostles (vs. 1-12)
2. The Lord's instructions and counsel to the Quorum of Twelve Apostles:

   a. Be faithful to the Lord and magnify their callings (vs. 13-15, 22-29, 33-34)

   b. The Twelve and the First Presidency (vs. 16-21, 30-32)

Historical Setting

Joseph Smith, Jun.

At this time the spirit of speculation in lands and property of all kinds, which was so prevalent throughout the whole nation, was taking deep root in the Church. As the fruits of this spirit, evil surmisings, fault-finding, disunion, dissension, and apostasy followed in quick succession, and it seemed as though all the powers of earth and hell were combining their influence in an especial manner to overthrow the Church at once, and make a final end. Other banking institutions refused the "Kirtland Safety Society's" notes. The enemy abroad, and apostates in our midst, united in their schemes, flour and provisions were turned towards other markets, and many became disaffected toward me as though I were the sole cause of those very evils I was most strenuously striving against, and which were actually brought upon us by the brethren not giving heed to my counsel.

No quorum in the Church was entirely exempt from the influences of those false spirits who are striving against me for the mastery; even some of the Twelve were so far lost to their high and responsible calling, as to begin to take sides, secretly, with the enemy.

In this state of things, and but a few weeks before the Twelve were expecting to meet in full quorum, (some of them having been absent for some time), God revealed to me that something new must be done for the salvation of His Church. And on or about the first of June, 1837, Heber C. Kimball, one of the Twelve, was set apart by the spirit of prophecy and revelation, prayer and laying on of hands, of the First Presidency, to preside over a mission to England, to be the first foreign mission of the Church of Christ in the last days . . .

(HC, Vol. 2, pp. 487-489)

The same day that the Gospel was first preached in England I received the following . . .

(HC, Vol. 2, p. 499)

Joseph Fielding Smith

. . .The day that the British Missionaries preached the first sermons, in England, July 23, 1837 the Lord gave a revelation to the Prophet Joseph Smith directed to Thomas B. Marsh as president of the council of the apostles. In this revelation Elder Marsh was instructed to teach the brethren in his council and point out to them their duty and responsibilities in proclaiming the Gospel. Some of the apostles had forsaken their responsibilitiy and had turned their attention to schemes of speculation....This revelation to Thomas B. Marsh was a warning and a call to him to bring his brethren back into the line of their duty as apostles of Jesus Christ...

(CHMR, Vol 3, p. 101)

Sacred Truths

Introduction

At the time of this revelation (1837) the church was being attacked from sides as well as from some of the members within. The Lord inspired the

Prophet Joseph Smith to send Elder Heber C. Kimball to England as a missionary. His efforts and the labors of subsequent missionaries would bring new life into the church, as many thousands of converts would join the church.

One illustration of the prophetic calling of Joseph Smith and the inspired source of his information concerning the missionary efforts in England was described by Elder Harold B. Lee as follows:

> In one year, 1840 to 1841—one year and fourteen days, to be exact—nine members of the twelve were called to labor in the British Mission. If you remember the history here at home, those years marked the period of some of the severest persecution that the Church was to undergo in this dispensation. In that one year and fourteen days the nine members of the twelve, with their associates, established churches in every noted town and city in the kingdom of Great Britain. They baptized between 7000 and 8000 converts. They printed 5000 copies of the Book of Mormon, 3000 hymnbooks, and 50,000 tracts, and they published 2500 volumes of the *Millennial Star* and emigrated 1000 souls to America. (CR, April 1960, p. 108)

While Elder Kimball was away on his first mission to England, the Lord spoke to his quorum president in Kirtland, Ohio. The counsel given by the Lord to President Thomas B. Marsh is contained in Section 112 of the Doctrine and Covenants. It can be conveniently arranged, for study purposes, into two categories, as recorded in the Overview of Section Content at the beginning of this chapter.

The Lord Instructs A Quorum President

The Lord acknowledged the prayers of President Marsh that were offered in behalf of his quorum members. (See D&C 112:1) He also reminded the President that he needed to keep his life in harmony with the Lord by following the Lord's counsel that was given to him at that time. (See D&C 112:2-10)

The Lord further instructed this quorum president as follows: (See D&C 112:11-12)

1. Be impartial towards the quorum members.
2. Love the quorum members as self.
3. Pray for the quorum members.
4. Admonish the quorum members for all their sins.

A responsive quorum president should be sensitive to the directions of the Lord and the needs of his quorum. He will be concerned about the welfare of the soul of each quorum member. As he prays for his quorum, he is concerned about not only the temporal but also the spiritual welfare of each quorum member. The Nephites were taught and practiced this principle:

> And the church did meet together oft, to fast and to pray, and to speak one with another concerning the welfare of their souls. (B of M, Moroni 6:5)

The Lord further expects the quorum presidents to admonish, correct, and encourage quorum members so that they might overcome their sins. When President Marsh was directed by the Lord to admonish his quorum members, there were several apostles who were not in harmony with the Lord. In obedience to this expectation, President Marsh labored in behalf of his brethren and the resultant fruits are described in the following commentary:

> Our Lord instructs the President of the Council to continue to pray for the members, and also to admonish them "sharply." Admonition without prayer is barren of results. He promised to feel after them, when they had passed through the tribulations awaiting them because they had yielded to temptations. And then, if they would not harden their hearts, they would be converted and healed.
> Orson Hyde, who had imbibed of the spirit of speculation, freely acknowledged his faults and asked forgiveness. Parley P. Pratt, too, at one time was overcome by the evil spirit, of strife, but, he says, "I went to Brother Joseph Smith in tears, and with a broken heart and contrite spirit, confessed wherein I had erred. He frankly forgave me, prayed for me, blessed me." Others did not repent. Luke S. Johnson, Lyman E. Johnson, and John F. Boynton were rejected and disfellowshipped by the Church on the 3rd of September, 1837, less than a month and a half after this Revelation was given. (DCC, p. 734)

There were those who heeded and those who did not heed the admonition of President Marsh. Regardless of the response of the quorum members, the quorum president could stand approved of the Lord because of his efforts to follow the Lord's counsel. His actions have demonstrated his impartial love for his quorum.

The Lord Instructs the Quorum of the Twelve

The Quorum of theTwelve have a special calling that differs from any other quorum in the church. They are to be special witnesses of the name of Christ in all the world. (See D&C 107:23) In this revelation (Section 112) they are reminded that they should so conduct their lives in order that they might magnify their callings. By so doing, they would be free from the blood and sins of this generation. (See D&C 112:13-15, 22-29, 33-34)

The Lord also informed the Twelve of their relationship with His First Presidency. The President of the Quorum of the Twelve was reminded that he held the keys pertaining to the missionary responsibility of the Twelve to take the gospel to all nations of the earth. However, he was also reminded that he and his quorum members were to function under the presiding direction of the First Presidency whom the Lord had appointed as counselors over all of the work of the Lord's kingdom. (See D&C 112:16-20, 30-32)

Summary and Conclusion

This revelation contains information and counsel from the Lord that can be applied by every quorum president in the Lord's church. Heeding this instruction, each president will stand approved before the Lord and will be the means of helping quorum members obtain eternal blessings for themselves and members of their families.

The specific instructions given to the President of the Quorum of the Twelve is being implemented in the church in this dispensation. The Quorum of the Twelve is directing the worldwide missionary efforts of the church under the direction of the Lord's First Presidency.

Chapter 42

Doctrine and Covenants Section 113

Suggested Title

Insights to the Book of Isaiah

Overview of Section Content

1. The stem, the rod, and the root of Jesse (vs. 1-6)
2. The power, authority, and responsibility of priesthood holders (vs. 7-8)
3. Scattered Israel exhorted to return to the Lord (vs. 9-10)

Historical Setting

Joseph Smith, Jun.

On the 14th of March, as we were about entering Far West, many of the brethren came out to meet us, who also with open arms welcomed us to their bosoms. We were immediately received under the hospitable roof of Brother George W. Harris, who treated us with all possible kindness, and we refreshed ourselves with much satisfaction, after our long and tedious journey, the brethren bringing in such things as we had need of for our comfort and convenience. (HC, Vol. 3, pp. 8-9)

Sacred Truths

Introduction

Shortly after the Prophet Joseph Smith arrived in Far West, while in conversation with some of the brethren, he gave some inspired answers to some questions pertaining to the writings of Isaiah. These questions were centered on two chapters of Isaiah, namely 11 and 52. Section 113 of the Doctrine and Covenants constitutes the record of the questions and answers that were provided. Verses 1 through 6 and 9 through 10 are basically self explanatory with the exception of the reference to the "rod" in verses 3 and 4. One possible explanation of the meaning of this term was provided by the late Sidney B.Sperry as follows:

> By "stem of Jesse" Isaiah has reference to Christ, and by "rod" he has reference to a servant of Christ. But just who is the servant? A careful reading of verses 4 to 6 in the explanation convinces me that Joseph Smith is meant, for who fulfills the conditions of these verses, especially verse 6, better than he? Surely he had the lineage to which rightly belongs the priesthood (cf. D&C 86:8-11); he received the keys of the kingdom (D&C 65:2) for an ensign (standard; D&C 45:9) and for the gathering of the Lord's people in the last days (D&C 110:11) Moreover, the situation under which Moroni quoted the chapter from Isaiah favors Joseph Smith as being the "rod."[See P of GP, JS-History 1:40] He would logically be the "servant in the hands of Christ" who was to receive the instruction from Moroni and be prepared to understand the ancient prophecies concerning his mission in the latter days. (Book of Mormon Compendium, p. 223)

In this chapter, we will discuss verses 7 and 8 as it pertains to the priesthood.

Power, Authority, and Responsibility of Priesthood Holders

Elias Higbee asked two questions pertaining to Isaiah 52:1. He wanted to know what was meant by the use of the term "strength" and secondly, he asked to know what people were being addressed by Isaiah. (See D&C 113:7)

The inspired answer was given in reverse order. (See D&C113:8) The people were identified as the holders of the priesthood in the Lord's church in the last days. To "put on her strength" means to gain access to and utilize the power of the priesthood in the Lord's church in the last days.

Every ordained priesthood holder in The Church of Jesus Christ of Latter-day Saints has received authority from God to act in His name. This authority has been restored to the earth in the last days to make possible the ordinances and covenants that establish a binding relationship between God and man. There is another dimension to this priesthood. Righteous priesthood holders can have access to the power of God that will bless the lives of all the children of the Lord. Isaiah was pleading for the priesthood holders to do more than just hold the priesthood. He plead for them to serve in their priesthood callings in such a way as to be the means of providing blessings to Father's children.

There are at least two ways this priesthood power can serve as a blessing to Zion.

1. There is a strength and power to be received from Heaven through the priesthood that heals mortal bodies, rebukes evil, provides prophecy, inspirational counsel, etc.

2. Blessings will flow from Heaven through the righteous priesthood holder to the inhabitants of Zion when the priesthood holder magnifies his calling in both word and deed. To illustrate this concept, we refer to an experience of Elder Harold B. Lee. Before he was called as a General Authority of the church, he was asked by the First Presidency to assist in formulating a welfare program that would provide appropriate assisstance to the membership of the church. He described his strugglings in the formulation process as follows:

> ...I rode in my car (spring was just breaking) up to the head of City Creek Canyon into what was then called Rotary Park; and there, all by myself, I offered one of the most humble prayers of my life.
>
> There I was, just a young man in my thirties. My experience had been limited. I was born in a little country town in Idaho. I had hardly been outside the boundaries of the states of Utah and Idaho. And now to put me in a position where I was to reach out to the entire membership of the Church, worldwide, was one of the most staggering contemplations that I could imagine. How could I do it with my limited understanding?
>
> As I kneeled down, my petition was, "What kind of an organization should be set up in order to accomplish what the Presidency has assigned?" And there came to me on that glorious morning one of the most heavenly realizations of the power of the priesthood of God. It was as though something were saying to me, "There is no new organization necessary to take care of the needs of this people.

All that is necessary is to put the priesthood of God to work. There is nothing else that you need as a substitute."

With that understanding, then, and with the simple application of the power of the priesthood, the welfare program has gone forward now by leaps and bounds, overcoming obstacles that seemed impossible, until now it stands as a monument to the power of the priesthood, the like of which I could only glimpse in those days to which I have made reference. (CR, October 1972, p. 124)

Just as President Lee declared that the priesthood has been and is a moving power for good in the welfare program, so also effective priesthood holders can obtain power as they magnify their respective priesthood callings in all programs of the church. Home teachers, bishops, priesthood leaders, counselors, etc. can, through this power, be a blessing to the membership of the church. By so doing, Zion gains and puts on strength from the Lord.

Summary and Conclusion

It is a blessing and an honor to have access to and hold the priesthood of God. It is a greater blessing and honor to use that priesthood in such a way that it provides blessings and power from Heaven in the lives of Father's children.

Chapter 43

Doctrine and Covenants Section 114

Suggested Title
David W. Patten—A Man of Faith

Overview of Section Content
1. The Lord called David W. Patten to serve a mission (vs. 1)
2. Unfaithful servants will be replaced (vs. 2)

Historical Setting

Joseph Smith, Jun.

    April 17.—I received the following:

(HC, Vol. 3, p. 23)

Hyrum M. Smith and Janne M. Sjodahl

    David W. Patten is instructed to settle up his affairs and be prepared to take a mission. He was born in the State of New York, about the year 1800, and was baptized June 15th, 1832, by his brother, John Patten. He performed several missions and gradually rose to prominence. On February 15th, 1835, he was ordained an Apostle. He was absolutely fearless. His testimony was powerful and through him God performed many mighty works. In 1838, the mobbings in Missouri commenced anew, and Patten was foremost in the defense of the Saints.

(DCC, p. 739)

Sacred Truths

Introduction

On April 17, 1838, the Lord informed David W. Patten that he was to settle up his business affairs and prepare for a mission the following Spring (1839). (See D&C 114:1) However, circumstances transpired that prevented his fulfilling his mission in mortality. His mission, no doubt, was in the spirit world on the other side of the veil. In the fall of 1838, mobocracy prevailed against the saints in the vicinity of Far West, Missouri. While assisting in the defense of the saints in a battle at Crooked River, Elder Patten was mortally wounded. The events that transpired and the conversations that took place at the time of his death provide great insight to the faith of this apostle.

A Man of Faith

At a time when some of the saints in Missouri were unfaithful to their covenants, David W. Patten looms as a man who stood steadfast in his commitment to the Lord. As he lay suffering and facing imminent death, he bore strong testimony and left no doubt of his loyalty to his faith to the end. He said:

> For I feel that I have kept the faith, I have finished my course, henceforth there is laid up for me a crown, which the Lord, the righteous Judge, will give me. (LHCK, p. 214)

Anyone who faces death with a comparable faith has no fear of death. Noting that David Patten enjoyed such a blessing led Elder Heber C. Kimball to comment as follows:

> The principles of the Gospel which were so precious to him before, afforded him the support and consolation at the time of his departure, which deprived death of its sting and horror. (LHCK, p. 213)

When a person has such an abiding faith and testimony in Christ as did David Patten, the welfare of the souls of others is uppermost upon his mind. Even when the shadows of death are closing in upon him, he is mostly concerned about the spiritual needs of others. This level of spiritual stature was never more evident than when the Savior was upon the cross, or in the closing moments of the lives of Mormon, Moroni, and David W. Patten. Referring to Elder Patten's level of concern, Elder Heber C. Kimball noted:

> Speaking of those who had fallen from their steadfastness, he [David W. Patten] exclaimed, 'O that they were in my situation! For I

feel that I have kept the faith, I have finished my course, henceforth there is laid up for me a crown, which the Lord, the righteous Judge, will give me.' Speaking to his beloved wife, he said, 'whatever you do else, Oh do not deny the faith.' (LHCK, pp. 213-214)

David W. Patten was the first apostolic martyr for the Savior in this last dispensation. This was his desire. According to Wilford Woodruff, Elder Patten had requested such a privilege from the Lord:

David made known to the Prophet that he had asked the Lord to let him die the death of a martyr, at which the Prophet, greatly moved, expressed extreme sorrow, "For," said he to David "when a man of your faith asks the Lord for anything, he generally gets it." (Life of David W. Patten, p. 53, see also Wilford Woodruff, History of His Life and Labors, p. 352)

Summary and Conclusion

Perhaps the greatest tribute that could be paid to anyone is to emulate their faith and reflect their conviction of the teachings of the Savior. Such reflection of the faith of David W. Patten is worthy of our consideration. We note the words of the Savior concerning Elder Patten's status following his death: "[He is]...with me at this time,..." (D&C 124:19)

As a man of faith, he died faithful to the Savior. He sought the privilege of sealing his testimony as a martyr in the cause of the kingdom. His greatest desire was to labor for the souls of his fellowmen. Such were the Christ-like attributes of this man of faith.

Chapter 44

Doctrine and Covenants Section 115

Suggested Title

The Name of The Lord's Church—Far West, Missouri Temple

Overview of Section Content

1. Those to whom this revelation is addressed (vs. 1-3)
2. The official name of the Lord's church in this dispensation (vs. 4)
3. A paramount responsibility of a member of the Lord's church (vs. 5)
4. A purpose of a stake of Zion (vs. 6)
5. Far West, Missouri to be built up as a holy and consecrated place (vs. 7, 17)
6. Instructions pertaining to the building of the Far West Temple (vs. 8-16)
7. Additional stakes of Zion to be appointed by the Lord through His prophet (vs. 18-19)

Historical Setting

Joseph Smith, Jun.

April 26.—I received the following:

(HC, Vol. 3, p. 23)

Joseph Fielding Smith

> ...On the 26th of April the Prophet received a very important revelation of instruction for the First Presidency, the apostles, the bishop, and the members of the Church. It will be noted that the counselors named to serve with the Prophet were Sidney Rigdon and Hyrum Smith. In the fall of the year 1837, Frederick G. Williams lost his standing because he had become disaffected and Hyrum Smith was called and sustained in his stead...
>
> (CHMR, Vol. 3, p. 114)

Sacred Truths

Introduction

The year 1837 has been called by some, "The year of the Great Apostasy in Kirtland." Many saints had become disaffected with the leadership of the church. Many left the church and sought to overthrow it. Commenting on this apostasy and time of trouble, Elder Wilford Woodruff has said:

> I passed through that scene [great apostasy in Kirtland], as did some others who are now with us, and I wish now to refer to it because it is something we should lay to heart. Even Apostles took occasion to rise up and endeavored to dictate and direct the Prophet of God. Here...was a manifestation—and a very strange one, too—of the power that the devil had over the leading men whom God raised up to assist in laying the foundation of this Church and in bringing forth the Book of Mormon. Those who testified to the Book of Mormon were led away through not keeping the commandments of God and thinking that they themselves were great men. Some of them were learned men; some of them considered themselves very smart men, and they were so smart that they wanted to dictate and direct the Prophet of God. The consequence of all this was that they turned aside from the commandments of God. Some of them had been true and faithful in their labors in the ministry. I have heard Oliver Cowdery testify of the Book of Mormon by the power of God, when it seemed as if the very earth trembled under his feet. He was filled with the Holy Ghost and the power of God while he was faithful, and so were many of these men. But Oliver Cowdery yielded to the temptation of the evil one, and we may say he apostatized. So did Martin Harris, and several others connected with them. They left the Church, they turned against Joseph and they said he was a fallen prophet, and they themselves wanted to direct the Church. I have remarked that

there was a time when there were but two of the quorum of the Twelve Apostles then in [the] town of Kirtland who stood by Joseph Smith and upheld him as a Prophet, Seer and Revelator. I was not a member of that quorum at that time; I was a Seventy. Several of these men called upon me in that time of this apostasy and asked me to join them against the Prophet; the Prophet was fallen, they said. Now, I had seen enough myself of the Prophet of God and I had read enough of the revelations of God through him, to know that he was a Prophet of God and not a fallen prophet. I saw that these men were yielding to the devil, and I told them so. Said I: "You will all go to hell unless you repent. Joseph has been raised up by the power of God and to the Church and kingdom of God here on the earth, and you will fall and go to perdition unless you repent of your sins and turn from the position you are in today." A good many of them did fall. I will here name one instance. I saw one of these Apostles in the Kirtland Temple, while the Sacrament was being passed, stand in the aisle and curse the Prophet of God to his face while he was in the stand, and when the bread was passed he reached out his hand for a piece of bread and flung it into his mouth like a mad dog. He turned as black in the face almost as an African with rage and with the power of the devil. What did he do? He ate and drank damnation to himself. He did not go and hang himself, but he did go and drown himself, and the river went over his body while his spirit was cast into the pit where he ceased to have the power to curse either God or His Prophet in time or in eternity. (*Millennial Star* 57:339-340, May 30, 1895, Quoted in Roy W. Doxey, *The Latter-day Prophets and The Doctrine and Covenants,* Vol. 4, pp. 214-215)

Under these trying circumstances in Kirtland, the Prophet Joseph Smith was obliged to flee for his safety to Far West, Missouri. In a revelation given to Joseph in Far West (D&C Section 115), the Lord directed all members of the church to gather in and build up the city and area surrounding Far West. (See D&C 115:1-3, 7, 17-18) Thus, the Lord established a new gathering place for His saints at that time.

Since the temple in Kirtland had been defiled, the Lord also directed the saints to build a temple unto Him in Far West. (See D&C 115:8-16)

In this chapter we will discuss the following:

1. The name of the Lord's church
2. A purpose of a stake of Zion

The Name of The Lord's Church

When the church was officially organized on April 6, 1830, the saints clearly understood that it was to bear the name of Jesus Christ. They had learned that fact from the Book of Mormon. (See B of M, 3 Nephi 27:3-8)

Elder B. H. Roberts described the various ways by which the church had been identified during the first eight years of its existence prior to this revelation. (D&C Section 115) He wrote as follows:

> It will be observed that in verses three and four of this revelation the Lord gives to the Church its official name, "The Church of Jesus Christ of Latter-day Saints." Previous to this the Church had been called "The Church of Christ," "The Church of Jesus Christ," "The Church of God," and by a conference of Elders held at Kirtland in May 1834 (see Church History, vol. 2, pp. 62-3), it was given the name "The Church of the Latter-day Saints." All these names. however, were by this revelation brushed aside, and since then the official name given in this revelation has been recognized as the true title of the Church, though often spoke of as "The Mormon Church," the "Church of Christ," etc. The appropriateness of the title is self evident, and in it there is a beautiful recognition of the relationship both of the Lord Jesus Christ and of the Saints to the organization. It is "The Church of Jesus Christ." It is the Lord's; He owns it, He organized it. It is the Sacred Depository of His truth. It is His instrumentality for promulgating all those spiritual truths with which He would have mankind acquainted. It is also His instrumentality for the perfecting of the Saints, as well as for the work of the ministry. It is His in all these respects; but it is an institution which also belongs to the Saints. It is their refuge from the confusion and religious doubt of the world. It is their instructor in principle, doctrine, and righteousness. It is their guide in matters of faith and morals. They have a conjoint ownership in it with Jesus Christ, which ownership is beautifully recognized in the latter part of the title. "The Church of Jesus Christ of Latter-day Saints," is equivalent to the "The Church of Jesus Christ," and "The Church of the Latter-day Saints." (HC, Vol. 3, pp. 23-24)

On April 26, 1838, the Lord revealed the official name of His church. (See D&C 115:4) It is not to be understood that the Lord was giving His name to the church for the first time. Rather, the Lord standardized the way by which His name should be used to designate His church in the latter days.

Speaking of the importance of using the designated title as the Lord has given it to the church, Elder Joseph Fielding Smith taught:

> ...the Lord called the attention of all the councils to the fact that he had given the Church its name and by that name it should be called. It is a very easy matter for us to adopt some other title, apparently for convenience, as the correct name is rather lengthy.

For instance we have, in these later days, fallen into the habit of speaking of the Church as the "Mormon Church," or as "the Restored Church," setting aside the correct title. It is true that even back in the days of the Prophet the Church was at times called the "Mormon Church," but this was rare, although we were quite generally referred to as "Mormons," and we answered to that title. Since the Lord felt it important to remind the councils of the Church of its correct name and inform them that by that name it should be known in the last days, we should endeavor to carry out this commandment more nearly than it is the custom for many of us to do. (CHMR, Vol. 3, pp. 114-115)

The official name of the church bears another message of particular importance to the members as well as to the world. Elder James E. Talmage spoke of an implied meaning of the name of the church:

But I pray you consider what the real name means—"The Church of Jesus Christ of Latter-day Saints." We can understand, easily, what "Latter-day" means—modern day, this day; but what does the word "Saint" mean? By derivation, by acceptation, and by the best authority in the language, it means directly, used as an adjective, "holy," and when used as a noun, "A holy one;" and we, therefore, profess to be a body of holy men, holy women. We proclaim ourselves in the name of Jesus Christ to be the holy ones of the last days, a significant proclamation, blasphemous in the extreme if it be not justified. But that name was given us of God. We do not apologize for it, nor do we preach the doctrines of the gospel, committed to the Church to be preached, in any apologetic manner. We preach in simplicity, in humility, but not by way of apology. I agree, from my own observation, with the attitude assumed by many, referred to and described so tersely by Elder McKay. We have no apology to offer for our name nor for our membership in the Church, nor for our scriptures that have been given by revelation through the prophets of the Lord unto the people.

What should it mean to you and me, to be thus called a holy man, a holy woman? As thus applied, the term does not mean that the one who bears it is necessarily without weakness or devoid of blemish. An authorized usage of the term "holy" is that it shall apply to anyone or anything that is authoritatively appointed and set apart for exclusive service in the cause of God, and such we profess to be, set apart amongst men and nations as the people of God. However, all peoples and all nations may be one with us and may thus be set apart, if they only will, and so become entitled to bear that distinguishing name. (CR, April 1922, p. 72, Quoted in Roy W. Doxey. *The Latter-day Prophets and The Doctrine and Covenants,* Vol. 4, p. 160)

A Purpose of a Stake of Zion

The city of Zion (New Jerusalem) is to be established in Missouri. The Lord refers to this city as "the center place." (See D&C 57:2-3) Thus, stakes are referred to as stakes of Zion, or stakes of the center place. Zion and her stakes symbolize a huge tent that is held secure by the strategic locating of stakes, tied and connected with the center pole. Further, it symbolizes that protection is afforded to all who come under its protective covering.

We learn from this revelation, that the Lord will gather His people, not only in Zion but in each of the stakes thereof in order that the people may be afforded "...a defense, and...a refuge from the storm, and from wrath, when it shall be poured out without mixture upon the whole earth." (D&C 115:6; see also D&C 29:7-8; 101:20-21) President Harold B. Lee said that a purpose of a stake of Zion is:

> ...for a defense against the enemies of the Lord's work, both the seen and the unseen. (CR, April 1973, p. 5).

One reason that a stake of Zion provides such defense for the saints, is that within the stake will be found the full program of the church. President Harold B. Lee encouraged the saints all over the world to look to and be involved in their individual stakes as a source for their protection:

> Down on the coast and elsewhere, we constantly have people who are saying that somebody has said we must flee to the Rocky Mountains for safety, leave the coast, the wickedness of the world, and come to the mountains. The Lord hasn't said that you have to come here in the shadow of the Salt Lake Temple to be safe. It is not *where* you live, but *how* you live that is important. You can be just as safe in Texas, New York, Chicago, or on the coast as you can here, provided you put in gear the full program of the Church. (Address to Seminary and Institute Faculty, BYU, June 17, 1970, p. 2)

Summary and Conclusion

Every Latter-day Saint should be grateful to have his name on the membership rolls of the church that bears the name of Jesus Christ according to the designated title authorized by the Savior. Those who honor that name should live worthy of the designation given to the members of the church as "saints." These shall be gathered unto places called stakes where they can be protected from the evil onslaught of satanic forces and find refuge within the revealed programs and practices of the Lord's church.

Chapter 45

Doctrine and Covenants Section 116

Suggested Title
Adam-ondi-Ahman

Overview of Section Content
The place where Adam shall come to visit his people.

Historical Setting

Joseph Smith, Jun.

Adam-ondi-Ahman is located immediately on the north side of Grand River, in Daviess county, Missouri, about twenty-five miles north of Far West. It is situated on an elevated spot of ground, which renders the place as healthful as any part of the United States, and overlooking the river and the country round about, it is certainly a beautiful location. (HC, Vol. 3, p. 39)

Joseph Fielding Smith

...Adam-ondi-Ahman was not just a small spot resting on the brow of the hill, but this name has reference to the surrounding territory. One can obtain a beautiful view from this ancient altar overlooking the valley through which courses Grand River. It was in this valley where Adam called together the faithful of his posterity three years before his death and blessed them. (D&C 107:53) (CHMR, Vol. 3, p. 118)

Sacred Truths

Introduction

Adam-ondi-Ahman is a special and sacred place. It is the place where Adam made his abode after he and Eve left the Garden of Eden. (See D&C 117:8) Elder Bruce R. McConkie has discussed the term "Adam-ondi-Ahman" as follows:

> ...*Ahman* is one of the names by which God was known to Adam. *Adam-ondi-Ahman*, a name carried over from the pure Adamic language into English, is one for which we have not been given a revealed, literal translation. As near as we can judge—and this view comes down from the early brethren who associated with the Prophet Joseph Smith, who was the first one to use the name in this dispensation—*Adam-ondi-Ahman means the place or land of God where Adam dwelt.* (Mormon Doctrine, p. 19)

The name "Adam-ondi-Ahman" was revealed to Joseph Smith, designating the place where Adam shall come to visit his people. (See D&C Section 116)

A Sacred Place

This area is very sacred. It has a great deal of historical as well as future significance. We note three important happenings or events associated with this place:

1. A place of beginnings

It was at Adam-ondi-Ahman that the family of mortals had its beginning. It was there that mortal man learned to work by the sweat of his brow. It was there that the first mortal children were born to the first mortal parents. Mortal man first learned to communicate with his God in those valleys. It was there that Adam built an altar and began to offer righteous sacrifice. On one occasion, Joseph Smith identified the site of Adam's altar. Elder Heber C. Kimball recalled being with the prophet in Daviess County, Missouri, and described the experience as follows:

> The Prophet Joseph called upon Brother Brigham, myself and others, saying, "Brethren, come, go along with me, and I will show you something," He led us a short distance to a place where were the ruins of three altars built of stone, one above the other, and one standing a little back of the other, like unto the pulpits in the Kirtland Temple, representing the order of three grades of Priesthood; "There," said Joseph, "is the place where Adam offered up

sacrifice after he was cast out of the garden." The altar stood at the highest point of the bluff. I went and examined the place several times while I remained there. (LHCK, pp. 209-210)

The area of Adam-ondi-Ahman was the site of the first death and murder on this earth. The blessings of the Savior's atonement took on added significance there, for the members of Adam's family. The first family relationships and associations were developed. In short, this area was truly a place of beginnings.

2. A place of departure

The Lord revealed to the prophet Joseph Smith that it was at Adam-ondi-Ahman that Adam called his righteous posterity together three years prior to his death. While gathered together, the Lord appeared and ministered unto them. (See D&C 107:53-57; See also HC, Vol. 3, p.388)

Commenting on the gathering of Adam's family before Adam's departure from mortality, Elder John Taylor said:

> ...Adam, before he left the earth, gathered his people together in the Valley of Adam-ondi-ah-man, and the curtain of eternity was unfolded before him, and he gazed upon all events pertaining to his descendants, which should transpire in every subsequent period of time, and he prophesied to them. He saw the flood and its desolating influence; he saw the introduction again of a people in the days of Noah; he saw their departure from the right path. He saw Abraham, Moses and the Prophets make their appearance and witnessed the results of their acts; he saw nations rise and fall; he saw the time when Jesus would come and restore the Gospel and when he would preach that Gospel to those who perished in the days of Noah; and in fact he saw everything that should transpire upon the earth, until the winding up scene. He was acquainted with the day in which we live and the circumstances with which we are surrounded. (JD, Vol. 17, p. 372)

3. A place of return

It will be at Adam-ondi-Ahman that Adam will return to this earth prior to the ushering in of the Lord's millennial reign. A special meeting will be held at this special place. When Adam returns, he will be coming home. He will be returning to the place where he presided as a priesthood holder.

Joseph Smith explained the importance and sacred nature of this meeting:

Daniel in his seventh chapter speaks of the Ancient of Days; he means the oldest man, our Father Adam, Michael, he will call his children together and hold a council with them to prepare them for the coming of the Son of Man. He (Adam) is the father of the human family, and presides over the spirits of all men, and all that have had the keys must stand before him in this grand council. This may take place before some of us leave this stage of action. The Son of Man stands before him, and there is given him glory and dominion. Adam delivers up his stewardship to Christ, that which was delivered to him as holding the keys of the universe, but retains his standing as head of the human family. (HC, Vol. 3, pp. 386-387)

Summary and Conclusion

Adam-ondi-Ahman is a sacred place. The identity of its location was of such importance that the Lord gave a revelation pertaining to it. We have learned that the Lord's work among mortals began there. We have also learned that the Lord's millennial work will have its beginning there.

Chapter 46

Doctrine and Covenants Section 117

Suggested Title
The More Weighty Matters

Overview of Section Content
1. Counsel given to Newel K. Whitney and William Marks concerning their immediate duties (vs. 1-11)
2. Counsel and promises extended to Oliver Granger (vs. 12-15)
3. Counsel given to Kirtland saints to keep the Lord's temple holy (vs. 16)

Historical Setting

Joseph Smith, Jun.

> Also I received the following:...
> Revelation given to William Marks, Newel K. Whitney, Oliver Granger and others, at Far West, July 8, 1838...
>
> (HC, Vol.3, p. 45)

Hyrum M. Smith and Janne M. Sjodahl

> The Lord had commanded the Saints to gather and build up Far West speedily (see D&C Sec. 115:17). A company of 515 souls, known as the *Kirtland Camp*, left Kirtland on the 6th of July, 1838, for

Zion. On the 14th of September, it appears only 260 members were left, the others having been scattered "to the four winds." The camp arrived in Adam-ondi-Ahman on the 4th of October. Neither Marks, Whitney, nor Granger were members of this company. Joseph Smith at Far West had no means of knowing, at that time, who had, or who had not, left for Zion; but the Lord knew.

(DCC, p. 744)

Joseph Fielding Smith

...It is quite evident that these two brethren [Marks and Whitney] had fallen under the spell of speculation and temptation so rife in Kirtland in 1837, and which was the downfall of so many of the leading brethren of the Church. However, they had not lost their faith and when the Lord gave them this call, they proceeded to obey the command...

(CHMR, Vol. 3, p. 124)

Sacred Truths

Introduction

As noted in the Historical Setting of this chapter, Far West, Missouri, had been designated by the Lord as the gathering place for His saints at that time. (See D&C 115:17) Joseph Smith received this revelation two days after the Kirtland Camp had responded to the Lord's directive and had departed for Far West. Neither Newel K. Whitney nor William Marks had left with the camp, but had remained behind in Kirtland. Several hundred miles separated Joseph Smith in Far West from the Kirtland Camp in Ohio. There was no telephone, telegraph, or any other immediate means of communicating with the camp. Joseph had no way of knowing who was in the group. But the Lord knew. What a testimony of the prophetic calling of Joseph Smith.

In this revelation (Section 117), the Lord gave instructions to both of these brethren who were still in Kirtland. He directed them to "...settle up their business speedily and journey from the land of Kirtland...if they tarry it shall not be well with them." (D&C 117:1-2)

In His counsel to these brethren, the Lord spoke of "...the more weighty matters..." (D&C 117:8) This will be the focus of our discussion in this chapter.

The More Weighty Matters

It should be understood that the brethren mentioned in this revelation were good men. Newel K. Whitney was the Bishop in Kirtland. William Marks later served as a Stake President in Nauvoo, Illinois. However, like all of us, these men needed to be reminded that programs and properties are but means to an end. The more weighty matters should always be given priority attention. What were the more weighty matters at that time? They needed to give heed to the counsel of the Lord as given through His mouthpiece, the Lord's prophet, which was to let the Kirtland property go. There was a greater priority for them. They were to leave Kirtland and gather with and support the saints in Far West. (See D&C 117:1-8)

As an illustration of being sensitive and giving heed to the more weighty matters, Elder Harold B. Lee related the following:

> One of the General Authorities had a son working on the railroad that went up Emigration Canyon to the mines in the early days. This boy was found crushed to death under the train. He was working as a switchman. His mother had the feeling that someone had pushed him under the train and taken his life. When the services were held, she was not comforted. But after some weeks, the mother said this boy appeared to her. He said, "Mother, I've been trying to get to Father to tell him it was just an accident. I had thrown the switch and was running to catch on to the hand bars, but my foot tripped against a root at the side of a rail and I was thrown underneath the train. It was a pure accident. I've been trying to get to Father, but he's too busy at the office. I can't reach him." President McKay said, "Brethren, don't you get so busy at the office that spiritual forces are not able to reach you." (Relief Society Courses of Study, 1979-80, pp. 32-33)

Another illustration of the more weighty matters is also taught in this revelation. The Lord's people ought to be true to their covenants with the Lord. He told Bishop Whitney that he ought to be "...ashamed of the Nicolaitane band and of all their secret abominations, and all his littleness of soul before me, ...and be a bishop unto my people, saith the Lord, not in name but in deed, ..." (D&C 117:11) The Lord's reference to the Nicolaitane band is understood to mean the church members who desire to be affiliated with the church in name, but live after the manner of the world. (See Bruce R. McConkie, *Doctrinal New Testament Commentary*, Vol. 3, pp. 446-447)

The Lord's counsel to Bishop Whitney is a reminder to all of us that nothing should take precedence over the keeping of our covenants. Whatever our responsibilities are to the Lord, we ought to be faithful to them. The keeping of covenants is a more weighty matter.

Oliver Granger is an example of one who reaps the blessings of faithfulness to the more weighty matters. He was told by the Lord "...that his name shall be had in sacred remembrance from generation to generation, forever and forever, ..." (D&C 117:12) Oliver Granger lived and died as a faithful Latter-day Saint. His name was placed upon the records of the Lord's church and will so remain there forever among those who are true and faithful to the Lord.

Summary and Conclusion

The Lord teaches and instructs His people by revelation through His prophet. Those who hearken to His instruction are those who give heed to the more weighty matters.

Chapter 47

Doctrine and Covenants Section 118

Suggested Title

Twelve Apostles—Faith and Obedience

Overview of Section Content

1. Vacancies in the Quorum of Twelve Apostles are filled (vs. 1, 6)
2. Instructions to Thomas B. Marsh (vs. 2)
3. Instructions and promises to the Quorum of the Twelve Apostles (vs. 3)
4. Future mission of the Quorum of Twelve Apostles (vs. 4-5)

Historical Setting

Joseph Smith, Jun.

>   Also I received the following:
>   Revelation given at Far West, July 8, 1838, in answer to the question, Show unto us thy will O Lord concerning the Twelve...
>   (HC, Vol. 3, p. 46)

Joseph Fielding Smith

>   ...In answer to the supplication: "Show us thy will, O Lord, concerning the twelve," the Lord commanded that a conference be

285

held immediately to fill the places vacated by those who had fallen...Men were selected to fill the vacancies caused by the excommunication of William E. M'Lellin, Luke S. Johnson, John F. Boynton, and Lyman E. Johnson.

(CHMR, Vol. 3, p. 126)

Sacred Truths

Introduction

During the years 1837 and 1838 apostasy had taken deep root in the quorums of the priesthood. (See chapter 41 this volume.) The Quorum of Twelve Apostles had lost some of its members and the Prophet Joseph Smith had sought to know the will of the Lord concerning replacement members. This revelation (Section 118) is the Lord's answer to the prophet's inquiry.

In this chapter, we will discuss the following two topics:

1. Men appointed to the Quorum of Twelve Apostles
2. The Quorum of Twelve Apostles appointed to a mission

Men Appointed to the Quorum of Twelve Apostles

The Prophet Joseph Smith did not take upon himself the responsibility or liberty to appoint men to be apostles and members of the Quorum of the Twelve. Though Joseph was the presiding priesthood authority and the Lord's mouthpiece upon the earth, he did not choose or select men to occupy these positions. The reason is simple and clear. Such men were not to be representatives of Joseph Smith. They were to be special witnesses of the name of Jesus Christ. (See D&C 107:23) Only the Lord could give a man the special witness needed to adequately perform his role in such a high and sacred calling. Such a call would have to come by revelation from the Lord.

In this revelation, the Lord gave Joseph Smith the names of the men who should be called. (See D&C 118:1, 6)

One illustration of these calls having come from the Lord was given by President Wilford Woodruff, one of the four men who was called in this revelation:

> In the time of the great apostasy in Kirtland the Spirit of the Lord said to me, "Get you a partner and go to Fox Islands." I knew no more what was in Fox Islands than what was in Kolob. I went there, however, baptized a hundred and brought them up to Zion with me. It was upon that island where I received a letter from Joseph Smith, telling me that I was called by revelation to fill the place of one of the twelve who had fallen. You will see it in the Doctrine and Covenants. That thing was revealed to me before I received the letter

from Joseph Smith, but I did not feel disposed to tell it to any mortal man, for I knew it was my duty to keep such things to myself. Through all my life and labors, whenever I have been told to do anything by the Spirit of the Lord, I have always found it good to do it. I have been preserved by that power.(CR, April 1898, p.31)

The Savior is the head of His church. It is He who directs His church through a living prophet. This pattern, or order of church government, dictates the way by which men and women are called to various positions in the church as typified by the appointment of the members of the Quorum of the Twelve Apostles.

The Quorum of Twelve Apostles Appointed to a Mission

In this revelation, the Lord also directed that the members of the Quorum of Twelve should leave for a mission on April 26, the following year. (1839) They were to assemble on that date at the Far West Temple site and embark upon their mission from that place. (See D&C 118:4-5)

This is the only revelation in the Lord's book that has a day, month, and year given when certain things were to be accomplished. The significance of the Lord's setting of this date was explained by President Wilford Woodruff as follows:

> The Twelve Apostles were called by revelation to go to Far West, Caldwell county, to lay the foundation of the corner stone of the Temple. When that revelation was given this Church was in peace in Missouri. It is the only revelation that has ever been given since the organization of the Church, that I know anything about, that had day and date given with it. The Lord called the Twelve Apostles, while in this state of prosperity . . .[to go on a mission April 26, 1839] to go to Far West to lay the corner stone of the Temple; and from there to take their departure to England to preach the Gospel. Previous to the arrival of that period the whole Church was driven out of the State of Missouri, and it was as much as a man's life was worth to be found in the State if it was known that he was a Latter-day Saint; and especially was this the case with the Twelve . . .
>
> The general feeling in the Church, so far as I know, was that, under the circumstances, it was impossible to accomplish the work; and the Lord would accept the will for the deed. This was the feeling of Father Smith, the father of the Prophet. Joseph was not with us, he was in chains in Missouri, for his religion. When President Young asked the question of the Twelve, "Brethren, what will you do about this? the reply was, "The Lord has spoken and it is for us to obey."

We felt that the Lord God had given the commandment and we had faith to go forward and accomplish it, feeling that it was His business whether we lived or died in its accomplishment...

We performed that work by faith, and the Lord blessed us in doing it.

...We had to travel by faith in order to fulfill the mission to which we had been called by revelation. But the Lord sustained us; He did not forsake us. (JD, Vol. 13, pp. 159-160)

On another occasion, President Woodruff explained further:

On the 18th of April, 1839, I took into my wagon Brigham Young and Orson Pratt; Father Cutler took into his wagon John Taylor and George A. Smith, and we started for Far West. On the way we met John E. Page, who was going with his family to Quincy, Illinois. His wagon had turned over, and when we met him he was trying to gather up with his hands a barrel of soft soap. We helped him with his wagon. He then drove into the valley below, left his wagon, and accompanied us on our way. On the night of the 25th of April we arrived at Far West, and spent the night at the home of Morris Phelps. He had been taken a prisoner by the mob, and was still in prison.

On the morning of the 26th of April, 1839, notwithstanding the threats of our enemies that the revelation which was to be fulfilled this day should not be fulfilled; notwithstanding ten thousand of the Saints had been driven out of the state by the edict of the governor; and notwithstanding the Prophet Joseph and his brother Hyrum Smith, with other leading men, were in the hands of our enemies in chains and in prison, we moved on to the Temple grounds in the city of Far West, held a council, and fulfilled the revelation and commandment given to us. We also excommunicated from the Church thirty-one persons who had apostatized and become its enemies. The 'Mission of the Twelve' was sung, and we repaired to the southeast corner of the Temple ground, where, with the assistance of Elder Alpheus Cutler, the master workman of the building committee, we laid the southeast chief cornerstone of the Temple, according to revelation. [See D&C 115:8-11] There were present of the Twelve Apostles: Brigham Young, Heber C. Kimball, Orson Pratt, John E. Page, and John Taylor; they proceeded to ordain Wilford Woodruff and George A. Smith to the apostleship.

Darwin Chase and Norman Shearer, who had just been liberated from Richmond prison, were then ordained to the office of seventy...

Bidding good-by to this small remnant of the Saints who remained on the Temple ground to see us fulfill the revelation and commandment of God, we turned our backs on Far West, Missouri, and returned to Illinois. We had accomplished the mission without a dog moving his tongue at us, or any man saying, "Why do ye so?" We crossed the Mississippi river on the steam ferry, entered Quincy on the 2nd of May, and all of us had the joy of reaching our families once more in peace and safety. Thus the word of god was complied with.

While on our way to fulfill the revelation, Joseph, the Prophet and his companions in chains were liberated, through the blessings of God, from their enemies and prison, and passed us. We were not far distant from each other, but neither party knew it at the time. They were making their way to their families in Illinois, while we were traveling to Far West into the midst of our enemies; so they came home to their families and friends before our return. (Wilford Woodruff—*History of his life and labors*, pp. 101-102)

The history surrounding this event is exciting to teach and exciting to hear. However, if we do not learn the spiritual message that will encourage lives to change and to become more Christ-like, we have only learned history for history's sake.

What is the spiritual message and how can it be applied to our lives today? The following are suggestions:

1. *The Apostles' Faith and Obedience*

We are reminded of the spirit and faith that prevailed with these brethren as we remember the words of President Wilford Woodruff:

The Lord has spoken and it is for us to obey. We felt that the Lord had given the commandment and we had faith to go forward and accomplish it, feeling that it was his business whether we lived or died in its accomplishment. (JD, Vol. 13, p. 159)

How convenient was it, at that time, for the Twelve to leave on their mission? The saints had just been driven from the state of Missouri and were desperate for food and shelter. Yet under those circumstances, faith and obedience took precedence.

Someday it may be our privilege to shake the hands of these brethren and thank them for their faith and obedience in responding to the call under such trying circumstances. It is because of these brethren that many of us are in The Church of Jesus Christ today. Their response to the Savior's command opened gospel doors to European nations. As a result of that effort many Latter-day Saints trace their membership in this great kingdom to a convert from those countries.

2. Our Faith, Obedience

Is our relationship with Jesus Christ sufficient that we, also, can say, "The Lord God has spoken it and it is for us to obey . . . it was his business whether we lived or died in its accomplishment."? (JD, Vol. 13, p. 159)

Will we serve the Lord on a mission at the time we are called? Are we willing to support a missionary son or daughter? Will we obey the Lord's standard in dress and grooming? Will we cease our Sunday shopping and recreational activities? Someday might our own sons and daughters say to us, "Thank you, father and mother, for your faith and obedience. I know that it was not convenient for you all the time but because of you I am in The Church of Jesus Christ today."

3. God's Commandments

. . .I will go and do the things which the Lord hath commanded, for I know that the Lord giveth no commandments unto the children of men, save he shall prepare a way for them that they may accomplish the thing which he commandeth them. (B of M, 1 Nephi 3:7)

Summary and Conclusion

No one in the kingdom of God is indispensable, no one is forced to keep covenants in the kingdom. Those not willing to keep their covenants will be replaced. The Lord's work will go forward under His direction through His living prophet.

Those who choose to remain faithful must exercise their faith unto obedience. Obedience is a sign of divine ownership.

Chapter 48

Doctrine and Covenants Sections 119 and 120

Suggested Titles

Section 119—The Lord's Law of Tithing
Section 120—Disbursement of Tithing Funds

Overview of Section Content

Section 119

1. Surplus property and the law of tithing (vs. 1-4)
2. Observance of the law of tithing required of all members of the Lord's church (vs. 5-7)

Section 120

The Lord appoints a council to be responsible for the disbursement of tithing funds.

Historical Setting

Section 119

Joseph Smith, Jun.

...I inquired of the Lord, "O Lord! Show unto thy servant how much thou requirest of the properties of thy people for a tithing," and received the following answer, . . .

(HC, Vol. 3, p. 44)

Joseph Fielding Smith

. . .July 8, 1838, the Prophet prayed to the Lord saying: "O Lord! Show unto thy servant how much thou requirest of the properties of thy people for a tithing," and he received a revelation known as Section 119. The Lord had given to the Church the law of consecration and had called upon the members, principally the official members, to enter into a covenant that could not be broken and to be everlasting in which they were to consecrate their properties and receive stewardships, for this is the law of the celestial kingdom. Many of those who entered into this solemn covenant broke it and by so doing brought upon their heads, and the heads of their brethren and sisters, dire punishment and persecution. This celestial law of necessity was thereupon withdrawn for the time, or until the time of the redemption of Zion. While suffering intensely because of their debts and lack of means to meet their obligations, Joseph Smith and Oliver Cowdery, November 29, 1834, in solemn prayer promised the Lord that they would give one tenth of all that the Lord should give unto them, as an offering to be bestowed upon the poor; they also prayed that their children, and children's children after them should obey this law. (DHC, 2:174-5.) Now, however, it became necessary for the law to be given to the whole Church so the Prophet prayed for instruction. The answer they received in the revelation . . .[Section 119]

(CHMR, Vol. 3, pp. 119-120)

Hyrum M. Smith and Janne M. Sjodahl

The law of tithing, as now understood, had not been given to the Church previous to this Revelation. The term "tithing" in the prayer quoted in the headlines, and in previous Revelations (64:23; 85:3; 97:11), is, therefore, synonymous with "free-will offering," or "contribution" to the Church funds. The question presented in the petition to the Almighty was not how much a tenth part of the property of the people amounted to, but how much of that property He required for sacred purposes. The answer was this Revelation on the Law of Tithing . . .

(DCC, p. 749)

Section 120

Joseph Smith, Jun.

    Also I received the following:
    Revelation, given July 8, 1838, making known the disposition of the properties tithed as named in the preceding revelation. [Section 119].

(HC, Vol. 3, p. 44)

Joseph Fielding Smith

    The same day, July 8, 1838, the Prophet inquired again, and received the following commandment in relation to the distributing of the tithing: . . .

(CHMR, Vol. 3, p. 121)

Sacred Truths

Introduction

    We will discuss these two sections together since they both pertain to the law of tithing.
    As noted in the Historical Setting of this chapter, Joseph Smith inquired of the Lord as to what was expected of the saints pertaining to their tithing responsibilities.
    The question might be asked: "Why would the Prophet Joseph Smith inquire of the Lord for guidance on this matter?" One answer might be as follows: Since the year 1831, the saints had been governed by the law of consecration as a means of taking care of their temporal necessities. The history reveals that collectively the saints had failed to live this law. Having been driven from Jackson County, Missouri, as well as Kirtland, Ohio, they were assembled in Far West, seeking to know the Lord's will pertaining to the disposition of their properties. These two revelations (Sections 119 and 120) constitute the Lord's response to their inquiries.
    In this chapter we will discuss the following:

1. A tithe
2. Disbursement of tithes
3. Tithing and Zion

A Tithe

    The Lord informed the Prophet Joseph Smith that, at that time, the saints were to place their surplus property that had accrued under the law of consecration, into the hands of the Bishop. (See D&C 119:1) Then, they were to pay "...one-tenth of all their interest annually;..." (D&C 119:4)

1. Surplus property

What was meant by "surplus"? Elder Franklin D. Richards, of the Quorum of Twelve Apostles, has explained as follows:

> Let us consider for a moment this word "surplus." What does it mean when applied to a man and his property? Surplus cannot mean that which is indispensably necessary for any given purpose, but what remains after supplying what is needed for that purpose. Is not the first and most necessary use of a man's property that he feed, clothe and provide a home for himself and family? This appears to be the great leading objects for which we labor to acquire means, and as, until the time that this revelation was given, all public works and raising of all public funds had been by consecration, was not "surplus property," that which was over and above a comfortable and necessary subsistence? In the light of what had transpired and of subsequent events, what else could it mean? Can we take any other view of it when we consider the circumstances under which it was given in Far West in July, 1838?
>
> (JD, Vol. 23, p. 313)

2. Tithing

What is the tithe? Elder Howard W. Hunter, of the Quorum of Twelve Apostles, explained as follows:

> The law is simply stated as "one-tenth of all their interest." Interest means profit, compensation, increase. It is the wage of one employed, the profit from the operation of a business, the increase of one who grows or produces, or the income to a person from any other source. The Lord said it is a standing law "forever" as it has been in the past.
>
> (CR, April 1964, p. 35)

Disbursement of Tithes

The proper handling of the tithes was of such importance that the Lord's prophet sought for divine guidance on the matter. In answer to this inquiry, the Lord revealed that the disbursement of tithing funds was to be accomplished by a priesthood council. This council was to consist of the First Presidency, the Presiding Bishopric, and the Quorum of Twelve Apostles. (See D&C Section 120) The Lord had previously revealed some of the purposes for which tithing funds should be used. (See D&C 119:2)

Tithing and Zion

One meaning of the word "Zion" is "the pure in heart." (D&C 97:21) One identifying characteristic of a person who is pure in heart is that he is a full tithe-payer. This is one of the requirements for those who would obtain an inheritance in the Lord's Zion and her stakes. (See D&C 119:5-7) Stressing the need for Latter-day Saints to be honest before the Lord in the payment of their tithes, President Joseph F. Smith taught:

> By this principle the loyalty of the people of this Church shall be put to the test. By this principle it shall be known who is for the kingdom of God and who is against it. By this principle it shall be seen whose hearts are set on doing the will of God and keeping His commandments, thereby sanctifying the land of Zion unto God, and who are opposed to this principle and have cut themselves off from the blessings of Zion. There is a great deal of importance connected with this principle, for by it it shall be known whether we are faithful or unfaithful. In this respect it is as essential as faith in God, as repentance of sin, as baptism for the remission of sin, or as the laying on of hands for the gift of the Holy Ghost.
> (CR, April 1900, p. 47)

Summary and Conclusion

The things of the earth are needed for man's comfort and welfare. They are essential to his survival. However, the acquisition of temporal things must not become the object of his existence. It is God who made the earth and all things therein available to man. Payment of tithes represents man's recognition of the true provider of all things and the source to which he looks for his sustenance. Integrity with this law is one means by which men's hearts remain pure.

Chapter 49

Doctrine and Covenants Sections 121, 122, 123

Suggested Titles

Section 121—Constitution of the Priesthood
Section 122—Why Suffering?
Section 123—Anti-Christ Literature and Works

Overview of Section Content

Section 121

1. The prophet's plea for the suffering saints (vs. 1-6)
2. Peace and promises extended to the Prophet Joseph Smith (vs. 7-10)
3. Judgments await those who assail the work of God (vs. 11-25)
4. Great knowledge to be revealed to the faithful saints (vs. 26-33)
5. Constitution of the priesthood (vs. 34-46)

Section 122

1. The Lord and His people to stand by Joseph Smith forever (vs. 1-4)
2. Blessings are to be derived from persecution and suffering (vs. 5-7)
3. The extent of the suffering of the Son of Man (vs. 8)
4. Promises extended to the Prophet Joseph Smith (vs. 9)

Section 123

1. The saints to gather libelous publications and record sufferings and abuses from enemies (vs. 1-5)
2. Several purposes for gathering libelous publications and recording sufferings and abuses from enemies (vs. 6-15)
3. Mans efforts—God's power (vs. 16-17)

Historical Setting

Joseph Smith, Jun.

> The Prophet's Epistle to the Church, Written in Liberty Prison.
> Liberty Jail, Clay County, Missouri
> March 25, 1839.
>
> To the Church of Latter-day Saints at Quincy, Illinois, and Scattered Abroad, and to Bishop Partridge in Particular: ...
> (HC, Vol. 3, p. 289)

Joseph Fielding Smith

...While the Prophet Joseph Smith and his companions, Hyrum Smith, Lyman Wight, Caleb Baldwin, Alexander McRae and part of the time, Sidney Rigdon, were confined in Liberty jail awaiting trial on false charges, and suffering unspeakable abuse from the wicked and filthy guards who attended them, they were, notwithstanding all the abuse, permitted to see some of their friends occasionally. These friends who were permitted to come to the jail were also permitted at times to bring letters from the prisoner's families. They were also able to forward communications in this way to their friends. One of these communications from the Prophet to the Church at Quincy—for the Saints had been driven from Missouri—was written March 25, 1839, and was signed by all of his companions. This is one of the greatest letters that was ever penned by the hand of man. In fact it was the result of humble inspiration. It is a prayer and a prophecy and an answer by revelation from the Lord. None other but a noble soul filled with the spirit of love of Christ could have written such a letter. Considering the fact that these prisoners had been confined several months; were fed on food at times not fit for a pig, and at times impregnated with poison and once being offered human flesh, evidently from the body of one of their brethren, it is no wonder that the Prophet cried out in the

anguish of his soul for relief. Yet, in his earnest pleading, there breathed a spirit of tolerance and love for his fellow men . . .
(CHMR, Vol. 3, pp. 196-197)

Hyrum M. Smith and Janne M. Sjodahl

In the *History of the Church* (Vol. III, pp. 289-305), an epistle is found, addressed "to the Church of Latter-day Saints at Quincy, Ill., and Scattered Abroad, and to Bishop Partridge in Particular." It is signed by Joseph Smith, Jr., Hyrum Smith, Lyman Wight, Caleb Baldwin, and Alexander McRae, and dated, "Liberty Jail, Clay County, Missouri, March 25, 1839." The letter, it appears, was commenced on the 20th and finished on the 25th. Sections 121, 122, and 123 are extracts from this communication . . .
(DCC, p. 753)

Sacred Truths

Introduction

These three sections of the Doctrine and Covenants (121, 122, 123) are extracts from a letter written by Joseph Smith from a jail in Liberty, Missouri.

In this chapter we will discuss the contents of these three sections under the following categories:

1. The prophet's plea
2. The Lord's answer

The Prophet's Plea

As one reads the prophet's plea unto the Lord, one cannot help but be impressed with the spiritual stature of the Prophet Joseph Smith. He knew there was but one source to which he might go in seeking help for the suffering saints in Missouri. It is clear that Joseph had plead with the Lord before and had received divine assistance from Him on other occasions.

It is significant that Joseph did not question the Lord as to why he and the saints were being subjected to affliction and persecution. His spiritual maturity provided contentment that the Lord's will would be done. Instead, Joseph simply asked, "How long?" (See D&C 121:1-6)

It is a common thing for people who are struggling for spiritual maturity to wonder why they must experience the trials and tribulations that come from time to time. However, when people are able to place their total confidence and trust in the Lord, their faith provides sufficient strength for the moment and their concern is expressed in the question, "O Lord, how long?"

The Lord's Answer

The remaining portions of these three sections constitute the Lord's answer to Joseph's plea. Contained within these inspired verses are many subjects. For convenience of discussion we have selected and grouped the following:

1. Promises to Joseph Smith
2. Why suffering
3. The Lord's anointed
4. Constitution of the priesthood
5. Enemies to the Lord's work

1. *Promises to Joseph Smith* (See D&C 121:7-9, 26-33; 122:1-3, 9)

Within these verses, there are many promises extended to the prophet. It would be well to remember that it was the Savior who extended these promises. Many have been fulfilled, and others will yet come to pass in the process of time. Witnessing the fulfillment of any of these promises is further testimony that Joseph Smith received revelation from the Lord.

A sampling of these promises affirms the above conclusion. To illustrate:

a. Under the sentence of death, the prophet was promised that his friends would greet him again "...with warm hearts and friendly hands." (D&C 121:9) And where were his friends in March 1839? They had been driven from the state of Missouri and had mostly settled in Illinois. Therefore, in order for Joseph to be greeted by his friends, such a reunion would have to be somewhere besides in a jail in Missouri. Joseph was thereby assured of his release from prison and a reuniting with the saints. This assurance was recorded in the letter that was sent to the scattered saints some time before Joseph's release from the Liberty jail. As an additional witness of the divine source of this promise, Elder Parley P. Pratt recorded the following conversation that took place the morning Joseph Smith and the other prisoners were placed in custody to be transported to a Missouri jail:

> As we arose and commenced our march on the morning of the 3rd of November, Joseph Smith spoke to me and the other prisoners, in a low, but cheerful and confidential tone; said he: "Be of good cheer, brethren; the word of the Lord came to me last night that our lives should be given us, and that whatever we may suffer during

this captivity, not one of our lives should be taken." Of this prophecy I testify in the name of the Lord, and, though spoken in secret, its public fulfillment and the miraculous escape of each one of us is too notorious to need my testimony. (APPP, p. 192)

b. Another promise extended to the prophet was that "The ends of the earth shall inquire after thy name, . . ." (D&C 122:1) This promise was made to a man in an obscure dungeon in a little-known country town on the western frontier of the United States. Its fulfillment is a marvel to behold. Since that day in 1839, untold millions of people, representing the nations of the world, have inquired of his name. Their inquiries have not only been made to the church over which he presided, but the inquiries have also been made to the God of Heaven who directed Joseph Smith in the work of the Lord upon the earth.

c. Still further, the Lord promised Joseph Smith " . . .the pure in heart, and the wise, and the noble, and the virtuous, shall seek counsel, and authority, and blessings constantly from under thy hand." (D&C 122:2) Joseph Smith was the mortal vessel through whom the Lord restored His priesthood making possible the restoration of His church and kingdom. Thus, the counsel, the authority, and the blessings that are bestowed upon the Lord's saints today, are a result of the Lord's work that began through the Prophet Joseph Smith. The Lord said "constantly," and it is literally being fulfilled today. There is not a single 24-hour period, but what someone, somewhere on the earth, is seeking counsel, authority, or blessings from the Lord's authorized representatives in His church. The temples, the missionaries, local and general authorities, parents and all who are empowered to represent the Lord are a constant source of spiritual power and assistance to the people of the earth. These blessings flow throughout the world in this dispensation as a result of that which the Lord restored through the Prophet Joseph Smith.

2. *Why suffering* (See D&C 121:10; 122:4-8)

There is a common tendency among mortals who experience periods of crisis and stress to conclude that they have a monopoly on trials and tribulations. Many feel their situation is unjust compared to others in the world.

The Lord inspired Joseph to write some great insights which afford us divine counsel in crises which can be beneficial to both our physical and spiritual well-being. Notice the strength and power that can come from applying the following principles contained in this inspired letter:

a. Adversities of mortality occupy but a small moment of eternity. (See D&C 121:7) When we wonder "how long," we are comforted in knowing it won't be too long. It won't be a longer time than the individual can endure.

b. Do more than just endure adversity—endure it well. (See D&C 121:8) All who face adversity will endure—they really have no choice. But to endure it well is to demonstrate and develop personal strength and discipline in the face of opposition. By so doing, the adversity, or trial, becomes a useful experience that serves as an opportunity for our personal growth and thus, it is for our good. (See D&C 122:7)

c. Our tribulations may seem monumental until we compare them with some others. Joseph Smith's trials in the Missouri prison were horrendous in the eyes of mortal men. Yet, even under these difficult circumstances, the Savior reminded His prophet that others may have suffered more. The Lord told Joseph: "thy friends do stand by thee, . . .Thou art not yet as Job; thy friends do not contend against thee, neither charge thee with transgression, as they did Job." (D&C 121:9-10)

d. A faithful Latter-day Saint is never really alone. The Lord will be with the righteous forever. The Lord has suffered more than any of us and He understands our experiences. We always have access to His understanding and to His comforting power and sustaining influence through His spirit. (See D&C 122:8-9; see also D&C 62:1; B of M, Alma 36:3)

e. Avoid the spirit of bitterness. The Lord's counsel is " . . .let us cheerfully do all things that lie in our power; and then may we stand still, with the utmost assurance, to see the salvation of God, and for his arm to be revealed." (D&C 123:17)

The need to follow the Lord's counsel in times of crises was emphasized and illustrated by Elder Orson F. Whitney as follows:

> It remained for the Prophet Joseph Smith to . . .set forth the why and wherefore of human suffering; and in revealing it he gave us a strength and power to endure that we did not before possess. For when men know why they suffer, and realize that it is for a good and wise purpose, they can bear it much better than they can in ignorance . . .
>
> It is for our development, our purification, our growth, our education and advancement, that we buffet the fierce waves of sorrow and misfortune; and we shall be all the stronger and better when we have swum the flood and stand upon the farther shore. . . .
>
> When we want counsel and comfort, we do not go to children, nor to those who know nothing but pleasure and self-gratification. We go to men and women of thought and sympathy, men and women who have suffered themselves and can give us the comfort that we need. Is not this God's purpose in causing [allowing] his children to suffer? He wants them to become more like himself. God has suffered far more than man ever did or ever will, and is therefore the great source of sympathy and consolation: "Who are these

arrayed in white, nearest to the throne of God?" asked John the Apostle, wrapt in his mighty vision. The answer was: "These are they who have come up through great tribulation, and washed their robes and made them white in the blood of the Lamb."

There is always a blessing in sorrow and humiliation. They who escape these things are not the fortunate ones. "Whom God loveth he chasteneth." When he desires to make a great man he takes a little street waif, or a boy in the backwoods, such as Lincoln or Joseph Smith, and brings him up through hardship and privation to be the grand and successful leader of a people. Flowers shed most of their perfume when they are crushed. Men and women have to suffer just so much in order to bring out the best that is in them. (IE, Vol. 22, pp. 5-7, November 1918)

3. *The Lord's anointed* (See D&C 121:11-25)

What mortal man may think of the Lord's anointed (authorized leaders of the Lord's church) is of no consequence when compared with the Lord's opinion of His anointed. Unto those who would cast censure upon His chosen leaders and remain unrepentant, the Lord has decreed a curse. Because of their disobedient attitude and behavior, they shall be cut off from the priesthood and its ordinances, despised by their colleagues in unrighteousness, and shall not escape the damnation of hell. (See D&C 121:16-23)

One illustration of loyalty to the Lord's anointed is graphically portrayed in an episode in the life of a faithful Latter-day saint mother:

> John Andreas Widtsoe was only 6, and his brother two months old, when his father died in 1878. His mother, Anna Karine Gaarden Widtsoe, received the gospel in her native Norway and then emigrated to Logan, Utah.
>
> There she raised her two boys, educated them and taught them the ways of the Lord. John was later to become an apostle of the Lord Jesus Christ.
>
> Elder John A. Widtsoe later wrote of his mother's devotion to the gospel and to the leaders of the Church.
>
> "About 1896," Elder Widtsoe wrote, "Moses Thatcher, an apostle of the Church, was suspended from service in the Quorum of the Twelve Apostles. Brother Thatcher, a man of unusual gifts and most charming personality, was very popular in his home town of Logan, as throughout the Church. His suspension caused widespread discussion, and many of his intimate Logan friends felt that he had been treated unjustly, and took his side against the action of the authorities of the Church.

"The temporary upheaval was tempestuous. Men's feelings ran high. While the excitement was at its height, two of the elders called at the Widtsoe home as ward teachers. The widow's two sons were home, and the whole family assembled to be instructed by the visiting teachers.

"Soon the visitors began to comment on the 'Thatcher episode,' as it was called, and explained how unjustly Brother Thatcher had been treated. The widow answered not a word, but there was a gathering storm in her stern eyes and high-held head.

"After some minutes of listening to the visitors find fault with the Quorum of the Twelve with respect to Brother Thatcher, she slowly rose from her chair and walked to the entrance door. She threw it wide open. With eyes now blazing she turned to the two brethren and said: 'There is the door. I want you to leave this house instantly. I will not permit anyone in this house to revile the authorities of the Church, men laboring under divine inspiration. Nor do I wish such things spoken before my sons whom I have taught to love the leaders of the Church. And don't come back until you come in the right spirit to teach us the gospel. Here is the door. Now, go!'

"In defense of the gospel, Sister Widtsoe knew no fear." (Church News, April 16, 1977, Editorial page)

It would be well for all members of the Lord's church to give heed to the counsel and teachings of Elder Harold B. Lee. He said:

> In the Master's Sermon on the Mount, he made another very expressive declaration when he said:
>
> "Blessed are the pure in heart: for they shall see God."
>
> You will remember that in his lifetime there were some who saw him only as the son of the carpenter. There were some who said that because of his words he was drunken with strong wine—that he was a winebibber. There were some who even thought him to be possessed of devils. Only those who were the pure in heart saw him as the Son of God.
>
> So it is today. There are some who look upon the leaders of this Church and God's anointed as men who are possessed of selfish motives. By them the words of our leaders are always twisted to try to bring a snare to the work of the Lord. Mark well those who speak evil of the Lord's anointed for they speak from impure hearts. Only the "pure in heart" see the "God" or the divine in man and accept our leaders and accept them as prophets of the Living God. (CR, October 1947, pp. 66-67)

4. Constitution of the priesthood (See D&C 121:34-46)

Joseph Smith and his brethren were in jail in Liberty, Missouri because of their enemies. Some of those enemies were members of the church who were also holders of the priesthood. In this inspired letter, Joseph Smith discussed the proper use of priesthood. It contained a warning to those who misused the priesthood or who were untrue to the principles which accompany the bestowal of the Lord's power.

The inspired explanation given of these priesthood principles has been referred to by some as the constitution of the Priesthood. In these verses we are taught that "...there are many called, but few are chosen." (D&C 121:34) There are many brethren who are called and given the rights or authority of the priesthood, but few of them are also chosen for an inheritance of eternal life. Those who are to receive eternal lives must first learn and apply the fundamental principles upon which the priesthood must function.

A man who has been given the authority of the priesthood has the right of access to the powers of God in the heavens. However, he can only obtain those heavenly powers when he complies with revealed principles of righteousness and keeps himself worthy to be the vessel through whom the powers can be utilized. (See D&C 121:36)

This concept, as described above, together with some principles of righteousness as contained in this revelation is illustrated in the accompanying diagram:

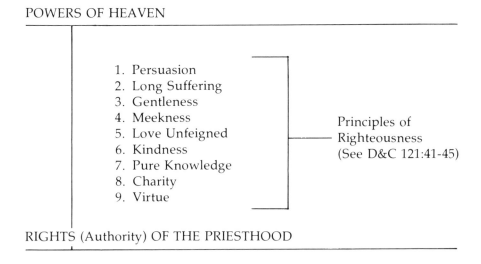

POWERS OF HEAVEN

1. Persuasion
2. Long Suffering
3. Gentleness
4. Meekness
5. Love Unfeigned
6. Kindness
7. Pure Knowledge
8. Charity
9. Virtue

Principles of Righteousness (See D&C 121:41-45)

RIGHTS (Authority) OF THE PRIESTHOOD

Priesthood holders whose lives are in harmony with principles of righteousness have power in their priesthood and have claim upon the promises of the Lord as follows: (See D&C 121:45-46)

a. Confidence in the presence of God

When a righteous elder of the priesthood presents himself before the Lord in the temple to have his worthy sweetheart sealed to him, he has confidence that such sealing will be fulfilled. This confidence is a result of the application of principles of righteousness in his previous life. Or, when a worthy elder administers a blessing to the sick, he will have the confidence that the blessing pronounced is a reflection of the mind and will of the Lord.

b. Doctrine of the priesthood

The doctrine of the priesthood has been explained as follows:

> What, then, is the doctrine of the priesthood?
> It is the doctrine that those who hold this power and authority will be chosen for an inheritance of eternal life if they exercise their priesthood upon principles of righteousness; if they walk in the light; if they keep the commandments; if they put first in their lives the things of God's kingdom and let temporal concerns take a secondary place; if they serve in the kingdom with an eye single to the glory of God.
> It is the doctrine that even though men have the rights of the priesthood conferred upon them, they shall not reap its eternal blessings if they use it for unrighteous purposes; if they commit sin; if the things of this world take pre-eminence in their lives over the things of the Spirit. It is a fearful thing to contemplate this priesthood truth: *Behold, many are called to the priesthood, and few are chosen for eternal life.* (IE, February 1961, p. 115)

c. The Holy Ghost–A constant companion

Who could ask for a better companionship than to have a member of the Godhead constantly with him?

d. An eternal dominion

The power promised to a righteous priesthood holder in mortality will continue with him into eternity. He will attain unto eternal life and preside in righteousness forever and ever.

5. Enemies to the Lord's Work (See D&C 123:1-13)

The saints were counseled to gather information pertaining to the abuses that were inflicted upon them by their enemies in Missouri. (See

D&C 123:1-5) The purposes for gathering such information were revealed by the Lord as follows: (See D&C 123:6-13)

a. That they might publish such information to the heads of government and to all the world.

b. That the nation might be left without excuse.

c. That the saints might be justified in calling upon the Lord to send forth His power in their behalf.

d. That the saints might fulfill their duty before the Lord, angels, wives, children, and the rising generation.

Whatever total use the Lord may make of this information in the future, we do not know. We do know it was essential to the Lord's plans. The prophet counseled as follows:

> Let no man count them as small things; for there is much which lieth in futurity, pertaining to the saints, which depends upon these things. (D&C 123:15)

Summary and Conclusion

The enemies of the Lord's church endeavored to stop the Lord's work by placing His prophet in prison. They placed him beyond the reach of the members of the church when they drove the saints from the state of Missouri. One thing they could not do—they could not place him beyond the reach of his God. Revelation from the Heavens continued to flow unto the prophet in prison, thus making his place of confinement a place of inspiration, a sanctuary for truth. The efforts of the Lord's enemies were to no avail. They were powerless to stop the work of the Lord's kingdom. Well did the prophet write:

> How long can rolling waters remain impure? What power shall stay the heavens? As well might man stretch forth his puny arm to stop the Missouri river in its decreed course, or to turn it up stream, as to hinder the Almighty from pouring down knowledge from heaven upon the heads of the Latter-day Saints. (D&C 121:33)

Chapter 50

Doctrine & Covenants Section 124

Suggested Title
Nauvoo Temple—Being Accepted of the Lord

Overview of Section Content
1. A solemn proclamation of the gospel to be made to all rulers of the earth (vs. 1-11)
2. Special assignments, counsel, and acknowledgements given to several brethren (vs. 12-21)
3. The Nauvoo House (vs. 22-24, 56-83, 119-122)
4. The saints are commanded to build a temple at Nauvoo (vs. 25-44)
5. The saints admonished to give heed to the Lord and His servants (vs. 45-48)
6. Works accepted by the Lord (vs. 49-55)
7. Instructions, assignments, and callings extended to several brethren (vs. 84-118)
8. Officers of the priesthood named (vs. 123-145)

Historical Setting

Joseph Smith, Jun.

   I received the following revelation:

Revelation given to Joseph Smith at Nauvoo, January 19th, 1841 . . .

(HC, Vol. 4, p. 274)

Joseph Fielding Smith

. . .Almost as soon as the Prophet and his brethren arrived in Nauvoo from their imprisonment and persecutions in Missouri, the Lord gave instructions that a temple should be built in Nauvoo. By this time the fulness of the doctrine of salvation for the dead had been revealed and the importance of performing ordinances for the dead was impressed upon the mind of the Prophet and by him, in discourses and letter, upon the saints. No doubt Joseph Smith had been praying to the Lord on this subject, and this revelation (Sec. 124) is an answer to his pleadings . . .(CHMR, Vol. 4, pp. 79-80)

Sacred Truths

Introduction

After the saints were driven from the state of Missouri, the main body of them settled in the state of Illinois. Eventually, they were able to purchase land in the area of Commerce, Illinois which was later named Nauvoo. The saints worked diligently to build homes and a community where they could regroup, rebuild, and reestablish themselves. While engaged in this endeavor, the Lord gave this revelation to the Prophet Joseph Smith.

In this revelation the Lord gave instructions on a variety of subjects. Among other things, the Lord reaffirmed the need for a temple, a full complement of church authorities, and stressed the need for the saints to follow the Lord's authorized leaders and obey counsel, that their works might be acceptable before Him.

In this chapter, we will discuss the following topics:

1. A solemn proclamation of the gospel
2. The Nauvoo house
3. The Nauvoo temple
4. Being accepted of the Lord
5. The Lord's leaders

A Solemn Proclamation of the Gospel

Joseph Smith was directed by the Lord to make a solemn proclamation of the gospel. (See D&C 124:1-11) This announcement of the restored gospel and the establishment of the Lord's kingdom was to be sent to the leaders of the nations of the world. The world's people were to be advised of the great advent of the gospel restoration. The Prophet Joseph and others worked on the preparation of this document from time to time until the martyrdom in June, 1844. Following the prophet's death, the Quorum of Twelve Apostles proceeded with the preparation of the proclamation and published it on April 6, 1845. It was then sent to those addressed in the revelation.

President Ezra Taft Benson referred to this proclamation and quoted the first portion thereof. This brief quotation provides an insight to the message and spirit of the proclamation:

> In the spirit of this divine direction, on the sixth day of April 1845, and shortly after the Prophet Joseph Smith and his brother Hyrum had mingled their blood with that of the other martyrs of true religion, the Council of the Twelve made such a proclamation. They address it:
>
> "To all the Kings of the World;
> To the President of the United States of America;
> To the Governors of the several States;
> And to the Rulers and People of all Nations:"
>
> In it they said:
> "Know ye:
> "That the kingdom of God has come: as has been predicted by ancient prophets, and prayed for in all ages; even that kingdom which shall fill the whole earth, and shall stand for ever.
>
> "The great Eloheem ... has been pleased once more to speak from the heavens; and also to commune with man upon the earth, by means of open vision, and by the ministration of Holy Messengers.
>
> "By this means the great and eternal High Priesthood, after the Order of His Son, even the Apostleship, has been restored; or, returned to the earth.
>
> "This High Priesthood, or Apostleship, holds the keys of the kingdom of God, and power to bind on earth that which shall be bound in heaven; and to loose on earth that which shall be loosed in heaven. And, in fine, to do, and to administer in all things pertaining to the ordinances, organization, government and direction of the kingdom of god.
>
> "Being established in these last days for the restoration of all things spoken by the prophets since the world began; and in order to prepare the way for the coming of the Son of Man.
>
> "And we now bear witness that his coming is near at hand; and not many years hence, the nations and their kings shall see him coming in the clouds of heaven with power and great glory.

"In order to meet this great event there must needs be a preparation.

"Therefore we send unto you with authority from on high, and command you all to repent and humble yourselves as little children, before the majesty of the Holy One; and come unto Jesus [Christ] with a broken heart and a contrite spirit; and be baptized in his name, for the remission of sins (that is, be buried in the water in the likeness of his burial and rise again to newness of life, in the likeness of his resurrection), and you shall receive the gift of the Holy Spirit, through the laying on of the hands of the Apostles and elders, of this great and last dispensation of mercy to man.

"This Spirit shall bear witness to you, of the truth of our testimony; and shall enlighten your minds, and be in you as the spirit of prophecy and revelation. It shall bring things past to your understanding and remembrance; and shall show you things to come.

"By the light of this Spirit, received through the ministration of the ordinances—by the power and authority of the Holy Apostleship and Priesthood, you will be enabled to understand, and to be the children of light; and thus be prepared to escape all the things that are coming on the earth, and so stand before the Son of Man.

"We testify that the foregoing doctrine is the doctrine or gospel of Jesus Christ, in its fulness; and that it is the only true, everlasting, and unchangeable gospel; and the only plan revealed on earth whereby man can be saved." (Messages of the First Presidency, 1:252-254) (CR, October 1975, pp. 46-47)

The Nauvoo House

The Lord directed the saints to build a hotel (Nauvoo House) for the convenience and comfort of those who might come as visitors to their city. The purpose for having such facilities was revealed as follows:

> And it shall be for a house for boarding, a house that strangers may come from afar to lodge therein; therefore let it be a good house, worthy of all acceptation, that the weary traveler may find health and safety while he shall contemplate the word of the Lord; and the corner-stone I have appointed for Zion. (D&C 124:23)

Making provision for the Nauvoo House made it possible for a stranger to visit the city of the saints and have a pleasant and positive experience with the church. This was a fellowshipping opportunity whereby the gospel could be taught by example as well as by precept.

Latter-day Saints have an opportunity to provide a "Nauvoo House" experience with their own homes. The outward appearance of the grounds, the buildings, the fences, etc. as well as the spirit of the interior can provide an inviting atmosphere for others to have a pleasant experience while visiting a "Nauvoo House" of the saints. President Spencer W. Kimball has counseled the saints concerning the appearance and atmosphere associated with their properties as follows:

> Now, brothers and sisters, we have launched a cleanup campaign. We are a throw-away people. Trash piles grow faster than population by far. Now we ask you to clean up your homes and your farms. "Man is the keeper of the land, and not its possessor."
> Broken fences should be mended or removed. Unused barns should be repaired, roofed, painted or removed. Sheds and corrals should be repaired and painted, or removed. Weedy ditch banks should be cleared. Abandoned homes could probably be razed. We look forward to the day when, in all of our communities, urban and rural, there would be a universal, continued movement to clean and repair and paint barns and sheds, build sidewalks, clean ditch banks, and make our properties a thing of beauty to behold.
> We have asked leaders of youth groups, auxiliary organizations, and priesthood quorums to give power to this concentrated action for beautification.
> The Lord said:
> "The earth is the Lord's, and the fulness thereof." (Ps. 24:1)
> "And I, the Lord God, took the man [Adam], and put him into the Garden of Eden, to dress it, and to keep it." (Moses 3:15)
> Therefore, we urge each of you to dress and keep in a beautiful state the property that is in your hands. (CR, October 1974, pp. 4-5)

The Nauvoo Temple

The saints had hardly begun to make permanent settlement in Nauvoo, when the Lord instructed them and invited other saints to come and participate in the building of a house unto Him in Illinois. (See D&C 124:25-27) The temple in Nauvoo was unique, in that it was the first "full-ordinance" temple built in this dispensation. Baptisms for the dead, as well as other priesthood ordinances for both the living and the dead, were to be performed in this temple. The Lord desired to restore to His children these ordinances that had been kept hidden from the world since the beginning of time. The ordinances are sacred and are not performed nor displayed in the presence nor before the eyes of the world. They are of such a sacred nature that they are to be performed only in such places appointed by the Lord.

Hence, the Lord authorized and directed the building of a house unto Him. (See D&C 124:28-30,39-41)

One of the identifying characteristics of the Lord's people and His church is the presence of a House of the Lord in their midst. The Savior revealed that His people "...are always commanded to build [my holy house] unto my holy name."(D&C 124:39) The Lord's Prophet, Joseph Smith, echoed this divine instruction when he said:

> ...What was the object of gathering the Jews, or the people of God in any age of the world?...
>
> The main object was to build unto the Lord a house whereby He could reveal unto His people the ordinances of His house and the glories of His kingdom, and teach the people the way of salvation; for there are certain ordinances and principles that, when they are taught and practiced, must be done in a place or house built for that purpose. (TPJS, pp. 307-308)

The Lord also revealed that, with His kingdom now restored, there would be temples built throughout the world. He has authorized His church, and no other, to build these temples in Zion, her stakes, and in Jerusalem. (See D&C 124:36)

Speaking of the temple to be built in Jerusalem, Elder Bruce R. McConkie has said:

> Who shall build this temple? The Lord himself shall do it by the hands of his servants the prophets. "Behold the man whose name is the BRANCH;...he shall build the temple of the Lord"—and, be it remembered, the Branch is one of the Messianic designations by which the Promised Messiah is known—"Even he shall build the temple of the Lord; and he shall bear the glory, and shall sit and rule upon his throne." And whence shall the workmen come to build the sanctuary? "They that are far off shall come and build in the temple of the Lord." (Zech. 6:12-15)
>
> Who are those "that are far off" who shall come to Jerusalem to build the house of the Lord? Surely they are the Jews who have been scattered afar. By what power and under whose authorization shall the work be done? There is only one place under the whole heavens where the keys of temple building are found. There is only one people who know how to build temples and what to do in them when they are completed. That people is the Latter-day Saints. The temple in Jerusalem will not be built by Jews who have assembled there for political purposes as at present. It will not be built by a people who know nothing whatever about the sealing ordinances

Section 124

and their application to the living and the dead. It will not be built by those who know nothing about Christ and his laws and the mysteries reserved for the saints. But it will be built by Jews who have come unto Christ, who once again are in the true fold of their ancient Shepherd, and who have learned anew about temples because they know that Elijah did come, not to sit in a vacant chair at some Jewish feast of the Passover, but to the Kirtland Temple on April 3, 1836, to Joseph Smith and Oliver Cowdery. The temple in Jerusalem will be built by the Church of Jesus Christ of Latter-day Saints. "They that are far off," they that come from an American Zion, they who have a temple in Salt Lake City will come to Jerusalem to build there another holy house in the Jerusalem portion of "the mountains of the Lord's house." (D&C 133:13) (The Millennial Messiah, pp. 279-280)

Further commentary on the subject of the Jerusalem temple was written as follows:

The building of the temple in Jerusalem will be an important step in the Lord's latter-day work, but it will be directly related to the Gospel as restored through the Prophet Joseph Smith and to the glorious Second Coming of the Lord.

It will not be part of any form of sectarianism, either Christian or Jewish, and will never be clouded by any uncertainties as to its purpose.

Any temple of the Lord is a House of the Lord, and every House of the Lord will be His abiding place, His sanctuary, His designated dwelling wherein ordinances of salvation will be performed. All of this requires His revealed direction and the services of His properly ordained and divinely authorized priesthood.

Who believes in the current revelation which would be required for this work? Who has living prophets among them? Who holds the keys of temple ceremonies? Whose ordinances assist in the salvation of both the living and the dead?

The authorized temple builders!

Only through them can any acceptable temple be built and operated, whether in Jerusalem, Missouri or Utah. (Church News, August 7, 1971, p. 16)

In retrospect, the command to build the temple in Nauvoo was one more step towards the building of temples throughout the world and the performance of priesthood ordinances that will be continued into the millennial reign of the Savior, whose work this is.

Being Accepted of the Lord

What does it mean to be accepted of the Lord? We remember that the Lord commanded us to be perfect. (See B of M, 3 Nephi 12:48) Can we be accepted of the Lord while we struggle up the long path towards perfection? Or must we wait for such a status of acceptance until we arrive at the decreed destination? Many people feel frustration and failure because they don't understand they can be accepted of the Lord in their imperfect state. The reason for their frustration is that they have not yet accomplished or performed their tasks of life consistent with the performance level that they know is attainable.

The Lord has revealed that His acceptance of the work of imperfect mortals is not based upon perfect performance only, but also upon faithful and diligent efforts towards the accomplishment of any God-given task. (See D&C 124:49) With this understanding, then, mortals need not be confounded and confused. Anyone who is accepted of the Lord is not a failure. He is, as Moroni taught, "perfect in Christ." (See B of M, Moroni 10:32-33)

Elder Neal A. Maxwell addressed Latter-day Saints on this subject by saying:

> Now may I speak, not to the slackers in the Kingdom, but to those who carry their own load and more; not to those lulled into false security, but to those buffeted by false insecurity, who, though laboring devotedly in the Kingdom, have recurring feelings of falling forever short.
>
> Earlier disciples who heard Jesus preach some exacting doctrines were also anxious and said, "Who then can be saved?" (Mark 10:26.)
>
> The first thing to be said of this feeling of inadequacy is that it is normal. There is no way the Church can honestly describe where we must yet go and what we must yet do without creating a sense of immense distance. Following celestial road signs while in telestial traffic jams is not easy, especially when we are not just moving next door—or even across town.
>
> In a Kingdom where perfection is an eventual expectation, each other's needs for improvement have a way of being noticed....
>
> Some of us who would not chastise a neighbor for his frailties have a field day with our own. Some of us stand before no more harsh a judge than ourselves, a judge who stubbornly refuses to admit much happy evidence and who cares nothing for due process. Fortunately, the Lord loves us more than we love ourselves....
>
> Yes, brothers and sisters, this is a gospel of grand expectations, but God's grace is sufficient for each of us. Discouragement is not

the absence of adequacy but the absence of courage, and our personal progress should be yet another way we witness to the wonder of it all!

True, there are no *instant* Christians, but there are *constant* Christians! (CR, October 1976, pp. 14, 16)

The Lord's Leaders

The church had been through a refiner's fire in Missouri. The saints had been persecuted not only because of the unrighteous treatment from enemies outside of the church, but also, in part at least, because of the traitorous actions of some of the members of the church. Some of the apostate saints would not follow or render obedience to the Lord's appointed leaders.

In this revelation (D&C Section 124) the Lord reviewed and reemphasized the importance of giving heed to and following His authorized leaders. Several principles were stressed by the Lord:

1. The Lord's people are assured of an eternal place in the church and kingdom of God when they hearken to the voice of His servants whom he has appointed to lead His people. (See D&C 124:45-46)

2. Any member of the Lord's church who teaches and counsels contrary to the teachings and counsel of the Lord as given through His First Presidency is not accepted before the Lord. He describes such a person as a promoter of false gods as objects of worship. (See D&C 124:84)

3. Revelation (oracles) from the Lord to His church comes through the Quorum of the First Presidency, the prophet being the Lord's mouth-piece. Lest there be any confusion as to the identity of those men who occupied the positions in the leading quorums of the church at that time, the Lord specifically named each member of those quorums. (See D&C 124:125-129).

Perhaps, few people in the church would fail to hearken to and obey the Lord if the Lord spoke or appeared personally to them. But the elect of God are those who follow His counsel and recognize that such counsel comes through His appointed leaders (See D&C 1:38; 29:7)

Summary and Conclusion

The Lord loves all of His children, those who are on the earth now, those who have been here previously, and those who are yet to come.

The Lord has made ample provision for all of His children to hear the gospel message as it is proclaimed by His authorized servants. He has also provided the means by which the priesthood ordinances of salvation can be performed for the living and the dead. Those who respond to the leaders of the Lord's church can be recognized and identified for they are distinctively set apart from the world by the way they live, the appearance of their properties, their participation in the erecting and using of sacred temples of the Lord, and their striving towards perfection as an accepted people of the Lord.

Chapter 51

Doctrine and Covenants Section 125

Suggested Title

Saints in Iowa

Overview of Section Content

1. A question concerning the saints in Iowa (vs. 1)
2. Faithful saints will be directed by the Lord through His prophet as to where to gather (vs. 2-4)

Historical Setting

Joseph Smith, Jun.

>About this time I received a revelation, given in the City of Nauvoo, in answer to the following interrogatory—"What is the will of the Lord, concerning the Saints in the Territory of Iowa?"...
>
>(HC, Vol. 4, p. 311)

Sacred Truths

Introduction

As the saints were driven from Missouri, many of them settled on both sides of the Mississippi River, many in Nauvoo, Illinois, and others in the territory of Iowa. In January 1841, the Lord had directed that His saints should gather to Nauvoo for the purpose of erecting a temple unto Him. (See D&C 124:25-28) The saints who had already settled on the Iowa side of the river, wondered what the Lord would have them do.

In this revelation, the Lord permitted the saints to remain in Iowa and counseled them to build up settlements there. (See D&C 125:1, 3-4) From His instructions we are taught an important principle about the gathering of the Lord's people.

A Principle of Gathering

By 1841, the church had been commanded on several occasions to gather in various locations (Ohio, Missouri, Illinois). Faithful saints had learned the importance of being where the Lord wanted them to be. They had also learned from past experience, that the place they should gather would be directed by the Lord through His prophet. This revelation reaffirmed such a pattern. (See D&C 125:2)

The places of gathering of the Lord's people are still being revealed by Him today through His living prophet. Every member of the church is assigned a place of membership within the geographical boundaries of the various church organizations. Every person is directed to gather with the saints within an assigned ward or branch, stake or mission. The name and place of such designated gatherings is given by inspiration through those appointed to lead the Lord's church.

When saints are obedient and properly respond to this principle of gathering, they have the blessings of the programs of the church. For instance, under the direction of authorized leadership, the saints have access to priesthood counsel, home teaching visits, temple attendance, etc.

Those who do not heed this principle of gathering, may find themselves losing some of the privileges and blessings of their church membership. They simply need to remember that the Lord also directs His church in such matters as places of gathering.

Summary and Conclusion

The Lord is intimately involved in all facets of the functioning of His kingdom. Pertaining to the gathering places of His people, He has assigned each member of the church a place where he can reap the benefits of his church membership. This assignment comes by appointment of the Lord's authorized leadership.

Chapter 52

Doctrine and Covenants Section 126

Suggested Title
Brigham Young—His Acceptable Offering to the Lord

Overview of Section Content
1. The Lord acknowledges Brigham Young's offerings and labors (vs. 1-2)
2. Brigham Young is to remain home and send the Lord's word abroad (vs. 3)

Historical Setting

Joseph Smith, Jun.

Thursday, July 1.—Elders Young, Kimball, and Taylor arrived at Nauvoo, after an interesting mission to England. The accounts of their missions are highly satisfactory . . . .

Revelation given to Joseph Smith, in the house of Brigham Young, in Nauvoo City, July 9, 1841 . . . .

(HC, Vol. 4, pp. 381-382)

Sacred Truths

Introduction

The twelve apostles had been called by the Lord to fill missions to the European nations. (See D&C 118:4-5) Two years later, after having completed successful missions, they returned to their families and the church at Nauvoo, Illinois. One of the Twelve was Brigham Young, to whom this revelation (D&C Section 126) was addressed.

In this chapter, we will discuss the following topics from the revelation:

1. The Lord's acceptance of Brigham Young
2. Missionary families

The Lord's Acceptance of Brigham Young

Previous to this revelation, Brigham Young's calling as President of the Quorum of the Twelve Apostles was reaffirmed by the Lord. (See D&C 124:127) In this position, he stood next to the First Presidency of the church. The Lord instructed President Young to remain at home with the body of the church and from there he was to direct the missionary efforts of the church. (See D&C 126:1, 3) The timeliness of this important instruction has been emphasized as follows:

> In order to grasp fully the significance of this Revelation, an incident from the first meeting, in 1832, between the Prophet Joseph and his successor should be recalled. They had spent the evening in conversation on the gospel, and when the time for parting had come, Brigham Young was invited to lead in prayer. While he was praying, the Spirit of the Lord came upon him, and he spoke in tongues—the first instance of the bestowal of that gift upon anyone in this dispensation. Afterwards, it is asserted, the Prophet said, "A time will come when Brother Brigham will preside over this Church" (Whitney's *Hist. of Utah*, Vol. I., p. 112).
>
> It should, further, be remembered that, at a Conference held at Nauvoo, August 16th, 1841, the Prophet Joseph, with this Revelation in mind, stated that, "The time has come when the Twelve should be called upon to stand in their place *next to the First Presidency*, and attend to the settling of emigrants and the business of the Church at the Stakes, and to assist to bear off the kingdom victoriously to the nations" (*Hist. of the Church,* Vol. IV., p. 403). By this Revelation, therefore, Brigham Young, the President of the Twelve (Sec. 124:127), was called to stand next to the First Presidency. Why? To take his place, whenever the prophet should be called to another sphere of action. By this Revelation, the Spirit indicated that

Section 126

Brigham Young was to be the successor of Joseph Smith, as the Prophet had predicted in 1832. (DCC, p. 797)

In this revelation, the Lord also made it known that Brigham Young's offering was acceptable to Him. (See D&C 126:1-2) To better appreciate the extent of the offering he made in behalf of the Lord and His church, we refer to the following comments by President Young:

> I came into this Church in the spring of 1832. Previous to my being baptized, I took a mission to Canada at my own expense; and from the time that I was baptized until the day of our sorrow and affliction, at the martyrdom of Joseph and Hyrum, no summer passed over my head but what I was traveling and preaching, and the only thing I ever received from the Church, during over twelve years, and the only means that were ever given me by the Prophet, that I now recollect, was in 1842, when brother Joseph sent me the half of a small pig that the brethren had brought to him, I did not ask him for it; . . .
>
> I have traveled and preached, and at the same time sustained my family by my labor and economy. If I borrowed one hundred dollars, or fifty, or if I had five dollars, it almost universally went into the hands of brother Joseph, to pay lawyers' fees and to liberate him from the power of his enemies, so far as it would go. Hundreds and hundreds of dollars that I have managed to get, to borrow and trade for, I have handed over to Joseph when I came home. That is the way I got help, and it was good for me; it learned me a great deal, though I had learned, before I heard of "Mormonism," to take care of number one. . . .
>
> In company with several of the Twelve I was sent to England in 1839. We started from home without purse or scrip, and most of the Twelve were sick; and those who were not sick when they started were sick on the way to Ohio; brother Taylor was left to die by the road-side, by old father Coltrin, though he did not die. I was not able to walk to the river, not so far as across this block, no, not more than half as far; I had to be helped to the river, in order to get into a boat to cross it. This was about our situation. I had not even an overcoat; I took a small quilt from the trundle bed, and that served for my overcoat, while I was traveling to the State of New York, when I had a coarse sattinet overcoat given to me. Thus we went to England, to a strange land to sojourn among strangers.
>
> When we reached England we designed to start a paper, but we had not the first penny to do it with. I had enough to buy a hat and pay my passage to Preston, for from the time I left home, I had worn

an old cap which my wife made out of a pair of old pantaloons; but the most of us were entirely destitute of means to buy even any necessary article. (JD, Vol. 4, pp. 34-35)

Before the Twelve Apostles ever left for their missions to Europe, the Prophet Joseph Smith beheld in vision, their labors, their sacrifices, and their destitute conditions as they labored in behalf of the Lord and His work in foreign lands:

> ...I saw the Twelve Apostles of the Lamb, who are now upon the earth, who hold the keys of this last ministry, in foreign lands, standing together in a circle, much fatigued, with their clothes tattered and feet swollen, with their eyes cast downward, and Jesus standing in their midst, and they did not behold Him. The Savior looked upon them and wept. (HC, Vol. 2, p. 381)

From the above commentaries, we can better understand why Brigham Young's offering was acceptable unto the Lord and why the Lord referred to President Young as "Dear and well-beloved brother..." (D&C 126:1)

Missionary Families

In this brief revelation, the Lord twice made reference to Brigham Young's family. (See D&C 126:1, 3) We realize that the Lord is aware of the sacrifice and efforts made by the family that supported Brigham Young and made it possible for him to extend an acceptable offering unto the Lord. This is true of all families who are represented by missionaries who render their service unto the Lord. The Lord is aware of the sacrifice made by families who share in this offering.

It was important for Brigham Young to be reminded of his obligation towards his missionary family. So also, should every missionary make a conscientious effort to recognize and appreciate the efforts, the prayers, the concerns, the love, and the sacrifice that is offered by family members in his behalf. Emphasizing the importance of this concept, Elder A. Theodore Tuttle taught:

> I hope I can always remember the scene that Brother Packer and I saw several years ago. While we were waiting in the Deseret Book Company for some materials, we saw a slender young man, bronzed from exposure to the sun except for the pale border that a recent haircut revealed, purchasing his missionary supplies. He was dressed in a new suit, new shirt, new tie, new shoes, and new hat. That he was obviously from the farm was also evident from his parents who accompanied him. His father's rough, gnarled hands

Section 126

spoke eloquently of the years of hard, manual labor. His solicitous mother wore a tidy but faded housedress. His father's old-styled suit, frayed shirt, and run-down heels on his shoes bore mute testimony that sending their son on a mission was not going to be easy. This mother and father hovered around their son suggesting this or that book. Having purchased the standard works and his I.P. book and some miscellaneous things, we heard his father say, "Now, is there anything else you need, son?"

I have thought of that little episode in the lives of those three people--and it could be multiplied hundreds, and I suppose thousands of times--and I have thought, "Yes, there is something more that son needs--a grateful heart and a firm resolve to prove worthy of his heritage!" (BYU, *Speeches of the Year*, November 26, 1968, pp. 5-6)

Summary and Conclusion

The Lord loves those who labor in His name for the souls of mankind. Their labors and sacrifices, as well as those of their families, do not go unnoticed by the Lord.

Chapter 53

Doctrine and Covenants Sections 127 and 128

Suggested Titles

Section 127—Baptisms for the dead—Witnesses and Recordings
Section 128—Baptisms For the Dead—Records in Heaven—Review of the
Restoration

Overview of Section Content

Section 127

1. Some of the persecutions and tribulations of the Prophet Joseph Smith (vs. 1-3)
2. The Lord's work to continue regardless of persecutions (vs. 4)
3. Records pertaining to baptisms for the dead (vs. 5-7, 9)
4. A promise of additional priesthood blessings (vs. 8)
5. The desires and prayer of the Prophet Joseph Smith (vs. 10-12)

Section 128

1. Witnesses and recorders for baptisms for the dead (vs. 1-5)
2. Records kept on earth and in heaven (vs. 6-9)
3. Power to bind on earth and in heaven (vs. 10-11)
4. Baptism for the dead a similitude of the grave and the resurrection (vs. 12-14)

328 Sacred Truths of the Doctrine and Covenants

5. Salvation for the living and the dead inseparably connected (vs. 15-18)
6. A review of some of the events of the restoration of the gospel of Jesus Christ (vs. 19-21)
7. Rejoicing over the restoration of the gospel of Jesus Christ (vs. 22-23)
8. Saints to make an acceptable offering unto the Lord (vs. 24-25)

Historical Setting

Section 127

Joseph Smith, Jun.

> Thursday, September 1, 1842.—During the forenoon in the Assembly Room, and in the afternoon at home, attending to business. [I] wrote the following:
> A Letter from the Prophet to the Saints at Nauvoo—Directions on Baptism for the Dead....
>
> (HC, Vol. 5, p. 142)

Joseph Fielding Smith

> ...During the summer and fall of 1842, the prophet Joseph Smith was forced to go into hiding because of the attempt on the part of Missouri mobocrats to get him in their clutches. He had been accused by ex-governor Boggs as being an accessory and Orrin Porter Rockwell as the principal in the shooting of Boggs, May 6, 1842. This was a conspiracy to get the Prophet back into the hands of the Missourian mobbers. Governor Carlin of Illinois, had joined in this conspiracy contrary to every principle of correct law, as it was later shown in the trial which was held in Springfield, [Illinois]....From this place of concealment the Prophet wrote these two letters (Section 127 and 128 in the Doctrine and Covenants) by revelation to the Church....
>
> (CHMR, Vol. 4, p. 134)

Section 128

Joseph Smith, Jun.

> Tuesday, September 6, 1842,—I wrote as follows:
> Letter of the Prophet to the Church—Further Directions on Baptism for the Dead....
>
> (HC, Vol. 5, p. 148)

Sections 127 and 128 329

Sacred Truths

Introduction

Sections 127 and 128 of the Doctrine and Covenants are separate letters written by Joseph Smith while in concealment from his enemies. As to the nature of this persecution, see Historical Setting, this chapter. (See also D&C 127:1-3)

Satan is an enemy to God. He attempts to destroy every good thing that would assist the saints in their quest for salvation. One of the means utilized by him is to stir up the people in anger against that which is good. (See B of M, 2 Ne. 28:20) The results are often manifested in persecution against the church and its leaders. Even though the prophet was forced, by this satanical persecution, to leave the mainstream of activity in the church, still the progress of the church could not be thwarted. The work of the kingdom still goes on in spite of the physical absence of a prominent leader of the organization. The work of saving souls is not to be impeded. The Lord said:

> ...Let the work of my temple, and all the works which I have appointed unto you, be continued on and not cease; and let your diligence, and your perseverance, and patience, and your works be redoubled, and you shall in nowise lose your reward, saith the Lord of Hosts. And if they persecute you, so persecuted they the prophets and righteous men that were before you. For all this there is a reward in heaven. (D&C 127:4)

While avoiding his enemies, the Lord's prophet continued to provide inspired direction to the church through the means of writing letters to the saints. We will discuss these two sections together, since both of these letters pertain to the subject of baptism for the dead. In this chapter, we will discuss the following topics:

1. Baptisms for the dead—witnesses and recordings
2. A promise of additional priesthood blessings
3. Records on earth and in heaven
4. Salvation for the living and the dead inseparably connected together
5. Review of the restoration
6. The Lord's expectations of His saints

Baptisms for the Dead—Witnesses and Recordings

In this dispensation, the Lord has revealed again that "...in the mouth of two or three witnesses shall every word be established." (D&C 6:28) This law of witnesses was to be observed in the performance of the ordinance of baptism for the dead. (See D&C 127:5-7, 9; 128:2-4)

What are the functions of a witness? The following are included:

1. To verify that the ordinance was performed. This provides a protection for the recipient of the ordinance. He does not stand alone.
2. To verify that the ordinance was performed by an authorized priesthood holder. This is a protection against deception.
3. To verify that the ordinance was performed properly. This is a protection against error in performance.
4. To verify the time and the place that the ordinance was performed.

The importance of the role of witnesses of priesthood ordinance work was taught by the Prophet Joseph Smith:

> I have one remark to make respecting the baptism for the dead to suffice for the time being, until I have opportunity to discuss the subject at greater length—all persons baptized for the dead must have a recorder present, that he may be an eyewitness to record and testify of the truth and validity of his record. It will be necessary, in the Grand Council, that these things be testified to by competent witnesses. Therefore let the recording and witnessing of baptisms for the dead be carefully attended to from this time forth. If there is any lack, it may be at the expense of our friends; they may not come forth. (HC, Vol. 5, p. 141)

A Promise of Additional Priesthood Blessings

The full temple endowment and other temple ordinances were not yet available to all of the members of the church at the time this section was written. A few of the leaders of the church were privileged to be the first recipients of the full endowment in May, 1842. (See HC, Vol. 5, pp. 1-2) To the membership at large, the Lord indicated He was "...about to restore many things to the earth, pertaining to the priesthood,...." (D&C 127:8)

Mankind had not had access to these temple priesthood ordinances for many centuries. One can only imagine the happiness and the excitement that must have filled the hearts of the saints when the Lord promised the return of these sacred ordinances.

Records on Earth and in Heaven

There may be many reasons for keeping records, but one very important reason is that a record verifies an action. Ordinances are a prerequisite to salvation, but there must also be a record made in order to verify that the ordinance was performed. Since the kingdom of God is not established for mortality only, the work of the kingdom must be verified by records both on earth and in heaven.

The responsibility for accurate record keeping is clearly upon the shoulders of mortal saints. Until the ordinances are properly performed and accurately recorded on earth, there cannot be and will not be a record in heaven. Thus, the opportunity for salvation is denied an individual until an accurate record verifies his worthiness and eligibility for a place in the kingdom of our Father. The records prepared on earth, then, become the source of judgment information. (See D&C 127:7; 128:7-9)

Salvation for the Living and the Dead Inseparably Connected Together

All children of God who have lived or who will yet live on this earth will have come here to a state of probation. Many leave mortality and enter the spirit world still in a probationary condition. For instance, those who have not had full opportunity to hear and accept the gospel of Jesus Christ still must make proper decisions in order to have access to the fulness of the blessings promised to righteous saints. The ordinance work necessary for those in the spirit world who accept and desire salvation must be performed by righteous saints in mortality.

Members of the church have been given the authority and responsibility to perform the ordinances for and in behalf of the departed dead. Our obligation is to share the benefits of the gospel with both the living and the dead. God is no respector of persons and neither should we be. Salvation for both the living and the dead depends in part, upon the faithful obedience of God's covenant children in discharging their sacred responsibilities toward their brothers and sisters who are still without covenant blessings in Father's kingdom. Until all people have had the opportunity to hear and accept the gospel and its covenants, their period of probation is not over. Their obligation to "keep their second estate" has not ceased. (See P of GP, Abraham 3:26) Therefore, we must view salvation as an opportunity for both living and dead, inseparably connected together. "For we without them cannot be made perfect; neither can they without us be made perfect." (D&C 128:18)

Furthermore, the righteous saints of all dispensations must be sealed together as members of God's eternal family. A person can only have the fulness of salvation as a member of this eternal family. (See D&C 128:18)

Review of the Restoration

Over the several millennia of the earth's temporal existence, the Lord has commissioned certain men bearing His holy priesthood to direct the many and various phases of His work. These authorized servants of the Lord, held priesthood keys of the kingdom that were essential to the conduct of the work of salvation during the various dispensations. In the dispensation of the fulness of times, there was to be a restoration of all things. Thus, the keys of previous dispensations needed to be restored by those who previously held them.

In Section 128 of the Doctrine and Covenants, Joseph Smith reviewed some of the events associated with the restoration process. He also identified many heavenly messengers who appeared to him in bringing about this restoration. (See D&C 128:19-21)

The importance of bringing back the keys of salvation by these authorized servants of the Lord was emphasized by President John Taylor as follows:

> Joseph Smith in the first place was set apart by the Almighty according to the councils of the Gods in the eternal worlds, to introduce the principles of life among the people, of which the gospel is the grand power and influence, and through which salvation can extend to all peoples, all nations, all kindreds, all tongues, and all worlds. It is the principle that brings life and immortality to light, and places us in communication with God. God selected him for that purpose, and he fulfilled his mission and lived honorably and died honorably. I know of what I speak, for I was very well acquainted with him and was with him a great deal during his life, and was with him when he died. The principles which he had placed him in communication with the Lord, and not only with the Lord, but with the ancient apostles and prophets; such men, for instance, as Abraham, Isaac, Jacob, Noah, Adam, Seth, Enoch, and Jesus, and the Father, and the apostles that lived on this continent, as well as those who lived on the Asiatic continent. He seemed to be as familiar with these people as we are with one another. Why? Because he had to introduce a dispensation which was called the dispensation of the fulness of times, and it was known as such by the ancient servants of God. (The Gospel Kingdom, p. 353)

The Lord's Expectations of His Saints

The Lord has restored all things necessary for the salvation of His children. The knowledge and power of the gospel has been given once more to mortals. The work of salvation of souls is the greatest cause the earth has ever known. (See D&C 128:22) The Lord expects the custodians of His gospel teachings and power to make such available to all His children. Further, He also expects proper and faithful records to be kept of the righteous works of those seeking salvation. (See D&C 128:24)

Summary and Conclusion

The Lord is no respecter of persons. He loves all His children. He has made provision for the salvation of all. Through the restoration of the gospel of Jesus Christ essential ordinances and proper records for both the living and the dead can be accomplished.

[Handwritten note: Read many of the cross references to Old + New Testament re baptism for the dead.]

Chapter 54

Doctrine and Covenants Section 129

Suggested Title
Three Grand Keys By Which Messengers May Be Known

Overview of Section Content
1. Resurrected and spirit beings in heaven (vs. 1-3)
2. Keys by which good and evil messengers may be known (vs. 4-9)

Historical Setting

Joseph Smith, Jun.

Spent most of the day in conversation with Parley P. Pratt and others. [Section 129 follows]

(HC, Vol. 5, p. 267)

Sacred Truths

Introduction
Following the restoration of the Lord's church to the earth, Satan and his evil spirits made great efforts to deceive people who came in contact with the gospel of Jesus Christ. Many times he would cause people to think that a revelation or some supernatural experience was of the Lord, when in reality

it was a result and a manifestation of the powers of Lucifer. On occasion Satan and his followers have appeared to mortal man and have represented themselves as messengers from the Lord. To protect the saints from being deceived under these circumstances, the Lord gave this revelation. (Section 129)

In this chapter we will discuss two topics from the revelation:

1. Beings in heaven
2. Keys by which messengers may be known

Beings In Heaven

There may be many kinds of beings in heaven. In this revelation, the Lord identified two kinds:

1. "...Angels who are resurrected personages, having bodies of flesh and bones—"(D&C 129:1)
2. "...spirits of just men made perfect, they who are not resurrected,..." (D&C 129:3)

Commenting on the nature of these beings, President Charles W. Penrose said:

> ...the quotation...from section 129, verse 1, of the Doctrine and Covenants...will show that it is not there stated that "all" angels are resurrected beings... The theme discoursed upon is the presence in heaven of two kinds or classes of beings, namely, first, resurrected beings and, second, spirits who are not resurrected. It is not asserted that there are no other kinds of persons in heaven than they, but the subject treated is of the two classes mentioned. (IE, Vol. 15, p. 949, August 1912; Quoted in Latter-day Prophets and the Doctrine and Covenants, Vol. 4, p. 370)

Keys By Which Messengers May Be Known

Three keys by which messengers may be accurately identified are summarized as follows:

1. Identification of angels (See D&C 129:4-5)
2. Identification of righteous spirits (See D&C 129:6-7)
3. Identification of evil spirits (See D&C 129:8)

The first two keys are self-explanatory. However, there may be a question about the third key. Some may wonder if an evil spirit would follow this pattern since he would know what is revealed in this revelation. It should be remembered, however, that the Lord said:

If it be the devil as an angel of light, when you ask him to shake hands, he *will* offer you his hand, and you will not feel anything; you may therefore detect him. (D&C 129:8; italics added)

When the Lord states that something *will* be done, it will be done. Evil spirits cannot vary from the restrictions placed upon them by the Lord. They have their bounds. Elder Orson F. Whitney commented on this concept as follows:

> There are bad spirits as well as good, and the vital question is: How can we know the difference between them? Let us at this stage consult an expert—for there are such—one who came in contact with spiritual forces to a marvelous extent, not only receiving messages from other worlds, but also interviewing the messengers. Joseph Smith knew the difference between good and evil communicants, and here is his testimony concerning them: [Sec. 129:4-8, quoted.]
>
> In another place, the Prophet says: "Wicked spirits have their bounds, limits and laws, by which they are governed; and it is very evident that they possess a power that none but those who have the priesthood can control." (Hist. Ch. Vol. 4, p. 576) (Latter-day Prophets and the Doctrine and Covenants, Vol. 4, p. 374)

Summary and Conclusion

Through living prophets, the Lord has revealed unto His children sufficient knowledge and understanding in order that they may be protected and avoid the deceptions of Lucifer. Section 129 of the Doctrine and Covenants provides one of the means afforded to us as a protection against the deceptive devices of the evil one.

There are true messengers of the Lord who may also appear unto mortal men. In this revelation, the Lord has provided His children with sufficient knowledge and understanding in order that authorized messengers of the Lord might be recognized and their messages received.

Chapter 55

Doctrine and Covenants Section 130

Suggested Title

The Godhead—Some Conditions in Heaven

Overview of Section Content

1. The Savior is an exalted man (vs. 1)
2. Mortal and immortal sociality (vs. 2)
3. Future appearance of the Father and the Son (vs. 3)
4. God, Angels, and man—time and residence (vs. 4-8)
5. Inhabitants of the sanctified earth (vs. 9-11)
6. Prophecy of the U.S. Civil War (vs. 12-13)
7. The time of the Lord's second coming not known to man (vs. 14-17)
8. Intelligence and the resurrection (vs. 18-19)
9. The law of blessings (vs. 20-21)
10. Nature of the Godhead (vs. 22-23)

Historical Setting

Joseph Smith, Jun.

At ten a.m. went to meeting. Heard Elder Orson Hyde preach, comparing the sectarian preachers to crows living on carrion, as they were more fond of lies about the Saints than the truth. Alluding to the coming of the Savior, he said, "When He shall appear, we shall be like Him, & c. He will appear on a white horse as a warrior, and maybe we shall have some of the same spirit. Our God is a warrior. (John xiv, 23.) It is our privilege to have the Father and Son dwelling in our hearts, & c."

We dined with my sister Sophronia McCleary, when I told Elder Hyde that I was going to offer some corrections to his sermon this morning. He replied, "They shall be thankfully received."[Section 130:1-17 follows]

(HC, Vol. 5, p. 323)

Joseph Smith, Jun.

"At one p.m. attended meetings. . . .

"Then corrected Elder Hyde's remarks, the same as I had done to him privately. . . .

"At seven o'clock meeting. . . .[Sec. 130:17-23, follows]"

(HC, Vol. 5, pp. 324-325)

Sacred Truths

Introduction

As noted from the Historical Setting of this chapter, Section 130 is an amalgamation of a number of subjects, which Joseph Smith discussed on two separate occasions.

For the purposes of our discussion in this chapter, we will group these subjects as follows:

1. The Godhead
2. Some conditions in Heaven

The Godhead

1. Nature of the Godhead

This revelation came at a time when the nature of the Godhead was generally misunderstood by mankind. Many false notions were, and still are, prevalent about the nature of Diety. Through the restoration process in this dispensation, a correct understanding of God was given once more to the people of the earth. Nowhere in holy writ is there a more clearly defined description of the Godhead than is given in this revelation.

We learn there are three distinct and separate beings in the Godhead. The Father and Son are resurrected beings having bodies of flesh and bones, and when they appear, they are seen as exalted men. The Holy Ghost is a personage of spirit and does not have a tangible body of flesh and bones. (See D&C 130:1, 3, 22)

The importance of having this correct understanding of God was emphasized by the Prophet Joseph Smith. He taught that it was a pre-requisite to faith in God:

> Let us here observe, that three things are necessary in order that any rational and intelligent being may exercise faith in God unto life and salvation.
>
> First, the idea that he actually exists.
>
> Secondly, a *correct* idea of his character, perfections, and attributes.
>
> Thirdly, an actual knowledge that the course of life which he is pursuing is according to his will. For without an acquaintance with these three important facts, the faith of every rational being must be imperfect and unproductive; but with this understanding it can become perfect and fruitful, abounding in righteousness, unto the praise and glory of God the Father, and the Lord Jesus Christ. (Lectures on Faith, Lecture Third, para. 2-5, p. 33)

2. *The Savior's second coming*

One of the great truths restored in this dispensation is the reality of the second coming of Jesus Christ. This revelation reinforces what had been previously revealed—the Savior lives and is coming to reign on the earth, though no one knows the exact time. Even though Joseph Smith inquired concerning the time of this great event, such information was withheld from him. (See D&C 130:14-17; 49:5-7)

Some Conditions in Heaven

1. *Sociality*

The world has little understanding regarding the type of life to be experienced in the hereafter. Only through the knowledge provided by divine revelation can mankind have a correct understanding of life beyond mortality. In this revelation, the Lord declared:

> ...that same sociality which exists among us here will exist among us there, only it will be coupled with eternal glory, which glory we do not now enjoy. (D&C 130:2)

Elder Orson Pratt has provided insight to some aspects of the conditions of sociality that might be experienced in Heaven:

It is, indeed, comforting to know whence we came, and have a correct understanding in regard to our future. This interesting and most important knowledge is only to be obtained by divine revelation. God has abundantly revealed these things that man might rejoice in them. There are no people upon the earth who have so great reasons to rejoice as the Saints; for to them God has spoken, and plainly manifested much concerning both the past and the future; and hence, they know what kind of an existence to pray for, what blessings to hope for, and where they shall receive their everlasting inheritance.

A Saint, who is one in deed and in truth, does not look for an immaterial heaven but he expects a heaven with lands, houses, cities, vegetation, rivers, and animals; with thrones, temples, palaces, kings, princes, priests, and angels; with food, raiment, musical instruments, etc.; all of which are material. Indeed the Saints' heaven is a redeemed, glorified, celestial material creation, inhabited by glorified material beings, male and female, organized into families, embracing all the relationships of husbands and wives, parents and children, where sorrow, crying, pain, and death will be known no more. Or to speak still more definitely, this earth, when glorified, is the Saints' eternal heaven. On it they expect to live, with body parts, and holy passions: on it they expect to move and have their being; to eat, drink, converse, worship, sing, play on musical instruments, engage in joyful, innocent, social amusements, visit neighboring towns and neighboring worlds: indeed, matter and its qualities and properties are the only being or things with which they expect to associate. If they embrace the Father, they expect to embrace a glorified, immortal, spiritual, material Personage; if they embrace the Son of God, they expect to embrace a spiritual Being of material flesh and bones, whose image is in the likeness of the Father; if they enjoy the society of the Holy Ghost, they expect to behold a glorious spiritual Personage, a material body of spirit; if they associate with the spirits of men or angels, they expect to find them material. (Millennial Star, Vol. 28, p. 722, November 17, 1866)

2. *Time*

Time is important. If it were not so, the Lord would not have provided for it. Time is relative and may be variously measured according to the place of residence that is used as a point of reference. (See D&C 130:4-5)

Man is expected to utilize his time wisely. For instance, he is not allotted a never-ending supply of time while in his second estate. This is the time provided for us to work out our salvation and we have been commanded not

Section 130

to procrastinate this eternal work. This time period will eventually come to an end, and then no more work for salvation can be done. (See B of M, Alma 34:31-35) It has been well said:

> To every thing there is a season, and a time to every purpose under the heaven:
> A time to be born, and a time to die; a time to plant, and a time to pluck up that which is planted;
> A time to kill, and a time to heal; a time to break down, and a time to build up;
> A time to weep, and a time to laugh; a time to mourn, and a time to dance;
> A time to cast away stones, and a time to gather stones together; a time to embrace, and a time to refrain from embracing;
> A time to get, and a time to lose; a time to keep, and a time to cast away;
> A time to rend, and a time to sew; a time to keep silence, and a time to speak;
> A time to love, and a time to hate; a time of war, and a time of peace.
> What profit hath he that worketh in that wherein he laboureth?
> I have seen the travail, which God hath given to the sons of men to be exercised in it.
> He hath made every thing beautiful in his time: also he hath set the world in their heart, so that no man can find out the work that God maketh from the beginning to the end.
> I know that there is no good in them, but for a man to rejoice, and to do good in his life.
> And also that every man should eat and drink, and enjoy the good of all his labour, it is the gift of God.
> I know that, whatsoever God doeth, it shall be for ever: nothing can be put to it, nor any thing taken from it: and God doeth it, that men should fear before him.
> That which hath been is now; and that which is to be hath already been; and God requireth that which is past. (Bible, Ecclesiastes 3:1-15)

3. Angels

God's house is a house of order. The Lord controls who comes to this earth. The world worries about invasions of people and forces foreign to this planet. How comforting to know that only those come here who are authorized by the Lord to minister to the inhabitants of this earth. (See D&C 130:5-7)

4. The future state of the earth and its inhabitants

Through revelation, we are taught the true destiny of this earth upon which we reside. It will be sanctified and become a celestial dwelling place for those who have come unto Christ and been true and faithful to their covenants with the Lord.

This earth is to become a celestial depository of knowledge for the benefit and use of the celestial inhabitants thereof. The citizens of the earth at that time will have access to the knowledge of the Gods. (See D&C 130:9-11; see also D&C 76:55-59, 94-96; 84:38; 93:20, 27-28; 132:20)

5. Principles of intelligence

Intelligence might be defined as "the righteous application of knowledge."

From this revelation, we learn that man's diligence and obedience are pre-requisites to his obtaining this intelligence. The spiritual level of man's understanding is determined by his faithful responses to God's commandments. Accordingly, his level of intelligence is the determining factor of the level of his resurrection and the degree of glory for which he has prepared and is capable of inheriting. Those who are more diligent and more obedient than others in this life, will obtain greater advantages in the world to come. (See D&C 130:18-19)

6. The law of blessings

Once more we are reminded in this revelation, that the law of the Lord is not a restriction, it is an opportunity. Obedience to law is the means whereby God can bless man. (See D&C 130:20-21)

The importance of understanding and applying this principle was emphasized by President N. Eldon Tanner as follows:

> All the laws of God and the laws of nature and the laws of the land are made for the benefit of man, for his comfort, enjoyment, safety, and well-being; and it is up to the individual to learn these laws and to determine whether or not he will enjoy these benefits by obeying the law and by keeping the commandments. My whole purpose today is to show that laws exist for our benefit and that to be happy and successful we must obey the laws and regulations pertaining to our activities; and these laws will function either to our joy and well-being or to our detriment and sorrow, according to our actions....
>
> As someone has said, you do not break the law, but actually break yourself by refusing to respect it as it applies to your condition. The law applies, and our actions determine the result. Too often we are not prepared to discipline ourselves and do that which

is necessary to accomplish the things which we desire most. (CR, April 1970, p. 62)

Summary and Conclusion

Through the restoration of the gospel, many great and eternal truths have been revealed for the benefit of man. Man need not seek in vain to know the true and living God. God has been revealed and man can place his faith in Him. Man has an eternal destiny and a hope in a life after death. Man's faith and obedience ultimately determine and presently assure him of an eternal reward in the sharing of all that Father has in a celestial world.

Chapter 56

Doctrine and Covenants Section 131

Suggested Title
Three Heavens in the Celestial Kingdom—The More Sure Word of Prophecy

Overview of Section Content
1. Three degrees in the celestial glory (vs. 1)
2. The new and everlasting covenant of marriage is essential to obtain the highest degree of glory (vs. 2-4)
3. The more sure word of prophecy (vs. 5)
4. Man cannot be saved in ignorance (vs. 6)
5. Spirit is matter (vs. 7-8)

Historical Setting

Joseph Smith, Jun.

[Tuesday, 16 May 1843]...Before returning, I gave Brother and Sister Johnson instructions on the priesthood; and putting my hand on the knee of William Clayton, I said: [Section 131:1-4 follows]...

Wednesday, 17, [May 1843]...At ten a.m. preached from 2nd Peter, 1st chapter and showed that knowledge is power; and the man who has the most knowledge has the greatest power. [Section 131:5-6 follows]

In the evening went to hear a Methodist preacher lecture. After he got through, offered some corrections as follows: [Section 131:7-8 follows] (HC, Vol. 5, pp. 391-392)

Sacred Truths

Introduction

As noted in the Historical Setting, this section is a compilation of inspired statements made by the Prophet Joseph Smith on three separate occasions. We will discuss each of these segments as follows:

1. Three degrees in the celestial glory
2. The more sure word of prophecy
3. A man cannot be saved in ignorance
4. Spirit is matter

Three Degrees in the Celestial Glory

The vision given to Joseph Smith and Sidney Rigdon, as recorded in Doctrine and Covenants Section 76 provides a great scriptural insight to the breadth of man's potential eternal destiny. From that vision we learn that there are three degrees of glory to which the majority of mankind will eventually become heirs:Celestial, Terrestrial, Telestial. (See also Bible, I Corinthians 15:40-42; II Corinthians 12:2) Our understanding of the Celestial glory is further broadened by the information contained in Section 131. We learn:

1. There are three heavens in the Celestial glory. (See D&C 131:1)
2. Eternal marriage is a pre-requisite for an inheritance in the highest heaven. (See D&C 131:2-3)
3. Only in the highest heaven will it be possible for eternally married people to have the blessings of eternal increase (children). (See D&C 131:4)

The sweetness of eternal marriage relationships will be enhanced through the spiritual use of the God-given creative powers of increase. Such marriages will be blessed with the opportunity of creating spirit-children posterity. Commenting on this husband-wife priesthood relationship, the Prophet Joseph Smith said:

> Except a man and his wife enter into an everlasting covenant and be married for eternity, while in this probation, by the power and authority of the Holy Priesthood, they will cease to increase when they die; that is, they will not have any children after the resurrection. But those who are married by the power and authority

of the priesthood in this life, and continue without committing the sin against the Holy Ghost, will continue to increase and have children in the celestial glory. (HC, Vol. 5, p. 391)

Elder Melvin J. Ballard also discussed the concept of eternal increase. He said:

> What do we mean by endless or eternal increase? We mean that through the righteousness and faithfulness of men and women who keep the commandments of God they will come forth with celestial bodies, fitted and prepared to enter into their great, high and eternal glory in the celestial kingdom of God; and unto them through their preparation, there will come spirit children. I don't think that is very difficult to comprehend. The nature of the offspring is determined by the nature of the substance that flows in the veins of the being. When blood flows in the veins of the being the offspring will be what blood produces, which is tangible flesh and bone; but when that which flows in the veins is spirit matter, a substance which is more refined and pure and glorious than blood, the offspring of such beings will be spirit children. By that I mean they will be in the image of the parents. They will have a spirit body and have a spark of the eternal or divine that always did exist in them.
>
> Unto such parentage will this glorious privilege come, for it is written in our scriptures that the glory of God is to bring to pass the immortality and eternal life of man. So it will be the glory of men and women that will make their glory like unto His. When the power of endless increase shall come to us, and our offspring grow and multiply through ages that shall come, they will be in due time, as we have been, provided with an earth like this wherein they too may obtain earthly bodies and pass through all the experiences through which we have passed. Then we shall hold a relationship to them the fulness and completeness of which has not been revealed to us; but we shall stand in our relationship to them as God our Eternal Father does to us, and thereby this is the most glorious and wonderful privilege that ever will come to any of the sons and daughters of God. (Melvin J. Ballard, Crusader for Righteousness, pp. 211-212)

The More Sure Word of Prophecy

In this revelation, we learn that the term "more sure word of prophecy" means "...a man's knowing that he is sealed up unto eternal life by revelation and the spirit of prophecy, through the power of the Holy Priesthood." (D&C 131:5)

The phrase "More Sure Word of Prophecy" is synonymous to the phrase "Calling and Election Made Sure." Understanding the terms used in this latter phrase helps to explain the meaning of the former one. To be called, is to be invited by the Lord to become a member of the church and kingdom of God. Those who accept His invitation and become a member of His church have received their calling. In a general sense, these are the elect of God. However, a more strict interpretation of the term "elect" was given by the Lord to identify the elect as those who ". . .hear my voice and harden not their hearts;" (D&C 29:7--See also D&C 33:6) In other words, the elect of God are those who favorably respond to the Lord's call and continue to hearken to His voice.

When a person is called into the kingdom he enters into a covenant with the Lord. He makes certain promises and in turn is assured of certain rewards (including eternal life) if he is faithful and keeps the conditions of his covenant. Thus, the rewards offered by the Lord are conditional at that time.

As the covenant member of the church continues to remain faithful to the conditions of his covenant, he will eventually prove himself worthy of unconditional promises of the Lord. He will receive the assurance by revelation, that his calling and election (membership standing in the church and kingdom of God) is made sure. He is thus sealed up unto eternal life. This is the more sure word of prophecy.

The Prophet Joseph Smith explained this principle and process as follows:

> After a person has faith in Christ, repents of his sins, and is baptized for the remission of his sins and receives the Holy Ghost, . . .then let him continue to humble himself before God, hungering and thirsting after righteousness, and living by every word of God, and the Lord will soon say unto him, Son, thou shalt be exalted. When the Lord has thoroughly proved him, and finds that the man is determined to serve Him at all hazards, then the man will find his calling and his election made sure, . . .(TPJS, p. 150)

There are many other ramifications of the above principle. For further insights and additional understanding see: Doctrinal New Testament Commentary, Vol. 3, pp. 323-355.

A Man Cannot Be Saved In Ignorance

The Lord informed us in this revelation that His children cannot be saved in ignorance. (See D&C 131:6) The question might be asked: "Ignorance of what?" Elder Spencer W. Kimball provided information that serves as an answer to this question:

> One may acquire knowledge of space and in a limited degree conquer it. He may explore the moon and other planets, but no man can ever really find God in a university campus laboratory, in the physical test tubes of workshops, nor on the testing fields at Cape Kennedy. God and his program will be found only in deep pondering, appropriate reading, much kneeling in devout, humble prayer, and in a sincerity born of need and dependence.
>
> These requirements having been fully met, there is no soul between the poles nor from ocean to ocean who may not positively obtain this knowledge, this hidden treasure of knowledge, this saving and exalting knowledge.
>
> President Joseph Fielding Smith, speaking at Brigham Young University, quoted from latter-day revelation: "It is impossible for a man to be saved in ignorance" (D&C 131:6), and then asked the question:
>
> "Ignorance of what? By that, do we mean that a man must become proficient in his secular learning—that he must master some branch of education? What does it mean?"
>
> We mean this: "That a man cannot be saved in ignorance of the saving principles of the Gospel. We cannot be saved without faith in God. We cannot be saved in our sins. . . .We must receive the ordinances and the covenants pertaining to the Gospel and be true and faithful to the end. Eventually, if we are faithful and true, we shall gain all knowledge, but that is not required of us in this brief, mortal life, for that would be impossible. But here in faith and integrity to the truth, we lay the foundation upon which we build for eternity."
>
> Real intelligence is the creative use of knowledge, not merely an accumulation of facts.
>
> The ultimate and greatest of all knowledge, then, is to know God and his program for our exaltation. . . .
>
> To have both the secular and spiritual is the ideal. To have only the secular is like Jude said: ". . .clouds they are without water, carried about of winds; trees whose fruit withereth." (Jude 12.)
>
> Desirable as is secular knowledge, one is not truly educated unless he has the spiritual with the secular. The secular knowledge is to be desired; the spiritual knowledge is an absolute necessity. We shall need all of the accumulated secular knowledge in order to create worlds and to furnish them, but only through the "mysteries

of God" and these hidden treasures of knowledge may we arrive at the place and condition where we may use that knowledge in creation and exaltation. (CR, October 1968, pp. 130-131)

Spirit Is Matter

Many religionists teach that God created man, the earth, and all things in the universe out of nothing. By revelation, the Prophet Joseph Smith learned from the living God that creation was a process of organization. He learned that "There is no such thing as immaterial matter. All spirit is matter, . . ." (D&C 131:7) This revealed truth has been echoed by scientists who say that matter cannot be created nor destroyed—only its form may be changed. Elder Orson Pratt taught this concept as follows:

> The materials out of which this earth was formed, are just as eternal as the materials of the glorious personage of the Lord himself. . . .This being, when he formed the earth, did not form it out of something that had no existance, but he formed it out of materials that had an existence from all eternity: they never had a beginning, neither will one particle of substance now in existence ever have an end. There are just as many particles now as there were at any previous period of duration, and will be while eternity lasts. Substance had no beginning; to say that laws had no beginning would be another thing; some laws might have been eternal, while others might have had a lawgiver.But the earth was formed out of eternal materials, and it was made to be inhabited and God peopled it with creatures of his own formation. (JD, Vol. 19, p. 286)

Summary and Conclusion

The Lord said ". . .he will give unto the faithful line upon line, precept upon precept; . . ." (D&C 98:12) True to His word, He has provided continued revelation to the church that bears His name.

The marvelous and eternal truths revealed in this revelation are an illustration of the Lord's keeping His promise. Knowledge which saves souls is knowledge that comes from God. Anyone who hopes for an eternal inheritance within the environments of the Gods, must first righteously apply the revealed truths that save.

Chapter 57

Doctrine and Covenants Section 132

Suggested Title
Celestial Marriage

Overview of Section Content

1. Joseph Smith's inquiry concerning the ancient practice of plural marriage (vs. 1-2)
2. The new and everlasting covenant of marriage and its blessings (vs. 3-14, 19-25)
3. Marriage for time only (vs. 15-18)
4. Sin against the celestial marriage covenant (vs. 26-27)
5. Saints directed to do the works of Abraham (vs. 28-33)
6. Plural marriages authorized by the Lord in ancient times (vs. 34-39)
7. Punishment for adultery (vs. 40-44)
8. Joseph Smith has the power to seal on earth and in heaven (vs. 45-48)
9. Joseph Smith sealed up to his exaltation (vs. 49-50, 57)
10. Emma Smith admonished to be faithful (vs. 51-56)
11. The law of the priesthood pertaining to the plurality of wives (vs. 58-66)

Historical Setting

George A. Smith

In 1843 the law on celestial marriage was written, but not published and was known only to perhaps one or two hundred persons. It was written from the dictation of Joseph Smith, by Elder William Clayton, his private secretary, who is now in this city. This revelation was published in 1852, read to a general conference, and accepted as a portion of the faith of the Church. Elder Orson Pratt went to Washington and there published a work called the "Seer," in which this revelation was printed, and a series of articles showing forth the law of God in relation to marriage...(JD, Vol. 14, pp. 213-214)

William Clayton (Andrew Jenson)

"On the morning of the 12th of July, 1843, Joseph and Hyrum Smith came into the office in the upper story of the 'brick store,' on the bank of the Mississippi River. They were talking on the subject of plural marriage. Hyrum said to Joseph, 'If you will write the revelation on celestial marriage, I will take and read it to Emma, and I believe I can convince her of its truth, and you will hereafter have peace.' Joseph smiled and remarked, 'You do not know Emma as well as I do.' Hyrum repeated his opinion and further remarked, 'The doctrine is so plain, I can convince any reasonable man or woman of its truth, purity or heavenly origin,' or words to their effect. Joseph then said, 'Well, I will write the revelation and we will see.' He then requested me to get paper and prepare to write. Hyrum very urgently requested Joseph to write the revelation by means of the Urim and Thummim, but Joseph, in reply, said he did not need to, for he knew the revelation perfectly from beginning to end.

"Joseph and Hyrum then sat down and Joseph commenced to dictate the revelation on celestial marriage, and I wrote it, sentence by sentence, as he dictated. After the whole was written, Joseph asked me to read it through, slowly and carefully, which I did, and he pronounced it correct. He then remarked that there was much more that he could write, on the same subject, but what was written was sufficient for the present...(Historical Record, Vol. 6, pp. 225-226)

Section 132   355

Sacred Truths

Introduction

The Prophet Joseph Smith inquired of the Lord concerning some aspects of marriage. He wondered about plural marriage in ancient times, adulterous sins against the marriage covenant and perhaps other issues pertaining to marriage. (See D&C 132:1-2, 41)

This revelation pertaining to the new and everlasting covenant of marriage can be conveniently discussed under the following topics:

1. Plural marriage
2. The Lord's law of celestial marriage
3. Sins against the marriage covenant
4. Blessings and works of Abraham

Plural Marriage

Much could be written pertaining to plural marriage. In this revelation, much has been revealed on the subject. We will discuss some aspects of this God-ordained practice in this chapter.

1. Significant dates pertaining to this revelation

As noted in the Historical Setting of this chapter, this revelation was committed to writing in 1843 as dictated by the Prophet Joseph Smith. The revelation was published and made available for public reading in 1852. However, the date the Prophet Joseph Smith received the revelation from the Lord was much earlier. There is ample evidence that the revelation was given soon after the church was organized. For instance, Elder B. H. Roberts has written as follows:

> The date in the heading of the Revelation on the Eternity of the Marriage Covenant, Including the Plurality of Wives, notes the time at which the revelation was committed to writing, not the time at which the principles set forth in the revelation were first made known to the Prophet. This is evident from the written revelation itself which discloses the fact that Joseph Smith was already in the relationship of plural marriage, as the following passage witnesses:
>
> "And let mine handmaid, Emma Smith, receive all those that have been given unto my servant Joseph, and who are virtuous and pure before me."
>
> There is indisputable evidence that the revelation making known this marriage law was given to the Prophet as early as 1831.

In that year, and thence intermittently up to 1833, the Prophet was engaged in a revision of the English Bible text under the inspiration of God, Sidney Rigdon in the main acting as his scribe. As he began his revision with the Old Testament, he would be dealing with the age of the Patriarchs in 1831. He was doubtless struck with the favor in which the Lord held the several Bible Patriarchs of that period, notwithstanding they had a plurality of wives. What more natural than that he should inquire of the Lord at that time, when his mind must have been impressed with the fact—Why, O Lord, didst Thou justify Thy servants, Abraham, Isaac and Jacob; as also Moses, David, and Solomon, in the matter of their having many wives and concubines (see opening paragraph of the Revelation)? In answer to that inquiry came the revelation, though not then committed to writing. (HC, Vol. 5, Introduction, pp. XXIX—XXX)

2. *The principle and practice of plural marriage*

Anyone who accepts the Bible as a depository of revealed truth, acknowledges that, on occasion, plural marriage has been sanctioned by the Lord. At various times in certain dispensations, the Lord has commanded that this principle should be put into practice. (See D&C 132:34-39; Bible, Genesis 25:1-6; Genesis chaps. 29 & 30; II Samuel 12:7-8) On other occasions, He has forbidden this practice. (See B of M Jacob 2:27-30)

In this dispensation of the fulness of times, the Lord has revealed that He would "...gather together in one all things in Christ, both which are in heaven, and which are on earth;..." (Bible, Ephesians 1:10; see also Bible, Acts 3:20-21) The practice of plural marriage is part of the restoration of all things spoken of by the Lord.

It is clear that the principle of plural mariage, as taught and practiced in this dispensation, was revealed and commanded by the Lord. Those who righteously obeyed this law did so by divine decree. (See D&C 132:3-14, 58-66)

3. *Revocation of plural marriage*

One of the fundamental truths that is evident in the functioning and operation of the kingdom of God is that the Lord commands and revokes as He sees fit. (See D&C 56:4; 58:30-33; 124:49) Any commandment or revocation of a commandment given by the Lord for His people will be revealed through the mouth of His living prophet. (See D&C 21:1-6; 28:2; 43:1-7; 90:1-4; 107:91; 124:45-46, 125-126)

The Lord revealed to the Prophet Wilford Woodruff that the practice of plural marriage should cease in that no additional plural marriages would be sanctioned by the Lord. An official statement was issued by the church in 1890 entitled the Manifesto that announced the revocation of the practice of solemnizing plural marriages. Based upon the divine principle of common consent (see D&C 26:2), this manifesto was presented to and sustained by the membership of the church. (See D&C, Official Declaration-1; see also Excerpts From Three Addresses by President Wilford Woodruff Regarding the Manifesto which follow Official Declaration-1)

Just as the implementation of the practice of plural marriage was of divine origin, even so certainly was the revocation of the practice given by the Lord. Just as those who obeyed His command to practice plural marriage stood approved by the Lord, even so do those who violate His revocation stand condemned before Him.

Inasmuch as plural marriage is no longer a practice of the Lord's church, there would be little value to an extended discussion of this subject.

The Lord's Law of Celestial Marriage

In this revelation on celestial marriage the Lord described three different kinds of marriage and the conditions and promises associated therewith.

1. Marriage for mortality only

The law under which this kind of marriage is contracted is only valid to the extent that man has authority or power to control some of the affairs of life. Such power or control is limited to mortal life and does not extend beyond the grave. Such a law of marriage is not of the Lord. (See D&C 132:15) The law that creates this kind of marriage does not have the power to bind the marriage beyond this life. The spouses in this marriage will find themselves alone and without claim upon any marriage relationships in the resurrection. They will serve, instead, as angels to those who have received higher degrees of exaltation. (See D&C 132:16-17)

2. A counterfeit celestial marriage

It is an eternal truth that marriage can endure for eternity when people comply with the conditions the Lord has set. Some people have assumed that the power to perform such a marriage is available through sources that are not authorized by the Lord. Lucifer has deceived some people to the extent that they perform such marriages when they do not have the authority from the Lord to do so. This kind of marriage will also have an end when men are dead. (See D&C 132:18)

3. Celestial marriage

Unique among the doctrines and practices of the world, is the Lord's concept of marriage as provided in the Lord's church and kingdom upon the earth. (See D&C 132:19; 131:1-4) He has revealed that His law provides eternal relationships for families which have been created under His law of marriage. He referred to this eternal marriage law as a gate. (See D&C 132:21-22) It is only by entering this gate that a couple gains access to eternal marriage blessings. Commenting upon this gate, Elder Bruce R. McConkie has said:

> We understand from the revelations that those who come up in immortality as husband and wife will grow, enlarge, advance, and progress until they inherit what is termed the "fulness of the Father." Then no power, no dominion, no truth will be withheld from them. But those who do not so inherit will come up in immortality, separately and singly, that is unmarried, without exaltation, in whatever degree of reward they merit, but forever denied the eternal fulness.
>
> Thus celestial marriage is the gate to exaltation. It opens the door. Those who have a continuation of the family unit in eternity have exaltation. If the family unit does not continue in eternity, there is no exaltation, or in other words, there is no eternal life. By definition, eternal life is God's life. It is the type, kind, status, and quality of existence which he enjoys as an exalted being. . . .
>
> Celestial marriage, like baptism, is a gate. You enter in at the first gate when you are baptized. This puts you on the path which leads to the celestial world; and you do not inherit a celestial glory unless you traverse the length of the path, or as the revelations say, "endure to the end."
>
> As with baptism, so it is with celestial marriage. It opens the door, a second door. It starts one out in the direction of exaltation. It puts one on the path that leads to eternal life. You cannot get on the path without entering the gate, but having entered the gate then you must traverse the length of the path. The process of going up that path is the process of keeping the covenant made in connection with this holy order of matrimony. It is the process of obeying the laws, commandments, principles, and ordinances of the gospel. (BYU Speeches of the Year, April 20, 1960, pp. 4,6)

The conditions and promises associated with this law are as follows:

   a. Proper authority—The power to bind a man and woman in wedlock for time and eternity is vested in one man upon the earth, the Lord's prophet. He, in turn, may delegate such authority to others who may then perform these sacred marriage ceremonies. (See D&C 132:7)

   b. Worthiness—Men and women obtain access to the eternal powers of the Lord under His law of marriage only when they comply with certain standards of personal worthiness. The criteria for an acceptable level of worthiness is established by the Lord through His prophets.

c. Holy Spirit of Promise—When the above two conditions are complied with, the Holy Ghost puts a stamp of approval upon the marriage ordinance with the promise that the participants in the ordinance will reap the reward of eternal life if they continue faithful. (See D&C 132:7, 19)

d. Sealed up to eternal life—A husband and wife who are true and faithful to their celestial marriage covenants will eventually have their calling and election made sure. They are sealed up to their eternal lives. (See D&C 132:19; See also 131:5-6)

e. Blessings of eternal life—Obedience to God's laws is not without reward. To have eternal lives is to experience life like unto God. A continuation of the seeds (children) will be forever. All powers and dominions will be bestowed upon the exalted and eternally-married couple. All that God has shall be given unto them. (See D&C 132:19-24)

Sins Against the Marriage Covenant

As noted above, there are many blessings associated with the marriage covenant. Those who are true and faithful to the conditions of that covenant will be sealed up to their exaltations. However, certain grievous sins might be committed against the covenant that would destroy the seal and promise of eternal life. (See D&C 132:19, 26-27, 41)

There are three such sins that were discussed by Elder Bruce R. McConkie as follows:

> ...the revelation [Section 132] speaks of that obedience out of which eternal life grows, and still speaking both of celestial marriage and of making one's calling and election sure says: "Verily, verily, I say unto you, if a man marry a wife according to my word, and they are sealed by the Holy Spirit of promise, according to mine appointment"—that is, if they are both married and have their calling and election made sure—" and he or she shall commit any sin or transgression of the new and everlasting covenant whatever, and all manner of blasphemies, and if they commit no murder wherein they shed innocent blood, yet they shall come forth in the first resurrection, and enter into their exaltation; but they shall be destroyed in the flesh, and shall be delivered unto the buffetings of Satan unto the day of redemption, saith the Lord God." (D. & C. 132:26.)
>
> ...even though a man's calling and election has been made sure, if he then commits blasphemy against the Holy Ghost, he becomes a son of perdition, because when he was sealed up unto eternal life it was with a reservation. The sealing was not to apply in the case of the unpardonable sin.
>
> As to the fact that the sealing power cannot seal a man up unto eternal life if he thereafter commits murder and thereby sheds

innocent blood (not in this case the blood of Christ, but the blood of any person slain unlawfully and with malice) the Prophet says: "A murderer, for instance, one that sheds innocent blood, cannot have forgiveness. David sought repentance at the hand of God carefully with tears, for the murder of Uriah; but he could only get it through hell; he got a promise that his soul should not be left in hell.

"Although David was a king, he never did obtain the spirit and power of Elijah and the fullness of the priesthood; and the priesthood that he received, and the throne and kingdom of David is to be taken from him and given to another by the name of David in the last days, raised up out of his lineage." (*Teachings, p. 339.*) Thus, even though a man's calling and election has been made sure, if he then commits murder, all of the promises are of no effect, and he goes to a telestial kingdom (Rev. 21:8; D. & C. 76:103), because when he was sealed up unto eternal life, it was with a reservation. The sealing was not to apply in the case of murder.

And as to the fact that the sealing power cannot seal a man up unto eternal life if he thereafter commits adultery, the Prophet says: "if a man commit adultery, he cannot receive the celestial kingdom of God. Even if he is saved in any kingdom, it cannot be the celestial kingdom." (*History of the Church*, vol. 6, p. 81.) Thus, even though a man's calling and election has been sure if he then commits adultery, all of the promises are of no effect, and he goes to a telestial kingdom, because when he was sealed up unto eternal life, it was with a reservation. The sealing was not to apply in the case of subsequent adultery. In other cases, through repentance, there is forgiveness for this sin which is second only to murder in the category of personal sins. (I Cor. 6:9-11; 3 Ne. 30; D. & C. 42:24-26.) (Doctrinal New Testament Commentary, Vol. 3, pp. 344, 346-347)

Blessings and Works of Abraham

In this revelation, the Lord made it known to the Prophet Joseph Smith that the blessings promised to Abraham would be available to this dispensation. The full realization of these blessings would be contingent upon entering into the law of celestial marriage and being true to the conditions of that marriage covenant. (See D&C 132:29-33) When a worthy couple kneel at the sacred marriage altars of the temple, they are given the right to eternal companionship and are promised the same blessings that were bestowed upon Abraham in ancient days. That is, they are assured of an eternal posterity, the rights and powers of the priesthood of God, and an eternal family relationship based upon the patriarchal order. (See Personal Study Guides for Melchizedek Priesthood Quorums 1977-78, pp. 14-15; 1980-81, p. 102)

The requirements for obtaining access to all of these Abrahamic blessings was specifically declared by the Lord when He said:

> Go ye, therefore, and do the works of Abraham; enter ye into my law and ye shall be saved.
> But if ye enter not into my law ye cannot receive the promise of my Father, which he made unto Abraham. (D&C 132:32-33)

President Spencer W. Kimball discussed some of the major works of Abraham that each of Father's children need to emulate. Based upon President Kimball's article, a list of some of those works is provided as follows:

1. He followed Jesus Christ
2. He sought for priesthood and priesthood blessings. (Patriarchal Power)
3. He gave prompt obedience
4. He received revelation for his family
5. He presided over his family in righteousness
6. He taught his family the gospel by example and precept
7. He gave missionary service
8. He acted as a peacemaker
9. He possessed integrity—kept covenants at all costs
10. He was honest with others
11. He paid a full tithe—He put God first
12. He exercised faith (See Ensign, June 1975, pp. 3-7)

When this revelation on the law of celestial marriage was given to the Prophet Joseph Smith it was a unique doctrine among the religious organizations of the earth. No other people in the world understood such a beautiful concept as the potential eternal relationships of husbands and wives.

Expressing his overwhelming delight at being taught such a doctrine of heaven, Elder Parley P. Pratt recorded:

> ...In Philadelphia I had the happiness of once more meeting with President Smith, and of spending several days with him and others, and with the Saints in that city and vicinity.
> During these interviews he taught me many great and glorious principles concerning God and the heavenly order of eternity. It was at this time that I received from him the first idea of eternal family organization, and the eternal union of the sexes in those inexpressibly endearing relationships which none but the highly intellectual,

the refined and pure in heart, know how to prize, and which are at the very foundation of everything worthy to be called happiness.

Till then I had learned to esteem kindred affections and sympathies as appertaining solely to this transitory state, as something from which the heart must be entirely weaned, in order to be fitted for its heavenly state.

It was Joseph Smith who taught me how to prize the endearing relationships of father and mother, husband and wife; of brother and sister, son and daughter.

It was from him that I learned that the wife of my bosom might be secured to me for time and all eternity; and that the refined sympathies and affections which endeared us to each other emanated from the fountain of divine eternal love. It was from him that I learned that we might cultivate these affections, and grow and increase in the same to all eternity; while the result of our endless union would be an offspring as numerous as the stars of heaven, or the sands of the sea shore.

It was from him that I learned the true dignity and destiny of a son of God, clothed with an eternal priesthood, as the patriarch and sovereign of his countless offspring. It was from him that I learned that the highest dignity of womanhood was, to stand as a queen and priestess to her husband, and to reign for ever and ever as the queen mother of her numerous and still increasing offspring.

I had loved before, but I knew not why. But now I loved—with a pureness—an intensity of elevated, exalted feeling, which would lift my soul from the transitory things of this grovelling sphere and expand it as the ocean. I felt that God was my heavenly Father indeed; that Jesus was my brother, and that the wife of my bosom was an immortal eternal companion; a kind ministering angel, given to me as a comfort, and a crown of glory for ever and ever. In short, I could now love with the spirit and with the understanding also. (APPP, pp. 297-298)

The importance of entering into the law of celestial marriage was graphically illustrated by President Heber J. Grant when he said:

I shall always be grateful, to the day of my death, that I did not listen to some of my friends when, as a young man not quite twenty-one years of age, I took the trouble to travel all the way from Utah County to St. George to be married in the St. George Temple. That was before the railroad went south of Utah County, and we had to travel the rest of the way by team. It was a long and difficult trip in those times, over unimproved and uncertain roads, and the journey each way required several days.

Many advised me not to make the effort—not to go all the way down to St. George to be married. They reasoned that I could have the president of the stake or my bishop marry me, and then when the Salt Lake Temple was completed, I could go there with my wife and children and be sealed to her and have our children sealed to us for eternity.

Why did I not listen to them? Because I wanted to be married for time and eternity—because I wanted to start life right. Later I had cause to rejoice greatly because of my determination to be married in the temple at that time rather than to have waited until some later and seemingly more convenient time.

Some years ago the general board members of the Young Women's Mutual Improvement Association were traveling throughout the stakes of Zion speaking on the subject of marriage. They urged the young people to start their lives together in the right way by being married right, in the temples of the Lord.

I was out in one of the stakes attending a conference, and one of my daughters, who was the representative of the Young Women's general board at the conference, said: "I am very grateful to the Lord that I was properly born, born under the covenant, born of parents that had been properly married and sealed in the temple of the Lord."

Tears came into my eyes, because her mother died before the Salt Lake Temple was completed and I was grateful that I had not listened to the remarks of my friends who had tried to persuade me not to go to the St. George Temple to be married. I was very grateful for the inspiration and determination I had to start life right.

Why did it come to me? It came to me because my mother believed in the gospel, taught me the value of it, gave me a desire to get all of the benefits of starting life right and of doing things according to the teachings of the gospel.

I believe that no worthy young Latter-day Saint man or woman should spare any reasonable effort to come to the house of the Lord to begin life together. The marriage vows taken in these hallowed places and the sacred covenants entered into for time and all eternity are proof against many of the temptations of life that tend to break homes and destroy happiness. (Gospel Standards, pp. 359-360)

Summary and Conclusion

Celestial marriage is ordained of God. Husbands and wives are assured the continuation of their marriage relationship beyond this life, provided they will enter into and live the Lord's law of celestial marriage. By so doing, they will receive all the blessings promised to Abraham.

Chapter 58

Doctrine and Covenants Section 133

Suggested Title

The Appendix—The Gathering and the Second Coming

Overview of Section Content

1. The Lord calls upon all His children to gather and prepare for His second coming (vs. 1-16)
2. The Savior's second coming and some events associated therewith (vs. 17-35)
3. The restoration of the gospel for the purpose of warning and preparing mankind for the Lord's second coming (vs. 36-74)

Historical Setting

Joseph Smith, Jun.

It had been decided by the conference that Elder Oliver Cowdery should carry the commandments and revelations to Independence, Missouri, for printing, and that I should arrange and get them in readiness by the time that he left, which was to be by—or, if possible, before—the 15th of the month [November]. At this time there were many things which the Elders desired to know relative to preaching the Gospel to the inhabitants of the earth, and concerning the gathering; and in order to walk by the true light, and be instructed from on high, on the 3rd of November, 1831, I inquired of the Lord and received the following important revelation, which has since been added to the book of Doctrine and Covenants, and called the Appendix: . . . (HC, Vol. 1, p. 229)

Joseph Fielding Smith

. . . Section 133, of the Doctrine and Covenants was received at the close of the conference of November 1, 1831, and two days after the Preface, or section one, was given. It was called "The Appendix" because it was received after the revelation approving the selection of revelations to be published, and has occupied the position near the end of the volume in all editions, and out of its chronological order. The tenor of this section is very similar to that of section one, in fact is largely a continuation of the same theme . . . (CHMR, Vol. 2, p. 34)

Sacred Truths

Introduction

As noted in the Historical Setting of this chapter, this revelation is largely a continuation of the theme of Section One of the Lord's book of revelations. (Doctrine and Covenants) The primary theme is that the gospel of Jesus Christ has been restored to warn and prepare the people of the earth for the Lord's second coming. For study purposes, this revelation can be grouped into two major categories:

1. The gathering in preparation for the Lord's second coming.
2. The Lord's second coming and some events associated therewith.

The Gathering in Preparation for the Lord's Second Coming

The Lord has restored His church and kingdom to the earth and has given it three major functions or missions to perform:

1. Teach the gospel—Missionary responsibility
2. Perfect the saints
3. Perform ordinances of salvation for the dead

In Section 133, the Lord gave emphasis to the first two of the three roles of the church as listed above.

1. Teach the gospel—Missionary responsibility

The Lord stressed the missionary responsibiity of the church. The elders of Israel were to go to all nations of the earth and warn the inhabitants thereof. They were to invite all to accept the gospel message, gather to the stakes of Zion, flee from the wickedness of the world, and prepare for the Lord's second coming. (See D&C 133:8-15, 57-60; See also D&C 1:2, 4, 23; 90:10-11) No one will be adequately prepared who fails to heed this message of the Lord as delivered by His authorized messengers.

When this requirement was revealed in 1831, the church was scarcely a year and a half old. A world-wide missionary responsibility must have loomed as an awesome concept to a mere handful of faithful saints in 1831. A century and a half later, the church could rejoice in being able to see a partial fulfillment of the Lord's directive. Faith and testimony should be strengthened in anticipation of the completion of this sacred task. Once more, the Lord is fulfilling His decree that " . . .the prophecies and promises which are in them [revelations in the D&C] shall all be fulfilled." (D&C 1:37)

Reflecting upon the progress made by the church in fulfillment of the Lord's injunction to take the gospel to all the world, President Spencer W. Kimball observed:

> On April 6, 1830, a small group assembled in the farmhouse of Peter Whitmer in Fayette Township in the state of New York. Six men participated in the formal organization procedures, with Joseph Smith as their leader. From that modest beginning in a rural area, this work has grown consistently and broadly, as men and women in many lands have embraced the doctrine and entered the waters of baptism. There are now almost four and a half million living members, and the Church is stronger and growing more rapidly than at any time in its history. Congregations of Latter-day Saints are found throughout North, Central, and South America; in the nations of Europe; in Asia; in Africa; in Australia and the islands of the South Pacific; and in other areas of the world. The gospel restored through the instrumentality of Joseph Smith is presently taught in forty-six languages and in eighty-one nations. From that small meeting held in a farmhouse a century and a half ago, the Church has grown until today it includes nearly twelve thousand organized congregations. (CR, April 1980, p. 75)

2. Perfect the Saints

Not only is the church responsible to teach the people of the earth in order that they may gather to the stakes of Zion, it is also responsible to assist in the perfecting of the saints who are already gathered into the kingdom.

In this revelation, the Lord counseled His saints to sanctify themselves, flee spiritual Babylon (wickedness), and be clean as designated vessels of the Lord. (See D&C 133:4-5, 7, 14)

There are at least two reasons why the Lord counsels His saints to become a sanctified people. First, that they might be prepared for His second coming. Such preparation is necessary whether the individuals are on the earth when He comes or in the spirit world and prepared to return with Him. Second, the Lord needs a worthy people to invite others to flee spiritual Babylon and be prepared for His second coming. His people will be pure in heart, pure in doctrine, and pure in their commitment to follow His authorized servants. These are the elect of God.

In the proclamation sent to the nations of the world by the Quorum of Twelve Apostles in April 1845, the declaration is made that the gospel has been restored and is being offered to all people that they may prepare themselves for the Savior's second coming: (See Messages of the First Presidency, Vol. 1, pp. 263-264)

The Lord's Second Coming and Some Events Associated Therewith

1. The Lord's Second Coming

The Lord's appearance to the earth will take place in at least three phases:

a. The Lord shall appear to the sanctified Latter-day Saints. (See D&C 133:18, 21; See also D&C 45:45-46, 56-57; 77:11)

b. The Lord shall appear to the Jews at Jerusalem. (See D&C 133:21; see also D&C 45:47-53)

c. The Lord shall appear to the world. (See D&C 133:21-25; see also D&C 45:74-75)

2. Some Events Associated with the Lord's Second Coming

It is folly to assume that we know the specific time or sequence of the events associated with the Lord's second coming. Suffice it to say they will take place in connection with the ushering in of the Lord's millennial reign. Some of the specific events mentioned by the Lord in this revelation are as follows: (See D&C 133:17-35, 56, 62-64)

a. The appearance of 144,000 high priests
b. The voice of the Lord shall be heard throughout the earth
c. The earth's surface shall be changed
d. Return of the lost tribes from the north countries
e. The tribe of Judah will be sanctified
f. The resurrection of the saints and their appearance with the Lord
g. The cleansing of the wicked from the earth

Though the above list of events is not exhaustive, still it does provide a further glimpse of some of the magnificent events, that the saints can look forward to with great anticipation. The second coming of the Savior is among the greatest and most significant events that the earth's history will record. The gospel has been restored that Father's children might share in that great experience with joyful delight.

Summary and Conclusion

There are two absolute truths we should remember:

1. The Savior is coming—He has so declared.
2. The Savior's church is the way—the only way—whereby mankind can obtain the saving principles of the gospel and thus be adequately prepared for the great day of the Lord.

Chapter 59

Doctrine and Covenants Section 134

Suggested Title

Governments and Man's Laws—Religion and Divine Laws

Overview of Section Content

1. Governments and man's laws (vs. 1-8)
2. Separation of church and state (vs. 9-10)
3. Men are justified in defending themselves from unlawful oppression (vs. 11)
4. The Lord's servants have the right to teach the gospel, but not with subversive motives (vs. 12)

Historical Setting

Joseph Smith, Jun.

A general assembly of the Church of Latter-day Saints was held at Kirtland on the 17th of August, 1835, to take into consideration the labors of a committee appointed by a general assembly of the Church on the 24th of September, 1834, for the purpose of arranging the items of the doctrine of Jesus Christ for the government of the Church. The names of the committee were: Joseph Smith, Jun., Sidney Rigdon, Oliver Cowdery, and Frederick G. Williams, who, having finished said book according to the instructions given them, deem it necessary to call a general assembly of the Church to see whether the book be approved or not by the authorities of the Church: that it may, if approved, become a law and a rule of faith and practice to the Church. Wherefore, Oliver Cowdery and Sidney Rigdon, members of the First Presidency, (Presidents Joseph Smith, Jun., and Frederick G. Williams being absent on a visit to the Saints in Michigan,) Appointed Thomas Burdick, Warren Parrish, and Sylvester Smith clerks, and proceeded to organize the whole assembly...

President Oliver Cowdery then read the following article on "Governments and Laws in General," which was accepted and adopted and ordered to be printed in said book, by a unanimous vote: [Section 134 follows]

(HC, Vol. 2, pp. 243,247)

Joseph Fielding Smith

A Declaration of Belief. At a conference of the Church held in Kirtland, Ohio, August 17, 1835, the Doctrine and Covenants was presented to the assembled conference for their acceptance or rejection. After the brethren there assembled had carefully and studiously considered the matter, the revelations which had been previously selected by the Prophet Joseph Smith were accepted as the word of the Lord by the unanimous vote of the conference, and were ordered printed. On the occasion of this conference, Joseph Smith the Prophet and his second counselor, Frederick G. Williams, were not present. They were on a brief mission to the Saints in Michigan, and because of this were not familiar with all the proceedings of this conference. After the conference had accepted the revelations, an article on marriage, which had been written by Oliver Cowdery, was read by Elder William W. Phelps and was ordered printed in the book with the revelations.

When this action had been taken, Oliver Cowdery arose and read another article, also written by himself, on "Governments and Laws in General." This article the conference also ordered printed in the book of Doctrine and Covenants. Unfortunately, a great many people, because these articles appeared in the Doctrine and Covenants, readily concluded that they had come through the Prophet Joseph Smith, and hence were to be received on a par with the other parts of the book of revelations. Because of this misinformation articles have been published from time to time declaring that these words on Government and Laws have come to us with the force of revelation having been from the mouth of the Prophet Joseph Smith. This article and the one on "Marriage" were not considered as revelations by the conference, but were published as an expression of belief of the members of the Church at that time.

The article on Governments and Laws has appeared in each edition of the Doctrine and Covenants since 1835, and has been accepted, as the preamble of the article states, as a declaration of belief of the Latter-day Saints....

(The Progress of Man, pp. 367-368)

Sacred Truths

Introduction

Section 134 is not a revelation given through the Prophet Joseph Smith. It is an article written by Oliver Cowdery that has been adopted by the church as "A declaration of belief regarding governments and laws in general...." (D&C 134, Superscription) This article is a part of the scriptural standard works of the church.

This section will be discussed in the following two categories:

1. Governments and man's laws
2. Religion and divine laws

Governments and Man's Laws

The concept of government is ordained of God that peace might prevail. (See D&C 134:1-2) However, not all constituted governments are of God. We note the following characteristics of governments and man's laws that are approved of the Lord:

1. Purpose of Government

Any government approved of the Lord will secure for the individual the following three things: (See D&C 134:2, 6-8, 11)

    a. Free exercise of conscience
    b. Right and control of property
    c. Protection of life

Stressing the importance of these individual rights, President David O. McKay has said:

> I believe with others that government, institutions, and organizations exist primarily for the purpose of securing to the individual

his rights, his happiness, and proper development of his character. . . .

Former United States Supreme Court Justice George Sutherland, from our own State [Utah], carefully stated . . . the individual—the man—has three great rights, equally sacred from arbitrary interference: the right to his life, the right to his liberty, and the right to his property. The three rights are so bound together as to be essentially *one* right. To give a man his life, but deny him his liberty, is to take from him all that makes life worth living. To give him liberty, but take from him the property which is the fruit and badge of his liberty, is to still leave him a slave." (From George Sutherland's speech before the New York State Bar Association, January 21, 1921.) (CR, October 1962, pp. 5-6)

2. Man's responsibilities to government

Man has an obligation before His maker to sustain and maintain any government that provides protection to him of his inalienable rights. (See D&C 134:1, 5, 8) When a man exercises his right to vote, or openly expresses righteous opinions on various political issues, or in various ways participates in the political process, he is fulfilling his responsibility for government before the Lord. (See D&C 98:5-10; B of M, Mosiah 29:11)

3. Limits of governments and man's laws

There are certain boundaries beyond which governments cannot go and stand approved of the Lord. Some such limits are:

   a. Man's laws are not to prescribe rules and forms of worship. (See D&C 134:4)
   b. Man's laws are not to endeavor to control the conscience or suppress the freedom of the soul. (See D&C 134:4)
   c. Man's laws are not to restrict man's rights and freedoms of worship so long as his religious worship does not encourage or promote sedition or anarchy. (See D&C 134:7)
   d. Man's laws are not to discriminate among various religious societies. (See D&C 134:9)

Religion and Divine Laws

Religion is ordained of God. All religious truths come from Him. (See D&C 134:4) However, not all constituted religious organizations or forms of worship are of God. We note the following characteristics of religion and divine laws that are approved of the Lord:

1. Divine laws

a. Divine laws have their origin in Heaven and are given to man through the process of revelation from God. (See D&C 134:6)

b. The purpose of divine laws is to prescribe rules of behavior pertaining to spiritual concerns in order to promote and develop individual faith and worship. (See D&C 134:6)

c. Man is accountable before God and His authorized representatives for his conduct relevant to divine laws. (See D&C 134:4, 6)

2. Limits of divine laws

a. Religious freedom does not imply nor provide license to infringe or impose upon the rights and liberties of others. (See D&C 134:4)

b. Religious organizations do not have the right to exercise jurisdictional authority over man's life or property. (See D&C 134:10)

3. Rights under divine laws

a. Religious organizations have the right to establish rules and criteria for membership in their religious society. They may impose restrictions upon membership privileges including excommunication from the society. (See D&C 134:10)

b. Religious institutions have the right to teach the gospel and warn the nations of impending judgments. (See D&C 134:12)

Summary and Conclusion

This section of the Doctrine and Covenants provides insights to the purpose of Governments and laws. Whether those governments and laws have a divine origin or are the results of man's endeavors, the underlying justification for their function is the same. They are to protect man's life, liberty, and property, whether it be temporal or spiritual in nature.

Chapter 60

Doctrine and Covenants Section 135

Suggested Title
Martyrdom—Joseph and Hyrum Smith

Overview of Section Content
1. The announcement of the martyrdom of the prophets Joseph and Hyrum Smith (vs. 1-2)
2. The divine mission of the Prophet Joseph Smith (vs. 3)
3. The testimony of innocent blood (vs. 4-7)

Historical Setting

Hyrum M. Smith and Janne M. Sjodahl

This article on the Martyrdom of the Prophet Joseph Smith and his brother Hyrum, the Patriarch, touches the heart of every sincere believer in the Gospel of Jesus Christ and the restoration of the Church. This article was written by Elder John Taylor who offered his life with his beloved brethren in this tragedy in Carthage, Illinois. President Taylor was severely wounded and carried the balls with which he was wounded to his grave. His devotion and willingness and that of his companion, Willard Richards, bear a strong testimony of their conviction and integrity to the truth of the mission of the Prophet Joseph Smith . . .

(DCC, p. 855)

Sacred Truths

Introduction

Elder John Taylor is credited with the authorship of the article constituting Section 135 of the Doctrine and Covenants. Elder Hyrum M. Smith of the Quorum of Twelve Apostles and grandson of Hyrum Smith stated that this article was written by John Taylor. (See Historical Setting for this chapter) This article constitutes an " . . .official statement of the Martyrdom of the Prophet and the Patriarch." (HC, Vol. 6, p. 629)

In this chapter we will discuss the following three topics from this section:

1. The martyrdom—A seal
2. Joseph Smith—The Savior's prophet
3. A willing sacrifice—Innocent blood

The Martyrdom—A Seal

Whatever else may be effected by the martyrdom of these two prophets, their deaths constituted a seal of the divinity of the work they espoused.

1. *The scriptures*

Through the Prophet Joseph Smith the Lord brought forth an ancient record out of the ground, written by ancient prophets on the American continent. This record was anticipated and foreseen by certain Biblical prophets who spoke of it's coming forth in ancient prophetic language. (See Bible, Isaiah chap. 29; Ezekiel chap. 18)

An additional book of scripture, containing many revelations from the Lord to His prophet in this dispensation, has also been published in these latter days.

The aforementioned books of scripture are known as the Book of Mormon and the Doctrine and Covenants. As a seal and witness of the divine source and content of these published volumes of holy writ, the Prophet Joseph Smith and his brother Hyrum gave their lives. (See D&C 135:1)

2. *The restoration*

A further, or broader, aspect of the seal effected by the Martyrdom pertains to the restoration of the kingdom of God in these last days. To

Joseph Smith, the Lord sent heavenly beings who restored to him all of the keys, powers, and authority of all previous dispensations of the earth's history. (See D&C 128:21) These keys gave Joseph Smith the authority to direct and regulate the affairs of the Savior's church on the earth and in the Heavens.

However, these keys of the kingdom were not bestowed upon Joseph alone. Oliver Cowdery received them jointly with Joseph and held them in concert with him as long as he remained faithful in his calling and assignment as second elder, or assistant president of the church. Following Oliver's transgressions and subsequent excommunication, those same keys were bestowed upon Hyrum Smith in accordance with the Lord's instructions. (See D&C 124:94-95) Hence, when these two prophets were martyred, their deaths constituted a final and permanent witness and seal as to the divinity of the Lord's work of restoration in this dispensation. (See D&C 135:6-7)

The martyrdom of these two men should be seen as a fulfillment of the requirements of the divine law of witnesses. (See D&C 6:28) By way of insight and explanation of this law and some of its dimensions, President Joseph Fielding Smith has taught:

> *Every time keys were restored, two men received them. Why? Because it was necessary according to the divine law of witnesses for Joseph Smith to have a companion holding those keys*; otherwise it would not have happened. So, as Oliver Cowdery states, when John the Baptist came, he and Joseph Smith received the Aaronic Priesthood under his hands; and when Peter, James, and John came, he was with Joseph Smith.
>
> It was Oliver Cowdery and Joseph Smith who received the keys in the Kirtland Temple on the 3rd of April, 1836, when Christ appeared, when Moses appeared, when Elias appeared, when Elijah appeared. And every time when the keys of a dispensation were bestowed it was to Joseph Smith and Oliver Cowdery—not Joseph Smith alone. Why? Just because of what the Savior said: "If I bear witness of myself, my witness is not true." [Bible, John 5:31]
>
> *If Joseph Smith had said, "I testify, and I testify alone," his testimony would not be true. There had to be two, that the testimony might be valid.*
> OLIVER COWDERY STOOD AS ASSISTANT PRESIDENT OF CHURCH. Now let me call your attention to this. In the Kirtland Temple in 1836, when Joseph Smith and Oliver Cowdery were behind the pulpit and received keys from heavenly messengers there was a First Presidency of the Church and the Prophet had counselors, Sidney Rigdon and Frederick G. Williams. But Sidney Rigdon and Frederick Williams did not go behind the veil, or the curtain, when it was drawn; they were not asked to kneel there

behind the pulpit. It was Joseph Smith and Oliver Cowdery. Why? Because that was Oliver Cowdery's place.

Now I am going to call your attention to something that is not, I regret to say, generally known. Oliver Cowdery was called to be what? The "Second Elder" of the Church, the "Second President" of the Church. We leave him out in our list of Presidents of the Church, we do not include Oliver Cowdery; but *he was an Assistant President. Oliver Cowdery's standing in the beginning was as the "Second Elder" of the Church, holding the keys jointly with the Prophet Joseph Smith.* He preceded the counselors in the First Presidency in authority, standing next to the Prophet Joseph Smith. December 5, 1834, Oliver Cowdery was ordained by Joseph Smith, by the command of the Lord, an Assistant President of the High Priesthood, to hold the keys of Presidency jointly with the Prophet in the ministry. I am going to read that record to you.

"The office of Assistant President is to assist in presiding over the whole Church, and to officiate in the absence of the President, according to his rank and appointment, viz.; President Cowdery, first; President Rigdon, second; and President Williams, third, as they were severally called. *The office of this priesthood is also to act as spokesman, taking Aaron for an example. The virtue of the above priesthood is to hold the keys of the kingdom of heaven or of the Church militant."* That is copied from the history of the Church.

So Oliver Cowdery, through that place as the "Second President," preceded the counselors in the Presidency—naturally so. Why shouldn't he? *He had the same authority, had received the same keys with the Prophet Joseph Smith every time the heavens were opened, and he was an Assistant President of the Church and the second witness of the dispensation of the fulness of times,* which is the greatest of all dispensations, for it was necessary that there be *two Presidents, two witnesses standing at the head of this dispensation....*

Unfortunately—at least unfortunately for Oliver Cowdery, who was called to this wonderful and responsible position, jointly associated with Joseph Smith holding all the authority and presidency in this dispensation—Oliver, in a spirit of rebellion and darkness, turned away. He lost his fellowship in the Church, the power of the priesthood was taken from him, and for a season he stood excommunicated from the Church. Fortunately he eventually overcame this spirit of darkness, but never again was he privileged to receive the keys of power and authority which once were placed upon him.

That this testimony of witnesses might be continued and made complete, the Lord chose another to take the place of Oliver Cowdery, and that other witness was the Patriarch Hyrum Smith. By revelation through Joseph Smith, Hyrum was called and ordained to the priesthood and standing once held by Oliver Cowdery.... [See D&C 124:94-95]

Hyrum Smith became a president of the Church with Joseph Smith, which place Oliver Cowdery might have held had he not wavered and fallen from his exalted station. I am firmly of the opinion that *had Oliver Cowdery remained true to his covenants and obligations as a witness with Joseph Smith, and retained his authority and place, he, and not Hyrum Smith, would have gone with Joseph Smith as a prisoner and to martyrdom at Carthage.*

The sealing of the testimony through the shedding of blood would not have been complete in the death of the Prophet Joseph Smith alone; it required the death of Hyrum Smith who jointly held the keys of this dispensation. It was needful that these martyrs seal their testimony with their blood, that they "might be honored and the wicked might be condemned...." [D&C 136:39]

But here is another point. He had to die. Why? Because we read in the scriptures that the testimony is not of force without the death of the testator—that is, in his particular case, and in the case of Christ. *It was just as necessary that Hyrum Smith lay down his life a martyr for this cause as a witness for God as it was for Joseph Smith, so the Lord permitted them both to be taken in that way and both sealed their testimony with their blood.* Both of them held the keys of the dispensation of the fulness of times jointly, and they will through all the ages of eternity. Then naturally the Council of the Twelve came into its place, and *by right* Brigham Young became President of the Church. (DS, Vol. 1, pp. 211-221)

Joseph Smith—The Savior's Prophet

Any honest scholar of the life of the Prophet Joseph Smith is faced with two obvious conclusions:

1. Joseph Smith accomplished and promoted an incredible amount of good in his short life time of 38 years. (See D&C 135:3; see also Elder Bruce R. McConkie, CR, April 1976, pp. 140-144)

2. Joseph Smith did not compile such an impressive record without divine assistance. No mortal man could have done it alone. He was called of God and directed by Him in his labors. (See D&C 1:17-23; 136:37-39)

Joseph Smith was but a mortal man. But he was the mortal man chosen by the Savior to assist in the restoration of the Lord's kingdom. Through him a knowledge of God was restored to the earth and once again the people of the world were given access to the knowledge that saves souls. A Latter-day Saint does not worship Joseph Smith—He worships the God of Heaven and

His Son Jesus Christ. But the Latter-day Saint is grateful for the work of Joseph Smith and bears testimony of his divine mission and His prophetic calling. Elder Bruce R. McConkie has taught:

> Now, let there be no misunderstanding. We are witnesses of Christ. He is our Savior. He is the door. He stands at the gate; "and he employeth no servant there; and there is none other way save it be by the gate; for he cannot be deceived, for the Lord God is his name." (2 Ne. 9:41.)
>
> But we are also witnesses of Joseph Smith, by whom we know of Christ, and who is the legal administrator to whom power was given to bind on earth and seal in heaven, that all men from his day forward might be heirs of salvation.
>
> We link the names of Jesus Christ and Joseph Smith in our testimonies. And we now testify, as God is our witness, that Joseph Smith is his prophet, and we do it in the blessed name of Him who is Lord of all and of whom we and all the prophets testify, who is Jesus Christ. Even So. Amen. (CR, April 1976, p. 144)

A Willing Sacrifice—Innocent Blood

Neither Joseph nor Hyrum Smith was under any obligation to mankind to die in a jail in Carthage, Illinois. Both went willingly and both knew the certain consequences that awaited them when they chose to go. In summary, both men willingly gave their lives to seal their testimony of the great work of God in this last dispensation. (See D&C 135:4-5)

These men stood approved before the Lord. Their souls were clean. Their blood was innocent. To slay them was to shed innocent blood which was an unforgivable condemnation unto those guilty of the martyrdom of two prophets of God. (See D&C 135:4-5, 7; 136:39)

Summary and Conclusion

The Church of Jesus Christ of Latter-day Saints is the Lord's kingdom upon the earth. The Lord called and ordained Joseph Smith to be His prophet and through him the Lord has once more revealed Himself to mankind. The prophets Joseph and Hyrum Smith willingly sealed their divine calling by giving their lives as a witness for Jesus Christ and the truthfulness of the restoration of the Lord's church to the earth.

Chapter 61

Doctrine and Covenants Section 136

Suggested Title

Covenants and Promises—Camp of Israel

Overview of Section Content

1. The organization of the Camp of Israel (vs. 1-16)
2. The covenants of the Camp of Israel (vs. 17-33, 41-42)
3. Rejection of the Lord's servants and their testimonies (vs. 34-36)
4. The calling and faithfulness of Joseph Smith (vs. 37-40)

Historical Setting

Hyrum M. Smith and Janne M. Sjodahl

...The Saints were driven from their homes in Nauvoo under the most trying circumstances and in poverty and destitution in large measure for they had been robbed by their enemies. Therefore it was extremely needful for a revelation from the Lord for their guidance in their journeyings to the Rocky Mountains. The Lord did not fail them in this hour of distress and gave this revelation to President Brigham Young to guide them in their journeyings and admonishing them to keep His commandments. All the members of the Church were to be organized in companies and were required to keep the commandments faithfully that they might have the guidance of His Spirit with them in all their trying circumstances. These companies were to be on the order followed by Zion's Camp in their remarkable march from Kirtland to Missouri, with captains, over hundreds, fifties and tens and all under the direction of the council of Apostles. (DCC, p. 857)

Sacred Truths

Introduction

This revelation is "The word and will of the Lord concerning the Camp of Israel in their journeyings to the West." (D&C 136:1) This revelation was given by the Lord through His Prophet Brigham Young to Latter-day Saints in the wilderness.

It should be remembered that Brigham Young was called by the Lord to be a member of the first Quorum of Twelve Apostles in this dispensation. Later, the Lord affirmed Brigham Young's position as President of the Quorum of Twelve and declared that he was accepted of the Lord. (See D&C 124:127; 126:1) Following the death of the Prophet Joseph Smith, Brigham Young presided over the church. He led the saints from Nauvoo to Winter Quarters when they were driven out by mobocrats in Illinois. While at Winter Quarters the Lord revealed His will pertaining to the Camp of Israel in the wilderness.

The following topics from Section 136 will be discussed in this chapter:

1. Organization of the Camp of Israel
2. Covenants of the Camp of Irael
3. Promises to the Camp of Israel
4. Rejection of the Lord's servants and their testimonies
5. The calling and faithfulness of Joseph Smith

Organization of the Camp of Israel

The Lord's house is a house of order, even while sojourning in the wilderness. In order for the saints to travel most effectively to their western abode, the Lord instructed them to organize in companies with captains over groups of tens, fifties, and hundreds. Over each company there was to be a presidency who were in turn directed by the Quorum of Twelve Apostles. (See D&C 136:2-3)

Each company had certain responsibilities, some of which were as follows:

1. Provide their own wagons, provisions, clothing and other necessities. (See D&C 136:5)

2. Arrange to take care of the needs of those who remained behind. (See D&C 136:6, 9)
3. Send some men as an advance party to plant spring crops. (See D&C 136:7)
4. Bear equal portion of the responsibility to take care of the poor, widows, fatherless children, etc. (See D&C 136:8)

Several lessons loom large. First, the Lord always provides adequate leadership for His people to accomplish whatever tasks they may be given. Their success is contingent upon their trusting the Lord by following His appointed representatives. Secondly, whether situations are temporary or permanent, the Lord expects His people to conduct the affairs of their lives in an orderly fashion. Third, all saints are important to God. The church looks after the temporal and spiritual needs of all of its members. Regardless of economic or other status distinctions, all worthy saints are alike unto God. All will move forward together.

Covenants of the Camp of Israel

One of the identifying characteristics of the Lord's people is that they are covenant-making people. Modern Israel in the wilderness was no exception. They were to journey according to the organizational structure revealed by the Lord while under covenant to keep the commandments and ordinances of the Lord. (See D&C 136:2-4)

Some of the specific requirements of their covenant were as follows:

1. Be humble—seek the counsel of the Lord. (See D&C 136:19)
2. Keep pledges or promises to fellowmen. (See D&C 136:20)
3. Do not covet goods or property of others. (See D&C 136:20)
4. Keep the Lord's name sacred. (see D&C 136:21)
5. Love fellowmen—control feelings. (See D&C 136:23)
6. Keep the Word of Wisdom. (See D&C 136:24)
7. Use edifying language. (See D&C 136:24)
8. Be honest with neighbors. (See D&C 136:25-26)
9. Be a wise steward over personal possessions. (See D&C 136:27)
10. Praise the Lord in all activities. (See D&C 136:28)
11. Seek comfort from the Lord when in sorrow. (See D&C 136:29)
12. Fear not enemies—have faith in the Lord. (See D&C 136:17, 30)
13. Learn wisdom by seeking the Lord's spirit. (See D&C 136:32-33)

Fulfilling these requirements of the covenants with the Lord will strengthen His people and assist them in obtaining mastery over the weaknesses of the flesh. It is not always an easy thing to be obedient and subject the flesh to the will of the Father. It is a trial for mortals to yield to the Lord's will. However, the Lord's people need to face trials in all things. Only by confronting tribulation can they conquer it. Thus, they are then prepared to receive the glory the Lord has prepared for them. (See D&C 136:31)

Promises to the Camp of Israel

A covenant involves two parties. After describing His expectations of His people, the Lord declared His portion of the covenant in the form of certain promises that would be fulfilled in His own due time. Some of the promises the Lord made to the Camp of Israel were as follows:

1. Necessities of Life

The saints were promised that obedience to the Lord's law would result in their having sufficient of the world's goods to provide for their needs. Wealth was not implied, but adequacy was assured. Food and clothing are essential to the well-being of a child of God. (See D&C 136:10-11)

2. Enemies

No mortal man can stop the work of the Lord. He told the saints there was no need to fear their enemies. The saints were promised that the work of the Lord will prevail. (See D&C 136:17)

3. Redemption of Zion

Since the beginning of the work of restoration in this dispensation, the Lord has spoken of the building and establishing of Zion. This revelation was directing the saints in a journey that would take them even further from the designated site of the city of Zion. Yet, the Lord reaffirmed His intention and promised the saints He would yet redeem Zion and fulfill His word pertaining to that anticipated work. (See D&C 136:18)

4. Glory of God

People who keep their covenants with the Lord are pure in heart. Such people were promised that if they remained pure, they would yet behold the glory of God. (See D&C 136:37)

These promises were given when the saints were living in very trying circumstances. They were suffering from the lack of physical comforts in life. They had been driven from one place to another by their enemies. The establishment of Zion that had once appeared to be a glorious hope was deteriorating to the realm of a lost cause. There was reason why some may wonder if this suffering group of Latter-day Israelites would ever enjoy the blessed presence of the Lord in their midst.

Under these very difficult conditions, the Lord delivered these specific promises to His covenant people while they wandered in the wilderness of discouragement and despair. Such promises loomed large as the basis for hope, both in their present trials, and in their anticipation of future fulfillment. The Lord has said that all of His promises will be fulfilled. (See D&C 1:37)

Now in retrospect, we see that the Lord has kept His promises. The saints are prospering; their enemies have not prevailed. We may also be assured that Zion will yet be redeemed and the glory of the Lord will ever be manifest in the lives and labors of His faithful covenant people.

Rejection of the Lord's Servants and Their Testimonies

It is a serious thing to reject the message and testimony of the Lord's servants.

We recall that ancient Nephites rejected the testimonies of two of the Lord's servants in the city of Ammonihah. When the wicked drove the righteous from their midst, they lost the protecting blessings that had come through the prayers of the faithful. The ultimate result was the total destruction of the city. (See B of M, Alma 10:22-23; 16:1-11)

In this last dispensation, a nation rejected the testimony of the Lord's servants, killed the Lord's prophets, and drove out the Lord's people. For these acts of wickedness, the Lord forewarned that calamity would befall that nation if they did not repent. (See D&C 136:34-36) History provides the evidence of the fulfillment of the Lord's warning. The great civil war caused the death and misery of many thousands of citizens as a result of the rejection of the Lord's servants at that time.

The Calling and Faithfulness of Joseph Smith

The Lord closed this revelation with His testimony of the mission and faithfulness of the Prophet Joseph Smith. (See D&C 136:37-39) Regardless of what others may say or think of Joseph Smith, the Lord testified that Joseph's mission and calling was of a divine origin. Further, the Lord declared that Joseph Smith died as a faithful prophet. He sealed "... his testimony with his blood, that he might be honored and the wicked might be condemned." (D&C 136:39) Well might the Latter-day Saints sing, "We thank thee O God for a prophet to guide us in these latter days."

Summary and Conclusion

The Lord always directs His church and counsels His people through a living prophet.

Following the death of the Prophet Joseph Smith, the Lord, through His Prophet Brigham Young, covenanted with modern Israel that through their faithfulness the glories of the kingdom would be theirs, notwithstanding their enemies and their trials.

Chapter 62

Doctrine and Covenants Section 137

Suggested Title

Joseph Smith's Vision of the Celestial Kingdom

Overview of Section Content

1. A vision of the celestial kingdom (vs. 1-4)
2. A vision of some who have and others who will yet inherit the celestial kingdom (vs. 5)
3. Heirs of the celestial kingdom (vs. 6-9)
4. Children who die before the age of accountability are saved in the celestial kingdom (vs. 10)

Historical Setting

On January 21, 1836, the Prophet Joseph Smith recorded: "At early candlelight I met with the Presidency at the west school room, in the [Kirtland] temple."(HC, Vol. 2, pp. 379-380) While assembled together a vision of the celestial kingdom was opened to their view. (See D&C Section 137)

Sacred Truths

Introduction

In order to more fully appreciate the doctrine revealed in this section, it would be well to reflect upon some of the teachings the Lord had previously revealed to Joseph Smith prior to this vision. Through his translation of the Book of Mormon, Joseph Smith had learned many principles of the restored gospel. He had learned that prerequisites for salvation included faith in the Lord Jesus Christ, repentance, baptism, etc. Through the process of the restoration of the church and the receiving of many revelations associated therewith, he learned of the need for man to make and keep covenants with the Lord. Further, he was permitted to see the ultimate destiny of Father's children as he witnessed the vision of the different degrees of glory. At that time he was informed of the requirements for entrance into Father's kingdom, or the celestial degree of glory. (See D&C Section 76)

When Joseph was permitted to see the celestial kingdom again in this vision (Section 137), he learned an important doctrinal principle pertaining to salvation of mankind.

We will discuss the content of this revelation as follows:

1. The glory of the celestial kingdom
2. The Prophet Joseph's question
3. The Lord's answer

The Glory of the Celestial Kingdom

The glory of the celestial kingdom is two-fold:

1. It is a glorious place of physical dimensions. It is not an immaterial heaven. It has streets, gates, thrones and people in a state of glorious resurrection. (See D&C 137:1-4)
2. It is inhabited by celestial people who are pure in heart. They have been spiritually born again through the atonement of Jesus Christ. (See D&C 137:2, 5)

The two-dimensional glory of the celestial kingdom was beautifully described by President David O. McKay as he shared an account of a celestial vision given to him.

> I...beheld in a vision something infinitely sublime. In the distance I beheld a beautiful white city. Though far away, yet I seemed to realize that trees with luscious fruit, shrubbery with gorgeously-tinted leaves, and flowers in perfect bloom abounded

everywhere. The clear sky above seemed to reflect these beautiful shades of color. I then saw a great concourse of people approaching the city. Each one wore a white flowing robe, and a white headdress. Instantly my attention seemed centered upon their Leader, and though I could see only the profile of his features and his body, I recognized him at once as my Savior! The tint and radiance of his countenance were glorious to behold! There was a peace about him which seemed sublime—it was divine!

The city, I understood, was his. It was the City Eternal; and the people following him were to abide there in peace and eternal happiness.

But who were they?

As if the Savior read my thoughts, he answered by pointing to a semicircle that then appeared above them, and on which were written in gold the words:

"These Are They Who Have Overcome The World—Who Have Truly Been Born Again!" (Cherished Experiences, p. 102)

The Prophet Joseph's Question

As the vision continued to unfold, Joseph was permitted to see certain people as heirs of the celestial kingdom. (See D&C 137:5) The presence of each of the heirs in the vision was consistent with Joseph's understanding of the requirements to be met for entrance into that kingdom. Each of them complied with the conditions as Joseph understood them. Even his own parents would eventually qualify because of their righteousness and faithful obedience to their covenants, though they were both still alive at the time of this vision.

There was one exception in Joseph's mind. His brother Alvin was seen. Alvin had not been baptized and therefore, based upon Joseph's knowledge at that time, Alvin would have had no claim upon the blessings promised to the faithful covenant people of the Lord. Alvin's presence was inconsistent with everything Joseph had previously understood. Thus he "marvelled" or questioned what he was seeing. (See D&C 137:6) It was as though Joseph were asking, "How can Alvin be there? He had not received the priesthood ordinances required for a celestial inheritance when he died."

The Lord's Answer

Up to this point in the vision, the Lord had not spoken. But as soon as Joseph could no longer understand and accurately interpret what he was seeing, the Lord provided the proper explanation. The Lord expected Joseph to understand things according to that which had been previously revealed. But when his experience exceeded his understanding, the Lord explained.

The Lord revealed the way by which salvation can come to people who have passed from this mortal existence without having the opportunity to receive priesthood ordinances unto salvation. These people are of two categories:

1. *Those who die without the gospel* (See D&C 137:7-9)

The Lord provides an opportunity for salvation to people who die without the privilege of hearing and receiving the gospel while in mortality. A required condition for these people is that they *would* have received it with all their hearts had they been permitted to tarry. Alvin's condition and situation was typical or representative of those people described in this revelation.

However, the Lord did not say that salvation will be available to those who have had an opportunity to hear and accept the gospel but rejected it while in mortality.

2. *Children who die before accountability* (See D&C 137:10)

Up to the time of this vision, there was no knowledge in the earth pertaining to hope for salvation for children who die in their infancy without the ordinances of salvation. Sweet as manna from heaven is the knowledge that children who die before the age of accountability will be saved or exalted in the highest degree of Father's kingdom. The Lord said that *all* children in this category will receive the reward of the faithful. None are excluded.

Through the atonement of Jesus Christ the following truths pertain to these little children:

a. All will be exalted in the celestial kingdom.
b. They will not need to be tested or tried.

(For further information and explanation on the Salvation of Children, see Elder Bruce R. McConkie, *Ensign,* April 1977, pp. 3-7)

Summary and Conclusion

Through the mercy and love of our Father in Heaven and his Son Jesus Christ, knowledge pertaining to the salvation of man has been restored to the earth again.

Our Father in Heaven knows all things, has all power, and is no respecter of persons. He has provided an opportunity for salvation for all His children under all circumstances.

Chapter 63

Doctrine and Covenants Section 138

Suggested Title
Joseph F. Smith's Vision of the Redemption of the Dead

Overview of Section Content

1. Circumstances surrounding the coming forth of this revelation (vs. 1-10)
2. Righteous spirits awaiting the visit of the Savior (vs. 11-17)
3. The Savior preached and ministered to the righteous spirits (vs. 18-19, 23-24)
4. The Savior did not go among the ungodly in the spirit world (vs. 20-22, 25-29)
5. Commission given to the righteous spirits to teach the gospel (vs. 30-37)
6. Specific righteous saints from ancient times were seen and identified (vs. 38-49)
7. Righteous spirits given power to be resurrected (vs. 50-52)
8. Specific righteous saints of the last dispensation were seen and identified (vs. 53-56)
9. Labors of righteous spirits of the last dispensation (vs. 57)
10. Redemption of the spirits who repent (vs. 58-59)
11. Testimony of Pres. Joseph F. Smith (vs. 60)

Historical Setting

This is a section that contains its own historical setting as recorded in the first eleven verses. It is interesting to note that this vision was given the day before the convening of the semi-annual conference of the church and approximately six weeks before the death of President Joseph F. Smith

Sacred Truths

Introduction

President Joseph F. Smith informed us that this vision came while he was pondering. (see D&C 138:1-11) Pondering, or meditating upon the things of God, opens doors to understanding. The mind and spirit are prepared to receive the promptings and guidance that emanates from the Holy Spirit. The importance of pondering and the reward thereof has been taught by President Marion G. Romney as follows:

> As I have read the scriptures I have been challenged by the word *ponder*, so frequently used in the Book of Mormon. The dictionary says that *ponder* means "to weigh mentally, think deeply about, deliberate, meditate." Moroni thus used the term as he closed his record:
> "Behold, I would exhort you that when ye shall read these things . . . that ye would remember how merciful the Lord hath been unto the children of men . . . and *ponder* it in your hearts." (Moro. 10:3. Italics added.)
> Jesus said to the Nephites:
> "I perceive that ye are weak that ye cannot understand all my words. . . .
> "Therefore, go ye unto your homes, and *ponder* upon the things which I have said, and ask of the Father, in my name that ye may understand. . . ." (3Ne. 17:2-3. Italics added.)
> Pondering is, in my feeling, a form of prayer. It has at least been an approach to the Spirit of the Lord on many occasions. Nephi tells us of one such occasion;
> "For it came to pass," he wrote, "after I had desired to know the things that my father had seen and believing that the Lord was able to make them known unto me, as I sat *pondering* in mine heart I was caught away in the Spirit of the Lord, yea, into an exceeding high mountain. . . ." (1 Ne. 11:1. Italics added.)
> Then follows Nephi's account of the great vision he was given by the Spirit of the Lord because he believed the words of his

Section 138 395

prophet father and had such a great desire to know more that he pondered and prayed about them.

President Joseph F. Smith tells us that "on the third of October, in the year nineteen hundred and eighteen, I sat in my room *pondering* over the Scriptures. . . ." He had particular reference at this time to Peter's statement that Christ "went and preached unto the spirits in prison" (1 Pet. 3:19) while his body lay in the grave.

"As I *pondered* over these things which are written," President Smith continued, "the eyes of my understanding were opened and the Spirit of the Lord rested upon me, and I saw the hosts of the dead, both small and great. . . ." He then gives us an account of his great vision concerning missionary work among the spirits of the dead. (Gospel Doctrine [Deseret Book Co. 1939], p. 472. Italics added.) (CR April 1973, pp. 117-118)

In this vision (Section 138), President Joseph F. Smith saw three groups of people in the spirit world. We will discuss the following:

1. The righteous in the spirit world from Adam to Christ.
2. The wicked in the spirit world from Adam to Christ.
3. The people in the spirit world from this dispensation.

The Righteous in the Spirit World From Adam to Christ

From this vision, there are several things to be learned about the condition and experience of the righteous spirits when the Savior visited the spirit world.

1. *Joyful condition of celestial saints* (See D&C 138:12-18)

All of these people had lived in obedience to celestial law while in mortality. This vast multitude had died firm in their testimony of Jesus Christ and consequently were filled with joyful anticipation of the Savior's advent into the spirit world. They knew that His coming meant the end of the separation of their spirit from their body. They were to be resurrected in conjunction with the Savior's own resurrection never again to suffer death. They were to receive a fulness of joy in their celestial inheritance. It is little wonder they were " . . .rejoicing in the hour of their deliverance . . ." (D&C 138:18)

2. *The Savior's declaration and preaching* (See D&C 138:18-19)

Of all the children of God who have walked in mortality, only one has conquered death and could declare liberty from the death that held all others captive. That one was Jesus Christ, the Son of God. The announcement of liberty was first declared to the celestial saints in the spirit world at the time Jesus appeared there.

The Savior preached to the faithful saints and reaffirmed the reason why they could be free. He reminded them that through His atonement He had overcome the effects of the fall by providing resurrection of the physical body to all mankind. Further, His atonement freed the righteous from their sins on condition of their repentance. Hence, the faithful saints were liberated through the grace and mercy of Jesus Christ, the Only Begotten Son of God, the great Jehovah.

3. *Rejoicing of the righteous* (See D&C 138:23-24)

It is one thing to be taught of the blessings of the atonement; it is quite another to experience those blessings. When the Savior stood in the midst of righteous spirits in the spirit world, they rejoiced over their freedom from both sin and death. These blessings were not only concepts to be understood; they had become a living experience and a reality in their lives. Hence, the reason for their joy.

The celestial saints acknowledged the source of their deliverance as Jesus Christ, the Son of God. He had given them what no man could provide. As a result of their obedience their countenance shown. Even the Lord's radiance was reflected upon them." . . . they sang praises unto his holy name." (D&C 138:24)

4. *Great and mighty ones* (See D&C 138:38-49)

In this vision, President Joseph F. Smith was privileged to see many great and mighty saints of the past who were faithful to Jesus Christ. There are several testimonies that come from this portion of the vision that serve as witnesses to us:

a. Those people are not just named characters in a book. They are living sons and daughters of God who lived on this earth in ages past.

b. The Lord has had living prophets on this earth in previous dispensations who bore testimony that salvation comes through the Redeemer, even Jesus Christ.

c. The flood is not just a figment of someone's imagination. It is not a myth. It is an historical event and a matter of fact.

d. The testimony of these prophets has been preserved and is contained within the scriptural record available to mankind today. The scriptures are of a divine source and stand as a witness of the Savior's work in all ages.

e. The ancient prophets foretold of the restoration of the kingdom of God in the last days with all of its teachings and ordinances. The kingdom is here—it is a literal fulfillment and restoration of ancient prophecy, keys, and powers.

5. *Immortality and eternal life* (See D&C 138:50-52)

Regardless of the level of righteousness of the individual, life in the spirit world constitutes a bondage. People there are living without a body. They cannot be released from such bondage without the Savior's atonement. (For a discussion on this subject, see Sacred Truths of the Doctrine and Covanants, Vol. 1, pp. 217-218)

When the Savior appeared amongst the righteous saints He gave them power, or keys, of resurrection, that they might follow Him through the process of resurrection. He gave them keys that are not to be found on earth among mortals. They could then be crowned with immortality and eternal life.

The Wicked in the Spirit World
From Adam to Christ

When the Savior went into the spirit world, He did not go among the wicked. The wicked constituted two classes of people:

1. Those who participated in the defilement of their mortal bodies and were not clean. (See D&C 138:20)
2. Those who rejected the testimony of Jesus Christ and warnings from His authorized representatives. (See D&C 138:21)

Even though these unrighteous people had rejected the Savior or had not complied with His teachings, still He did not forget them. He provided a way for them to be taught truths that would bless their lives beyond their current state of misery. He sent messengers to them to declare the principles and ordinances of the gospel. Their compliance with these teachings would serve as a means unto an inheritance of a degree of glory. Their hope of redemption would also come through the atonement of the Savior, regardless of the level of glory they attain. (see D&C 138:29-37) Every knee will bow and every tongue will confess that redemption for souls in every kingdom of glory will only be achieved through the atonement of Jesus Christ.

The People in the Spirit World
From This Dispensation

President Smith was also shown people in the spirit world who had lived in mortality during the dispensation of the fulness of times.

First, he saw departed presiding leaders of the church. They were not leaders by chance—they had been chosen for this noble calling in the pre-mortal spirit world before coming to the earth to labor for the souls of men. (See D&C 138:53-56) This vision provides further testimony of the foreordination and approval of the Lord of the ministries of prophets of this dispensation.

Secondly, President Smith observed the labors of departed faithful elders of this dispensation. They continue to teach and labor for the souls of the departed dead. They declare that redemption comes only through the atonement of Jesus Christ. They teach that eternal rewards are dependent upon the degree of compliance with the truths of the gospel. (See D&C 138:57-59) President Wilford Woodruff provided additional insight to the nature of the labors of the faithful elders of this dispensation who are fulfilling their priesthood callings in the spirit world:

> When Joseph Smith had laid the foundation of this work he was taken away. There are good reasons why it was so. Jesus sealed his testimony with his blood. Joseph Smith did the same, and from the day he died his testimony has been in force upon the whole world. He has gone into the spirit world and organized this dispensation on that side of the veil; he is gathering together the elders of Israel and the Saints of God in the spirit world, for they have a work to do there as well as here. Joseph and Hyrum Smith, Father Smith, David Patten and the other elders who have been called to the other side of the veil have fifty times as many people to preach to as we have on the earth. There they have all the spirits who have lived on the earth in seventeen centuries—fifty generations, fifty thousand millions of persons who lived and died here without having seen a prophet or apostle, and without having the word of the Lord sent unto them. They are shut up in prison, awaiting the message of the elders of Israel. We have only about a thousand millions of people on the earth, but in the spirit world they have fifty thousand millions; and there is not a single revelation which gives us any reason to believe that any man who enters the spirit world preached the gospel there to those who lived after him; but they all preach to men who were in the flesh before they were. Jesus himself preached to the antediluvian world, who had been in prison for thousands of years. So with Joseph Smith and the elders—they will have to preach to the inhabitants of the earth who have died during the last seventeen centuries; and when they hear the testimony of the elders and accept it there should be somebody on the earth, as we have been told, to attend to the ordinances of the house of God for them. (DWW, p. 151)

Section 138

Summary and Conclusion

The living and the dead can only realize the blessings of redemption from death and hell through the atonement and sacrifice of Jesus Christ, the great Jehovah. The work for the redemption of souls continues in mortality and the spirit world through the labors of His authorized representatives.

Appendix

Index of Suggested Titles for Doctrine & Covenants Sections 71-138

Suggested Titles	Sections
Adam-Ondi-Ahman	116
Acceptable offering to the Lord, His	126
Accepted of the Lord, Being	124
Anti-Christ literature and works	123
Apocrypha, The	91
Apostles, Twelve	118
Appearance of the Savior, The	110
Appendix, The	133
Baptisms for the dead—Records in heaven—Review of the restoration	128
Baptisms for the dead—Witnesses and recordings	127
Being accepted of the Lord	124
Bishop, Second	72
Blessings, A Law of	82
Book of the Law, The	85
Book of Isaiah, Insights to the	113
Book of Revelation, Insights to the	77

Brethren—Strengthen Your Brethren	108
Building—Chastisement for delaying the building of the Kirtland temple	95
Buildings, Church	94
Call—A special missionary call to Joseph Smith and Sidney Rigdon	71
Calling—Compensation for full-time calling	106
Callings—Power in our church callings	79
Camp of Israel	136
Camp—Zion's Camp	103
Cast out, Why	101
Celestial kingdom, Joseph Smith's vision of the	137
Celestial kingdom, Three heavens in the	131
Celestial Marriage	132
Chastisement for delaying the building of the Kirtland Temple	95
Children of light	106
Children, Salvation of	74
Children—Women and children under the Law of Consecration	83
Church buildings	94
Church callings, Power in our	79
Church court, A	102
Church government, Priesthood and	107
Church, Marriage within the	74
Church, The name of the Lord's	115
Church—Order of the church for the salvation of men	104
Church, Salvation only through the	85
Compensation for full-time calling	106
Conditions in heaven	130
Consecration, Purposes of the Law of	78
Consecration—Women and children under the law of Consecration	83
Constitution of the Priesthood	121
Corinthians—I Corinthians 7:14	74
Council—The first high council	102
Counselor, A	81
County—Jackson County	101
Covenants and promises	136

Index

Dead, Baptisms for the—Records in Heaven	128
Dead, Baptisms for the—Witnesses and Recordings	127
Dead, Joseph F. Smith's vision of the redemption of the	138
Dedicatory—The dedicatory prayer of the Kirtland Temple	109
Degrees of glory, The vision	76
Delaying—Chastisement for delaying the building of the Kirtland Temple	95
Disbursement of tithing funds	120
Dividing the French Farm	96
Divine—Religion and divine laws	134
Duties of missionaries	75
Effective use of time	73
Faith, A Man of	114
Faith and Obedience	118
Farm—Dividing the French Farm	96
Far West, Missouri Temple	115
First Corinthians 7:14	74
First High Council, The	102
First Presidency	81
Follies	111
Forgiveness, A principle of	82
Forgiveness—Law of Forgiveness, Retribution, War	98
For what purpose?	96
French Farm, Dividing the	96
Full-time—Compensation for full-time calling	106
Funds—Disbursement of tithing funds	120
Gathering and the second coming, The	133
Glory, The degrees of—The vision	76
Godhead, The	130
God, Oracles of	90
Government, Priesthood and church	107
Governments and man's laws	134
Heaven, Conditions in	130
Heaven, Records in	128
Heavens—Three heavens in the Celestial Kingdom	131

Heirs—Lawful Heirs to the Priesthood	86
High Council, The first	102
How and what to teach	100
How and what to worship	93
Insights to the Book of Isaiah	113
Insights to the Book of Revelation	77
Instructions—The Lord's instructions to a quorum president	112
Iowa, Saints in	125
Isaiah, Insights to the Book of	113
Israel, Camp of	136
Jackson County	101
Joseph F. Smith's vision of the redemption of the dead	138
Joseph Smith's vision of the celestial kingdom	137
Judged by what we know	82
Keys of the Kingdom—First Presidency	81
Keys of the Kingdom—Oracles of God	90
Keys restored	110
Keys—Three grand keys by which messengers may be known	129
Kingdom—Joseph Smith's vision of the celestial kingdom	137
Kingdom, Keys of the—First Presidency	81
Kingdom, Keys of the—Oracles of God	90
Kingdom—Three heavens in the celestial kingdom	131
Kirtland Temple, Chastisement for delaying the building of the	95
Kirtland Temple—Dedicatory prayer	109
Law of Blessings, A	82
Law, the book of the	85
Law of Consecration, Purposes of the	78
Law of forgiveness, retribution, war	98
Law, Purpose of the	98
Law of Representation	99
Law of Tithing, The Lord's	119
Lawful heirs to the priesthood	86
Laws—Governments and man's laws	134
Laws—Religion and divine laws	134
Leaf, The Olive	88
Light, Children of	106

Index

Literature—Anti-Christ literature and works	123
Lively member, A	92
Lord, Being accepted of the	124
Lord, His acceptable offering to the	126
Lord's instructions to a Quorum President, The	112
Lord's Law of Tithing, The	119
Lord's Church, The name of the	115
Man of Faith, A	114
Man's Laws, Governments and	134
Marriage, Celestial	132
Marriage Within the church	74
Marsh, Thomas B.—The Lord's instructions to a Quorum President	112
Martyrdom—Joseph and Hyrum Smith	135
Massachusetts, Mission to Salem	111
Matters, The more weighty	117
Member, A lively	92
Men, Order of the church for the salvation of	104
Messengers—Three grand keys by which messengers may be known	129
Mighty—One mighty and strong	85
Mission to Salem, Massachusetts	111
Missionaries, Duties of	75
Missionary—A special missionary call to Joseph Smith and Sidney Rigdon	71
Missouri Temple, Far West	115
More weighty matters, The	117
Name of the Lord's Church, The	115
Nauvoo Temple	124
Obedience, Faith and	118
Offering—His acceptable offering to the Lord	126
Olive Leaf, The	88
One mighty and strong	85
Oracles of God	90
Order of the church for the salvation of men	104
Patten, David W.	114
Power in our church callings	79
Prayer—The dedicatory prayer of the Kirtland Temple	109
Presidency, First	81
President—The Lord's instructions to a Quorum President	112

Priesthood	84
Priesthood and church government	107
Priesthood, Constitution of the	121
Priesthood, Lawful heirs to the	86
Principle of forgiveness, A	82
Promises	100
Promises, Covenants and	136
Prophecy, The more sure word of	131
Prophecy on Wars	87
Purpose—For what purpose?	96
Purpose of the law	98
Purposes of the Law of Consecration	78
Quorum President, The Lord's instructions to a	112
Recordings, Witnesses and	127
Records in Heaven	128
Redeemed—Zion not to be redeemed for a little season	105
Redemption—Joseph F. Smith's vision of the redemption of the dead	138
Redemption of Zion	103
Religion and divine laws	134
Representation, Law of	99
Restoration, Review of the	128
Restored, Keys	110
Retribution—Law of forgiveness, retribution, war	98
Revelation, Insights to the book of	77
Review of the restoration	128
Rigdon, Sidney—A special missionary call to Joseph Smith and Sidney Rigdon	71
Saints in Iowa	125
Salem—Mission to Salem, Massachusetts	111
Salvation of children	74
Salvation only through the church	85
Salvation—Order of the church for the salvation of men	104
Savior, The appearance of the	110
Second Bishop	72
Second Coming, The gathering and the	133
Smith, Hyrum—Martyrdom	135
Smith, Joseph—Martyrdom	135

Index

Smith, Joseph—A special missionary call to Joseph Smith and Sidney Rigdon	71
Smith, Joseph—Vision of the Celestial Kingdom	137
Smith, Joseph F.—Vision of the redemption of the dead	138
Special missionary call to Joseph Smith and Sidney Rigdon	71
Stewardships—Second Bishop	72
Strengthen your brethren	108
Strong—One mighty and strong	85
Suffering, Why	122
Tares—The wheat and the tares	86
Teach—How and what to teach	100
Teach and testify	80
Temple—Chastisement for delaying the building of the Kirtland Temple	95
Temple, Far West, Missouri	115
Temple, Kirtland—The Dedicatory prayer of the Kirtland Temple	109
Temple, Nauvoo	124
Testify, Teach and	80
Three grand keys by which messengers may be known	129
Three heavens in the celestial kingdom	131
Time, Effective use of	73
Tithing—Disbursement of tithing funds	120
Tithing, The Lord's Law of	119
Twelve apostles	118
Vision, The (Degrees of Glory, Etc.)	76
Vision—Joseph Smith's vision of the Celestial Kingdom	137
Vision—Joseph F. Smith's vision of the redemption of the dead	138
War—Law of forgiveness, retribution, war	98
Wars, Prophecy on	87
Weighty—The more weighty matters	117
Wheat and the tares, The	86
Why Cast Out	101
Why suffering?	122
Wisdom, The word of	89
Witnesses and recordings	127

Women and children under the law of consecration	83
Word of Prophecy—The more sure word of prophecy	131
Word of Wisdom, The	89
Works—Anti-Christ literature and works	123
Worship, How and what to	93
Young, Brigham	126
Zion	97
Zion not to be redeemed for a little season	105
Zion, Redemption of	103
Zion's Camp	103

SELECTED BIBLIOGRAPHY

Andrus, Hyrum. *They Knew the Prophet.* Salt Lake City: Bookcraft, 1974.

Ballard, Melvin J. *Crusader for Righteousness.* Salt Lake City: Bookcraft, 1968.

Bible, The.

Bible, Joseph Smith's Translation (Inspired Version). Independence, Missouri: Herald Publishing House, 1964.

Book of Mormon, The. Salt Lake City: The Church of Jesus Christ of Latter-day Saints.

BYU Speeches of the Year. Provo: Brigham Young University Press.

Cannon, George Q. *Gospel Truth.* 2 vols. Salt Lake City: Deseret Book, 1974.

Church News. Salt Lake City: Deseret News Press.

Clark, James R. *Messages of the First Presidency.* 6 vols. Salt Lake City: Bookcraft, 1965.

Conference Reports. Salt Lake City: Deseret News Press.

Cowley, Matthias F. *Wilford Woodruff, History of His Life and Labors.* Salt Lake City: Bookcraft, 1964.

Doctrine and Covenants, The. Salt Lake City: The Church of Jesus Christ of Latter-day Saints.

Doxey, Roy W. *The Latter-day Prophets and The Doctrine and Covenants.* 4 vols. Salt Lake City: Deseret Book, 1963.

Dyer, Alvin R. *Who Am I?* Salt Lake City: Deseret Book, 1970.

Elders Journal, vol. I. Kirtland, Ohio: The Church of Jesus Christ of Latter-day Saints, October 1837.

Ensign. Salt Lake City: The Church of Jesus Christ of Latter-day Saints.

Grant, Heber J. *Gospel Standards.* Salt Lake City: Deseret News Press, 1941.

Hinckley, Gordon B. Address to Church Educational System Religious Educators, Salt Lake City, 15 September 1978.

Historical Record. The Church of Jesus Christ of Latter-day Saints, Salt Lake City.

Improvement Era. Salt Lake City: Mutual Improvement Association.

Jenson, Andrew. *L.D.S. Biographical Encyclopedia.* 4 vols. Salt Lake City: Publishers Press, 1971.

Journal of Discourses. 26 vols. Los Angeles: General Printing and Lithograph Co., 1961.

Kimball Spencer W. *Men of Example.* Address to Religious Educators, Assembly Hall, Salt Lake City, 12 September 1975.

Kimball Spencer W. *The Miracle of Forgiveness.* Salt Lake City: Bookcraft, 1969.

Lee, Harold B. *Addresses to Seminary and Institute Faculty,* Brigham Young University, July 17, 1958; June 17, 1970.

Lee, Harold B. *Stand Ye in Holy Places.* Salt Lake City: Deseret Book, 1976.

Lee, Harold B. *Youth and the Church.* Salt Lake City: Deseret News Press, 1945.

Lundwall, N. B., comp. *Lectures on Faith by Joseph Smith.* Salt Lake City.

McConkie, Bruce R. *Doctrinal New Testament Commentary.* 3 vols. Salt Lake City: Bookcraft, 1970.

McConkie, Bruce R. "Honest Truth Seekers" Letter, 1 July 1980. Salt Lake City.

McConkie, Bruce R. *The Millennial Messiah.* Salt Lake City: Deseret Book, 1982.

McConkie, Bruce R. *Mormon Doctrine.* Salt Lake City: Bookcraft, 1958.

Melchizedek Priesthood Personal Study Guide. 1977-78; 1980-81.

Middlemiss, Clare. *Cherished Experiences from the Writings of David O. McKay.* Salt Lake City: Deseret Book, 1955.

Millennial Star. Manchester, England: The Church of Jesus Christ of Latter-day Saints.

Moyle, Henry D. Unpublished Address to California Mission, 2 June 1962.

New Era, The. Salt Lake City: The Church of Jesus Christ of Latter-day Saints, June 1973.

Pearl of Great Price, The. Salt Lake City: The Church of Jesus Christ of Latter-day Saints.

Pratt, Parley P. *Autobiography of Parley P. Pratt.* Salt Lake City: Deseret Book, 1966.

Selected Bibliography

Pratt, Parley P. *Key to Theology.* Salt Lake City: Deseret News, 1883.

Pratt, Parley P. *A Voice of Warning.* Salt Lake City: The Church of Jesus Christ of Latter-day Saints.

Readers Digest. March 1975.

Relief Society Courses of Study. The Church of Jesus Christ of Latter-day Saints, 1979-1980.

Roberts, Brigham H. *A Comprehensive History of the Church.* 6 vols. Salt Lake City: Deseret News Press, 1930.

Smith, Hyrum M. and Sjodahl, Janne M. *The Doctrine and Covenants Commentary.* Salt Lake City: Deseret Book, 1950.

Smith, Joseph. *History of the Church of Jesus Christ of Latter-day Saints.* 6 vols. Salt Lake City: Deseret News Press, 1951.

Smith, Joseph F. *Gospel Doctrine.* Salt Lake City: Deseret Book, 1963.

Smith, Joseph Fielding. *Answers to Gospel Questions.* 5 vols. Salt Lake City: Deseret Book, 1957.

Smith, Joseph Fielding. *Church History and Modern Day Revelation.* 4 vols. (Pamphlets) Salt Lake City: Deseret News Press, 1946.

Smith, Joseph Fielding. *Doctrines of Salvation.* 3 vols. Salt Lake City: Bookcraft, 1954.

Smith, Joseph Fielding. *Way to Perfection.* Salt Lake City: Deseret News Press, 1953.

Smith, Joseph Fielding., comp. *Teachings of the Prophet Joseph Smith.* Salt Lake City: Deseret Book, 1963.

Smith, Joseph Fielding. *The Progress of Man.* Salt Lake City: Deseret News Press, 1952.

Sperry, Sidney B. *Book of Mormon Compendium.* Salt Lake City: Bookcraft, 1968.

Talmage, James E. *Articles of Faith.* Salt Lake City: The Church of Jesus Christ of Latter-day Saints, 1952.

Taylor, John. *The Gospel Kingdom.* Salt Lake City: Bookcraft, 1943.

Times and Seasons. Nauvoo: The Church of Jesus Christ of Latter-day Saints, 1839-1846.

Whitney, Orson F. *Life of Heber C. Kimball.* Salt Lake City: Bookcraft, 1967.

Widtsoe, John A. *Priesthood and Church Government.* Salt Lake City: Deseret Book, 1954.

Wilson, Lycurgus A. *Life of David Patten.* Salt Lake City: The Deseret News, 1904.

Woodruff, Wilford. *The Discourses of Wilford Woodruff.* Salt Lake City: Bookcraft, 1969.